I0474141

BLOODFLOWERS

The Visual Arts of Africa and Its Diasporas
A series edited by Kellie Jones and Steven Nelson

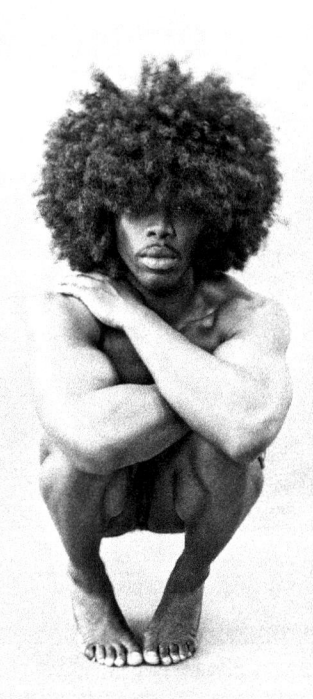

W. Ian Bourland

BLOODFLOWERS

ROTIMI FANI-KAYODE,

PHOTOGRAPHY, AND THE 1980S

Duke University Press / Durham and London / 2019

© 2019 Duke University Press

All rights reserved

Designed by Mindy Basinger Hill

Typeset in Garamond Premier Pro by Copperline Book Services

Library of Congress Cataloging-in-Publication Data

Names: Bourland, W. Ian, [date] author.

Title: Bloodflowers : Rotimi Fani-Kayode, photography, and the 1980s / W. Ian Bourland.

Other titles: Rotimi Fani-Kayode, photography, and the 1980s

Description: Durham : Duke University Press, 2019. | Series: The visual arts of Africa and its diasporas | Includes bibliographical references and index.

Identifiers: LCCN 2018032576 (print)

LCCN 2018037542 (ebook)

ISBN 9781478002369 (ebook)

ISBN 9781478000686 (hardcover)

ISBN 9781478000891 (pbk.)

Subjects: LCSH: Fani-Kayode, Rotimi, 1955–1989—Criticism and interpretation. | Photography of men. | Photography of the nude. | Homosexuality in art. | Gay erotic photography. | Photographers—Nigeria. | Photography—Social aspects.

Classification: LCC TR681.M4 (ebook) | LCC TR681.M4 B68 2019 (print) | DDC 779/.21—dc23

LC record available at https://lccn.loc.gov/2018032576

Frontispiece: Rotimi Fani-Kayode, *Untitled* (1985). © Rotimi Fani-Kayode / Autograph ABP. Courtesy of Autograph ABP.

Cover art: Rotimi Fani-Kayode, *Tulip Boy II* (1989). © Rotimi Fani-Kayode / Autograph ABP. Courtesy of Autograph ABP.

This book was made possible by a collaborative grant from the Andrew W. Mellon Foundation

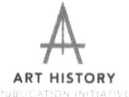

ART HISTORY
PUBLICATION INITIATIVE

CONTENTS

ACKNOWLEDGMENTS

This book represents some ten years of work, connecting a broader project on Afro-British art with intervening years of travel and scholarship across several continents. It would, of course, be impossible to adequately recognize the many, many people who have supported me or enabled this project along the way. I apologize to those who are not included here.

Foremost, I want to thank Steven Nelson, without whom the book in hand would not exist. His vital essay on Rotimi Fani-Kayode for the *Art Journal* in 2005 brought the artist to my attention, setting the stage and tone for the work that followed. During the subsequent years, Steven has tirelessly supported my and others' research on Fani-Kayode and on diaspora art more broadly, down to his crucial editorial guidance during this final version of the book. Steven exemplifies what it means to be a generous colleague and leader in our field.

During the course of this project, I also came to know a broader circle of Africanist art historians, including Jessica Martinez and Cécile Fromont, both of whom supported this work in the field from its earliest stages. On the whole, I had the good fortune to be part of the Chicago community during a time of decided transition toward investigations of both the contemporary and the Black Atlantic.

This was true of the University of Chicago itself, where my time with Darby English, Matthew Jesse Jackson, Margaret MacNamidhe, Tom Mitchell, Joel Snyder, and Ken Warren was transformative, and also of the larger network of interlocutors in the city. I am grateful to Hamza Walker for the memorable, impromptu conversations at the Renaissance Society, Naomi Beckwith, and Huey Copeland. The great Julia Langbein acted as draft editor and London pub guide during a pivotal few years. And I was especially lucky to meet Kate

Bussard, who remains a mentor and collaborator for whom I am continually grateful.

Books don't happen in a vacuum, and I can safely say that whatever degree of clarity or eloquence appears in the pages ahead are directly attributable to a decade of work as a critic, and to the editorial direction and feedback from which I benefited. Thank you to Lauren O'Neill Butler at *Artforum International* as well as Dan Fox, Evan Moffitt, and Jennifer Higgie at *frieze*. Thanks are also due to the friends and colleagues I met during my time at the Whitney ISP, where this project was formulated—especially Brendan Fernandes, Odili Donald Odita, and Nate Harrison, and my then-research assistant Jeewon Kim.

This project took shape while I was on faculty at Maryland Institute College of Art (MICA) and I am grateful to my colleagues there for their expertise and editorial support, notably David Brooks, Christine Manganaro, Jay Gould, Lynn Silverman, Fabienne Lasserre, Monica Amor, Firmin Debrabander, and Sarah-Neel Smith; to MICA alums Adam Golfer, Margaret Hines, and Adejoke Tugbiyele; and to my good friend Jared Thorne, whose conversations about race and photography have been invaluable.

A special thank-you is in order to everyone at Duke University Press, from Elizabeth Ault, who initially saw the potential in this project, to Ken Wissoker, Bonnie Perkel, and the many others who brought the manuscript from prospect to completion, and who facilitated the Andrew W. Mellon Art History Publication Initiative award that made possible the extensive use of images here.

I am indebted, too, to the many individuals and organizations who permitted their incredible photographic work to be reproduced—they are indicated in the pages that follow. Ajamu X, Eddie Chambers, and Robert Taylor went further, and spoke with me at length during draft phases of the manuscript, and their insight was profoundly helpful. Notably, Autograph-ABP greatly facilitated the visual component of this work and maintained Fani-Kayode's archive. Mark Sealy in particular has been a tireless advocate of these photographs and their enduring legacy over the past several decades. I owe Mark, Renée Mussai, Karin Bareman, and Steve Blogg specific thanks for their contributions to this and to the larger project of keeping Fani-Kayode's life and art in the foreground of contemporary discussions.

The final note goes to my family and friends and, especially, Barbara, for everything.

NOTHING TO LOSE

> If matter appeared to us as a perpetual flowering,
> we should assign no termination to any of our actions.
> Henri Bergson, *Creative Evolution*

BLOODFLOWERS

Consider two kinds of photograph. The first, printed in 1989, measures ten by twelve inches, about the size of a small painting. It is a Cibachrome, and its vivid color, deep shadows, and careful staging by the photographer, Rotimi Fani-Kayode (1955–1989), reinforce its lush quality. It is tonally rich, tenebristic in its use of light, like a lost artifact from the Baroque period. The figure in the picture—shirtless, gazing fiercely beyond the picture plane, bearing a small, vegetal blossom like a gift—could be one of the roguish saints or sinners commonly depicted by many seventeenth-century Italian masters. And the bloom that he bears calls to mind the *nature mort* so common to that era, especially in the then-ascendent Netherlands. Indeed, this photograph is called *Tulip Boy I*, named for an iconic flower charged with associations, from bulbous early modern commodity to pregnant symbol of springtime. The tulip is synonymous with sumptuous wealth, but even more so with the revivification of the cold earth after a deep winter. Another picture from this series, *Tulip Boy II* (figure Intro.1), provides a humorous counterpoint. Clearly from the same contact sheet, the figure here clinches the flower in his mouth, suspending it somewhere between consumption and display.

The second kind of photograph (Intro.2) is a variant on the first, produced in 1990 and signed in pencil by Alex Hirst (1951–1992), a Yorkshire-born novelist and writer, who reprinted *Tulip Boy* from the original negatives in the

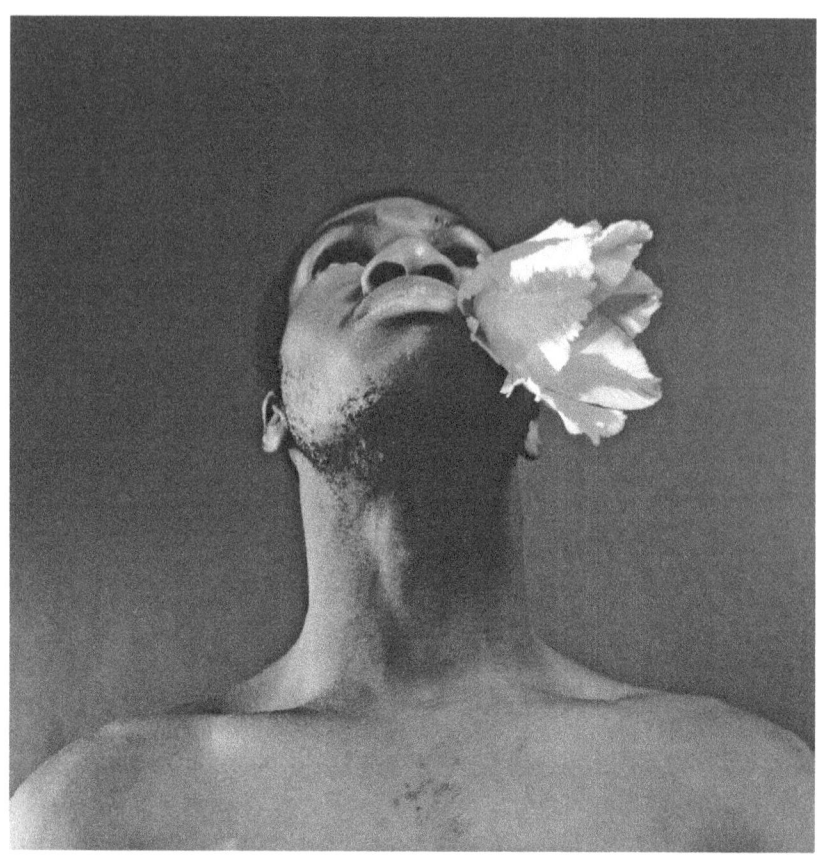

Figure Intro.1 Rotimi Fani-Kayode, *Tulip Boy II* (1989). © Rotimi Fani-Kayode / Autograph ABP. Courtesy of Autograph ABP.

year following Fani-Kayode's sudden death in late December 1989. Hirst's posthumous elaboration of Fani-Kayode's work is indicative both of the intensity of their collaboration as lovers and partners during those final years of the decade, and also of Fani-Kayode's turn to alternate processes toward the end of his life. The first photograph bears the high finish and chromatic clarity common to Cibachromes. By contrast, the 1990 version is rougher, stranger, exuding the telltale qualities of the gum-bichromate printing method. Then as now, such a protomodernist approach was uncommon. It hearkens to a more arcane, alchemical phase of the medium and relies on a distinct chemistry—potassium bichromate, suspended in layers of gum arabic, hand ap-

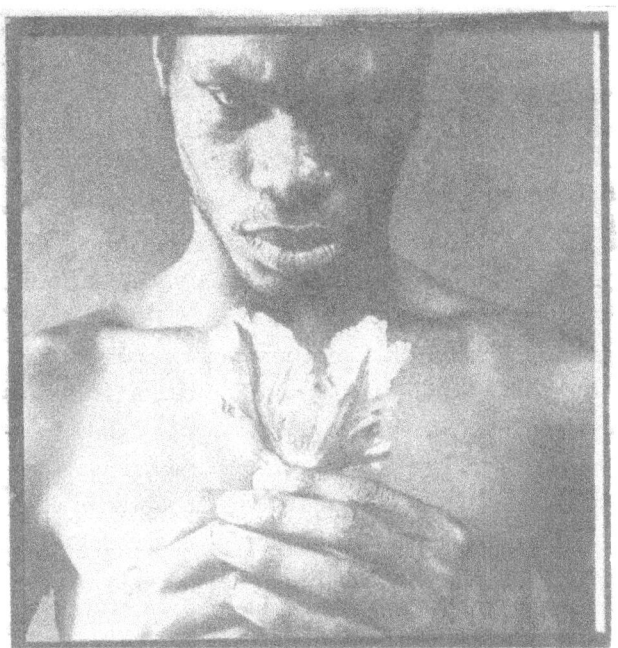

Figure Intro.2 Rotimi Fani-Kayode, *Tulip Boy I* (1989–1990).
© Rotimi Fani-Kayode / Autograph ABP. Courtesy of Autograph ABP.

plied in washes onto a surface, typically paper. The application of gum in multiple layers produces spectral color and leaves a trace of the artist's own manufacture.[1]

By using the gum process, the artist—in this case, Hirst—might lose the sharpness and tonal range expected of fine art photography, but gain a distinctive, dense materiality. A hallmark of the pictorialist camera clubs of the late nineteenth century who harnessed it to produce lyrical, haunting tableaux, this method was decidedly antique during Fani-Kayode's years of production, from 1983 to 1989, but had been revived in some of the darkrooms and workshops of South London. All the same, a picture such as *Tulip Boy I*, in its bichromate version, would have called to mind a parallel historical universe for most viewers. This photograph was not an example of the banal, postconceptual documentary or diaristic vérité characteristic of the 1980s but instead a callback to the minute, hand-tinted surrealism of Hans Bellmer, or the homoerotic studio portraiture of the Victorian-era commercial photographer F. Holland Day. Not merely a picture, the 1990 version is akin to a precious gem, scarcely enlarged and measuring roughly nine inches square. It renders the figure in a wash of ochre, floating amid a diaphanous haze.

A knowing viewer might see in these *Tulip Boy* pictures still other resonances: the pose is almost an exact reconstruction of an image from the ritualistic collaboration of the Japanese author Yukio Mishima and photographer Eikoh Hosoe from some twenty years prior. And Fani-Kayode's contemporaries in downtown New York or South London (then a haven of black and queer artists, critics, and activists) would have seen parallels to the famed Robert Mapplethorpe, whose *Black Book* portfolio was released in the summer of 1986—a chronicle of naked black men, many of whom posed with evocative white flowers as Mapplethorpe maneuvered them before his lens.

In all of their multiple resonances, these two photographs are emblematic of Rotimi Fani-Kayode's larger arc as an artist. He was a cosmopolitan and erudite photographer who started his life in Nigeria, the son of a Yoruban family prominent for both its political and religious connections. The "Fani" in his name refers to Ifá, the orisha and divination practice in Yoruba cosmology associated with the reading of one's destiny, and the drawing of *àshe* (creative energy) into the world. The Kayodes were also part of a shared governance structure of a Nigeria that gained independence from British rule in 1960, before the 1967 secession of the Igbo-led state of Biafra inaugurated a three-year conflict that resulted in famine, displacement, and tens of thousands of casualties.

Nigerian elites had long nurtured ties to the colonial center in London, and Fani-Kayode's family fled the chaos of the postcolonial state. A young Rotimi was educated in the English countryside and sent to Washington, DC, in the mid-1970s to study what he called a "respectable" field, economics. But to the dismay of his family, he found a different path, one that wended its way through the subcultures and counterpublics of the DC and New York undergrounds, through loft and warehouse parties, to the black salons of Dupont Circle and Harlem, from rough-and-tumble punk bars to the neighborhood galleries and community centers of London, where he settled from 1983 until his death.

During this time he seems to have used his photographs to conduct a wide symbolic and psychic journey through what theorists at the time had started to call the Black Atlantic, a zone of cultural transmission and translation through which the African diaspora, its labor, and its radical traditions dynamically shaped modernity during the seventeenth century and beyond.

Fani-Kayode first staked out his own practice in hallucinogenic color before moving to the comparatively cheaper modernist tones of gelatin silver, shooting black-and-whites in the streets and in a makeshift studio. Later, in collaboration with Hirst and facing his own imminent mortality, he began to experiment with more esoteric choices of composition, scale, and materiality. He left perhaps a hundred photographic works behind, many subsequently reprinted or reformatted by others, some lost or destroyed. There are negatives and contact sheets beyond these, but during his life, his photographs mostly populated collaborative spaces and the pages of journals and catalogs that circulated in gay bookshops and the libraries of nonprofit organizations such as Autograph: Association of Black Photographers (Autograph ABP), which he helped found in 1988.

In the years since his death, Fani-Kayode's photographs have taken on a second life. His contemporary, the critic Kobena Mercer, wrote widely on the artist, and his words accompanied reproductions in several catalogs and a monograph that brought them to a global audience in the decade after 1989.[2] Okwui Enwezor also included Fani-Kayode in a seminal exhibition of African photography, 1996's In/sight: African Photographers, 1940 to the Present at the Guggenheim Museum.[3] The curator later claimed that those pictures, which focused on contemporary manifestation of beauty, spirituality, and desire uniquely confounded expectations of African art, especially the troubling blend of voyeurism and pessimism that often accompanied it.[4] Throughout the 2000s, those same photographs were gradually taken on in emerging queer histories of art and the twentieth century and, more recently still, in surveys of the 1980s, which have begun to detail his contributions to the politically charged landscape of the era, making tentative art-historical connections as well.[5]

The book at hand, Bloodflowers, for the first time draws together these threads—Fani-Kayode the Atlantic errant, the queer visionary, the formalist synthesizer, and the art-rock rebel. What follows is an account of his practice, both on its own terms and in light of its contributions and formation in response to the profound political and cultural shifts underway during his brief, six-year career. Precisely because his work defied many of the binaries through which the culture of the decade is often understood—modernist versus postmodernist, the aesthetic versus the political, identity versus class, and so on—it has maintained an uncanny resonance for an audience that seems to grow with each passing year. Perhaps more important, in retrospect one can see Fani-Kayode's images not only as documents of, but as interventions in, the shifting cultural debates surrounding questions of gender and queerness, race and democratic inclusion, the enduring legacy of slavery and colonialism, visual responses to the AIDS crisis, the radical potential of photography as a medium, and the viability of transnational avant-gardes. In short, Fani-Kayode's photographs are early sites in which a present that now seems within reach was actively envisioned, negotiated, and captured in silver.

ROSES AND RESURRECTION

Fani-Kayode wrote only sporadically of his practice, typically enlisting Hirst to account for the photographs in text. Nonetheless, he left a definitive artist's statement that diagnosed the particular confluence of power and identity that circumscribed his life and compelled him to look toward visionary modes of subjectivity and artistic production. He incisively noted:

> On three counts I am an outsider: in matters of sexuality, in terms of geographical and cultural dislocation, and in the sense of not having become the sort of respectably married professional my parents might have hoped for. Such a position gives me a feeling of having very little to lose. . . . At the same time, traces of the former values remain, making it possible to take new readings on to them from an unusual vantage point. The results are bound to be disorientating.[6]

While Fani-Kayode was certainly correct that a crucial aspect of his pictures was their power to disorient and reorient the viewer, he was not, in the end, alone. Fani-Kayode's fellow travelers were Cuban *babalawos* and Afro-British video artists; American house DJs and punk rockers, or, back in London, the era's iconic frontmen—the perpetually morose and dandyish Smiths' crooner Morrissey or the Cure's Byronesque Robert Smith. The last was known for songs about loss and apparitional visitors, and such lyrics as "never fade / never die / you give me flowers of love / always fade / always die / I let fall flowers of blood."[7] The Cure were a fixture of the postpunk and goth scene in London from the late 1970s on, and listening to the aquatic tones of their nocturnal records on a fog-bound British evening, one could just as easily recall the words of the lyric poet Robert Herrick, "Gather ye rosebuds while ye may, / Old Time is still a-flying; / And this same flower that smiles today / Tomorrow will be dying."[8]

Hence the title of this book, which references those end-of-millennium Robert Smith lyrics but also connects to a deeper root structure. *Bloodflowers* conjures beauty and decay, death and resurrection, classicism and modernity, communion and commerce.[9] It suggests an uneasy balance between the vegetal and the sanguinary and nods in the direction of Fani-Kayode's play of subject and object, living and inert, and, more obviously, the HIV cells and ecstatic antibodies that punctuated the last years of his life. What's more, plant life is evident everywhere in Fani-Kayode's pictures—a floral crucifix in tight focus, or fronds and reeds revealed as glistening objects of sacrament. Ripe fruit appears as a symbol of offering and desire. Tulips, baby's breath, and wreaths of annuals form the regalia of the coterie of lovers, transsexual priests, and otherworldly figures who populate his endless twilight.

Accordingly, the echo of another time, of Charles Baudelaire's 1857 *Les fleurs du mal* is no accident.[10] Baudelaire's poetic stanzas foreground antipodes and refusals within a modernity populated by Paris's hidden rebels, its queers, artists, colonial creoles, prostitutes, and factory workers—those who militated against the alien, rational order of the Haussmannized city.[11] Like Baudelaire, Brassäi, Roy DeCarava, and many others who came before, Fani-Kayode would center and celebrate such figures in his own invisible cities. But as Hirst frequently alluded, a commonality that runs through all of these examples is a sense not of an infinite horizon but of fleeting time—loss, illness, heartbreak, even death. *Bloodflowers*, in the spirit of Baudelaire, suggests not our return to a classical beauty but, instead, a haunted one. Flowers bloom briefly and vividly but, ebbing with the spring, die all too soon. Then again, sometimes they return, like the tulips in the picture of the same name, a symbol of regeneration and resurrection.

OUT BEYOND THE BINARY

Fani-Kayode called his practice contemporary Yoruban art, and he specified his medium as "black, gay photography." These descriptions may seem superfluous in light of his subject matter, which is obviously homoerotic, featuring black men on both sides of the camera. But Fani-Kayode's self-description is telling, as well—it locates him, even within the constellation of marginalized publics and counterpublics of the 1970s and 1980s, as radically possessed of a singular vision. He was black but had to contend with lingering elements of homophobia and misogyny *within* the black radical tradition; he was gay

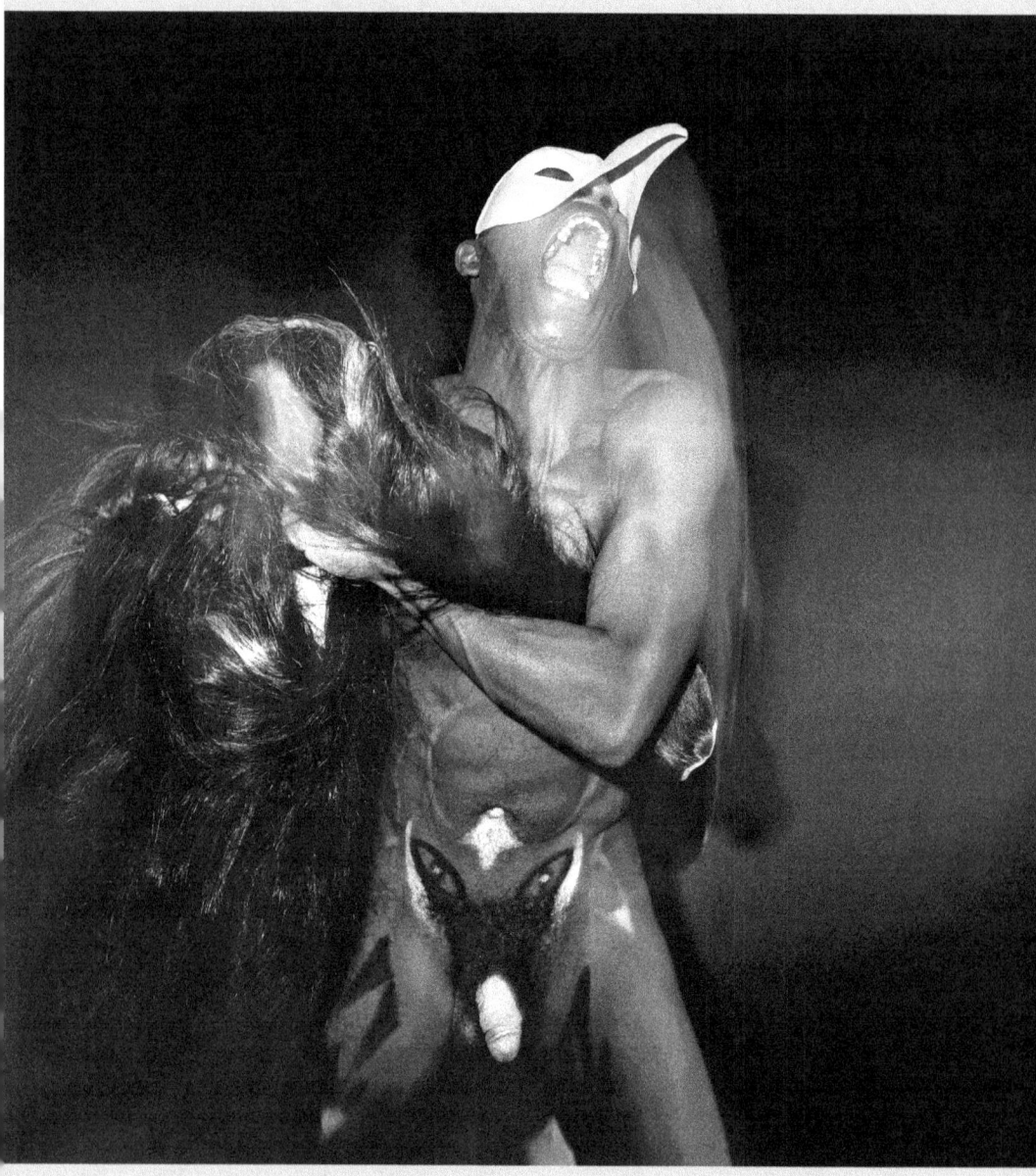

Figure Intro.3 Rotimi Fani-Kayode, *Golden Phallus* (1989). © Rotimi Fani-Kayode / Autograph ABP. Courtesy of Autograph ABP.

but was openly critical of racism and fetishism *within* the gay cultures of New York and London.[12] He was Nigerian, but by going home he would have risked familial shame and perhaps even personal harm.[13] He was a man but worked to complicate gender, actively drawing on feminist techniques and theories of subjectivity. Fani-Kayode's position was one of triangulated specificity, and he worked amid critical conversations that advocated for heterogeneity and freedom of vision over collectivist orthodoxies.

As a result, it can be difficult to define the nature of Fani-Kayode's practice. The editor Derek Bishton called him a black British artist, while Kobena Mercer dubbed him a "boundary rider of cultural difference," traversing the in-between spaces of alterity.[14] The art historian Steven Nelson sees in Fani-Kayode a desire for transcendence and an intentional transgression of limits and taboos.[15] All of these readings get at something central to the man and the work. From the perspective of the early twenty-first century, it seems clear that while Fani-Kayode's photography was aesthetically pathbreaking, it was also politically vital because it brought new subjectivities and new ethnicities into focus. It set the scale, technical precision, and historical rigor of earlier modes of photography in productive tension with radical sonics and the vestiges of early modern painting.

In so doing, he gave visibility to a range of publics otherwise excluded from art making in general, and who more typically appeared on the picture plane as objects of ethnographic knowledge, scopic pleasure, or coarse stereotype.[16] Again, it may be difficult to imagine, on the far side of the twentieth century, how significant a gesture this was, and how little support artists such as Fani-Kayode had. Now, in much of the world, nuanced depictions of black, queer, and postcolonial subjects are increasingly common. But in eighties London, such depictions were decidedly uncommon beyond an array of improvised conduits of production and reception. As Mark Sealy, the director of Autograph ABP, wrote in 1995, when Fani-Kayode tried "to generate interest in his photographs he experienced, more often than not, that the gatekeepers were out to lunch. . . . Curators found it difficult to grasp Kayode's terms of reference. Quite simply, his practice was not understood."[17]

And yet, black, queer, and diasporic subjects were always already integral to the history of the West and to modernity itself. What I argue here is that Fani-Kayode's photographs, beyond the story they tell of a time and place in recent history, beyond their evident beauty or technical virtuosity, are significant for their *relational* quality. They are important in their insistence on bridging seemingly unbridgeable binaries—of past and future, self and other, black and white—into dialogic relation. In this way, his photographs enact and open onto to possible futures while critically bringing to the surface submerged histories. During his time, Fani-Kayode staked out as a matter of necessity provisional zones that one might now recognize as intersectional, elaborating and complicating an archive of international black, gay, and Yoruban practice. That is, he made possible in his work precisely what seemed impossible to many during those years. The spaces and subjectivities recorded in Fani-Kayode's photographs self-consciously worked to queer the avant-garde art world and to critically unravel oppositional binaries and static identities. As Hirst put it in the introduction to Fani-Kayode's first artist's book in 1988, "Black–white: fantasy-races in which infinite difference reveals infinite affinity."[18] In place of the asymptotic horizon of essential difference, Fani-Kayode posits the self in a wider field of relation, a space in which subjectivity is performed, constructed, reversed, and revised.

In this way, Fani-Kayode's photographs begin to reanimate history as well, mining the past, drawing it into the present. The photographs stage a vast array of imagery, and he invokes the earliest days of modernity, in mercantile Europe and the first moments of the colonial enterprise and the Atlantic slave trade.[19] Others have Fani-Kayode disidentifying with and signifying in the terrain of art history and its layers of citation and elaboration of the past: Neoclassicism, Romanticism, pictorialism, primitivism, and surrealism are all here. What these references have in common is that they mark larger historical sites of recognition and misrecognition, points of inflection and rupture in a long, global timeline of encounter and exchange. Fani-Kayode's pictures insist—they visualize frame by frame—that the history of the West is not one of the dispersal or assimilation of difference but, instead, a dynamic landscape of collaboration, desire, and commingling. He suggests that frontiers are illusory. He reminds the viewer that there could be no Europe without Africa, no white without black. This formulation, in retrospect, tracks precisely with the theoretical and critical breakthroughs of roughly the same period in the 1980s.[20] And, as I will show, although Fani-Kayode had notable peers in the realms of art, music, and literature, his practice was in and of itself unique and, in its temporal and historical vision, profoundly ahead of its time.

Appropriately, then, Fani-Kayode seems to have allied himself with what Paul Gilroy has called "countercultures of modernity" and what Michael

Warner has designated as radical counterpublics—those working within the structures of modernity but who, nonetheless, constitute its antipodes. Such cultural formations create pockets of refusal, revision, and negation.[21] There are many words for such countercultures: they are Dionysian, they are avant-garde, they are marginal; they translate, retranslate, remix, echo, and generate "breaks."[22]

And while these modes of avant-garde practice have increasingly figured into accounts of modern art, for the purposes of thinking through Fani-Kayode's work it is worth making two qualifications here. First, one can understand modernity as a constellation of countless, singular microhistories, but there do seem, too, to be insistent nodes of resistance—outsiders and exiles who embody a will toward disruption that haunts modernity in spite of its self-narration as a history of progression or evolution. Second, many have argued that there is no "outside" of modernity, that radical politics are in a sense baked in and ultimately subordinate to the very systems they seek to unsettle. Maybe so. It is up to the reader to reckon with the ultimate efficacy of the work itself, and of the forerunners that Fani-Kayode variously resurrects and riffs on. Whatever version of modernity with which one tries and make Fani-Kayode fit, one thing is abundantly clear: he persistently attempted a form of disorientation, inaugurating zones of relation and open-endedness. Fani-Kayode's labor as a subject and an artist constituted a form of visionary praxis and cultural critique that sought to renegotiate inherited social realities.

ALCHEMICAL IMPRINTS

Treating Rotimi Fani-Kayode in art-historical terms raises several problems. As Sealy has argued, among his peers—especially photographers—Fani-Kayode was distinctive in producing work that holds up in a more explicitly aesthetic than documentary register.[23] Just as postwar African photography, with few exceptions, tended to be understood in terms of "struggle" journalism, then-emerging forms of black radical or gay liberation art also tended toward more literal approaches to representation or direct political engagement. By contrast, Fani-Kayode's own account suggests an idiosyncratic, if earnest, search for deeper truths. His method was almost certainly a consequence of what he perceived to be the limitations of the various subaltern communities with which he was in dialogue as he made his way through the circuits of the

Black Atlantic. Accordingly, he responded by looking back to his Yoruban heritage, which for him had been hidden from view by the cosmopolitan and modernizing agenda of the postcolonial Nigerian state and by his upbringing in elite schools in England and the United States.

In this way, Fani-Kayode was out of step with the contexts in which he found himself but, paradoxically, uniquely a product of them. One argument of this book is that Fani-Kayode's project can only be understood in light of the broader sociopolitical climate in which they were realized and that his works, in turn, provide indexes of specific sites and moments. But the photographs were not, in most instances, conceived as mere documents; they were never framed as clear windows onto the recent past. They are more like core samples, fossilized amber congealing and materializing a dynamic and dialectic engagement between Fani-Kayode and the people and places that were interspersed in his life.

There are a few important consequences here. For one, it means that Fani-Kayode's art may not seem, for many readers, overtly political in its orientation and execution, especially in contrast with the collectivist and activist models that would have served as both a precedent and direct parallel during his life. Yet conversely, Fani-Kayode was able to transcend the agonistic binaries of both identity-driven forms of resistance and the day-to-day of juridical politics. In various ways, the pages ahead argue that Fani-Kayode was perhaps best understood as an *errant*, Édouard Glissant's exilic subject. The errant is a figure of nomadic mobility or transoceanic passage, able to see beyond the rigidity of seeming difference. The errant points the way toward a space of rhizomatic, unexpected interconnections that are sometimes hidden from view but nonetheless form the substance of our shared modernity. For Glissant, this is "very much the image of the rhizome, prompting the knowledge that identity is no longer completely within the root but also in Relation."[24]

This seeking out of underlying spaces of relation—of finding and aligning points of convergence, dissonance, and symmetry between disparate traditions and temporalities—means that Fani-Kayode's work exudes a seemingly timeless quality. It refers to buried lifeworlds that precede and exceed the linear sweep of the modernist project and also reactivates the various technologies of modernity's many internal countercultures. This relational logic has also meant that Fani-Kayode's photographs shift in meaning and reception over time. While they were initially circulated in the community centers of

London and the pages of gay and lesbian publications, after the artist's death they took on a second life, as curators such as Sealy and Enwezor and scholars such as Nelson and Mercer brought them to the fore of what has become the fields of contemporary African art and African diaspora studies. And since the 2000s, those same works have found a much wider audience through digital pathways and renewed interest in Fani-Kayode on the part of major institutions and collectors. Like multilayered Rorschach tests, they offer different things to different viewers and cannot be accounted for as the patrimony of any one constituency. Such durability and reach would, perhaps, have been gratifying to Fani-Kayode, who sought to go beyond the quotidian to locate and elaborate more subtle membranes of connectivity through his practice.

It is tempting, then, to treat these photographs primarily as interpretive puzzles, attending to their rich iconographic citations, their familiar but distinctive play with canonical tropes, their literary or hagiographic allusions, and their technical precision. Fani-Kayode was clearly calling on and responding to the discourses around a transcultural set of art-historical codes. As such, close reading of the objects, their dense materiality and multiaccentual reference, is crucial. Indeed, a positive effect of the efforts of so many during the last several decades has been the gradual centering—however partial or complicated—of once marginal practices at the heart of the global contemporary. Accordingly, more traditional historical or interpretive work on artists such as Fani-Kayode is possible and long overdue. And given the progressive momentum of the 1990s and early 2000s, one could imagine writing this book ten years ago using more narrowly art historical parameters as a kind of political intervention in its own right, signaling a move from "black" or "diaspora" art to contemporary art tout court.

Certainly, Fani-Kayode's photographs provide more than enough material for such a sustained project of description and analysis. What's more, writing in 2005 Mercer himself argued that perhaps framing art in terms of more general social or political currents might be insufficient, that the next phase of historicizing diasporic and black radical culture is one of carefully attending to specific objects rather than holding them up as exemplary of a particular polemical or sociopolitical project.[25] This suggestion echoes Sealy's concern that the black British moment itself has been, to an extent, reified in recent years—that a revisionist fixity has been given to what was, in effect, a small network of often disparate and overlapping individual interventions.

Importantly, Fani-Kayode made his work in direct tension with the alignment of social and spatial forces of his own experience in the 1980s, with its particular blend of life in the United States—one inflected by openly public models of gay freedom, black gay consciousness, punk, and postmodernism—and the United Kingdom, with its postimperial melancholia, its multitudes of recent immigrants, its persistent but diminished legacy of left politics, and its new sonic and sartorial formations. This book argues that his was an art inextricably linked to that moment, an art that responded to and complicated the cultural politics of a decade by visualizing new forms of subjectivity.

Some thirty years on, more progress has been made on issues of equity in Western institutions and its art worlds than Fani-Kayode might have thought possible. Nonetheless, from our current vantage point, that progress seems by turns fragile or illusory. A younger generation attuned to a resurgence in ethnonationalism, Islamophobia, anticosmopolitan skepticism, and persistent violence against black bodies might understandably consider attempts to delink art from politics and power (even rhetorically) as naive or misguided. They might, indeed, find helpful precedent for the present situation in those first years after the conservative retrenchments of 1979–1980—when clashes with the police, confrontations with quotidian racism, and official discourses that propped up xenophobic and homophobic visions of Britishness galvanized action by artists, musicians, and writers. They might, finally, look to Fani-Kayode's photographs, which staked out the contours of a queer, diasporic, antimisogynistic, and inclusive world that is still being fought for today. Those photographs and Fani-Kayode's written work with Alex Hirst speak not to a utopian prospect but to a life in which the past is always present and progress itself is contingent, if not merely transient. For all that, in those same words and pictures tragedy is invariably counterbalanced by moments of rebellious self-determination, Dionysian communion, and small but powerful gestures of transgression and freedom. In practice, they contributed to a crucial process of negative dialectics while also seeking paths of transcendence.

My goal here, then, is to echo Fani-Kayode's method. I do not argue for the primacy of one position over another but follow the open-ended and rhizomatic connections manifest in the work wherever they lead. There are inevitable excursions into nested and contested histories of art, visual and sonic cultures, and the broader sociopolitical matrix through which they were constituted. In this way, *Bloodflowers* follows Paul Gilroy's suggestion to explore "the detailed unfolding of cultural formation. The aim of this is not to construct a history of simple hybridity to offset against the achievements of the homogenizers and purity seekers. Instead, local and specific intervention can contribute to a counterhistory of cultural relations and influence from which a new understanding of multicultural Europe [might emerge]."[26]

This book aims to balance close investigations of material cultures and the lived experience of them not to delink art from life but as a way of contributing what will, undoubtedly, be one of many close analyses of the constituent forms that have, in practice, articulated diasporic modes of subjectivity so effectively theorized by others in recent decades.

As a closely related note, it should be clear that while this book takes Rotimi Fani-Kayode as a focal point, it is not an attempt to retroactively canonize him or to subsume him within the more universalizing economy of authenticity and valuation that he and many around him carefully sought to subvert. For one, it is clear that while Fani-Kayode's photographs evince a singular confluence of semiotic and material interests, he himself seemed to draw not on conventions of originality so central to Western modernism but instead on what he and Hirst dubbed "premodern" models of storytelling, masquerade, and reinvention. Of course, such aesthetic strategies never really went away, surviving in the diasporic practice of signifying on received symbolic or narrative scripts, or through the more general principle in much West African cosmology of the artist as a medium for spiritual or creative energy as it enters the world. Moreover, Fani-Kayode frequently relied on masking and costuming his sitters and constructing tableaux of energetic transformation. He did this in order to undermine the very notion of static identity while, in the final years of his life, staging his process as a collaboration with Alex Hirst.

In a slightly more abstract register, I also agree with Kobena Mercer that a core strength of Fani-Kayode's work was its insistence on the proposition that "self and Other are always mutually implicated in ties of identification and desire . . . its emphasis on the constitutive hybridity of the postcolonial and diasporic subject."[27] Mercer elaborates how Fani-Kayode and contemporaries such as Lyle Ashton Harris, Marlon Riggs, and Isaac Julien worked at the confluence of traditions, cutting into and working against the grain of "master codes"—be they canonical or tied to identity-based forms of collectivity such as gay liberation or black (inter)nationalisms. In this way, to lionize Fani-Kayode according to the logic of Western art history or one of its categorical shorthands (black art, queer art, African art, modernist, postmodernist, and so on) is to miss the point. The following makes clear that Fani-Kayode, too, intentionally negotiated the relative margins of exile and the productive tension that he located at the intersections between existing categories. As such, he quite openly resisted affiliation with any particular group or ideology. It is therefore insufficient to simply note that he was a diaspora artist; rather, the task here is to find out what diaspora means at discrete moments of its articulation as part of a slower kind of historical work. This is the primary goal of the chapters ahead.

With that in mind, *Bloodflowers* is perhaps best understood as what the art historian George Baker termed an "anti-monograph." His writing on Francis Picabia centered "a marginal period, a marginal figure, a blind-spot for art history" so that from "this half-forgotten, not-yet-congealed historical moment can emerge a re-reading."[28] But a rereading of what? For Baker it is the terms of Dada itself; for *Bloodflowers* it is the specificity of diasporic practice between the years 1976 and 1989, a marginal period not unlike interwar Europe: seemingly stuck between more belabored historical moments, at once consciously optimistic but wearied, even traumatized by the long shadow of resurgent nationalism, a catastrophic virus, violence in the streets, and tectonic shifts in the political landscape.

Dada was (like diaspora) routed in upheaval, in the transnational, and in the transgression or appropriation of master codes. Fani-Kayode, in turn, explicitly tapped into the various countercultures of modernity activated in the interventions we retrospectively call Dada, using tactics of bohemian earnestness and bitter irony. And diaspora (like Dada) loses its edge as a revisionary force at the moment of its canonization: each forces the historian to chart the avowedly amorphous, to resist hypostatizing its adaptive and resistant energies without arresting it in the process. *Bloodflowers* attempts to do so by homing in on the layers encoded in different photographs, which are revealed, like Baker's Dada strategies, as dialogic, as "mediating forces" in a "much larger cultural phenomenon."[29]

A second ambition of *Bloodflowers* is to offer case studies in the formation of an emerging account of, indeed, a much larger phenomenon—the long 1980s itself. Fani-Kayode staged his work in response to debates around the role of art in pressing political conflicts (from institutional recognition for marginalized subjects to adequate responses to the AIDS crisis), and the resulting photographs prompt the viewer to reckon with the wider landscape of 1980s cultural production and the polemics that defined it. Fani-Kayode's practice provides powerful examples of ways in which then-contemporary art transcends some of the more ideological critiques of the period. For example, he notably did not make the sort of explicitly postconceptual photography that was championed by many prominent critics but, instead, drew on earlier conventions within a self-consciously aesthetic lineage. Fani-Kayode built on a range of countercultural practices within modernity, such as Romanticism and homoerotic portraiture, and materialized modes drawn from musical cultures, ranging from the black radical tradition to punk.

A long-standing concern among critics—especially those who came of age in the tradition of the neo-avant-garde and the New Left—was that with the fragmentation and stylistic eclecticism often associated with postmodernist practice meant the end of an era, and with it, a tradition of critique and political engagement. It is perhaps for this reason that a great deal of art historical writing of the past decade has tended to pick up on art produced in the early 1970s, or after 1989, with the efflorescence of projects dealing with questions of democracy, globalization, and participation.[30] And while there has, of course, been writing to date on the 1980s, much of it has emerged from the realm of criticism written at the time, or in the form of broader political retrospective. As Fani-Kayode's peer Keith Piper poignantly remarked: "The 1980s has emerged in our contemporary consciousness as a misread, misaligned, and misinterpreted decade. Trapped somewhere between the heat and light of the 1990s, when the strategic intervention of marketing moguls created an environment within which to be young, British, and an artist was to be conferred almost instant celebrity status, the 1980s has become a decade consigned to the murky shadows of prehistory."[31]

To some degree, the presence of such a blind spot is unsurprising. The 1980s was, for many, a decade out of time. To the seeming dispersion of modernism's linear flows, one might add that the popular culture of the decade was awash with nostalgia, from conservative fantasies embedded in discourse as far ranging as sitcoms and Saturday morning TV to the proclamations of iconic leaders such as Ronald Reagan and Margaret Thatcher. Both of the latter appealed to conceptions of society of which Christianity, the heterosexual nuclear family, and free-market capitalism were central pillars. The historian Sean Wilentz and theorist David Harvey, in different ways, have pointed to a "long 1980s" that began somewhere in the decade prior: the 1980s were borne out of a pushback against the gains of the civil rights and Stonewall era, the rollback of organized labor in the United States and England, the deregulation of financial markets, the emergence of the religious right, and a tragic—even willful—mishandling of the AIDS epidemic.[32] As such, many might recall these years as either a protracted nightmare, symbolized literally in the Eisenhower-age bromides and rampant consumerism of the film *Back to the Future* (1985), or else as prehistory—indeed, as the run-up to an unfettered neoliberal capitalism with postmodernist art as its visual culture.[33]

Nevertheless, while the 1980s can be seen as a critical period of transition, that transition was rarely uncontested. As a range of curatorial explorations have compellingly demonstrated, eclecticism often correlated with heterogeneity, a willingness to break with orthodoxy and transcend boundaries, in the process actively renegotiating inherited notions of identity, location, and value. The 1980s was a time of confluence between activism and cultural production during which the various strands of identity politics that emerged in the wake of the 1960s deepened in complexity, cross-pollination, and public address. Fani-Kayode's work was formed within this crucible, and it documents not only debates *within* key counterpublics of the era but potential futures and usable preludes that paralleled or were pushed to the edges during those years. Both his writing and Hirst's describe life in some of the world's wealthiest cities, where a chasm loomed between those who profited and those who were left behind—people of color, people with AIDS, people who had helped to build those cities but were nonetheless too recently arrived. Such histories were sketched eloquently at the time by theorists and critics such as Stuart Hall, Rosalyn Deutsche, and Gregg Bordowitz. With respect to Fani-Kayode's art, in particular, Hirst summed it up: "in this tangible Western world of not-enough light, the sight of human (and more specifically, male) flesh 'exposed' really is fantastic . . . a temporary and marvelous relief from the glare of analysis and the tyranny of capital gains."[34]

In short, I agree with Helen Molesworth in her contention that the 1980s was a decade marked not merely by excess, by regress, or by mere eclecticism.[35] It was, instead, a time in which art, politics, and (importantly) love—desire, fantasy, memory—all coalesced to do vital work. Her inclusion of Fani-Kayode in her landmark 2011 exhibition was no accident. So a second aim of this book, beyond drawing sustained attention to Fani-Kayode and his oeuvre, is to connect them meaningfully to larger histories of the 1980s. My goal here is not to periodize the decade as such but to argue that there are meaningful questions to be addressed through the lens of Fani-Kayode's photographs. For example, in what ways can the black radical tradition or surrealism be enlisted in the cultural politics of the day? What avenues beyond direct agitation could be pursued to address the AIDS crisis? Which extant knowledges or facets of traditional practice might be brought to bear productively after modernism? And what new syncretism could be unearthed or envisioned in so doing?

FULL BLEED

This chapter opened with two photographs called *Tulip Boy*, first processed as Cibachromes and then again as gum bichromate prints—one of the several "alternative" methods being taught in London during the late 1980s, along with platinum and Van Dyke brown processes. Fani-Kayode had experimented with printmaking as early as 1978. He and Hirst hand-tinted black-and-white prints more consistently in 1987, and gum bichromates in marine blues and earthy reds soon followed. And Hirst continued in this vein between 1989 and 1992 as a sort of afterimage of their collaboration. While these techniques are closely associated with the photographic vanguard of a full century prior, in procedure and effect their meaning was clear, marking a sharp contrast with a modernist standard that valorized precision, clarity, and tonal control.

In this way, falling on the far side of the modernist divide, Fani-Kayode's alternate process prints align more closely with what Kaja Silverman has theorized as the "liquid intelligence" of early photography.[36] She means liquid in a literal sense, as in the application of flowing collodion to glass plates, but also as a more ambient sensibility: of motion captured by open shutters, of the potential for chance, error, and perhaps even the occasional specter to irrevocably materialize as the fix is applied. This formulation also rhymes with what Derek Conrad Murray has elaborated as a contemporary aesthetic of "liquid blackness," in which subjectivity is understood as perpetually adaptive and contingent, where blackness itself is an unbounded, pliable affective force.[37]

While Fani-Kayode used technology that came into fashion some thirty years after wet collodion, he too partook of a liquid sensibility through the dynamism and dissolution of figures in his black-and-white prints, and in the gum bichromates, with their imprecise hand application of photo-sensitive metals. Neither technique relies on aqueous chemicals per se but on multiple or rapid exposures—the repeated snaps of the camera or the successive bursts of contact printing used to build additive chromatic layers in pictorialist prints. Multiple exposures capture time, in the blurred duration of movement

Nothing to Lose / 19

across frames, in recurrent pulsations and multiplicities, and in the physical accretion of surfaces, built on paper supports like sedimentary layers.

Metaphors of fluidity, admixture, spectrality, and mobility abound in the chapters that follow, but the framework of the book is based on the logic of multiple exposure itself: in this type of photograph, any one opening of the shutter registers a single image that is, in its way, real. But once the final image is processed, those single shots are revealed as incomplete. The coherence of the image is built through multiple returns to the same substrate. And so, rather than proceed in a linear or biographical fashion, the chapters that follow can be thought as individual exposures that accumulate and might be seen in hindsight as a provisional whole. As such, the same objects, people, or places are revisited, but they appear in different layers, inflected by shifts in time, in methodological filter, or in theoretical starting point. Again, part of the longevity of Fani-Kayode's photographs is their density of resonances and affinities. His gift was not so much for appropriation or remix as for drawing together referents seemingly alien to each other on a unified, viscid field.

The first half of the book is oriented spatially, around particular physical locations, sites of publicity and counterpublicity, and the transnational flows that gave rise to emerging forms of identity and their attendant aesthetics and politics. Exposure 1 charts the terrain of Brixton, South London, where Fani-Kayode settled and produced his entire body of mature work. I argue here that rather than representing Nigerian, African, or black art as they were defined in the 1970s and early 1980s, his photographs underscored and contributed to an emerging conception of ethnicity and black radicalism in London that built on earlier diasporic modalities while also responding to specific pressures of race and nation, as well as to the powerful theoretical and artistic discourses forged as subjects from the postcolonies settled in the city.

London after 1976 had, more generally, emerged as a cultural capital of underground sonic cultures formed through material flows and psychic affinities between England and the Americas—from the roots of early punk rock in New York and the pulsations emanating from Caribbean sound systems and a subterranean network of urban dance clubs and loft parties. Exposure 2 explores the ways in which avant-garde energies were reinvigorated through communities forged in relation to music, the spaces where it is played, and its diffusion through vernacular forms such as posters, magazines, clothing, and hair. Fani-Kayode was implicitly and explicitly in dialogue with such musical communities and, taken together, a picture of the 1980s begins to emerge that works against the grain of long-standing, commonplace narratives of art-world excess and post-1968 fatalism.

Exposure 3 considers the role Fani-Kayode played in the queer politics of the 1980s. Fani-Kayode's photographs first found purchase in the global circuits of gay literature and erotica—his work extended visual codes that obtained since at least the Victorian era and gained in visibility during the post-Stonewall years of the 1970s. In London, gay and lesbian liberation politics remained less overt but were nonetheless potent in an array of counterpublics. Fani-Kayode connected a transatlantic constellation of visual culture with nascent projects that dealt with the specific challenges and openings presented in the postcolonial metropolis. He did this, in no small part, by merging black American and specifically British articulations of liberation and black gay consciousness. As a result, he contributed to the emergence of intersectional and performative modes of subjectivity that would, in the following decade, be more fully theorized as disidentificatory and queer.

The second half of the book shifts to interpret the far-reaching citations and appropriations apparent in many of the photographs, theorizing Fani-Kayode's uses of a wide array of referents drawn from a geographically and temporally broad archive. While each of these three chapters undertakes sustained semiotic readings of the work, outlining Fani-Kayode's practice of subversion, signification, and juxtaposition, each also takes his own claims seriously—namely, that his was a contemporary practice or Yoruban spiritual invocation that he termed a "technique of ecstasy." As a result, Exposures 4 and 5 build from this self-understanding, which complicates Fani-Kayode's uses of arguably antiquated countercultural strategies within modernity and, indeed, helps to explain the reappearance of Romanticist and surrealist currents in the 1980s as much more than ironic or nostalgic revivalism.

One of the most notable harbingers of the end of modernism was the widespread rephrasing of antiquity as pastiche or site of semiotic play, notably with the return of Neoclassical motifs in architecture and the visual arts. Fani-Kayode was not immune to this impulse. But as the final chapter argues, this return to the premodern was for him not a matter of style, cynical self-mythologizing, or commentary on the exhaustion of originality. Instead, Fani-Kayode and Hirst sought in their last photographs to enlist techniques and forms of encounter that were then thought to be the province of theatricality or ritual but were once an integral function for the artist in Europe and Africa alike. These photographs amplify secret histories of "Western" art that could, if applied anew, reveal the marvelous in the world or, perhaps, even talismanically resist death, as in his final series, which was addressed to the AIDS crisis. In the process, Fani-Kayode worked in parallel with his contemporaries not as an activist but by turning back to art as a place of communion, interconnection, and unimaginable potential in an evidently tragic, disenchanted world.

BRIXTON

But thought in reality spaces itself out into the world.
It informs the imaginaries of people, their varied poetics,
which it then transforms, meaning, in them its risk becomes realized. . . .
Culture is the precaution of those who claim to think thought
but steer clear of its chaotic journey. Evolving cultures infer Relation,
the overstepping that grounds their unity-diversity.

Édouard Glissant, *Poetics of Relation*

I face the wardrobe. I open the windows behind me and
increase the camera's exposure setting slightly. A black lamp, gray striped
wallpaper, the wardrobe, a foldable luggage rack, black light switches, a
brazen handle on a black door. Arrayed like that, they look like an illustration
in a child's encyclopedia. This is a door. This is a ship. This is a lake. This is a
mountain. This is a room to which you long to be away, a room redolent
of fernweh. This is a man in a room, crouched behind the camera,
readying his shot, far away from home, not completely happy,
but happier perhaps than he would be elsewhere.

Teju Cole, "Far Away from Here"

FERNWEH

In 1988, Rotimi Fani-Kayode released the only solo collection of his works
to appear during his life, an arrangement of black-and-white reproductions
in a small, square volume called *Black Male/White Male*—a fitting title for a
book that references a century of photographic nudes of men, and one that
does so in the register of interracial homoerotic portraiture. At seventy pages,

Black Male/White Male includes some sixty pictures in portrait, landscape, and square formats, reproduced at roughly seven inches to a side. Several models—including activists, poets, fellow artists, and Fani-Kayode himself—recur either as themselves or as staged characters. Alex Hirst, then a writer and editor, provides a brief introductory text that sums up the collection as "Black–white: fantasy-races in which infinite difference reveals infinite affinity."[1] Fani-Kayode would display and publish several photographic series during the next two years, but *Black Male/White Male* was the definitive statement of his early years as an artist, and a slim résumé of finished work dating from 1983 to 1987. While archival records showed Fani-Kayode experimenting with printmaking and drawing—mostly in a full-color figurative mode, reverse-engineering the primitivist gestures of Henri Matisse—the book cataloged his decisive turn to black-and-white photography as both a tonal and an epistemological bedrock.

In browsing through this portfolio, one cannot but be struck by its peripatetic quality: while many of the pictures are rendered in the purgatorial darkness of a studio, these are juxtaposed with pieces produced on the go. Some are shot in the grainy tones of the snapshot, some playful and ad hoc, others quiet, bordering on the hagiographic. *Charles Forbes and David in Washington* (figure 1.1),[2] for instance, is the facing page of a studio work from Brixton. Probably shot around 1983, it closely frames a candid moment of loving embrace, hearkening to an early adulthood spent within the influential black gay scene of the American capital. Another portrait shows a young blond figure, shirtless and sandaled, gazing bemusedly into the lens as a plump nun dozes against the barrier on which he sits. *Station of the Cross, Vatican City* plays off ironic juxtaposition but also shows that Fani-Kayode embarked on his own "grand tour," reaching Italy, a nexus of Catholic history and a legacy of premodern cosmopolitanism.[3]

Two other facing images depict fishermen drawing their gear along the beach in western Africa. *Fishermen, Lomé* is an aestheticized portrait of a Togolese man, whose draped mesh suggests monastic vestments or the elaborate masquerade accoutrements typical of the wider region. *Fishermen, Bar Beach, Lagos* is panoramic, comprising a horizon of palms and men in shorts conversing amid their weighted nets. Beaches and ruined structures punctuate more abstract compositions in the book but remain nameless—they could be the shores of Brighton or the slave port of Elmina. What is clear is that many of the outdoor photographs in *Black Male/White Male* suggest departure and

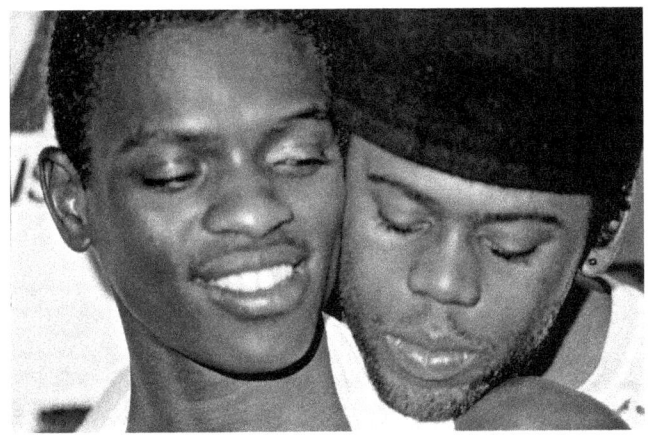

Figure 1.1 Rotimi Fani-Kayode, *Charles Forbes and David
in Washington* (ca. 1983). © Rotimi Fani-Kayode / Autograph ABP.
Courtesy of Autograph ABP.

arrival. While time and place may be uncertain, an undercurrent of maritime vastness prevails. In short, to the extent that Fani-Kayode's pictures have a place, that place seems to be the Atlantic triangle—the zone inaugurated by the slave trade and reinscribed through subsequent centuries of travel, migration, translation, observation, and appropriation.

For their part, the stillness and subtlety of Fani-Kayode's "travel pictures" suggest patience and immersion, a photographer at ease in many contexts, and inspired to roam. Of course, there are different names to this form of wandering artist: the angst-ridden Romantic, finding himself amidst misty mountains and derelict ruins; or the nomadic freedom of the post–studio artist, making her way from (air)port to (air)port. Both connote a sense of willful departure and, indeed, privilege.[4] One might be tempted now to think of Fani-Kayode as an "Afropolitan," the class of boarding school–educated internationals of African descent, as comfortable in New York or Brussels as Lagos or Accra. On paper, Fani-Kayode seemed to fit this bill: educated after 1966 at elite British schools such as Millfield in Somerset and, later, in economics at Georgetown University. He was not only the scion of a prominent Yoruban political family but heir to the lineage of Ifá, the class of diviner priests who helped order the Yoruban cosmos.

But his wandering was not marked by the privilege of the twenty-first-century elite. A young man searching for a place in the world, his movements

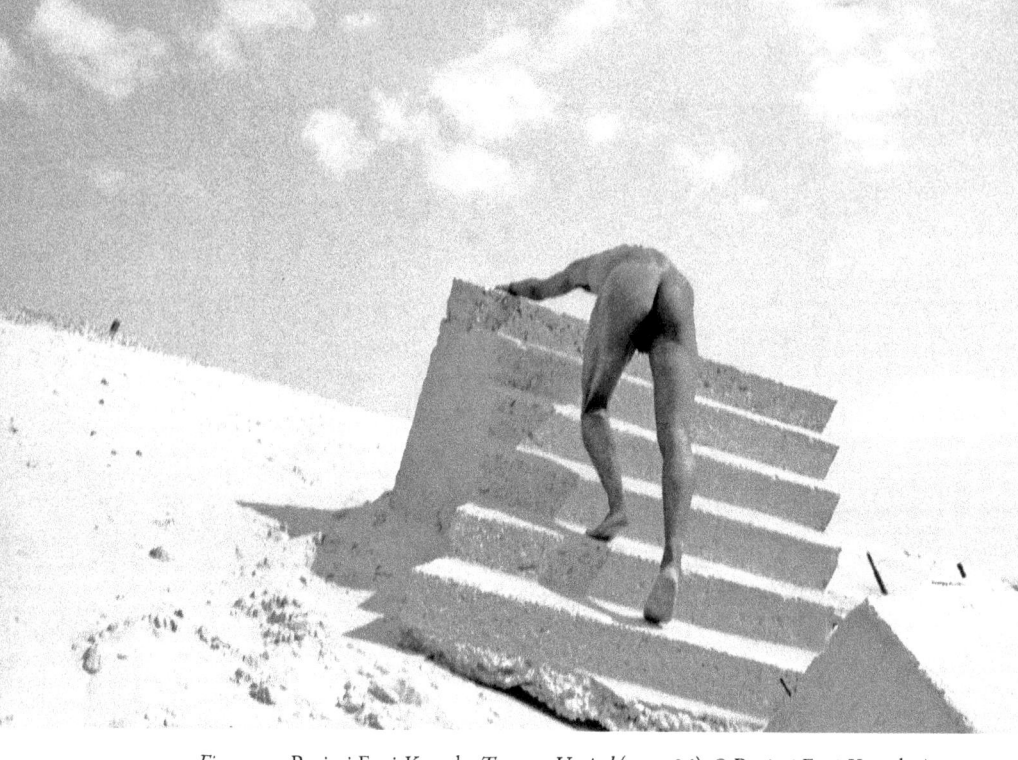

Figure 1.2 Rotimi Fani-Kayode, *Tongues Untied* (ca. 1986). © Rotimi Fani-Kayode / Autograph ABP. Courtesy of Autograph ABP.

were solitary, psychically laden in a manner suited to an earlier time. And, as Teju Cole argues, the first sort of movement might be characterized by wanderlust, which is "rooted in the German Romantic tradition and is strongly tied to walking out in nature." The second type, however, is characterized by *Fernweh*, a longing to be away from home, a desire to be in faraway places. *Fernweh* is similar to wanderlust but "has a sickish, melancholy tinge.... *Fernweh* is the silver lining of melancholia around the cloud of happiness about being far from home."[5] For Freud, melancholia suggested fixation, an inability to integrate grief and, thus, to belabor and, ultimately, relive it. Wandering is, reciprocally, the silver lining of those who cannot return home but cannot fully leave it behind, either.

Fani-Kayode left Nigeria the year before the Biafran secession—a political crisis that fragmented the nascent state and shattered the political balance between the western Yoruba, northern Hausa, and eastern Igbo. The war ended in 1970, but by the time Fani-Kayode reached adulthood, he could not return for other reasons. In his definitive artist's statement, he concluded that he was made an outsider on multiple levels, a person with no attachments and nothing to lose, whose history rested just beyond the veil, yet somehow still tangible. As he recounted, "traces of the former values remain, making it possible to take new readings on to them from an unusual vantage point. The results are bound to be disorientating."[6] What Fani-Kayode describes here is the position of the exile—the errant who cannot return home. His refusal to become a "respectably married professional" would have not only disappointed his parents but conceivably invited embarrassment and shame given their social standing in what was then a conservative society. His queerness would have meant alienation or perhaps even violence against him.[7]

And yet, like so many exiles of modernity, Fani-Kayode found his silver lining. He carried with him vestiges of his past but saw his natal home and adopted country from a sort of parallax, finding "new readings" from his "unusual vantage point." Which is why, according to Édouard Glissant (the great theorist of movement and creolization in the Atlantic), the mere nomad is "overdetermined by the conditions of his existence . . . rather than the enjoyment of freedom"; nomadism may instead be a "form of obedience to contingencies that are restrictive."[8] And while the exile and the errant share a lack of roots, the errant, far from losing home altogether, gains a new power, to transcend sharp dualities and static identities. The errant thus moves into a space of relation and dialectics. For the errant, in "taking up the problems of the Other, it is possible to find oneself."[9]

Errantry characterizes a great deal of Fani-Kayode's interventions in the world, and their critical stakes. By blending the distance of the exile and the mobility of the nomad, Fani-Kayode, a quintessential errant, was able to draw upon—find the points of relation between—seemingly disparate histories and topographies, thus revisualizing the contours not only of his lived subjectivity but also of a shared history of modernity itself. In seeing clearly the various trajectories of the black Atlantic triangle that articulated together Africa, Europe, and the Americas, his photographs become a staging ground of forgotten histories and occluded presents. For the viewer, his work functions as both a critical guide and also a knowing site of inversion and disruption. This position of errantry, this "unusual perspective," allowed Fani-Kayode to apply the lessons of a Nigerian childhood and an American education within his adopted home, the South London of the mid-to-late 1980s. This South London was a welter of performance, art, music, and political activism. While it is clear from the *Black Male/White Male* portfolio that although Fani-Kayode, like a latter-day Arthur Rimbaud, made his way around the streets of Europe and the shores of the Atlantic, he spent the final and most productive years deeply enmeshed in a British context, his pictures at once a document and an instrument of the expanding and contested terrain of life in England during a Conservative resurgence.

It is clear that Fani-Kayode drew considerable influence and energy from the varied communities that surrounded him there, with whom he worked in dialectical relation. His photographs reflected this world and channeled altogether new ones, merging elements of a Yoruban past and his wider travels in the Atlantic world with the florescence of British art production by the postcolonial citizens actively reshaping the sociocultural contours of "nation." Unsurprisingly, given the long-standing connection between black radical art and sonics,[10] the avant-garde and utopian pulse of the British musical underground was formative of Fani-Kayode's ostensibly visual output. And so, one can imagine Fani-Kayode, amid the housing cooperatives and squats along Railton Road, "a man in a room, crouched behind the camera, readying his shot, far away from home, not completely happy, but happier perhaps than he would be elsewhere."[11]

A LIVED CONTRADICTION

One can start to reconcile these two levels—the flows of a diasporic mobility and the specific cultural politics of British nationalism—by looking back to the work of another key figure who came to prominence at the same moment, theorizing and mediating the cultural politics of England in the 1980s. In *The Black Atlantic: Modernity and Double Consciousness* Paul Gilroy built on the methods of the Birmingham Centre for Contemporary Cultural Studies—with its emphasis on class formation and the power of subculture, popular music, and other "ephemera"—and borrowed its title from the work of W. E. B. Du Bois, a seminal theorist of cosmopolitanism and the political power of black art.[12] Gilroy outlined not only a capacious conception of blackness in Britain but also the conceptual and lived instability of Britishness itself.[13] He argued for an understanding of race based not on notions of purity but, rather, on hybridity, and for a history of the modern West that is, at root, rhizomatic . . . adaptive and multifaceted. For Gilroy, the "history of the black Atlantic yields a course of lessons as to the instability and mutability of identities which are always unfinished, always being remade."[14]

At the same time, the lived experience of blackness and the power of various black radical traditions—visual, sonic, and textual—remain vivid, central to Gilroy's larger narrative. In an essay for *The New Statesman* in 1990, he argued that, "in this climate, to be both black and British was thought to be an impossible compound identity. To be British is, in any case, to contract into a category of administrative convenience rather than an ethnic identity."[15] Gilroy's target is a biological racism that underscored decades of social and institutional exclusion of postcolonial subjects who had migrated during the years following World War II. When he writes of British "ethnic absolutism,"[16] he does so living in the shadow of urban uprising (like the 1958 Notting Hill Riots or those in Brixton in 1981 and 1985)[17] and legislation aimed at curtailing immigration or undermining the quotidian rights of black subjects to housing or employment.[18]

The Black Atlantic was foreshadowed during Gilroy's time in London's Elephant and Castle area, teaching sociology at South Bank Polytechnic as a decade of Tory political dominance drew to a close, during which racism had made its way into the day-to-day of school yard taunts and the euphemisms of political discourse.[19] With respect to the realm of art institutions and criticism, Jean Fisher recalled, when analyzing *The Other Story* exhibition at the Hayward Gallery in 1989, the supposed internationalism through which British modernism was conceived concealed a "dusty parochialism."[20] That parochialism effectively obscured the earlier work of black artists in England and amounted to the sustained institutional exclusion of artists from the Commonwealth. Many of the latter arrived as part of the so-called *Windrush* generation, named after the Atlantic-bound ship that brought a first-generation of Caribbean-born blacks to the United Kingdom;[21] others were more recent arrivals, exiles and errants from the African postcolony, such as the Fani-Kayodes, fleeing Nigeria in 1966.[22]

As the historian Eddie Chambers has argued, the postwar years were marked by the pointed absence in the official self-definition of British modernism of the various postcolonial artists who worked either from or in relation to the metropolitan center in London. By the 1970s, the beginning of a wider conception of blackness in England—one that comprised people drawn from the shores of South America, the Indian subcontinent, Africa, and the Caribbean—was being reinforced not only by the day-to-day of xenophobia and spatial segregation but also in the grouping of otherwise unlike artists under the heading of "ethnic art" in periodic group shows and critical write-ups. A black consciousness began to solidify at precisely this moment, building on the literary and activist legacy of the Caribbean Artists Movement and the British Black Panthers, which paralleled American counterparts in the late 1960s. External events were also galvanizing: the intensification of the struggle against apartheid in South Africa with the widely publicized crackdown on the Soweto uprising of June 1976, and the Second World Black and African Festival of Arts and Culture (Festac '77) held in Lagos in 1977. As Chambers argues, the late 1970s marked a shift in self-identification from Caribbean or Afro-Caribbean to "black British"—a classification that would become all the more politicized at the turn of the decade, which saw clashes between police and citizens in the streets of working-class black areas of many cities, and responses thereto in the form of art, music, and direct activism.[23] This emerging multitude was documented by, among others, the postpunk social photographer Syd Shelton, as in his rousing crowd-level picture of Darcus Howe (1943–2017), the Trinidadian-born community organizer and figure in the British Black Panther movement (figure 1.3). Here Howe stands above a mixed-race crowd with a bullhorn in hand, the massive housing blocks of the South London area of Lewisham hulking in the distance.

Chambers himself came from the Midlands and lived for a time in Bristol, working as an artist and critic. Citing his work on the anti-immigrant National Front party, included in *The Other Story*, Fisher notes that "by the 1980s post-conceptual, mostly British-born Black and Asian artists [were] politicised by a social milieu fraught with prejudice, discrimination and racial tension."[24] And so, it is unsurprising that by decade's end, Gilroy would diagnose the prospect of being "black and British" as "a lived contradiction," one that carried a considerable political weight. Such a politics was unifying for a heterogeneous constellation of practices known retrospectively as the "Black British Arts Movement"[25]—a cause for optimism and set of attempts to, in Stuart Hall's terms, reconfigure the "relations of representation."[26]

It is important to rehearse Gilroy's claims and to provide this overview of the social and institutional terrain of Britain in the 1980s because it suggests at least two frameworks for understanding Fani-Kayode's entire post-MFA practice. In one sense, *The Black Atlantic* provides a topography that maps more or less precisely onto that of Fani-Kayode's own travels, documented in his photographs. For Fani-Kayode (like Gilroy), this is a topography populated by errants and aliens, defined through an endless play of translation and relation.

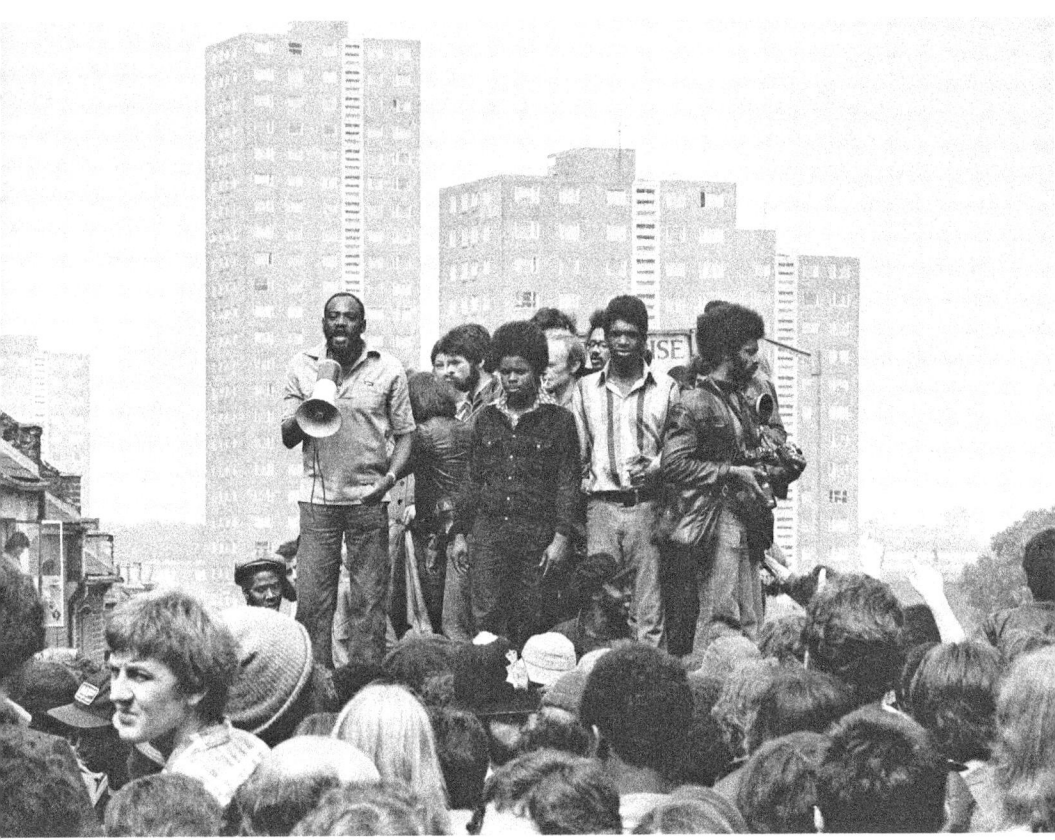

Figure 1.3 Syd Shelton, *Darcus Howe in Lewisham* (1977). © Syd Shelton / Autograph ABP. Courtesy of Autograph ABP.

In turn, Fani-Kayode was the sort of figure—at once cosmopolitan and exilic, free to roam but never to return, perched in a vantage of parallax to home and adopted home—that Gilroy might have been addressing when he argued that the "strange history" of the black English demanded that "we strive to integrate the different dimensions of our hybrid cultural heritage more effectively. ... In doing this we may discover that our story is not the *other* story at all, but *the* story of England in the modern world."[27]

For all of the difficulties faced on the national level by Britons from the Commonwealth, it is also clear that the 1980s marked a time of powerful cultural production across media. Cautioning against the reductions and elisions inherent in critical formulations such as "black art" or "Black Arts Movement,"[28] the multimedia artist Keith Piper notes that "the clearest outcome and perhaps the most tangible legacy of the Black Arts Movement is the partial assertion of its own visibility." Recalling his time in the Midlands, cofounding the BLK Art Group in 1979 and attending the First National Black Art Convention in 1982, Piper notes the heterogeneous character of the debates: from "early alliances around gender politics" to balancing "cultural nationalistic countertext to the instinctive racial pluralism of the emerging generation" and clashes with public funding bodies, such as West Midlands Arts.[29]

One can glean in Piper's writing the careful interplay of, on the one hand, older generations formed by the experience of anti-Caribbean racism and, on the other, a younger cohort marked by the confluence of intersecting identities and interests; of the tactical value of asserting a cogent black British identity and the artistic imperative of respecting creative autonomy. As these larger theoretical debates played out in Wolverhampton, Finsbury Park, Brixton, and beyond, what is clear is that Fani-Kayode had, by 1983, alighted on a wider terrain of counterpublics and practices that fostered and gave critical definition to his own practice. In the 1983–1984 season alone, he would have had access to exhibitions of Piper's and Chambers's work as the BLK Group (at the Battersea Arts Centre); absorbed the influence of African artists such as Lubaina Himid, Gavin Jantjes, and Uzo Egonu (at the Mappin Gallery, Sheffield); seen practices that explored gender and location by Ingrid Pollard, Sonia Boyce, and Claudette Johnson (Battersea); and encountered visualizations of postcolonial queerness in the images of the photographer Sunil Gupta, filmmaker Hanif Kureishi, and many others.

Such a constellation likely struck the twenty-eight-year-old Fani-Kayode as at once familiar and revelatory. After an eight-year residency in the United States beginning in 1975, he would have been acutely aware of the political and aesthetic praxis across media in the US Black Arts Movement (BAM), which responded to the failures of democratic inclusion elaborated in the American project and envisioned by a decade of civil rights struggle.[30] In spite of the gradual erosion of the political liberation project embodied in BAM and other groups, according to Stuart Hall,

> the Black Arts Movement . . . was enormously influential for black British artists like Eddie Chambers and Keith Piper and the formation of the Pan-Afrikan Connection in 1982.[31] However, the term "black" in the British context . . . always also reference[s] migrants from the Asian subcontinent

as well as the African diaspora, a fact that makes the politics of antiracism significantly different on both sides of the Atlantic.[32]

And Fani-Kayode was no stranger to Harlem, availing himself of the Studio Museum, founded in 1968, and the nearby Schomburg Center for Research in Black Culture. In other words, he had already sought out a confluence of deeper currents of black creative practice in the Harlem Renaissance and the explicitly community-oriented approach of the museum, which sought to connect diaspora art to daily life. Such visits likely stirred an interest for Fani-Kayode in earlier approaches to black figuration and surrealisms, as well as in more recent collective practices, such as Jeff Donaldson's psychedelic abstraction and writings for the AfriCOBRA group, which posited a trans-African connection, linking liberation struggles in the United States with those of anticolonial resistance on the continent. Donaldson proposed a revolutionary form of art making that supported a nation building guided by "the whole family tree of African people, the African family tree."[33] His language echoed that of Fani-Kayode's father, Remi, who published a short manifesto in 1965 called *Blackism*, a call to pan-African unity based on a careful analysis of the then-nascent European Economic Community. Here, the elder Fani-Kayode cautioned against the effective neocolonialism of African reliance on Europe, arguing instead that "African union is the life blood of the independent African states, and Blackish the spiritual inner force that must compel that union. . . . African union is the living air vital to the freedom of black men all over the world."[34] Importantly, *Blackism* brought together struggle photography that explicitly connected the American civil rights movement with the 1960 Sharpeville massacre and other moments of protest in South Africa.

While none of Fani-Kayode's photographs operate in a similar documentary mode—that would be the work of Vanley Burke, Syd Shelton, and others—his "Traces of Ecstasy" statement plainly borrows from the anti-imperialist and black internationalist rhetoric of BAM and *Blackism*. Similarly, while the theatrical, autobiographical, and homoerotic aspects of his pictures put him at odds with the explicitly politicized and generally heteronormative emphasis of earlier black nationalisms, Fani-Kayode did not see a contradiction. In an interview from 1987, he and Alex Hirst noted that they both faced scorn from their peers for being in an interracial relationship, but they reasoned that freeing one's desire and modeling positive black and white connection was a political gesture in its own right. Fani-Kayode concluded that

"Black people are trying to build their own identity, to develop in their own terms. You tend to forget though that your sexual preference has to be a choice that doesn't compromise your political beliefs. But you can be in a mixed race relationship and still believe in Black political consciousness."[35] And so, while Fani-Kayode's outlook was crucially informed by a globally minded sense of diasporic identity, it was framed by his experience in the United States and complicated by his specific position in England: African, gay, and in an inter-racial relationship, all while living in the heart of the South London black radical community.

LAMBETH

This specifically British frame crystallized in the very neighborhood where Fani-Kayode worked and lived, on Railton Road in the South London area of Brixton. As the Bronx-born activist and artist Rita Keegan has noted, "I like South London especially because of the cultural mix. You meet all types of people from all over the world. In a way, nobody belongs here, black or white. . . . everyone, in their own way, has that point of difference, and that difference in communities."[36] Keegan, a painter and digital artist, moved from New York in 1982, seeking a community in which to make her work. She stayed in Brixton for the opportunities then emerging, "the vibrant scenes . . . getting involved with a collective gallery, learning how to put on exhibitions, and meeting people from all parts of the world."[37]

The gallery was the Brixton Art Gallery, founded in June 1983 as a collabo-ration by artists and writers including Linton Kwesi Johnson, the Jamaican-born former British Black Panther and dub poet frequently associated (along with C. L. R. James, Kamau Brathwaite, and others) with the Caribbean Art-ists Movement. The gallery, which operates as a community-driven nonprofit, was formerly housed in the iconic arched structure of the overground train that runs along the one-quarter mile of Brixton Station Road. Fani-Kayode lived roughly fifteen minutes away by foot, off Shakespeare and Railton roads, just south of the arch. He was featured in several group exhibitions in the space, including during the 1985 season—his second show in London, and his fifth since finishing college in DC.

During these first few years in Brixton, Fani-Kayode alternated his time between community education and freelance work. His CV indicates that he took pictures for pop groups, "actors, artists, etc.," as well as the Inner London Education Authority (ILEA), an autonomous educational ministry under the supervision of the Greater London Council (GLC). The former was, from 1983 to 1986, led by Labour leader Frances Morrell, who used the body to promote greater gender equality in schools and used the ILEA budget to push back against Conservative austerity measures. Fani-Kayode also served throughout the then-marginal neighborhoods of the city, primarily as a photography tutor in several adult education programs in the South London boroughs of Wandsworth and Lambeth, and the East End's Tower Hamlets.[38] His studio practice tended, too, toward portraiture of the milieu.

One such photograph features Keegan herself, smiling broadly, draped in flowing clothes and heavy jewelry. She leans with her right arm on a well-lit table, a glass of white wine at the left of the frame. *Rita Keegan* (1989; figure 1.4) is a quintessential Fani-Kayode composition—square format with his subject defined in chiaroscuro. She is at ease, clearly engaged with the camera. While the table and glass are unique for a Fani-Kayode photograph (suggesting a quotidian domestic space), the theatrical blackout of the background subtly transports Keegan, lending her a kind of iconic serenity. Fani-Kayode would have known Keegan from the neighborhood and from the Brixton Art Gallery, perhaps sharing stories of the city they left and the borough they shared. Keegan had already made a place for herself in London and was active in promoting art production on a grassroots level. She recalls that she helped to

> set up an organisation called "Community Copyart" which, in the end, was based on Battlebridge Road behind King's Cross. Copyart began in '83/'84. We did a lot in the battle to save the GLC and had a short life after its demise. Copyart had two main prongs. One was to work with community organisations in creating their own publicity, making an affordable resource centre available for them, the other was working with artists that wanted to use the photocopier as a form of printmaking.[39]

The GLC, in particular, was one source of "opportunity" that Keegan and many other émigrés had sought in moving to Lambeth. Beyond larger sources of funding such as the publicly endowed Arts Council England, the GLC was one of several local councils that advocated for neighborhood constituencies and arranged for space, funding, education, financial relief, and other measures that logistically supported grassroots cultural production. The GLC had, since 1965, served as a governing body for a city that had extended well beyond its central core but lacked a mayoralty. Such councils were sites of local

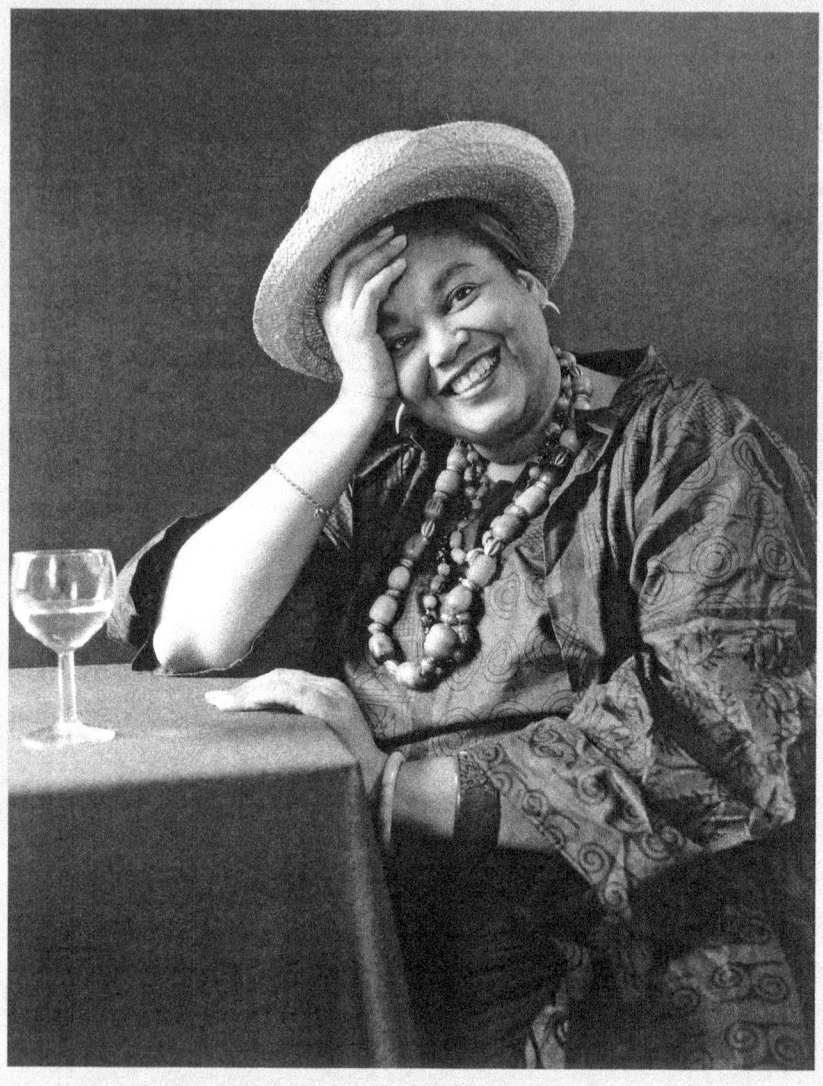

Figure 1.4 Rotimi Fani-Kayode, *Rita Keegan* (1989). © Rotimi Fani-Kayode /
Autograph ABP. Courtesy of Autograph ABP.

resistance to Tory governance. For example, the *Daily Mail* called the Walsall Council a "little Kremlin in the heart of England," and by 1981 the GLC was back under Labour control, led by future mayor Ken Livingstone, derided by some as "Red Ken." Under his leadership, many local initiatives were funded in spite of a broader climate of austerity, and Livingstone—who was subject to smear campaigns in the form of suggestions of IRA sympathies and queer sexual preferences—became a public champion for progressive economic and cultural policy.[40]

In 1986, however, the GLC was shuttered, following the Conservative Parliament's Local Government Act 1985, nominally aimed at austerity and local accountability. Some 250,000 people took to the streets of South Bank on 31 March of that year to celebrate the GLC and mourn its closure, which was seen by many as an example of national-level moves to curtail left-leaning Labour governance.[41] Livingstone and the GLC were emblematic of a specific moment in which Brixton was a hub where the Marxist left connected with the heart of black radicalism, and during a brief time when conflict in the streets, government reports, and subcultural agitation created a window for the official subsidy of projects by or about black artists.

Gradual shifts were under way as Fani-Kayode returned to London, echoing the work of spaces like the Brixton Art Gallery. While 1989 is remembered as a watershed year, earlier exhibitions brought together new work from an array of critically minded artists. *From Two Worlds*, for instance, ran in summer 1986 at the Whitechapel Gallery in the city's East End, featuring many who would continue on to international acclaim, and cocurated by the South African painter Gavin Jantjes and Nicholas Serota, the future director of the Tate Museum. In her introduction to the catalog, Adeola Solanke cites Keith Piper, who reflected that to "produce art and to eat simultaneously in Thatcher's Britain is to exercise privilege, and privilege without responsibility is a myth.... If you are not part of the solution, then you are part of the problem." She concludes: "Artists may be able to trace their roots back to two or more worlds but at the end of the day can be loyal only to one."[42]

While he himself was something of an iconoclast working at the edges of many tendencies, Fani-Kayode physically located himself within Lambeth's vibrant community of activists, critics, and artists. At the area's theaters, galleries, and museums, he witnessed the efflorescence of a scene that prioritized heterogeneity of voice and tradition but was also keenly aware of a sense of both privilege and revisionary possibility. He docked in to this milieu in a variety of ways, and shows with the Brixton Art Galley foregrounded a nascent organizational impulse that came to fruition most obviously as Fani-Kayode became the first chair of Autograph ABP. Autograph was founded in 1988 with the help of a £10,000 grant from the Arts Council and was initially housed at 444 Brixton Road—the storied Bonmarché building with its grand 1877 facade connected to a rail viaduct on the high street near the Northern line tube station.[43]

That organization was quite literally close to home, as one of Fani-Kayode's last listed addresses places him a mere ten-minute walk to the south,[44] amid the Victorian two- and three-flat townhouses that line the streets.[45] In turn, Autograph ABP was a one-time Fani-Kayode mailing address (although the association would find more permanent homes over the course of the next two decades, culminating in their current location at Rivington Place in Shoreditch). A year after his death, in 1990, a farewell exhibition of his photographs was held at 198 Railton, at the gallery of the same name founded in 1988 and then known as Roots Community, a place for elders to gather and for black artists to exhibit. He was also, early on, closely linked with the nearby Oval House Theatre, where he was a tutor in 1985 and 1986, and where he showed in group exhibitions in 1986 and 1987.[46]

Now called Ovalhouse, the theater was founded in 1963, and by the 1980s already a mecca for "fringe" and avant-garde productions, and it was known as a laboratory for black and queer theater groups. Ovalhouse's iconic, arch-shaped building served as a collaborative community space and rests on the edge of the Kennington Oval, a sporting pitch founded in 1845 and a long-time home to football and cricket test matches. The Oval is an urban landmark, documented in Fani-Kayode's black-and-white portraits, especially in a brightly lit portrait entitled *Errol, at the Oval* (1985; figure 1.5). Shot from below and at a slight angle, the picture neatly frames a muscular young man resting a wooden bow over his shoulders, standing in a cruciform in front of an anonymous brick fortification. Errol gazes coolly into the distance while wearing a studded black leather cap that, in all of its evocation of queer nightlife, contrasts playfully with his white vestment.

In spite of naming its subject, the *Errol, at the Oval* also preserves a kind of anonymity for the sitter—he is something of an archetype, larger than life. But the photograph also insists on a precise location familiar to any Londoner, a veritable citadel to sport and proper "Britishness" that was, at least during

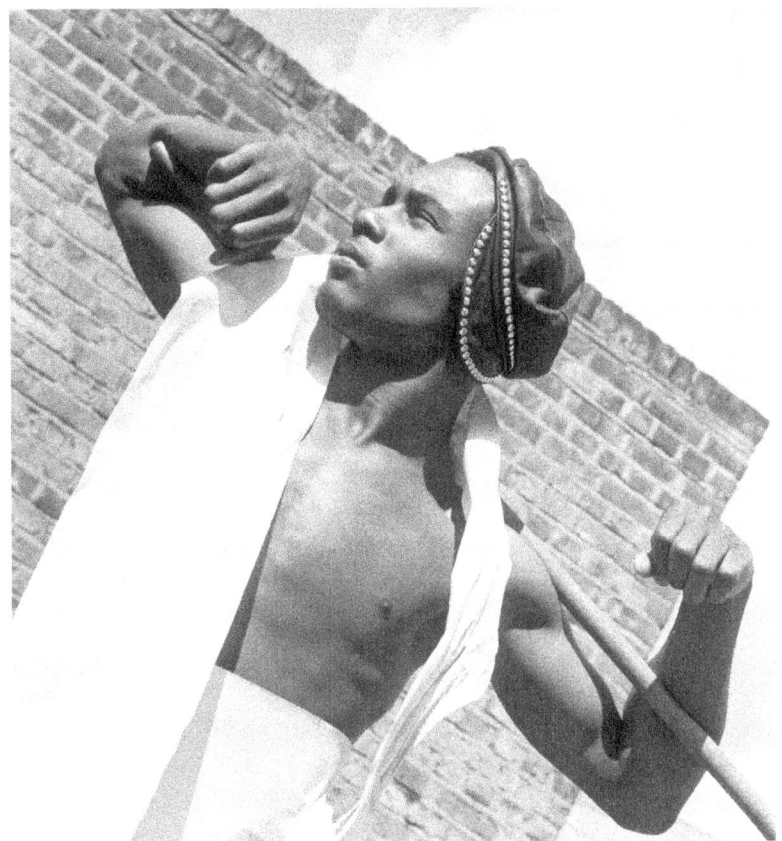

Figure 1.5 Rotimi Fani-Kayode, *Errol, at the Oval* (1985). © Rotimi Fani-Kayode / Autograph ABP. Courtesy of Autograph ABP.

the mid-1980s, also a stomping ground for Fani-Kayode and his interlocutors. In this sense *Errol, at the Oval* works more as social documentation, tracing a group of young men south of the Thames, at ease in the urban landscape. Other images are more placeless, shot in the studio, but still designated by neighborhood: *Richard Walker in Brixton*, a shirtless white figure with closely cropped hair peeking from behind a clock face; gay health advocate Dennis Carney with the American poet Essex Hemphill (1957–1995) in an intimate embrace, eyes downcast in *Dennis Carney and Essex Hemphill in Brixton*. In short, the borough of Lambeth provided Fani-Kayode a community and he was, at times, something of a scene photographer.

While Fani-Kayode engaged with London as an artist from the postcolony, his daily life might have resonated with his experience in the Americas: strands of Caribbean culture predominated in Brixton at the time. To anyone living nearby it would have been obvious, in mellifluous patois on street corners, in the smells of food wafting from corner shops, or in the sound of throbbing bass, angular guitars, and sinewy melodica . . . dub reggae drifting from open windows or weekend sound systems. Such sensorial cues would have complemented sartorial ones—the two tone of ska and its "rude boys," or the flowing dreadlocks associated, of course, with Rastafarianism and transgressive elements of Caribbean culture more broadly. It was the clash between the communities of Caribbean immigrants from the Commonwealth and ethnically narrow conceptions of Britishness that would define much of the early 1980s throughout England, as ideological tension between democratic inclusion and nationalist absolutism crosscut the quotidian realities of jobs, housing, and policing. For example, the summer of 1981 blazed with outbreaks of arson, looting, and conflict with area police, beginning on 10 April in Lambeth and Brixton in London and culminating with a string of uprisings in Moss Side near Manchester and Toxteth and Handsworth near Birmingham. (The Handsworth community would see rioting again in September 1985.) According to Mark Sealy, these disturbances marked a crucial turning point because they brought sufficient visibility to communities such as Brixton that patronage for the arts from groups such as the GLC suddenly became available as a sort of political expedient.[47]

The 1985 Handsworth disturbance was the starting point for a sixty-minute, montage-driven film, *Handsworth Songs*, by the Black Audio Film Collective (BAFC). According to director John Akomfrah, "Running throughout *Handsworth Songs* is the idea that the riots were the outcome of a protracted suppression by British society of black presence. It portrays civil disorder as an opening onto a secret history of dissatisfaction that is connected to the national drama of industrial decline."[48] Structuring the entire project is a relentless sonic component—the dense accents on screen, a dissonant and clattering score, and editing that mirrors the recursive echo and improvisatory repurposing of the "dub plates" so central to reggae, and the hip-hop culture it would engender on the streets of the Bronx.

BAFC's layering of the archive and recent events worked to visualize submerged histories and challenge dominant discourses that positioned immigrants from the Commonwealth as beyond the purview of British nationhood. In very obvious ways, films such as *Handsworth Songs* were of a piece with larger arcs in postwar black cultural production, often executed using formal maneuvers that resisted or recoded traditional or vernacular approaches. BAFC's and Keith Piper's use of slide tape, for one, evoked grammar-school presentations or shared family pictures; here such mnemonic and subjective media are brought into the gallery space, creating counternarrative portraits of nationhood and belonging. In this vein, Vanley Burke, who was born in Jamaica in 1951 and relocated to Birmingham in 1965, used a camera gifted to him by his grandmother to document a decaying Midlands.

Burke documented black communities that had long resided in Liverpool, a port city central to the transatlantic slave trade; elsewhere, he documented the desolated and graffiti-marked streets of Toxteth and Handsworth[49] that would be the sites of civil disturbance throughout the early years of the decade. His most celebrated work remains *Boy with a Flag: Wilfred in Handsworth Park* (1970), which portrays a scuffed but confident black adolescent, arms akimbo, bike propped against his knee. A tree-lined path dissolves into a soft depth of field, but a Union Jack waves in the breeze, mounted on the boy's handlebars and in center frame. The iconography here is overt, the portrait stirringly composed, and in the context of seventies England, a defiant declaration of identity. Here Wilfred and, by extension, Burke locate themselves as at once black and British. Such a documentary project is, in turn, continuous with the poetic and sonic modes attributed with the Caribbean Arts Movement.

Indeed, just as Burke depicted Handsworth, Linton Kwesi Johnson would write of the uprisings in Brixton in a dense patois, shifting the rhythm and meter of his stanzas to echo the vernacular of the streets he describes in militant terms as a site of local clashes with the police: "well now den run gain go plan countah-ackshan / but di plastic bullit an di waatah cannan / will bring a blam-blam / will bring a blam-blam / nevah mind Scarman / will bring a blam-blam."[50] Johnson's dub poetry is arguably one instance of what Fred Moten calls black performativity, part of a longer genealogy within modernity that works against the closures of a universalizing project of absolute meaning.

The phonetic slippages within Johnson's "outernational" use of language are of a piece with what Moten calls "a critique of the valuation of meaning over content and the reduction of phonic matter and syntactic 'degeneracy' in the . . . late modern search for a universal science of language." For Moten, this ambient pulse within the black Atlantic has been figured visually as well. For instance, in describing Beauford Delaney's Parisian paintings, Moten locates an *appositional force* at work on the canvases, at "the site of emergence of what [Delaney] called voices and forces, the painted sounds of the thought of the outside, the visual manifestation of phonic substance and the content it bears." Moten is interested, here, in "how what might be thought as the merely gestural . . . manifests itself in Delaney's paintings and texts as irreducible phonic substance."[51]

There are strong connections in Moten's analysis—the political force of fugitivity, as well as his privileging of Harlem, riding the A train, Delaney's experience of dreams and sexual longing—with Fani-Kayode's own peripatetic movements, during which he alighted on uptown Manhattan. More important, however, Moten's theorization of a sonic pulse made manifest within (rather than thrumming in exteriority to) visual practice clarifies Fani-Kayode's pictures and the more subtle ways in which sonics structured his method. In a very straightforward sense, for example, both house music and variations of punk were so ambient to his psychic landscape—nights spent dancing, records and tapes spinning away in one corner of the room, the sartorial cues of dyed hair and motorcycle jackets—that the next two chapters dwell on them at length. But in more immediate terms it seems clear that explicitly diasporic musics prefigure the black-and-white pictures.

The photograph *Dee Brown* (1987; figure 1.6), for example, is a stark study in tone, closely cropped on a man's back, which is brought into sharp relief against a dappled white background. His head is cocked slightly to the left, right hand holding his wireless headphones more closely to his head, like a DJ trying to find the beat. Brown is, apparently, unconcerned with the viewer, instead attuned to his soundscape; the scene is reminiscent of a lyrical fragment by Massive Attack's Robert del Naja, "My heavy brother get lighter than helium / Float above the world to break the tedium / Living in my headphones Sony's what I say to 'em / The surreal boom of the Budokan Stadium." Del Naja's song, "Daydreaming," is an encomium to drifting through the rough-and-tumble British city in a state of rhythmically induced reverie.

While this particular song was not released until 1991, Massive Attack provided a blend of the unfamiliar sounds that diffused the streets of Brixton and Bristol throughout the previous decade; they produced songs that included samples from Rastafarian musician Horace Andy's reverb-saturated croon, exemplified in his 1983 release in Europe of *Dance Hall Style*. Fani-Kayode's

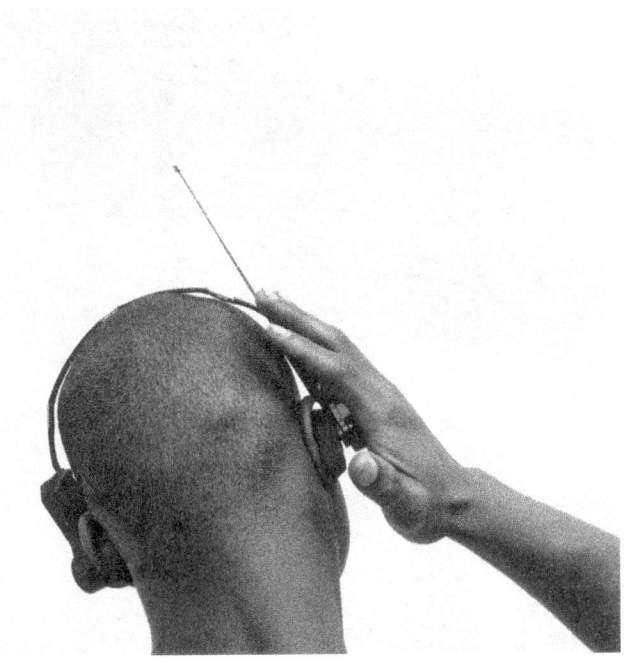

Figure 1.6 Rotimi Fani-Kayode, *Dee Brown* (1987). © Rotimi Fani-Kayode / Autograph ABP. Courtesy of Autograph ABP.

Dee Brown points, in turn, to the capacity for music—especially played over headphones—to create parallel sonic terrain in the city, subtly reorienting one in the landscape.[52] The figure here is living in his headphones, looking away and beyond, perhaps (in the words of del Naja) "seeking knowledge, not acknowledging the jetset / Silver papers of the sound within my Budokon headset."[53]

As such, the headphones are a relatively straightforward iconographic clue confirming, for all of *Dee Brown*'s suggestiveness, Moten's formulation that sound might operate more structurally, which helps us to understand photographs such as *Struggle* and *One in Three* (1985; figures 1.7 and 1.8). These images clearly rely on multiple exposure techniques (most likely in the camera itself), as the picture tracks subtle movement across the frame in an impossibly dilated instant. There is, too, a ghostly quality to the figures—evanescing on deep-black ground, their bodies are made unfamiliar, multiple and conjoined. Art historically, in both tone and technique these two works from *Black Male/White Male* mine the history of surrealist imagery, but they also

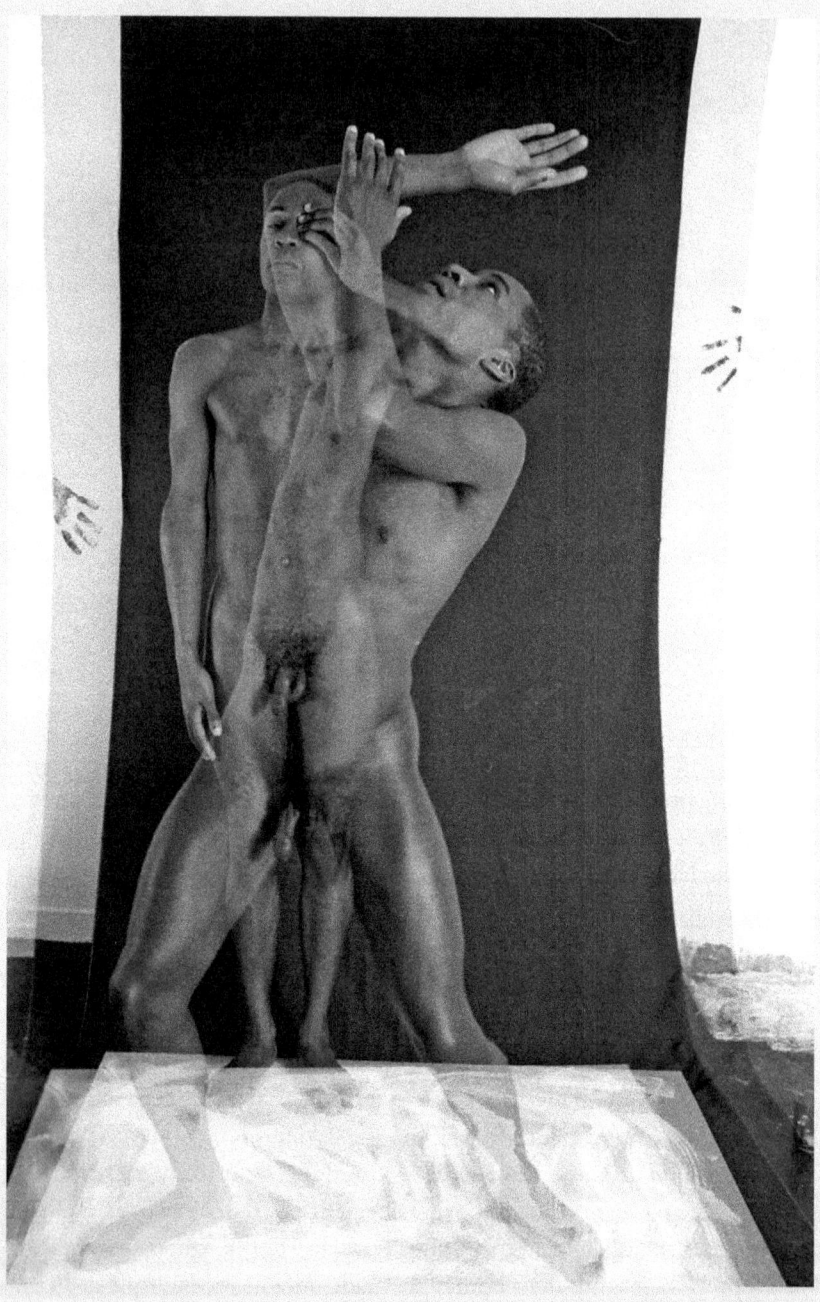

Figure 1.7 Rotimi Fani-Kayode, *Struggle* (1985). © Rotimi Fani-Kayode /
Autograph ABP. Courtesy of Autograph ABP.

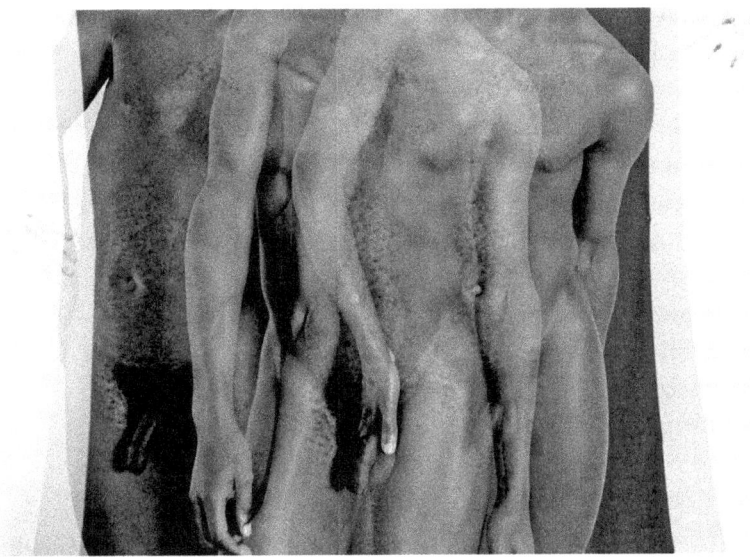

Figure 1.8 Rotimi Fani-Kayode, *One in Three* (1985). © Rotimi Fani-Kayode /
Autograph ABP. Courtesy of Autograph ABP.

offer a rejoinder to a more conventional history of portraiture that focuses on
a unified figure and insists on the of closure of signification. That is, insofar as
pictures supposedly denote reality (rather than coconstitute or envision it), a
portrait can powerfully affirm the sitter's social position in everything from
sartorial cues to carriage of the body, props, and so on.[54]

In contrast, both *One in Three* and *Struggle* enact openness, a deferral of
completeness in the figures: the former is literally faceless, a blur of corporeality that is in focus but unresolved; the latter literally depicts resistance, both
in the action-oriented flow of the body and in the figure's shift within the
frame from a closed-eyed space of contemplation to an upward glance—now
visionary, mobile, breaking free of the frame. This motion, this unresolution,
is, in turn, effected by a *beat* within the picture itself, the click-click-click of
the camera, bump-bump-bump from left to right. This repetition is visually
evident, but one might also imagine Fani-Kayode and his sitters in the studio,
the latter not frozen in place like the long-exposure daguerreotypes of old, but
free to move. Here, the act of photographing itself becomes activated, rhythmic, like improvisation within a jam session. Such associations would only
become more evident as Fani-Kayode moved into larger-scale color work in

1988–1989, as his photographs were staged as both records of and sites for the ecstatic communion, and the disorientation of subjectivity more commonly associated with Afro-Caribbean traditions such as Santeria and Voudou.[55]

Within the framework of contemporary art history, one can also think of this multiplication of bodies as an instance of *pulse*. For Yve-Alain Bois and Rosalind Krauss, such pulse is made operative early on by Marcel Duchamp's *Rotoreliefs*, which in their centripetal force generated an optical flicker that created a "visual equivalent of coitus."[56] They argue further that creating a photographic space in which "the unified visual field is agitated by a shake-up that irredeemably punctures the screen of its formality" means that one does not even need physical motion per se. For Bois and Krauss, "the same beat agitates the photographs" of many surrealist photographers, and "the same fragmentation of the body . . . disturbs the surrealists' 'exquisite corpses.'"[57] It seems clear in the pages of *Black Male/White Male* that Fani-Kayode used the pulse made available in postsurrealist modes of composition and capture precisely in order to make a libidinal beat evident through the screen of the static image. These ethereal but electric shots do not depict music as such, but in their implied movement, in the temporality they enact, they are akin to Delaney's "visual manifestation of phonic substance and the content it bears."

With that in mind, it is worth recalling that historically black musical formations have often been reductively conflated with sex as such—the demonization of Elvis' swinging hips (his *rock and roll*)[58] or the propulsive thrust of funk, with James Brown himself a self-described "sex machine" ("Movin' and doin' it, you know / Can I count it off? (Go ahead) / One, two, three, four!"). Even so, Fani-Kayode's pictures (above, and in general) seem to confirm Moten's contention that "photographs in general bear a phonic substance,"[59] and that such substance has an erotic component. For their part, Fani-Kayode's stills improvise on inherited modes—the sonics around him and the photographs by which he was influenced—in order to, in Moten's terms, "ongoingly [stage] the piercing insistence of the excluded . . . not only of excluded identity, but also of excluded sense."[60] By 1985, he had begun to experiment more rigorously with such multiple exposure methods, in effect rejoining earlier avant-garde strategies with their contemporary aural and anthropological source code. This reclamation is notable, for instance, in the iconic *Four Twins* (1985; figure 1.9). It elegantly indexes Moten's multisensory pulsations in the diasporic allegorical terrain of the trickster and the twins, here a know-

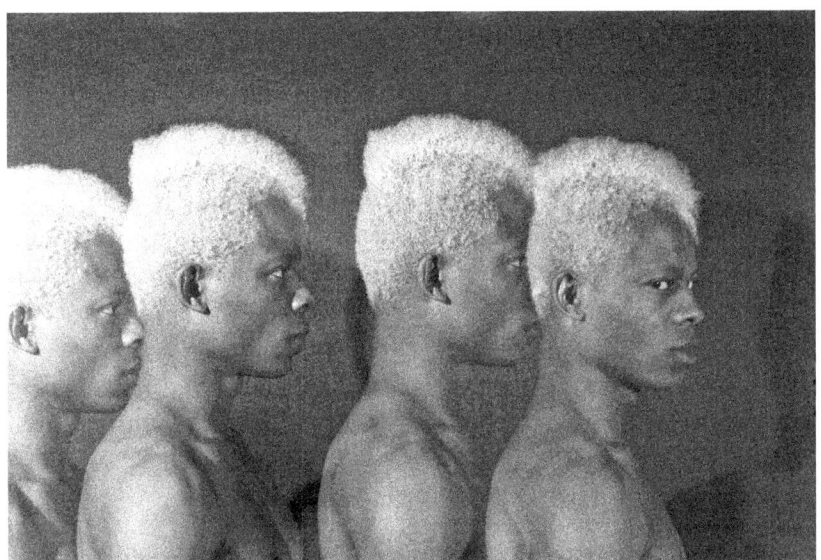

Figure 1.9 Rotimi Fani-Kayode, *Four Twins* (1985). © Rotimi Fani-Kayode /
Autograph ABP. Courtesy of Autograph ABP.

ing doubling of doubling, layers accreting upon layers. A version hangs in the
hallway of the Autograph ABP offices to this day.

This is Black Atlantic identity within Britain, of course, but also queer
identity within the black radical tradition; this is the sonic made visual, a
sense excluded but made evident nonetheless through erotic pulse. Such a
figuring of radical sonics marks a point of inflection between Fani-Kayode
and other postcolonial denizens of Brixton, who resisted exclusion on more
overtly musical terms, from ska and dancehall to the fluid patois of CAM-
inspired poetry, even as outernational sonics irrupted in turn into critical
theoretical accounts of the period. Gilroy's *"There Ain't No Black in the
Union Jack"* traced the economic and legislative moves that pictures such as
Burke's sought to visually contest as an act of witnessing. And the Jamaican-
born Stuart Hall formed his approach to cultural studies at Birmingham,
which specialized in Marxist analysis of sartorial and musical subculture. It
is likely not coincidental that the Trinidadian-born theorist and historian
of the Haitian revolution, C. L. R. James, himself lived at 164–167 Railton

Road, a housing cooperative also home to Linton Kwesi Johnson, the dub poet Jean "Binta" Breeze, and one Rotimi Fani-Kayode.[61]

T R A N S L A T I O N S

While it is clear, then, that Fani-Kayode's local community was substantially composed of a host of influential Caribbean-born artists, poets, and musicians, he was not part of the CAM as such, nor are his particular affiliations with reggae, dancehall, or ska subcultures totally clear. Moreover, as a Nigerian living in London, Fani-Kayode would have occupied a position of relative privilege, given his direct and comparatively immediate connections to the African continent, and the prominence of Nigerian communities within London that paralleled Caribbean neighborhoods such as Brixton. Nonetheless, as Fani-Kayode himself made clear, his status as Yoruban elite was also in a sense routed rather than inherited: he had to rediscover his own Africanness through research and in dialogue with black communities in the United States. Not so much an emissary direct from Yorubaland, Fani-Kayode both relied on quotidian signifiers of urban blackness and in his work enacted the transcultural syncretism so central to diasporic practice in the Americas. In some ways, these connections are quite obvious: in pictures such as *Ebo Òrìsà*, figures don various forms of dreadlocks or braids in their hair, marking clear distinction over the "white" hair styles of many English people at the time. Similarly, a rarely seen and untitled black-and-white picture from 1985 depicts a man squatting in the center of the (untypically for Fani-Kayode) white frame (figure 1.10). This picture is notable for the sitter's exaggerated Afro coiffure, so fulsome that it seems to crown his head in nearly of foot of hair in every direction, even obscuring his eyes. One cannot help but notice the near comical tension in the interplay of the figure's intense countenance and a symbolically laden 'do exaggerated into the terrain of camp. *Untitled* interweaves aspects of play and masquerade, and the immediate filmic backdrop of 1975's *Rocky Horror Picture Show*, with its leather-clad Dr. Frank N. Furter. This association is only heightened by arch photographs from the same period of leather-clad men or the nude white figure in Fani-Kayode's *Which Doctor? Herr Doktor Scheidegger*. At the same time, it is impossible not to consider the Afro as an invocation of black radicalism in the United States, in which natural black hair styles became clear signs of pride and, indeed, a turn away from straightened or cropped hair in more "European" or "white"

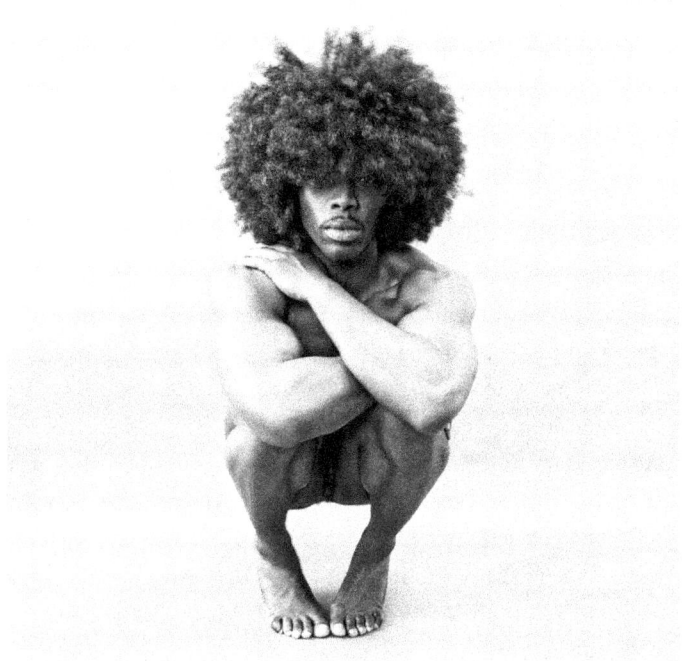

Figure 1.10 Rotimi Fani-Kayode, *Untitled* (1985). © Rotimi Fani-Kayode /
Autograph ABP. Courtesy of Autograph ABP.

modes. As a signifier of black power and black internationalism, the Afro was profound: it was the style of Angela Davis and Huey Newton in 1968, it made its way into the positive imagery of American painters such as Jeff Donaldson and Wadsworth Jarrell as a sign of revolutionary affinity, and it even appeared internationally, as captured, for example, in an apartheid-era picture by the South African photographer David Goldblatt.

Fani-Kayode seems to be riffing on these associations, staging this scene neither as one of pure revolutionary activism nor a merely theatrical joke but something in between—an ambivalence typical of the sartorial choices staged throughout his various portfolios. Such choices are indicative of what Kobena Mercer then termed "defiant dandyism," whereby the more stable categories of "black" or "white" hair become electively complicated through forms of creolization, conveying less a process of undiluted cultural retention but, instead, modes of appropriation and revision. Historically, Mercer connects this process to the urban American conk style, associated with Little Richard and Duke Ellington and, later, the permutations of classic crops, curls, and dreadlocks in the British context, themselves inflected by the aggressive cues of punk rock and the emergence of Mohawks, skinheads, and Day-Glo color palettes.[62]

Indeed, *Black Male/White Male* can easily be read as a catalog of coiffure, and such syncretized—and thus, in Mercer's estimation, oppositionally ambivalent—style is clearest in *Four Twins*, which flashes the same figure across the near-panoramic frame. The first three "twins" face forward, while the fourth casts a sidelong glance at the camera, his gaze at once weary and flirtatious—appraising us. *Four Twins* relies on a multiple exposure technique, likely with the figure walking through the camera's field as Fani-Kayode clicked the shutter open four times. The illusion is striking in its simultaneous spectrality and intimacy, but the tight focus on the upper body also means that the twins' hair is front and center: a neatly bleached crop adorned with a curly Mohawk. In one gesture, then, multiple associations are drawn together. This is hair that builds on the naturalistic curls of a part-Afro but adds punk rock insouciance and a sharpness that underscores its dandyish defiance.

These gestures are powerful for at least two reasons, according to Mercer. On the one hand, they are instances of the multiplicity within ethnicity so vital to constituting the new subjectivities of postcolonial Britain; on the other, such riffing merges here with homoerotic and queer signification in ways that also add complexity to earlier forms of black radicalism, from the BAM to reggae, in which heterosexism was, at times, taken as part and parcel of a politicized black identity.[63] Such questions of the intersectionality of masculine archetypes and racial pride were simultaneously taken up in the collage-based work of Keith Piper and the photographic practice of, for instance, Sunil Gupta, with whom Fani-Kayode exhibited in the *Same Difference* show at Camerawork in East London's Bethnal Green in July 1986.

But *Four Twins* is symbolically resonant as well: the motif of twins is recurrent in Hellenic mythology—Romulus and Remus, Castor and Pollux—but it is particularly potent in Yoruban cosmology, where twin births are statistically high and twins are seen as ambivalent augurs. At once profoundly connected to the spirit realm, even in waking life, twins are also associated with unstable forms of power and even mischief. To venerate and appease the twins (which in some formulations are even considered an orisha, or saintlike aspect of the divine), traditional *ere ibeji* figures have long been produced in Yorubaland as objects to which offerings can be made in the form of ornate accoutrements, indigo dye, and various foods. In the event of the death of a twin, Yoruba mothers may even carry such figures as a sort of metonymic substitute. These forms made their way into the Atlantic diaspora, and twins appear in an array of visual cultural forms, the *ibeji* syncretized in the manner of Santeria in Cuba or Voudou in Haiti, where depictions of Catholic saints become improvised sites of communion with African deities.[64]

Fani-Kayode certainly would have remembered such symbolism from his childhood and, indeed, travels after university. In New York he would have reencountered Yoruban and Fon culture in diasporic translation, notably in the Santero communities in Washington Heights and the Bronx, or among the Haitians who populated Crown Heights. And as his images of western Africa show, he made his way back to the beaches of Togo, capturing both the fishermen themselves and the Atlantic beaches that launched countless crossings. Earlier, those beaches inspired the spiritual imaginations of the Edo, Fon, and many others as a locus of divine activity. Mark Sealy, the director of Autograph ABP, has consistently argued that Fani-Kayode's "confidence came from being born to the Balogun chief of Ife. His family were deeply rooted in Yoruban culture . . . keeper of the Shrine of Yoruba Deities and priests of Ife. Kayode understood his cultural heritage. He did not have an 'identity crisis.'"[65] Indeed, Fani-Kayode staged scenes of Atlantic crossing in obvious ways, most notably in *Cargo of Middle Passage* (1989; figure 1.11). Its sanguinary associations are heightened by the gum bichromate format—shadowy crimson tones, the figure's malnourishment and wraithlike form underscored by highlights of bone white. It is an enduring image that for Fani-Kayode, it seems, held a double meaning. On the one hand, the gum method coaxes out associations less obvious in the silver gelatin version—it becomes an even more empathic meditation on the horrors of the trade itself, a systematic violence that he felt resonated in his present. He noted that it "touches me just as closely as the knowledge that millions of my ancestors were killed or enslaved in order to ensure European political, economic, and cultural hegemony in the world."[66] On the other, this invocation of the Atlantic trade is also a reminder of the openness and mutability of African cultures, shifting and forging new connections in ever-changing landscapes. Indeed, he cautioned against the temptation to reduce African art to stable, easily digestible interpretations.

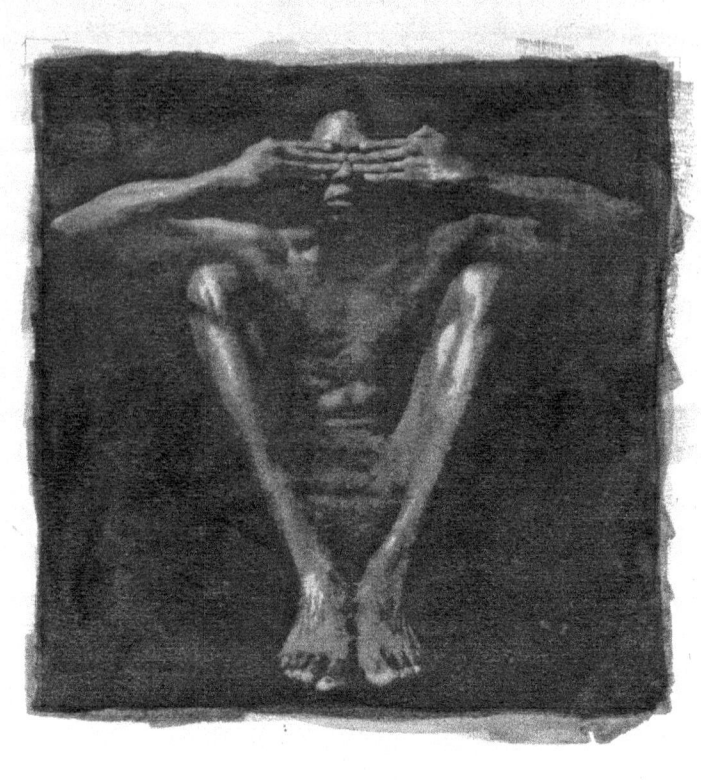

Figure 1.11 Rotimi Fani-Kayode, *Cargo of Middle Passage* (1989).
© Rotimi Fani-Kayode / Autograph ABP. Courtesy of Autograph ABP.

According to Sealy, Fani-Kayode was acutely aware of "the systems he was trying to penetrate," noting that "Europeans faced the dogged survival of alien cultures and as mercantile as they were in the days of the Trade, are now trying to sell our culture as a consumer product. I am inevitably caught up in this."[67] And so, he located a longer history of Euro-American commodification of blackness—first as dehumanized labor, then as visual sign—that in turn created a bind for him as he made work that sought to give visibility to postcolonial subjects while not reducing them under the aegis of pure difference. Sealy went as far as to argue that "Kayode was at the forefront of blowing apart the stereotype. He resisted categorization and labelling. . . . He was no afro-essentialist."[68] I return to *Cargo of Middle Passage* in more depth in the last chapter of this book, but it is important to note that in the field of black visual culture, the cargo container was then, as now, a potent and multivalent site of intervention, as in Pat Ward Williams's 1987 *32 Hours in a Box . . . and Still Counting* (1987) and Glenn Ligon's 1993 installation *To Disembark*. As Huey Copeland has argued in the case of Ligon's reactivation of the container as symbolic form, the disembarking of forced migration and diasporic movement means "not so much to reach the end of a journey as to endlessly retrace its course in search of openings always under the threat of disappearance."[69] According to Copeland, the antecedent of the displaced black body opens onto a more generalized mode of fugitivity, a "lack of location" that figures contemporary black queer subjectivity as a site of critical potential against the seemingly limited horizon of resistance in the aftermath of the 1960s. It is such a confluence that, I argue in the pages ahead, in no small measure activated a critical edge in Fani-Kayode's own practice.

Accordingly, then, Fani-Kayode's photographs tended toward creating locations of ambivalence and relation, finding inflection points between seemingly disparate cultural practices and temporalities, in effect short-circuiting reductive interpretations in much the same way that his own Yoruban traditions remained vital and adaptive in diasporic translation. Hence the portrait *Michael French of Arcachon* (1987; figure 1.12), of a figure whose loose, nascent dreadlocks radiate amid a halo of sunlight; he is pictured from below, on a stone wall with beach in the distant background. The setting evokes those fishermen on the shores of the Bight of Benin, but this is likely a seaside redoubt. His accoutrements are a mash-up of references—steady gaze behind large-framed sunglasses and neatly-cropped goatee, body draped in flowing

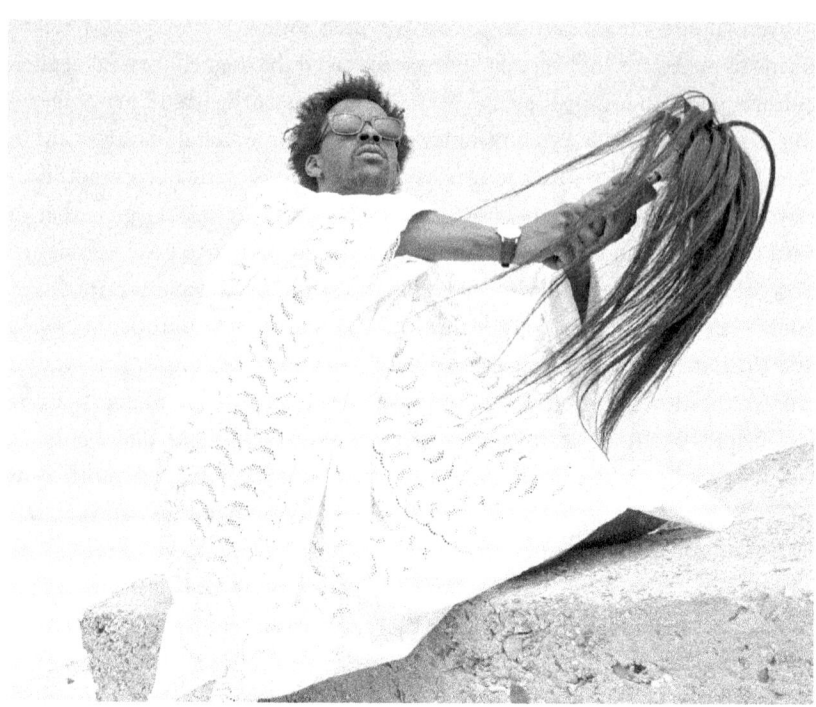

Figure 1.12 Rotimi Fani-Kayode, *Michael French of Arcachon* (1987). © Rotimi Fani-Kayode / Autograph ABP. Courtesy of Autograph ABP.

and elaborate fabric. He wears a chunky watch with a leather band but waves a large whisk (a horsehair flyswatter) in front of himself, contrasting neatly with his impeccable white garb. While the whisk and sunglasses seem to be drawn from a common store of theatrical props in Fani-Kayode's studio, here they are redeployed on the southern coast of France, and a young man routed through 1980s Europe is reborn as Yoruban royalty.

For the Yoruba, white cloth connotes *iwa*, the spotless reputation of good character; the flywhisk a practical scepter of the king. One might read this picture, in sum, as a depiction of coolness. This is a play on the mystery and confidence implied in French's shades (themselves a riff on the beaded masks Yoruban kings wear to protect subjects from their charged gaze). But coolness here also refers to the calm visage and closed eyes that suggest, in this context, a relaxed alertness found in Yoruban figuration at the court of Ife (dating to ca. 1200–1400), what historian Robert Farris Thompson identified as an "aes-

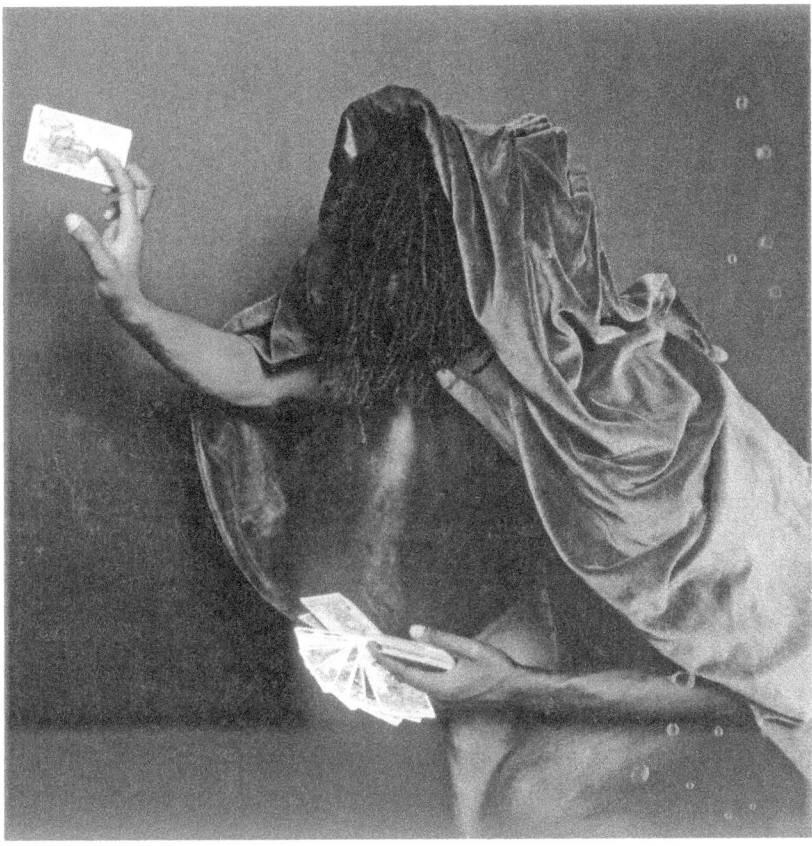

Figure 1.13 Rotimi Fani-Kayode, *Òrúnmilà* (1989). © Rotimi Fani-Kayode /
Autograph ABP. Courtesy of Autograph ABP.

thetic of the cool," indicating the good character of the subject, which can be localized to the seat of consciousness—the head.[70]

Kobena Mercer has argued in favor of this interpretation and, in light of the iconographic syncretisms enacted in his photographs, dubbed Fani-Kayode a "boundary rider of cultural difference" and "migrant translator."[71] From this vantage, then, other images emerge with new resonances. An untitled photograph from *Black Male/White Male* might be read simply as formal experiment—a nude figure with legs crossed and head ensconced in a deployed white umbrella. This piece is a model of composition, cropping, and contrasting tonal values. It is thus emblematic of earlier modernist concerns about demonstrating the camera's technical range first and foremost, and the stark whiteness of the umbrella makes it a handy prop. But then again, the sitter (almost certainly Fani-Kayode) has his face covered, implying both masquerade and the royal shielding of the visage. Umbrellas are predominant too in the courts of the Fon culture of Dahomey, recurring again in Haitian and American Voudou, decorated with cosmic *vèvè* drawings.[72]

More overtly still: a color piece from 1988–1989 shows a hooded figure, hair obscuring his face like a cascade of beads, reaching out from beneath a cloth and handing a card to someone beyond the frame (figure 1.13). This richly robed, spectral figure is, like many of the sitters in Fani-Kayode's later pieces, figuratively blinded in an oracular invocation. Indeed, he draws from a deck borne in the left hand, revealed as the elongated forms of the tarot, a Renaissance-era variation of playing cards, said to have divinatory power by way of their pictographic meaning. Fani-Kayode would have recognized immediately parallels with the Ifá system of divination, which relies on the casting of chains or *ikin*, palm nuts whose combinations reveal prophetic or diagnostic allegory to be interpreted by the diviner. The orisha or deity that brought this tool for communication between worlds to humanity was named Òrúnmìlà—the very title of Fani-Kayode's photograph.

At first blush, one might read the shift described here, from the streets of Brixton to multivalent portraiture, as a sort of withdrawal from collective struggle into zones of interiority and aesthetic expression. Travelogue and social documentary give way to studio tableaux and ever-tightening formalism. And, indeed, the rest of this book demonstrates the ways in which, even conceding such an interpretation, Fani-Kayode's work continued to be staged as a kind of radical and visionary form of intervention that alternately elaborated or complemented other modes of diasporic practice.

For now, it is clear that Fani-Kayode was, as the editor Derek Bishton has argued, a "black British artist," but not in any doctrinaire sense that shorthand of critical retrospect might suggest.[73] Insofar as he was recently arrived from the postcolony, he could not elude the larger tension of class and national belonging that created a reactionary climate for those who might visibly constitute "difference," be they black or South Asian, from the Caribbean or Africa. Fani-Kayode engaged an array of overlapping histories that came together spatially in the heavily Caribbean working-class neighborhood of Brixton, sharing gallery and theater space and living alongside activists and culture workers. And his practice, as a form of errantry, was diasporic precisely in its willingness to work against the grain of canonical images and forms, whether quintessentially European or drawn from the already hybrid practices of the Caribbean and Africa as they were figured and actively negotiated in London.

During those six years, that city was a vital crucible in which Fani-Kayode elaborated his art and his subjectivity, drawing on the contours of the neighborhood and calling on those around him as sitters for his portraits—portraits that increasingly generated spaces not only for diasporic translation but for locating the inflection points among seemingly disparate cultural formations. In so doing, Fani-Kayode contributed to and was allied with the larger project underscoring a diverse constellation of artists working in eighties England, challenging absolutist conceptions of nation. He did this by giving visibility to the very postcolonial subjects that conservative elements sought to downplay or erase from the fabric of Britishness.

But Fani-Kayode fundamentally worked at the confluence and margins of many interests and orientations, asking questions within questions. His sometimes model Ajamu, a photographer from the Midlands who lived in the same building in Brixton, has noted that for many in the South London scene, the cultural politics of race were an essential lens for understanding their context, but so too were the various individual permutations of "intersectional identities," especially where blackness crosscut with queerness.[74] And so, many might look at the untitled figure with the Afro and see Camp above all, or look at *One in Three* and see not sonic repetition but, instead, the duplication of homoerotic desire, not unlike Andy Warhol's repetition of large-scale screen prints of a gun-toting Elvis Presley from 1963—"visual coitus" made utterly manifest through photographic means. They would be right. Just as Fani-Kayode's photographs find relational ground and produce sites of generative friction or outright recognition between black and white, Greece and Yorubaland, the Romantic and the contemporary, they also generate further intersections, most notably with the heterotypic spaces of the club and London's queer counterpublics, comprising other realities still.

RAGE AND DESIRE

For anyone who actually experienced punk at the time of its subcultural
impact, its force—if not always clearly evident—was nonetheless inescapable.
There is a direct link between the visual arts and the social practices of youth
that encompasses much more than what the bands were doing. It is seen in an
indivisibility of experimental underground film, graphic art . . . fashion and
street styles, performance, and guerrilla politics in which the look, attitude,
or consciousness of what was being expressed were freely
and fluidly incorporated into contemporary art.

Carlo McCormick, 2007

Are you really satisfied with the life you're living. Look a bit harder. Racism is
as British as the Black and White Minstrel Show. We Brits love to think
we are being exploited by foreigners yet nothing is so historically untrue.
Scratch a patriot and what do you get? A finger nail full of hope and glory,
a pathetic hankering after a world that never existed and the need to take
frustration out on an inferior person (preferably black, female or queer).
The British "race" was bastard anyway and always has been.

David Widgery, *Temporary Hoarding*

Arriving in London from New York in summer 1983, Rotimi Fani-Kayode
already had a large portfolio of work—some painting, some photography,
mixed media, and other ephemera. He turned up on Alex Hirst's door wearing lemon-yellow trousers and a black leather cap, asking to share his work.
Soon thereafter, as Hirst recalls, "we became lovers and, a few months later,
we decided to live together."[1] It was a time of turmoil: famine in Ethiopia, US
deployment of missiles in Europe amid large protests, IRA bombings, youth-

led antiapartheid demonstrations—a nuclear era with landslide victories for conservative forces in England. Margaret Thatcher and the Tories won the June vote by a decisive margin. Fani-Kayode's portfolio did not take up these themes directly, was not political in the sense of being issue-oriented or aimed at movement orthodoxies. Instead, he identified with a more countercultural mode, proudly working against the grain of dominant norms, living a life of intensity at the margins. He and the figures he photographed embodied a deep current of rebellion, a bohemian strain of originality and individualism that had, nonetheless, been discredited in many corners of the art world by the demythologizing critique of modernism and its precursors during the 1970s.

But as a black queer artist, living frugally, shooting in improvised spaces with little access to institutional support, such a life of rebellion was not a choice, not a performative gesture. Hirst summed it up by stating that Fani-Kayode "used his imagination to work through the experiences of having lived in different places. I think of what he'd seen of power and its abuses he'd developed a dislike of authority and a distrust of power. He became a kind of political and sexual rebel. . . . He never saw himself as an insider." But then, rebellion is difficult to quantify—it is more of a disposition or attitude than a process or mode of production. Earlier attempts to harness such energies often resulted in tragedy, as in the brief lives of the poets and anarchists of the nineteenth century, the dissipation of the avant-garde in the wake of the world wars, or the futility of leftist struggle under late capitalism. By the 1980s, the momentum toward meaningful political change seemed, for many, to be coming to an end. It had been defeated in the streets and at the ballot box. And yet, a progressive spirit survived in other ways, in the subaltern and vernacular forms often associated with youth culture, with the urban underground, and with music in particular. This attitude of utopian transgression and insouciant negation—a form that resisted form—was alive and well, especially in the nocturnal clubland that linked New York, London, and dozens of other cities. It was this energy and these communities that animated Fani-Kayode's life as a site of social practice, and his photographs as part of an ongoing dialectic of countercultures within modernity.

To be more precise, it would be reductive to call Fani-Kayode a punk, full stop—he wasn't, exactly. Nor was he necessarily a product of the New York discos or "Madchester" warehouse parties that defined much of post-1976 nightlife. Both modes, the punk/postpunk and the loft party/disco had their own utopian and dystopian currents, racial antagonisms, and consumerist complicities. But Fani-Kayode drew inspiration—formal, stylistic, sartorial, attitudinal—from these dual threads of the sonic underground and the communities that supported them. Such affinities were not, it seems, a form of subcultural orthodoxy but, instead, what theorist José Esteban Muñoz called *disidentification*, a zone of multivalent play and adaption of larger social formations, whether hegemonic or ostensibly subversive. While Fani-Kayode productively worked in tension with both dominant and countercultural approaches, it is not difficult to understand why punk itself would be a crucial starting point. It was an ambient energy in lower Manhattan and London and, like many transatlantic practices before it, a register of collective solidarity that animated large segments of bohemian life. During the "postpunk" years of the early 1980s it worked to upend and destabilize existing categories. On the whole, the wake of punk produced new points of relation and negation through an underlying disposition of skepticism.

RAZOR

During those early years, those last months in Brooklyn and Harlem and the high summer of 1983, Fani-Kayode was drawing to a close what he considered the first period of his career, in which he saw himself to be "painting with light. . . . My work is about having a good time, experiencing life, sex."[2] The idea of painting with light as a photographic practice—or, for that matter, foregrounding desire—was hardly new. There was direct precedent to his work in both the European New Vision experiments of the 1920s and, in particular, in the photographs of Man Ray, an elaborate monograph of whose work appeared on the occasion of a retrospective in Paris in 1982. Man Ray's iconic *Space Writing* project (ca. 1930s; see, e.g., figure 2.1) captures a blur of motion, the background and figure blurred and overexposed while the open shutter admitted a stream of penlight, a photonic form of automatic writing dancing across the frame like neon. Fani-Kayode reproduced this effect as the cover for issue 3 of *Square Peg* (figure 2.2), the queer journal of which Hirst was an editor and frequent contributor. This smaller format image seems to be drawn from a larger body of work undertaken in during this first year in London, during which Fani-Kayode made a series of 20" × 24" color prints of 35 mm shots (some dating back to 1982) with the high gloss and ratio of an Ektachrome snapshot. Even in this more populist format, however, Fani-Kayode uses motion to re-create the kinetic effects so central to Man Ray and his work with Marcel Duchamp. Rather than a handheld source, these large prints reveal that the lattice of flowing light emanated from a more festive source—Christmas lights suspended across the room.[3]

More generally, the shift evident in these early works is from Man Ray's analytic translations of surrealist automatism (meant to record the index of autographic movement) to Fani-Kayode's explicit documentation of a frenetic, even hedonistic, energy. The squalls of gestural light in these works are akin to the psychedelic trails in an after-hours *boîte de nuit*. The darkened figure on the *Square Peg* cover is none other than Stedman Scribner, a model who went by the name Razor and sported an Afro Mohawk. Robert Mapplethorpe also photographed Scribner in 1982, but his version is staged from the side in the form of a sublimated mug shot, with such cool clarity as to be an exercise in the high aestheticism of modernist formalism.

By contrast, Fani-Kayode continued his *Square Peg* portfolio across two square-format inner pages of that 1983 issue under the title *Paint Cut React (Razor's Aftershave)* (figure 2.3). For this he used a cut-and-paste montage effect typical of both advertisements for gay clubs such as Heaven elsewhere in the magazine and of punk-rock zine style, recognizable for its lo-fi or highly processed images ripped and stitched together amid sinews of text. Here, Razor appears in multiple, face darkened in seeming homage to *Space Writing*, donning masklike forms that seem themselves to be a patchwork of *décollage*. He alternately wears the black hat of a desperado and is daubed in paint, suggesting a ghoulish mask and incandescent sigil across his chest.

Such "writing with light," merged with a play of montage and masquerade, appears again in a series of Polaroid pictures from this period, including six taken in quick succession (see figures 2.4–2.7). The figure here, evidently in the casual setting of an apartment (wood floors, uncontrolled lighting) is captured in rapid motion. In one, he is on the ground and holding several other photos; another is tightly cropped, revealing a fade haircut dyed purple and gold, accented with an elaborate array of lightning bolts and resembling a Mohawk. As in the "Razor's Aftershave" layout, his face is painted, now in demonic shades of red; in one blurred frame this figure (likely Scribner, but it is difficult to tell) seems to scream into the lens, taking on a fearsome countenance. The Polaroids are marked with white, producing undecipherable hieroglyphics and energetic vector lines, like graffiti or the radiant figures that Fani-Kayode's contemporary Keith Haring inscribed onto the trains and walls of Manhattan. Except for the black leather in which he seems to be draped,

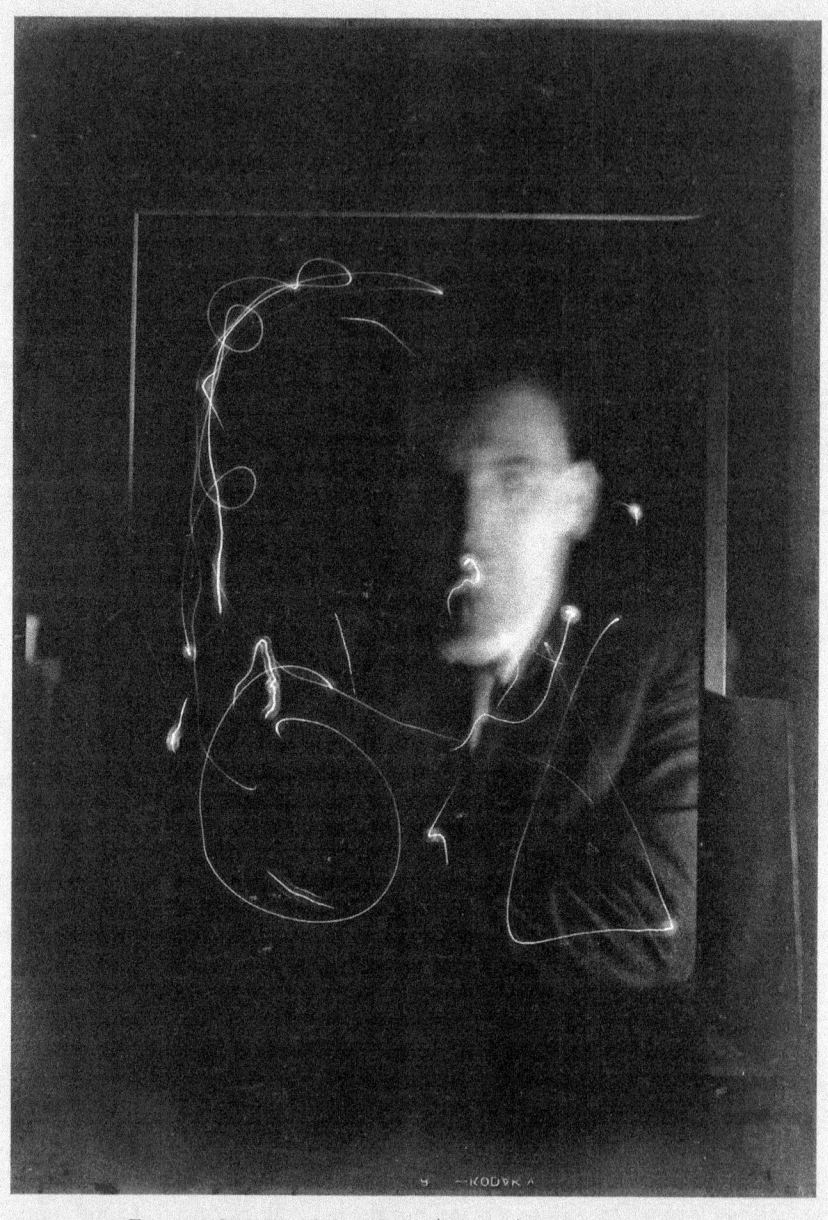

Figure 2.1 Man Ray, *Space Writing* (ca. 1930s). © Man Ray Trust /
Artists Rights Society (ARS), NY / ADAGP, Paris.

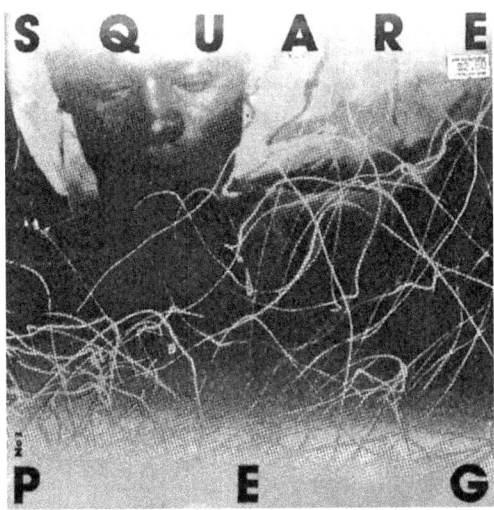

Figure 2.2 Cover of *Square Peg* 3 (1983).

one might assume that this figure is leaving for a costume party, or perhaps the street procession of Carnival celebrations in Crown Heights or Notting Hill.

Then again, for another type of viewer, the scene is proof of something else: he is off to a show. Perhaps Scritti Politti, the Stranglers, the Buzzcocks, or another early eighties band whose fans might, as a matter of course, blend into their wardrobe the glamorous and the gothic, dark humor with intellectual intensity. The clues here—garish colors, the leather jacket over belted jeans, the DIY immediacy and tonal limitation of the Polaroid itself—all point to a bit of punk rock portraiture, with the figure amping up before a night on the town. Or, a third reading still: this could be a one-off, part of Fani-Kayode's growing reliquary of saints and sinners. These six pictures could, indeed, be a study for Shango, the Yoruban king made orisha, or deity, in turn associated in the Americas with Santa Barbara. His colors are red and white, and he is symbolized with the Janus-faced and two-headed, a version of the doubled form atop the hammer that conjures concussive bolts of energy that he cascades from above.

But making such distinctions would have been, for Fani-Kayode, to miss the point. Music and mysticism, the explosive energy of the orishas, or the combustible reverie and nocturnal dirges that were circulating on the club circuit of Manhattan's Lower East Side and the edges of respectable London—they

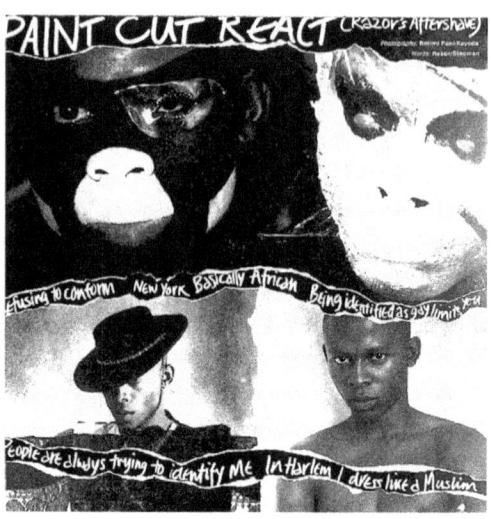

Figure 2.3 Rotimi Fani-Kayode,
Paint Cut React (*Razor's Aftershave*) (1983).

could disrupt the surfaces of polite society in equal measure. There is a distinct ratio of energy in the Polaroids and, later, the 1989 series such as *Nothing to Lose*; taken together they are at once violent, irreverent, and beautiful. Back in the pages of the *Square Peg* spread, Razor's textual interlude implores, "More to offer people than sex I have RAGE / the rage of being black / People need to deal with FEAR / A neutral sprit fantasy / A freer person."[4] One wonders what Fani-Kayode was reading, if not necessarily what he was listening to or looking at (the latter was, seemingly, more obvious). Given the Caribbean artists and critical voices surrounding him, or his father's own anticolonialist writings, might he have picked up a text from 1952? Would he have been reading Frantz Fanon's signal work, *Black Skin, White Masks*, written two years before the outbreak of war in French-controlled Algeria?[5]

There is one instance from Fanon's text that is less frequently noted than the sentences immediately surrounding it. This is the famed scene in which a small child has fearfully indexed Fanon, shouting "Look, a Negro!" to his mother. In that moment, the "white mask" of mimicry is revealed as inadequate to the transfiguring energy of the dermal schema. Fanon discovers his "livery for the first time. It is in fact ugly. [He] won't go on because who can tell [him] what beauty is?" This moment of disorienting revelation is interrupted, however, by the woman—and this is the important thing. She at-

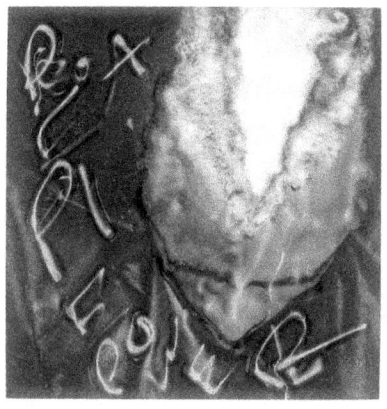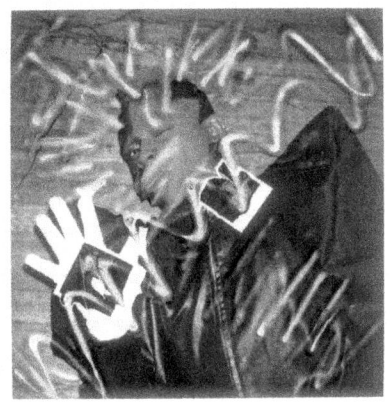

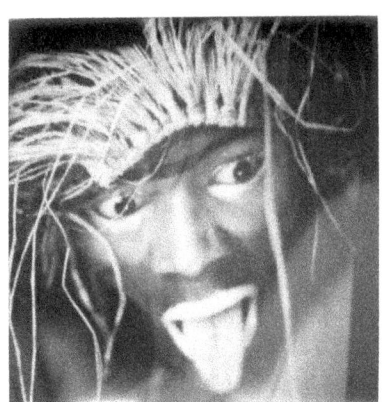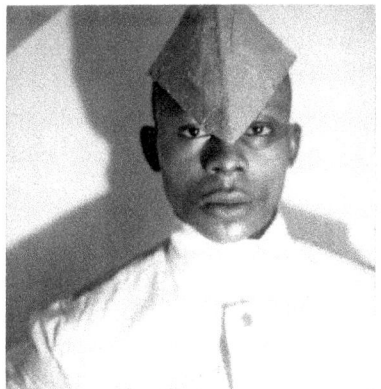

Figures 2.4–2.7 Rotimi Fani-Kayode, untitled Polaroids (1983–1984).
© Rotimi Fani-Kayode / Autograph ABP. Courtesy of Autograph ABP.

tempts a save, asking the boy to "Look how handsome that Negro is." Fanon is trembling, blood surging. "The handsome Negro says, 'Fuck you,' madame." He goes on, "At last I was freed from my rumination. I realized two things at once: I had identified the enemy and created a scandal. Overjoyed. We could now have some fun."[6] This is a moment of self-recognition, of rejection, of trampled propriety; the larger passage is often cited as a turning point, at once analytically rich and existentially vital. Read in the 1960s, it would have been notable for its oppositional quality, a militarism that resonated in Algiers and, in other ways, in the streets of Oakland or the South Side of Chicago. But as a clarion call of one era to another, an echo into the demimonde of the early 1980s, Fanon's words foreground another register still: they exude the revisionist impropriety, the oppositional defiance of punk, avant la lettre.

Fani-Kayode was consciously working on the far side of Fanon's dialectic, and he did so shooting and writing in very similar keys to Fanon himself: a mode at once knowing, impatient, and dissatisfied with the alignments and limitations of his present. While their means were absolutely distinct, at times they shared a tonal quality that blended ferocity and lyricism. And Fani-Kayode, like Fanon, often wrote in existentialist terms, though never, of course, from the vantage of the clinician. For the former, punk was the expression at the edges of late modernism that held his Romanticism in slight suspension, granting it a self-awareness and a critical edge, sanding away its forays into beauty like the abrasive pages of Guy Debord's 1959 protopunk multimedia work *Mémoires*.[7]

So, in many ways, one can locate punk most obviously as a sensibility for Fani-Kayode, one compatable with his own sense of postcolonial critique, and one that would have served as the background of his practice, animating and fueling the photographs. He lived in New York as punk's influence crested and then ramified into the various strains of postpunk, goth, new wave, synth pop, drone, no wave, and hardcore. Writing from London in 1989, he and Hirst noted the air of contradiction that Fani-Kayode registered back in the US, between the oppositional energies of its countercultures and the impersonal calculus of its booming banks. They mused that "America—bless her cotton-pickin' socks, despite the contradictions that produced them—has inadvertently provided people such as ourselves with the nerve to dare to differ openly from the tyrannies of culture and empire."[8] Elsewhere, Kobena Mercer has argued that Fani-Kayode cannot be understood without attending to a cultural landscape "convulsed" by the aftershocks of punk, which started in the United States in clubs such as CBGB and Max's Kansas City, crossed over to England in the form of tours and records by the Ramones, Iggy Pop, and Patti Smith, and then ignited a new generation of Britons tired by the excesses of progressive rock.[9]

Certainly Fani-Kayode would have been inundated with variants of punk culture during his time in the United States—he lived in DC as the city became home to Dischord Records (1980), the label where early political punk bands such as Minor Threat got their start. Black punk band Bad Brains, too, formed a year after Fani-Kayode started school at Georgetown. The university, in turn, was more traditional in bearing, but its radio station, WGTB, was a hotbed of antiwar and pro-LGBT sentiment and it broadcast across a district that was quickly becoming the center for a range of antiestablishment musical forms. The campus rests on a hilltop on the banks of the Potomac in one of DC's toniest neighborhoods and was, in those still quite segregated days, a rarefied if politically engaged enclave in a city that was very much at the center of the waves of social unrest and an emergent politics of identity that characterized much the 1970s and 1980s.[10]

After DC, as Fani-Kayode arrived in New York in 1980, punk would have been everywhere, especially for a young art student at school just across the Williamsburg Bridge from Manhattan's Lower East Side and East Village. Those neighborhoods were ground zero for a storefront and apartment gallery scene that blended elements from the uptown graffiti and hip-hop cultures with the dystopian chic of the music emanating from the then-working-class downtown. Lower Manhattan was an epicenter for such cross-pollination and was itself consciously framed by artists and critics as a kind of parallel world, a neobohemia that drew on avant-garde tropes of yore.[11] For some, this amounted to an aesthetic, encapsulated in raw Polaroid scenes of a debauched demimonde; for others it was a spatial strategy, a way of moving through and reclaiming the disenchanted city. This can be seen in David Wojnarowicz's self-portraits as a nineteenth-century French enfant terrible, staged in subway cars and dark alleys, wearing a photographic mask as *Arthur Rimbaud in New York* (1978–1979). In the ensuing several years, Keith Haring and Jean-Michel Basquiat inscribed city walls with paint stick and marker. Haring sketched high-contrast energy lines and stick figures, and Basquiat emblazoned cryptic aphorisms under the handle SAMO.[12]

In 1976 punk could be framed as something of a "class" music: for all of its periodic art-school pretensions it was, at root, youth driven—deskilled, democratic, and outraged. Punk's amplified, fast-paced blues were a vehicle for antiestablishment tirades,[13] and its signature iconography of cut-and-paste montage was not dissimilar to the World War I–era broadsides of Hannah Hoch and Raoul Hausmann, or the neo-avant-garde reformulations of Situationist *détournements* of mass culture in the postwar period. When, in 1977, the Sex Pistols released "God Save the Queen," the title of the two-hundred-year-old anthem was pasted like a ransom note against a cameo of Queen Elizabeth II over the Union Jack. This registered as a shocking cultural appropriation sealed with the sneering lyrics, "God save the Queen / The fascist regime / They made you a moron / A potential H-bomb / God save the Queen / She ain't no human being / There is no future / And England's dreaming."[14] The punk as an antisocial archetype would go on to pervade eighties popular culture, if only as a form of reactionary caricature.[15]

For its part, the Pistols' most famous song was fitting of a short-lived career that blended avant-garde criticality with foul-mouthed nihilism. There is a critical impulse here, but while the song breaks with the past it characteristically offers no utopian prospect. Which is to say, in its earliest British iterations, punk outlined a world with no future, one of atom bombs and mass delusion—it was a wake-up call, if not a fully elaborated project. Subsequently, the emergence of dozens (then hundreds) of bands on both sides of the Atlantic that took up the mantle of punk heralded improvements in musical quality, shifts in lyrical subject matter or cause, and cross-pollinations with other genres. The cultural critic Greil Marcus found common currents within punk itself, positing it as part a strain of dissent going back to the early days of Enlightenment Europe: a critical counterculture of which late Labour-era youth culture was simply a timely articulation.

Of the Sex Pistols, Marcus argued that they were a "carefully constructed proof that the whole of received hegemonic propositions about the way the world was supposed to work comprised a fraud so complete and venal that it demanded to be destroyed beyond the powers of memory to recall its existence."[16] He and others, such as Manchester-based Factory Records cofounder Tony Wilson, would credit the 4 June 1976 Sex Pistols show at the Lesser Free Hall in that city as a foundational moment when the British independent music scene of the ensuing decade was born, and with it the modern electronic dance club, New Romanticism, and so on. Punk bands played music; punk itself was a catalyst, an oppositional and improvisational force that suffused urban England during the years culminating in Fani-Kayode's return.[17]

For all of their iconic power, of course, the Sex Pistols embodied a mode of white working-class cynicism, later picked up in rather arch terms by many "young British artists" over a decade later.[18] At the time of its most obvious cultural salience in England—roughly the years 1976–1981—the politics around punk were protean and contested. As Autograph A B P director Mark Sealy recalls, those years were "one of the most intriguing and contradictory political periods in post–World War II British history. A time when racist skinheads danced to Jamaican ska, punks embraced reggae and black kids reached out to punk. Meanwhile disaffected white Britain turned to rightwing politics and a shopkeeper's daughter . . . became the Prime Minister."[19] Indeed, if 1976 is remembered as a watershed year in the formation of British punk, it is also notable for the first major summer riot around Caribbean Carnival—in this case, in London's Ladbroke Grove, which became an augur of clashes between police and immigrant communities that would mark the ensuing nine years.

It was at this moment, too, that antifascist and antiracist collectivities began to coalesce through the channels of Caribbean-routed music and punk rock, notably in the form of Rock against Racism. The latter was documented in photographs such as Syd Shelton's archive of photographs of the Notting Hill Carnival and antiracist demonstrations and exemplified in the zine *Temporary Hoarding* (see figure 2.8). Paul Gilroy, who wrote during those years under the nom de guerre G-Roy, recalls the importance of visual culture—graphic design, "badges," clothing, stickers—as a means transgressing existing boundaries of race and gender, and of generating elective communities that shared an ethos of plurality. He argued in 2015 that there "was an unprecedented connection between the spirit of political dissent and the novel ways in which it was being communicated and rendered. These tactics certainly drew from the brazen confidence . . . of Punk, but they also surpassed it in delivering viewers and participants beyond the limits of a world projected recursively in black and white."[20]

Shelton's photographs more broadly document the posters and graffiti that constituted the visual culture of punk in the streets of South and East London, and also moments of overlap in the stylistic codes of both black and white; the bands Steel Pulse and X-Ray Spex alike were nodes in a larger array

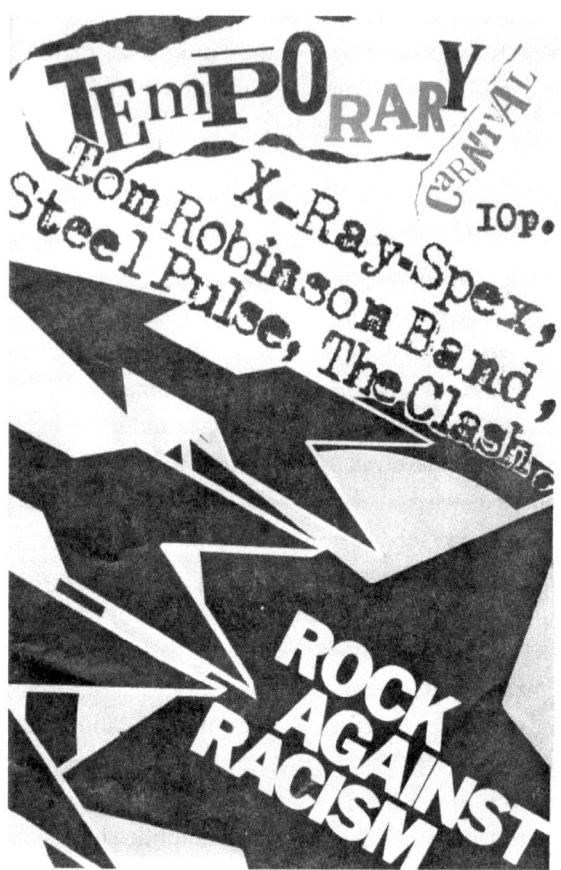

Figure 2.8 Temporary Hoarding Special Carnival Issue 1978
(1978). © The TH team.

of antiracist collectivity and radical sonics. They, in turn, fueled an ambient energy of protest and resistance in the neighborhoods where Fani-Kayode lived and worked. Further still, there were specific bands that emerged from this constellation that one can more closely connect with Fani-Kayode. His occasional portrait sitter, the photographer Ajamu X, for instance, remembers the housing cooperative on Railton Road where they lived, a place seemingly suffused by the spirit of *Temporary Hoarding*. Echoing the methods of an underground gallery scene emerging in the early years of the decade, the co-op embodied an ethos of resourceful improvisation and the oppositional occupation of space. It started as a series of "squats" and "short life housing," units that the local councils could not make habitable, and became home to a host of activists, artists, poets, and theorists. In these provisional spaces, Ajamu would pass by Fani-Kayode, Sonia Boyce, and the Trinidad-born broadcaster and community organizer Darcus Howe. Until 1988, Howe, with Linton Kwesi-Johnson and Farrukh Dhondy, published the bimonthly Marxist periodical *Race Today*, founded in 1969 by the Institute of Race Relations, an antiracist think tank. At Railton, residents created darkroom space, wrote, and organized, all to a soundtrack that included variants of punk—the gothic echoes of Nick Cave's Birthday Party, DC and New York hardcore by way of Bad Brains, and rocksteady-inflected bands such as The Specials.[21]

Such acts, and the labels they were associated with—Rough Trade and Two Tone (both founded in London in 1978), or Dischord (DC, 1980)—were synonymous with politicized hybrids of punk, first-wave ska (a fifties-era Jamaican blend of calypso and R&B), and dub reggae. Such cross-pollinations between seemingly disparate constituencies were unsurprising: on the one hand, London's and Manchester's various underground musics played out in close geographic proximity at large festivals such as the 1978 Carnival in Victoria Park, as well as the more quotidian spaces of town halls, pubs, and basements. The spacey sub-bass of dub echoed from sound systems as art students or rude boys slammed away in spartan, makeshift clubs.[22] Moreover, from its inception in New York in the early 1970s,[23] punk was something of a queering, boundary-rupturing force, making it a genre suited to syncretizing and allying with other audiences and styles. Of this multivalent scene in London, Gilroy recalls a life provisionally "reconfigured under the Union Jill, [where] the country yet to come would be other than black and white. It might be bondage-free, two-tone and inescapably plural, even genderless."[24] Back in New York, pioneers such as the New York Dolls pressed such transgression into sexual identity more broadly; they played gigs at the Mercer Arts Center, drawing on the glam-rock tones of David Bowie. Their onstage personas, according to a *New York Times* review, projected a "camp, prissy 100% homosexual group in black tights."[25]

Other groups, such as Bad Brains in DC, emerged from a fusion of jazz and reggae, and the band's frontman, H.R.—dreadlocked, shirtless, and explosively energetic—championed the motto "PMA," or Positive Mental Attitude. Their 1983 record *Rock for Light* reflected on their exclusion from capital-area rock clubs and their subsequent move in 1979 to New York, and hinted at the transatlantic possibilities for their music. The song "Banned in D.C."

proclaimed, "Banned in D.C. with a thousand other places to go / Gonna swim across the Atlantic cause that's the only place I can go." Other musicians recall the group coming out of their Southeast high school initially wearing sharp suits, which were later spattered in paint and shredded. Their sound was "frenetic, insane," with H.R. gyrating and conducting like "Cab Calloway on steroids."[26] His acrobatic engagement with the audience is captured in a 1982 photograph by Leslie Clague, who was something of a scene photographer during the key years of DC punk, from roughly 1979 to 1985 (figure 2.9). H.R. recalls of the period, "[We] quit our jobs, and we played music all the time. . . . We were creating. See this is the difference between a sellout and what's real."[27] Leo, of the Madam's Organ venue on Eighteenth Street, was even clearer about the inclusiveness and anticorporate ethos of the city's underground, its logic of utopian refusal. From the vantage point of 1986 he noted it "attracted all types of people . . . primarily kids who didn't want to be hippies, who didn't want to get fucked up on drugs, didn't want to be rednecks and didn't want to listen to Fleetwood Mac. They didn't want to be part of the 70's me generation. It was its own unique thing. It wasn't from LA."[28]

For all of its home-grown character, DC's cosmopolitan and countercultural dimensions had its congruences with the U.K. For instance, London's The Clash (formed in 1977) blended sonic textures drawn from music imported from overseas—jazz polyrhythms on the drums, reverb, and sharp guitar attack—mimicking dub and funk. Their 1980 song "Magnificent Seven" was written on a trip to New York, where the group claims to have been inspired by the breakbeats and verbal rapping of early hip-hop. Two years later, on their massively successful *Combat Rock*, the song "Straight to Hell" lamented the deindustrialization of the Midlands, discrimination against immigrants from the postcolonies, and American policy in Vietnam.[29] Many of their early-career songs explicitly examined the urban landscape of Caribbean cultural formations, from the Notting Hill Carnival to reggae shows at the Hammersmith Palais in West London.[30]

These bands shared a tonal quality as well as a praxis of antiracism as a world-altering force. Importantly, their visual equivalent is crystallized in many of Fani-Kayode's photographs, including *Lee Clover in Bristol* (ca. 1985; figure 2.10). The figure here, with tight Afro and stubble, leans against an exterior stone wall, seemingly under the glare of a streetlight in a side alley. His chin is cocked upward, eye closed, sinking into a moment or lost in a haze. . . . A partially smoked cigarette dangles between his right fingers, his left hand

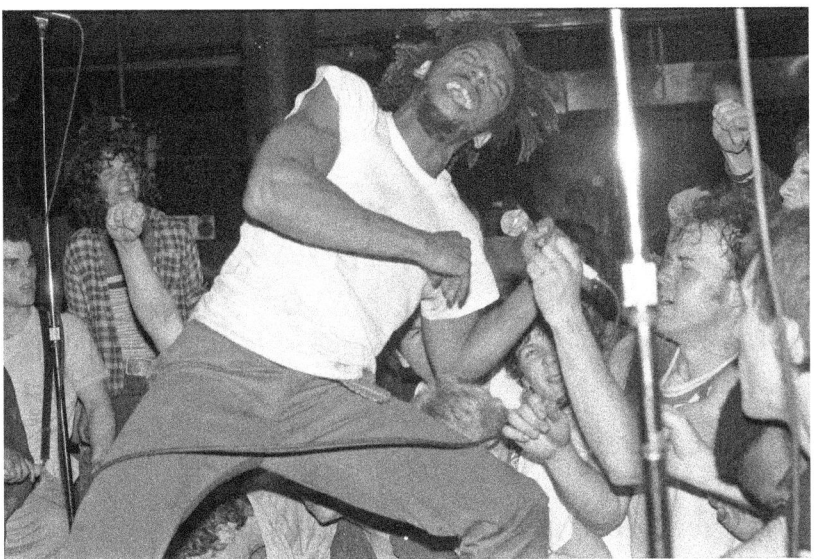

Figure 2.9 Leslie Clague, *HR of the Bad Brains Performing at the 9:30 Club in Washington, DC, on April 29, 1982* (1982). © Leslie Clague. Courtesy of the artist.

interlaced with thick, black leather suspenders. Lee Clover wears no shirt, but his pleated wool pants suggest a riff on the natty suits common to the rude boys and mods. The picture is erotic (even seductive), but Clover seems unconcerned with the camera—he is distant, hopelessly cool. The picture locates him in Bristol, a bustling university town on England's western shores built on the wealth of the Caribbean sugar trade, but by the 1980s home to its own iconic fusions of hip-hop, soul, and punk. Accordingly, Clover's clothes evoke a merger of subcultural references—the sartorial sharpness of ska and suggestive leather straps that bridged bondage with motorcycle gangs and rockabilly. This is eighties-era gay portraiture, but it importantly draws on transatlantic codes of blackness, queerness, and countercultural musics, and the various points of inflection (clubs, boutiques, bars) through which they were mutually constituted. On the whole, the photograph exudes a sense of nocturnal bohemianism and insouciant swagger.

Lee Clover echoes Shelton's pictures of black youth in Brixton during the years just before Fani-Kayode arrived in London. But where Shelton's rely on a lo-fi immediacy, there is more chiaroscuro to Fani-Kayode's, more of a spectral luster—but they frame the same streets, the same type of subject. And the at-

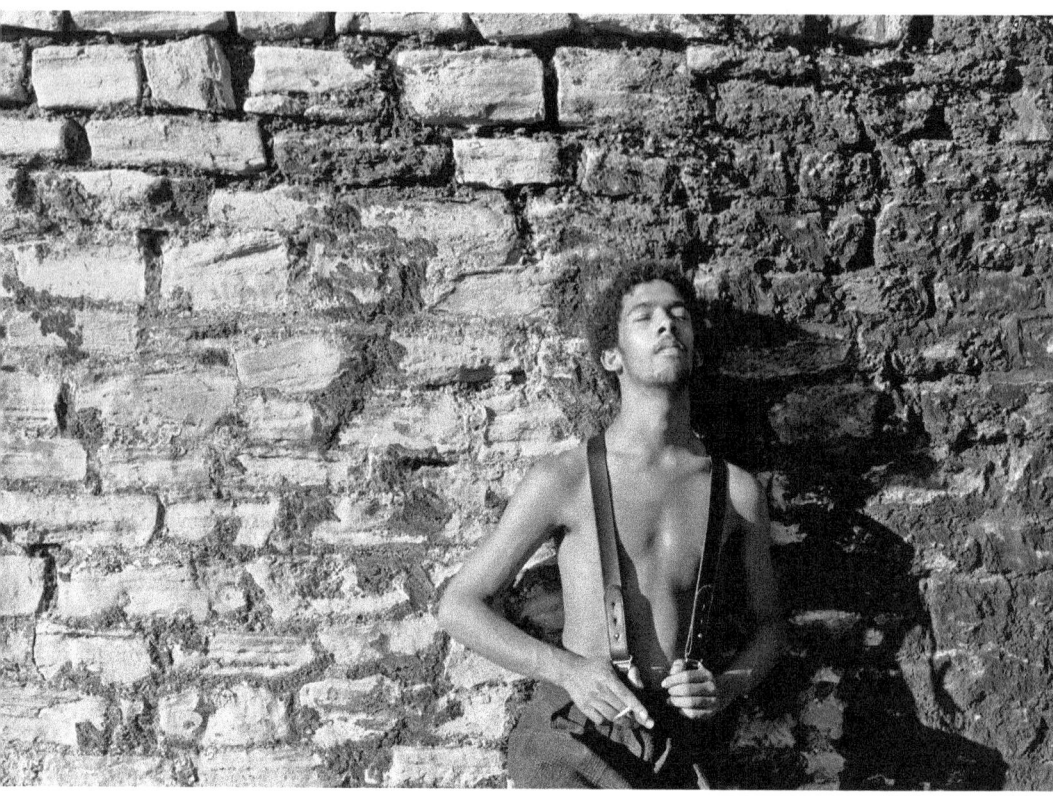

Figure 2.10 Rotimi Fani-Kayode, *Lee Clover in Bristol* (ca. 1985). © Rotimi Fani-Kayode / Autograph ABP. Courtesy of Autograph ABP.

titude of dissent crystallized in Shelton's photographs animates Fani-Kayode's writing, too. For instance, his definitive statement, "Traces of Ecstasy," is by turns diagnostic and reflective, but it is shot through with an undercurrent of outrage and criticality, a rejection of the status quo and a self-reclamation posited as an act of survival. Citing the grassroots organizations of which he was a part, which crosscut "issues of race and sexuality," he argued that such joint work could inspire new modes of creation. "It can also have the very concrete effect of providing the means for otherwise isolated and powerless artists to show their work and insist on being taken seriously."[31] After a short discussion of Nazi homophobia, he suggests that government policies of the 1960s and 1970s represented a backslide into fascistic values, posing a reductive vision of

Britishness against all forms of cultural difference, against, in his words, "anyone who represents otherness."

Fani-Kayode notes of his career that it is "Black, African, homosexual photography—that I must use not just as an instrument, but as a weapon if I am to resist attacks on my integrity and indeed, my existence on my own terms."[32] This is a view of art making not merely as an act of cultural analysis but of full-throated resistance, of counterattack. Fani-Kayode's language echoes the existential and militant stance of Fanon and also the bluntness and confrontational clarity of the lineage that Greil Marcus traces in the European avant-garde. Autograph ABP director Mark Sealy confirmed the defiant tone that suffuses Fani-Kayode's practice in an essay for the 1995 catalog *Communion*, in which he recalled that "Kayode's work was not seen as being in good taste or suitable for a gallery." Citing Fani-Kayode's appropriation of Paul Gauguin and Édouard Manet, he argues that this "work was a direct attack on institutional canons . . . a challenge which reads: 'I have done my homework; I have read your art history. This is what I want to do with that knowledge—invert, subvert and appropriate it—to suit my own concerns and experiences.'"[33]

FLAGS

Sealy's quotation is telling for a few reasons: in simplest terms, Fani-Kayode embraced punk's discontented and revisionist ethos, but he resisted incorporating into his photographs its stylistic modes, which generally elaborated the strategies of shock and fragmentation pioneered by elements of European Dadaism and, later, the Situationist International. He may have lived during his years in London in a squat populated by musicians and political radicals, and he may have, at times, dressed the part. But his photographs were never as bluntly programmatic or polemical as the multimedia approaches of many of his peers. That is, like the musics of the black radical tradition and gay discos of the era, punk is perceptible in his work as an attitude, and in the affect and dress of individuals, but rarely as an aesthetic per se. His photographs after 1984 seem to abandon the montage effect of the *Square Peg* layout, but not their underlying sociopolitical tenor.

Consider, for example, *Union Jack* (ca. 1987; figure 2.11), a black-and-white photograph shot in the studio and cropped to create a striking vertical axis

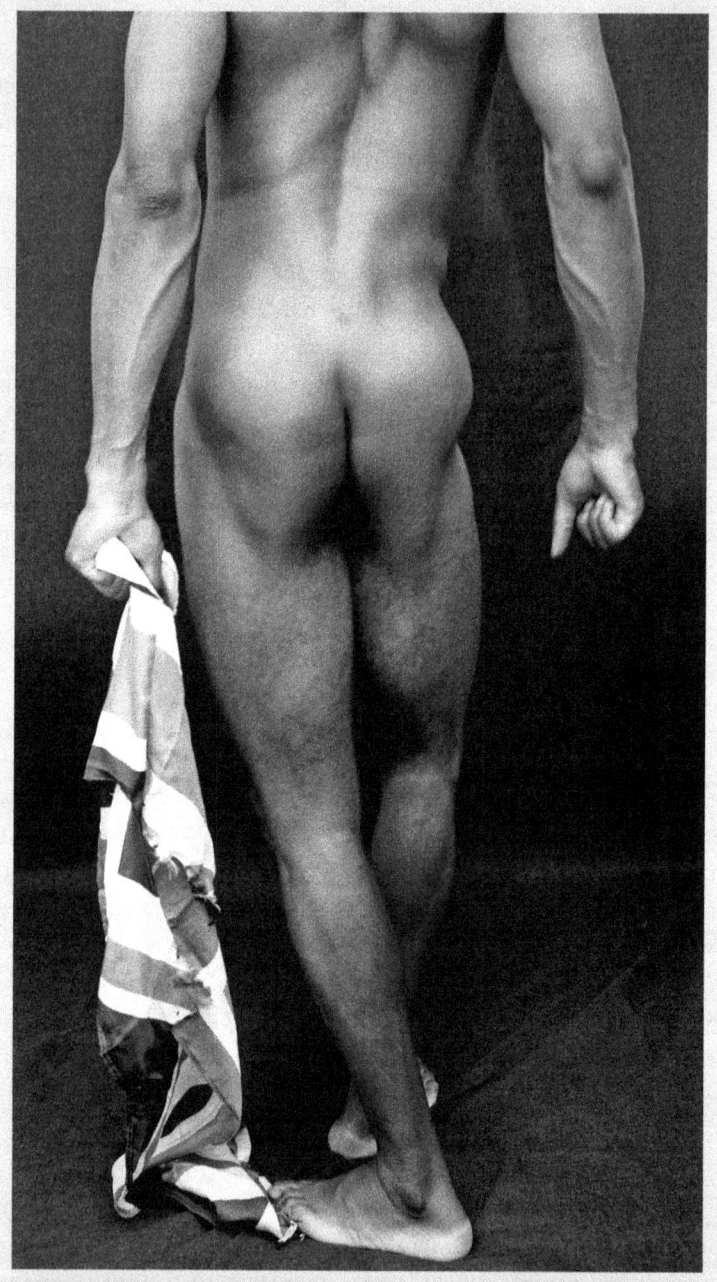

Figure 2.11 Rotimi Fani-Kayode, *Union Jack* (ca. 1987). © Rotimi Fani-Kayode / Autograph ABP. Courtesy of Autograph ABP.

that tracks the nude posterior of a black figure, from the luminous edges of his feet to the slight torsion of his trapezius muscles. His left hand grasps the British flag, which piles loosely on the floor and glances off the back of his knee; meanwhile the tonal density of the photograph draws the flag's white saltire into sharp relief against the obsidian background. The flag itself is symbolic of a composite identity, predicated on the internal colonization of Ireland and Scotland, and of a long-contested question of what it means to be British at all. Thinking back to Gilroy's formulation that "there ain't no black in the Union Jack," Fani-Kayode's *Union Jack* can be seen as a literal reclamation and *détournement*, an echo of Vanley Burke's famous picture of an immigrant boy on a bicycle in Liverpool, albeit stripped of both Burke's documentary immediacy and any remnants of sentimentality.

As a result, *Union Jack* also specifies Fani-Kayode's connection to punk tactics, in particular his shift away to the more abrasive and shocking mode of montage and cut-and-paste juxtaposition and into the tight control of studio portraiture. Yet the picture itself, despite its high finish, signals an attitude, an orientation toward the world, that resonates in the same key as the records on the platter. This is evident both in Fani-Kayode's knowing appropriation of a highly contested signifier of empire and in his handling of that flag, which is pulled across the floor rather than held aloft. It is noticeably tattered and burned along its outer edge. And while Fani-Kayode does not resort to the blunt ransom-note typography and spinning pupillary swastikas of Jamie Reid's Sex Pistols montage, one can gather from his statements that he drew parallels between fascism and then-contemporary English attitudes toward difference and deviance. In this instance, the British flag is repurposed with a blend of overtness and subtlety—a visually appealing photograph that signals dissent through distressed fabric here, and the saunter of its queer, black figure there.

Union Jack, then, is Fani-Kayode's "fuck you, madam" moment—one of many to follow, and also one that had clear parallels in both England and the United States. In the American context, the star-spangled banner served as a metonym for the failures of equity and representation in the liberal state—as a symbol of victory in the space race it was taken on by Faith Ringgold in her *Black Light* series. Her version of the flag, overlaid with text, reads "Die Nigger." Here, Ringgold co-opts the language of geometric abstraction while reading between the lines—that space exploration was a triumph for a system predicated on racial violence. As Lisa Farrington has observed of *Flag for the Moon*, it "expresses Ringgold's anger over the billions of dollars spent to put a man on the moon in 1969 while millions of Americans at home continued to live in poverty."[34] When it showed in 1970 at the Judson Memorial Church with other works that "critiqued U.S. military aggression in Vietnam and gender and racial oppression at home," she and two other members of the Art Workers' Coalition (AWC) showing in the exhibition were arrested on charges of "flag desecration."[35] David Hammons would go one to produce his own national colors, to subvert the boundaries of nation with his *Pan-African Flag* (1990), a version of the American tricolor reimagined in the black internationalist tones of red, green, and black. The flag hangs on 125th Street in New York, at the Studio Museum in Harlem.

Fani-Kayode's handling of the Union Jack is clearly framed in individual terms—his own experience or priorities—and, more generally, in the intersectional mode of black homoeroticism. In this sense, he builds on the subversive gesture in Ringgold's flag appropriations, but he does so without obvious reference to broader codes of collective resistance. He was, it should be noted, working outside of the specific framework of the Black Arts Movement or the AWC that prefigured the 1969 flag or, with respect to Hammons, without reference the explicit and long-standing signifiers of pan-Africanism. Nonetheless, resistant collectivity in the United States embodied by the AWC, AfriCOBRA, and the post-Stonewall gay liberation movement were likely the very blueprints that, as Hirst suggested, "provided people such as ourselves with the nerve to dare to differ openly from the tyrannies of culture and empire." Perhaps Fani-Kayode found corollaries for those US-specific collectivities in the individualist but galvanic energies of Rock against Racism, antiracist punk, reggae, and even New Romanticism.

For all that, the most obvious stylistic convention of punk design—the technique of cutting and rending—is not always immediately present Fani-Kayode's photographs. The visual aesthetic of punk was more evident in the work of his immediate contemporaries in New York (think Barbara Kruger's iconic feminist compositions of the period) or, in England, by Eddie Chambers. Chambers's use of media imagery and swastikas in collage-type paintings made during the early 1980s critiqued ascendant forms of xenophobia and racial absolutism (figure 2.12). Fani-Kayode, by contrast, seems to have enacted a parallel mode, one of reorienting well-established tropes and sanctified imagery and creating tableaux from the ground up. He did this rather than graft such signifiers from found visual culture, and his method granted the

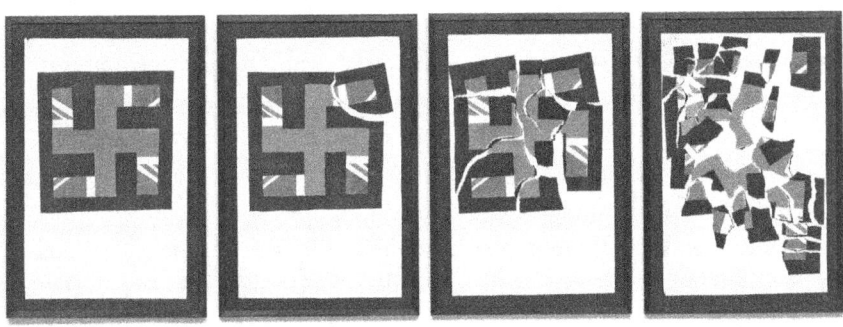

Figure 2.12 Eddie Chambers, *Destruction of the National Front* (1979–1980).
© Tate, London 2017.

photographs a depth of materiality and tone and (as the next several chapters argue) a capacity to exceed punk's engaged immediacy in favor of a broader temporal sweep.

Nonetheless, as the curator Rosetta Brooks has argued, the critical utility of rending and tattering cloth suggests that "punk's real resistance could somehow be found in its relationship with the commodity image and the implicit violence of the rip. . . . It is a way of demonstrating that the world is not alright." With respect to Fani-Kayode's flag, her conclusions resonate clearly: "the moment you incise the fabric with zips or orifices (holes) or tears, you draw attention . . . to the materiality. You render a different meaning to it. Something as familiar as the tartan becomes suddenly estranged."[36] At its most critically productive, then, punk and its related visual and affective variations provided a method of destabilizing social boundaries—of class and race—as well as formal ones, notably high and low culture. In this way, Greil Marcus is correct that punk built on a modernist framework but also enacted an aspect of what was then theorized as postmodernism, with its tendency toward hybridity and catholicity of source material. As Brooks would have it, these fusions exemplified a critical dimension of youth subculture, what the historian Jon Savage sees as a resistant tactic of bricolage within the matrix of late-capitalist mass media.[37]

But Brooks is also aware of the double-edged quality of punk as a potentially aesthetic rather than social practice. She concedes that "for those who understood cultural strategy . . . [punk was] a deliberate, strategic interruption that recognized the dialectic between violence and pleasure in consumption."[38] In this account, artists who adopted punk maneuvers were always already aware of the limits of avant-garde critique, but also the upside in terms of cachet and social capital to be had by adopting the conventions of outlaw and neobohemian self-representation. To wit, the very neighborhoods in which punk first thrived, such as Camden, Soho, the East Village, and the Lower East Side are now fashionable and wealthy enclaves.[39] The novelist Jay McInerney recalls his life in Manhattan's West Village (now one of the most affluent neighborhoods in the world) as late as early as 1991, rhapsodizing that

> at least half the neighbors were gay men and it was basically a neighborhood where breakfast was taken at eleven and whether you liked it or not the trannies from the adjacent meatpacking district were going to use your stairwell as their place of business and sooner or later you were probably going to get mugged. These minor inconveniences notwithstanding, this was the downtown fantasy that many of us non-native New Yorkers had moved to the city in search of, the New York of the Abstract Expressionists and the Talking Heads, because we'd heard of the Cedar Tavern and CBGB. We didn't want to be Jock Whitney or Carter Burden; we wanted to be Patti Smith or Jim Carroll.[40]

And so, it is unsurprising that many artists who adapted punk attitudes, motifs, and compositional strategies became successful among elite gallerists and collectors, sometimes meteorically so. Indeed, those who at first blush share some immediate contextual similarities to Fani-Kayode, such as Basquiat and Robert Mapplethorpe,[41] are virtually synonymous with the downtown scene and enjoyed a high level of exposure and remuneration before their untimely deaths (in 1988 and 1989, respectively). Both Basquiat (a black artist when black art was by and large institutionally marginalized) and Mapplethorpe (a gay artist who depicted scenes of intense, even graphic, homoerotic encounter) thrived in no small measure thanks to the confluence of wealth in the New York art market, and that market's appetite for work that embodied the dangerous and chic edges of a city that was then still palpably divided between uptown and downtown. In this context, Basquiat,[42] with his aggressive handling of paint and knowing play of signifiers seemed to blend art brut, crosstown graffiti, and punk rock affect (he played in a noise band called Gray) with the hip-hop culture that had made its way from the Bronx into the gallery settings of the East Village.[43] He even collaborated with the Ur–art rock celebrity Andy Warhol, by then an éminence grise living in the East Village, who, in turn, owned Basquiat's building on Great Jones Street—a perch from which the latter made work for sale, ultimately, at Mary Boone's blue chip gallery.

Mapplethorpe worked one block away at 24 Bond Street. And for all of his seeming extremity—amid all the leather and skulls—his photographs blended the high gloss of fashion with a timeless, Apollonian orientation toward classical beauty, from flowers to female musculature (see figure 2.13; Mapplethorpe's portrait of Stedman Scribner is described above). Mapplethorpe was a transgressive character in his daily life, but one who also produced series after series of strikingly palatable work. This along with his rapport with a sophisticated class of patrons and mentors meant that Mapplethorpe emerged from the more marginal life that typified his seventies-vintage experiments with montage and Polaroids to become what the curator Ingrid Sischy called "a society photographer in the largest sense." For example, one account of Mapplethorpe's early forays into photography has him being given a camera by the then curator of photography at the Metropolitan Museum of Art, John McKendry. The wealthy socialite Sam Wagstaff served as a mentor and patron from the late 1970s onward, giving Mapplethorpe both an income and an entrée.[44]

Fani-Kayode occupied the same geographic space, but his practice was prefigured by a topology that both intersected with and diverged from his contemporaries. Although schooled in and influenced by New York, on moving to Brixton he benefited from few of the advantages of one living and working in the former's booming art market. In contrast to the plenitude of patronage that many punk-influenced contemporary artists enjoyed in the United States, the London market for home-grown art remained comparatively inert, with its soon-to-be most notable speculator, Charles Saatchi, still investing in American work, and many of its artists still finding their way through state-sponsored competitions and juried exhibitions after graduate school. Of course, the tone and momentum in London would change by decade's end, in-

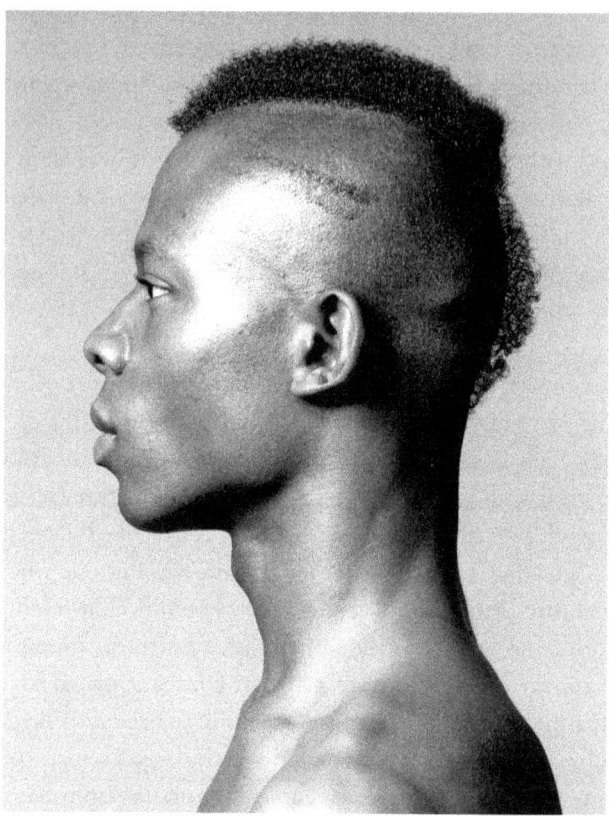

Figure 2.13 Robert Mapplethorpe, *Stedman* (1982). © Robert
Mapplethorpe Foundation. Courtesy Art + Commerce.

augurated by a cohort of artists born in the 1960s who, under the initial leadership of Damien Hirst at Goldsmiths, University of London, staged a series
of DIY exhibitions in postindustrial offices spaces near the Thames River, including the three-part *Freeze* at Surrey Docks in autumn 1988.[45] Nonetheless,
whatever Fani-Kayode sacrificed in terms of society connections and market
viability he gained in being part of a specific British cultural context quite unlike New York, in which antiracism, activism, and more individuated forms of
rebelliousness coalesced in the welter of music and visual culture to revivify a
spirit of utopianism under the sign of negation.

The above rehearsal of the working conditions of "punk-styled" artists in New York is important because it demonstrates crucial distinctions in access and visibility. Namely, in the years leading up to the breakthrough of the Goldsmiths-educated younger generation, artists such as Fani-Kayode who foregrounded the experiences of intersectional, black, Asian, feminist, and queer subjects displayed in de facto underground venues and, often, lived in the sort of provisional spaces described above. Such sites of reception mirrored New York's East Village landscape in their nominal outlook and practical resourcefulness, but not in terms of commercial viability. However, there are indeed productive parallels to be drawn between Fani-Kayode and the punk-influenced artists of another American hub—the so-called Boston School. The latter comprise photographers who emerged from that northeastern city and who experimented with diaristic and realist modes that were *demimondaine* in their subject matter, marked by nocturnal scenes, physical violence, hospital vérité, drug use, and sexual overtones. Such pictures were often similar to the Fani-Kayode snapshots with which this chapter started, most evidently in formal terms, including the group's common use of Polaroid film, montage effects, Day-Glo colors, and scrawled marginalia.

The most obvious overlap here is Nan Goldin, who took her camera everywhere and documented her downtown world with unflinching directness, showing the results in a nostalgic slide-carousel format called *The Ballad of Sexual Dependency* (1985). She later documented HIV-positive friends such as Cookie Mueller.[46] A more striking comparison still is Goldin's contemporary Mark Morrisroe, who was associated with both the New England punk scene as a zine editor and the drag circuit, both in Boston (as Sweet Raspberry) and in the East Village (as part of the "Clam Twins" with Stephen Tashjian). Morrisroe's photographs, like Goldin's, depict scenes of hard living, from chest X-rays and IV drips, to battered and emaciated bodies. Morrisroe himself would succumb to AIDS five months before Fani-Kayode's death in 1989. His attitude seemed to reflect an amoral nihilism many equated with punk (he swore that he would "coldly use and manipulate everyone who can help my career. No matter how much I hate them I will pretend that I love them"), and he wrote that his work was dismissed by a jury as unskilled and amateurish, that he "needed to learn composition and technique as well as simple color balance"—observations made, it seems, with acidic irony, even pride.[47]

Even so, Morrisroe was also known as something of a formalist, using novel development processes with images made on a Polaroid Land Camera to make "sandwich" prints that produced painterly effects reminiscent of nineteenth-century photographic pictorialism and Old Master figure studies. As a result, there is a timeless, Romantic quality to many of his individual works, not unlike Fani-Kayode's own gum bichromate experiments. Elsewhere, Morrisroe employs a "double negative" process whereby figures are multiplied in spectral gradation—another technique used by Fani-Kayode, in an update of surrealist process. On the whole, however, his oeuvre tended toward a stark realism, depicting other figures from his neobohemian landscape.[48]

One can, therefore, consider Fani-Kayode's Polaroids side by side with Morrisroe's—both draw on the directness and instantaneity of the medium, and both show figures who transgress the boundary between the beautiful and the monstrous, living and dead, male and female. Morrisroe's pictures are populated by nudes worthy of Egon Schiele, amid smoking women and vamping figures in drag. They share with Fani-Kayode's Polaroids a psychedelic drift of blurred overexposure and an interest in figures in states of ambivalent masquerade. This is true of the series of six images of the man with the lightning bolt coiffure described above, and also of another set, which shows a black man with a nearly bald head, wearing a clasped, high-necked and tightly tailored white tunic, eyes covered in round shades and lips tinted in deep purple. This latter figure is an enigma, embodying elements of Carnival-style adornment, garish makeup, and clothes that evoke a bondage-styled doctor or technician. And so, while Fani-Kayode's subject is not explicitly in drag (that is, in terms of the more explicit gender inversion frequently displayed in Morrisoe's pictures), he does partake in drag's play of identity and its performance of gender. He does so here (as does a figure in yet another Polaroid, who appears in ghostly white pallor and red glasses) with nods to a gamut of subcultural cues.

It is fortunate that such Polaroids have made their way into Fani-Kayode's larger body of work, because they are an important counterpoint to the highly finished photographs that have come to be emblematic of his career. In contrast, these rawer images reveal connections between Fani-Kayode and transatlantic punk, the New York downtown scene, and other queer photographers at work during the 1980s. More important, they affirm some overt connections to then-contemporary British artists such as the filmmaker Derek Jarman, whose play of Union Jacks, hardscrabble bohemians, and transgressive

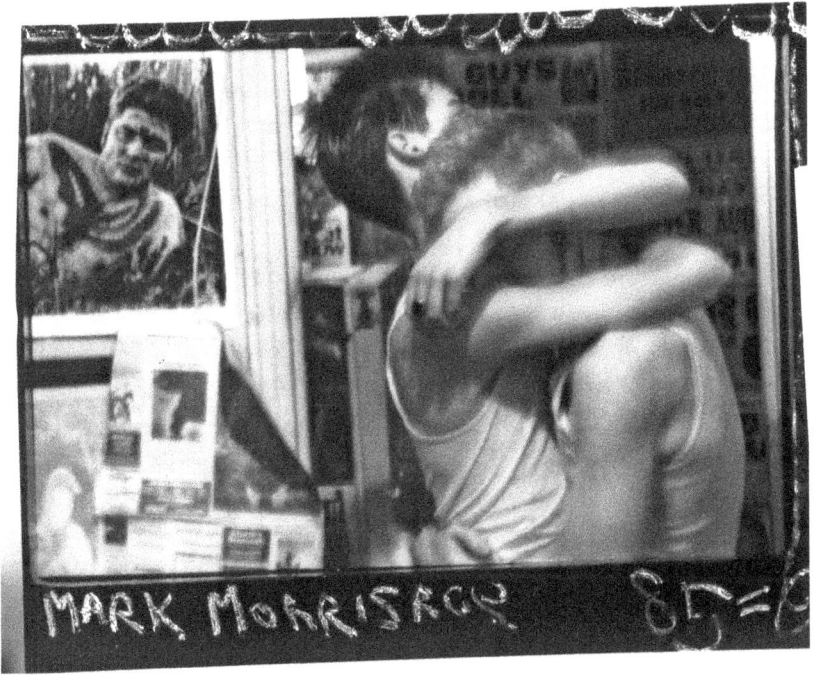

Figure 2.14 Mark Morrisroe, *Untitled [John S. and Jonathan]* (1985).
© The Estate of Mark Morrisroe (Ringier Collection) at Fotomuseum Winterthur.
Courtesy of Fotomuseum Winterthur.

sexuality drew on punk aesthetics and politics. Jarman also circulated within the queer zones of London of which Fani-Kayode was a crucial part. Fani-Kayode's photographs similarly partook of punk culture and disidentified with it, most notably in his rejection of pure fragmentation or negation in favor of an additive approach—one that showed an expanded field of subjectivities, buried histories of relation, and hidden spirit worlds.

Even this additive process was transgressive in its way, working to unsettle boundaries and disorient the viewer's perception of reality. As he and Hirst argued, the impetus to transgress in this way—sometimes using the camera as a weapon (as a "fuck you, madam"), sometimes with dark humor and irony—was inspired by Fani-Kayode's travels and larger sonic and social milieu. Such work, in turn, productively crosscut black and gay politics as a zone of visionary performance of everyday life. In opposition to the unvarnished polemics and sloganeering of earlier waves of punk-driven art, Morrisroe's and Fani-Kayode's pictures did not so much directly oppose dominant structures or postulate utopias beyond them but, in Muñoz's terms, "work[ed] on and against" those very structures from within, performing identity in ways that unsettle, rather than fix, relations of power and rigid demarcations of subjectivity.[49]

One final caveat: punk was at times an uneasy bedfellow for such an intersectional project and, as such, queers of color (to borrow Muñoz's formulation) have frequently worked to complicate not only mainstream ideological codes but also those within counterculture. For example, Muñoz charts the work of Vaginal Davis, a black man in "terrorist drag" who helped to cohere the early eighties Los Angeles punk scene even as she critiqued its more reactionary elements. But for all of its complexities and ramifications into the 1980s—into iterations of skinheads and rude boys, hardcore, goth, new wave—it is important to reiterate an observation made earlier, that punk also has its origin stories in those early days of the 1970s, with the "100% sissy" glam of the New York Dolls.

Not coincidentally, the heyday of the nascent New York scene correlated with the rise of another British art student, David Bowie, a musician whose protean identities embodied a new version of authorship, one that fused punk bravado and glam excess to create modes of performing the self that put pressure on commonplace notions of sexuality and gender. In chameleonic fashion, Bowie created a seemingly pan- and postsexual identity that shifted from year to year. His Ziggy Stardust character was enshrined in an eponymous record from 1972 and appeared again in 1973 on the cover of *Aladdin Sane*, with Bowie sporting striking red hair, with an electric bolt of red, purple, and black makeup bisecting his downturned face. The look is virtually identical with the figure in Fani-Kayode's Polaroid. It is fair to venture that Fani-Kayode looked to the immediate crucible of early eighties punk, but also its origins, in which new subjectivities began to emerge at the interstices of a range of underground subcultures.

In both London and New York, where punk could be seen in many instances as a site of white, class-bound nihilism, artists such as Fani-Kayode, Morrisroe, and Jarman all recognized the form's deeper affinity with currents within modernity that sought to disrupt and destabilize seemingly static social relations. In this light, it is no coincidence that as punk was driven from traditional rock venues in London it overlapped with the gay underground. As Jon Savage notes, "apart from the freedom of dress" that gay clubs offered, their spatial marginality and disidentification with a culture in which homosexuality was "partially criminalized" meant that haunts such as Chaguaramas ("a dingy dive where the worst transvestites in the world went") would become epicenters that were "part of the Punk remapping of London."[50]

THE SPIRIT OF THE CLUBHOUSE

Much of the above has described some stylistic and energetic aspects of resistant collectivities in the post-1976 West. But space itself has been equally important: the contested modes of public gathering such as Carnival or the rock festival, or the protean clubs that hosted a range of musical subcultures and served, at the same time, as a Venn diagram of convergent interests. So in thinking sonic cultures and Fani-Kayode together, it is fitting to end in two linked sites of the underground—the bathhouse and the disco. This was a nocturnal itinerary with which he was quite familiar (the key locations for which were DC, Chicago, New York, and London from the early 1970s through the mid-1980s), and one from which many of the stylistic and psychotropic cues in Alex Hirst's writing originate.[51]

One such bathhouse in London—Chariots—can scarcely be missed as one crosses under the viaduct at Vauxhall, walking south toward the Oval at the edge of Brixton. A Roman gladiator drives the titular carriage, and bands of rainbow colors demarcate it as both a place of hedonism and a neighborhood landmark. It is one of several such clubs in a franchise and was opened in 1996, as official policies of xenophobia and homophobia began to gradually recede under the "New Labour" government. Chariots—located across the street from an MI6 building—is just over a mile's walk from another local institution, Ministry of Sound. Founded in Lambeth in 1991, the Ministry is a palace of dance culture and was a locus (along with clubs such as Fabric and the aforementioned Heaven in London, or Limelight in New York) of increasingly popular variants of electronic music, such as dub-heavy drum and bass and the more commercially slick trance of the late 1990s. Now a multimillion-pound concern, Ministry of Sound, like Chariots, is indicative of an acceptance and commodification of what just a decade prior were channels of subcultural resistance.

Both the bathhouse and the dance club have long been key sites of collaboration and communion—both sexual and spiritual. Indeed, Muñoz later specified such spaces of transgression as crucial to bringing into being utopian forms of queer futurity that reject the here and now and open on to potential new worlds.[52] Derek Jarman recalls the club as a place where suddenly queers were not isolated, but instead constituted a critical mass, numbering in the thousands.[53] Tony Wilson, the iconic punk-era impresario and owner of Manchester's Hacienda, equated his parties to a kind of worship in postindustrial cathedrals, with crowds losing themselves in "the beatification of the beat."[54] These social spaces exist within and beyond "aboveground" cartographies—they reflect the "natural" order of things while also suspending or inverting them. This reflection proceeds by making the utopian "unreal" temporarily accessible and by carnivalizing the outside world. The brothel (or the bathhouse), the cemetery, the colony, the nightclub: these were spaces all theorized by Michel Foucault, who developed a term for them— the heterotopia, which he defined as: "places that do exist and that are formed in the very founding of society—which are something like counter-sites, a kind of effectively enacted utopia in which the real sites, all the other real sites that can be found within the culture, are simultaneously represented, contested, and inverted. Places of this kind are outside of all places, even though it may be possible to indicate their location in reality."[55]

Clubland of the 1970s and early 1980s was an *other* place of the highest order. It comprised underground chambers and postindustrial cathedrals in which outside social relations and hierarchies were dissipated in an atmosphere of inclusion and experimentation, propelled by DJs and records that moved through the linked conduits of the subcultural economy. While the bathhouse was a site of unbridled sexual freedom, the club provided a concretization of utopian affinities carried over from the 1960s. Its atmosphere cultivated recombination and interaction, from the aural alchemy on the PAS to the blurring of normative boundaries on the dance floor. New York's Loft, for example, was celebrated for, according to a recent history of dance culture, "its vividly unifying atmosphere (it was probably about sixty percent black and seventy percent gay). . . . The club's pansexual attitude was revolutionary in a country where up until recently it had been illegal for two men to dance together unless there was a woman present, where women were legally obliged to wear at least one recognizable item of female clothing in public."[56]

The model of the Loft was duplicated in a loose network of other cities. In the case of DC it was the Clubhouse, located in a nondescript industrial space in the northern part of the city. The Clubhouse opened its doors in 1975 around a code of tolerance and unity upheld, ironically, by making access to its Friday night parties membership or invitation only. Nonetheless, it seems that the Loft's balance of subcultural insularity and visionary frisson was alive and well in this venue to the south. One piece of folk history, a poem by a former member reads, "Like a well lubricated machine / Functioning smoothly-without friction / A journey in a natural world / Where the language is universal."[57] The popular touring producer and DJ Colonel Abrams cited it as "one of the hottest" clubs he played, fondly recalling the large banks of speakers around the dance floor with, atypically for the era, men dancing atop.[58] The Clubhouse, in any case, was sufficiently formative for Fani-Kayode, then a young student pushing against the doctrinaire wishes of his father,[59] that he dedicated *Black Male/White Male* to the place and his experiences therein.

That spirit—the collaborative and visionary futurity of the Clubhouse—was doubly important for Fani-Kayode: it extended directly in the tone and subject matter of *Black Male/White Male*; and it was the element that made such clubs vital, sites in which a sensibility is brought into being through the communion of its participants. In this sense, DC was crucial in the formation of a young Fani-Kayode's artistic and political consciousness. At the time, the city did not yet partake of the class anxieties, urban fashionability, and Caribbean undertones so central to London punk, but it did forge a politicized, antiwar, antiapartheid scene rooted in early hardcore that was the "house music" of the DIY punk and postpunk community. This scene specifically drew on Chocolate City's local music, go-go, a form named after the venue in which it was played. Go-go was not an extant style but rather a way of performing of a series of cover songs, fused by drum breaks and fills, and call-and-response in which audience and performers (such as Chuck Brown) cyclically generated a one-time set that could be recorded and circulated by bootleg, but never repeated. DC music was what emanated from its own heterotopias—it synthesized and riffed on existing genres and was transcendent, even revelatory in tone.[60] It was "scene music" in the same way that Fani-Kayode's photographs are a form of scene photography.

Once disco and house were absorbed into mainstream culture, clubs were transmuted into something more prosaic, into rooms that played dance music.[61] But while they lasted (precisely during Fani-Kayode's education in the US), these "other spaces" were critical nodes, temporary portals that coalesced around a critical carnivalesque of music and dance. Neither the Clubhouse's nor Fani-Kayode's projects manifested some permanent utopia on the horizon or outside the negative dialectics of the present. But as Muñoz observes, there is never really an outside, only disidentification from within. Foucault further specified this, arguing that utopias are sites without place; they perhaps usefully "present society itself in a perfected form, or else society turned upside down, but in any case these utopias are fundamentally unreal spaces."[62] But however fragile or temporary, the importance of the club—and of the discursive site articulated by Fani-Kayode's photography—is that they were real, physically present and accessible, the one the synecdoche of the other, manifestations of Foucault's heterotopia.

The heterotopia, of course, has its conceptual analogue in the form of what the theorist Michael Warner calls the "counterpublic," communities within a more dominant public sphere that develop their own forms of discourse and value, their own forms of reception, and their own spaces of gathering and exchange.[63] The counterpublic is "counter" precisely because it operates against the grain of a status quo that necessarily excludes it from its institutions and norms. Counterpublics generate or gather in heterotopic locales; and counterpublicity (zines, record covers, newsletters, posters) is the way in which resistant subcultures come into being until they are either commodified, change the contours of the mainstream, or both. In this sense, the sonic cultures—reggae, punk, dance music—outlined above at once crosscut Fani-Kayode's personal and visual practice and can be defined as counterpublic at different moments in their histories. But the most obvious such sphere with which Fani-Kayode identified and, often, disidentified, was London's network of queer communities. To these, he brought his own experiences in DC and New York, and a broad knowledge of transatlantic, homoerotic image making.

MAGNOLIA AIR

Some Western photographers have shown that they can desire Black males
(albeit neurotically). But the exploitative mythologising of Black virility on
behalf of the homosexual bourgeoisie is ultimately no different from the
vulgar objectification of Africa that we know at one extreme from the work
of Leni Riefenstahl and, at the other, from the "victim" images that constantly
appear in the media. It is now time for us to reappropriate such images
and to transform them ritualistically into images of our own creation.

Rotimi Fani-Kayode, "Traces of Ecstasy"

When I die, my angels, immaculate Black diva drag queens,
all of them sequined and seductive, some of them will come back
to haunt you, I promise, honey chil'.

Essex Hemphill, *The Tomb of Sorrow*

Rotimi Fani-Kayode was a gay artist. The homoerotic cast of more-or-less
every single photograph that was released to a wider viewership makes such
a statement so superfluous that it actually bears repeating. At a time when
struggles for the recognition and inclusion of queer and trans subjects are
bearing cultural and legislative fruit, it is important to look back on the 1980s,
a decade of profound crisis, opportunity, and transition. Positioned midway
between the militancy and identity politics that typified the post-Stonewall
generation and the emergence of intersectional and queer reformulations of
the theoretical agenda, the period during which Fani-Kayode worked was a
crucial time. On the one hand, the AIDS crisis crystallized the existential immediacy of gay rights in societies in which laws and dominant discourses remained stubbornly heterosexist; on the other, art and theory provided key

sites not only for galvanizing political projects but for reformulating the very contours of subjectivity and its histories.

Fani-Kayode's life was, to an extent, defined by the limitations and potential liberations of being a gay man in eighties England, a reality reflected in his activism and his art. But what kind of "gay photography" was he making, and to what end? Certainly, his work was initially distributed in the alternative circuits of gay presses and bookstores, and at the time his pictures occupied the liminal space between art and erotica, consciously staged in dialectic with Robert Mapplethorpe's notorious *X Portfolio* (1978) and *Black Book* (1986). This legacy is borne out thirty years on: an internet search for Fani-Kayode finds that he persists in the archives of LGBT websites. His inclusion in two major surveys in the early 2010s—the definitive tome *Art and Queer Culture* and the 2012 traveling exhibition *This Will Have Been*[1]—solidified these connections in terms of contemporary art history, emphasizing Fani-Kayode's canonical status in new accounts of queer art. For example, Catherine Lord, in analyzing *Ebo Òrìsà* (figure 3.1), emphasizes Fani-Kayode's collaboration with "young men" such as Alex Hirst and the poet Essex Hemphill, arguing that the picture's *gelede* mask functions as both a "tired metaphor for the closeted Western homosexual" and, in its upending, as "a proclamation of queer diasporic modernity." She reiterates the language from Fani-Kayode's statement, "Traces of Ecstasy," that his was a "Black, African, homosexual photography."[2]

But what is queer diasporic modernity? And beyond contributing to a lineage of the male nude and the homoerotic portrait, how did Fani-Kayode's photographs contribute to the larger sociopolitical context of activism, the politics of representation, and the formulation of queer subjectivities? Lord's prompt is a productive starting point because diaspora has largely been theorized along lines of nation and ethnicity. Nonetheless, its theoretical emphasis on communities spatially dispersed but nonetheless connected by ongoing, dialogic engagement around questions of shared identity also specifies the transnational flow of queer cultural practice. More important, Fani-Kayode's specific mode of image making consciously uses humor, homage, and appropriation to critically interrogate not only heteronormative master codes but also the more racially determined conventions associated with gay subcultural formations for much of the nineteenth and twentieth centuries. This gesture, of interrogating and reformulating signs as a genealogy that "cuts in" to hegemonic cultural forms, is, for Kobena Mercer, a hallmark of black diasporic art.[3] Which is to say that, in one sense, transnational queer-

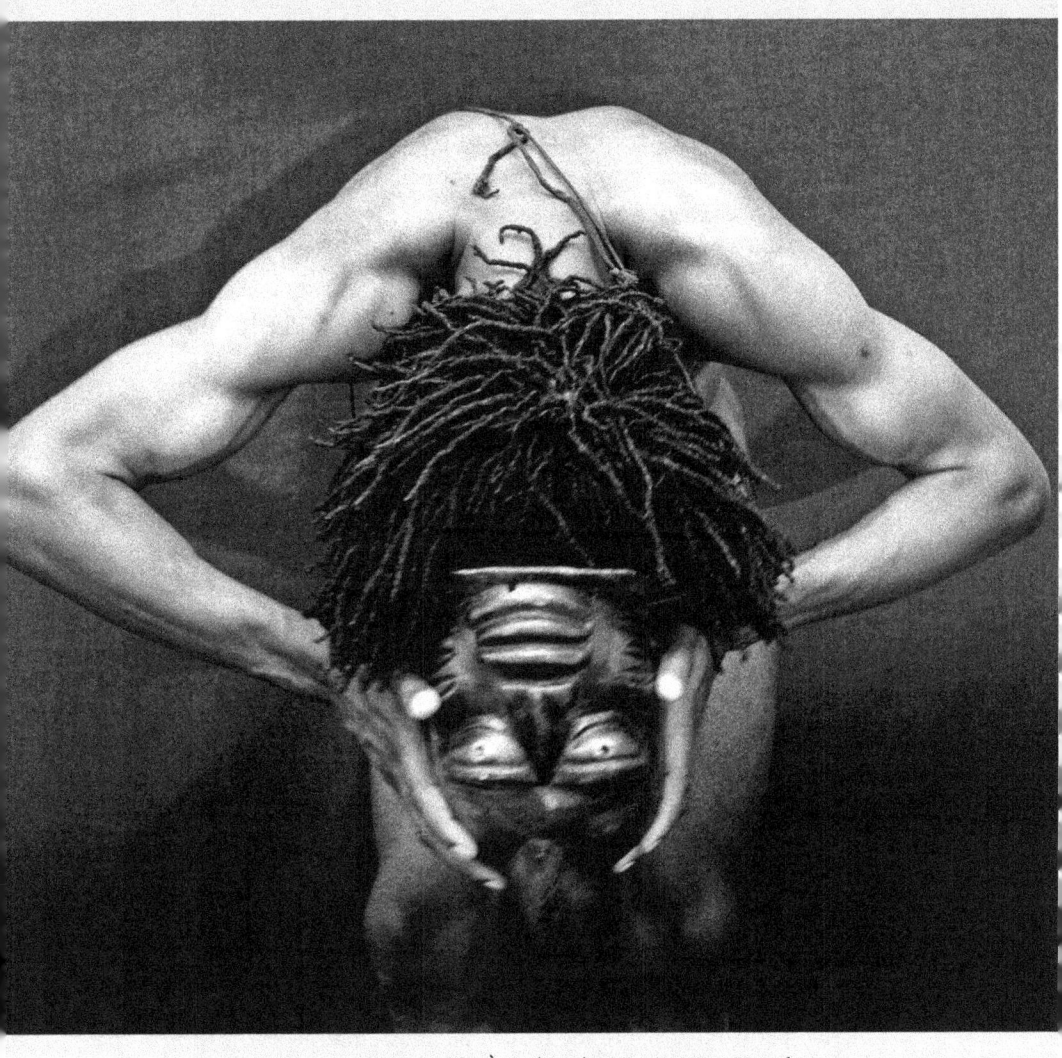

Figure 3.1 Rotimi Fani-Kayode, *Ebo Òrìsà* (1987). © Rotimi Fani-Kayode /
Autograph ABP. Courtesy of Autograph ABP.

ness and diasporic practice are in many ways homologous, and, in another, Fani-Kayode's position as a black gay artist in the 1980s allowed him to forge a subversive synthesis of these often parallel worlds, drawing them into relation and productive dissonance. He did this by elaborating methods familiar to earlier iterations of black internationalism. Accordingly, this chapter tracks multiple layers in this process: translating and signifying existing gay visual culture; pursuing a new syntax for specifically black, gay image making; and elaborating on material culture as it moved and circulated across borders and through noninstitutional channels. Ultimately Fani-Kayode operated at a pivotal juncture between the codes of Western, gay culture and an emerging formulation of queerness that put pressure on the very possibility of static or collective definitions of identity.

The resulting photographs thus worked as sites on which queer subjectivity, with its manifold histories and futures, could be ramified and materialized. In contrast to the civil rights model that predominated in the United States, Fani-Kayode's approach was at once consonant with—and a vital record of—a specifically British queer politics. It was one way of generating spaces of discourse and presence where they by and large did not exist. Catherine Lord is correct, then, in pointing to Fani-Kayode's bypassing of the "tired" dyad of being closeted or out—he relied instead on more anarchic process of "upending." This should already be unsurprising in light of the confluence of radical sonics and antiracist discourse through which Fani-Kayode framed his praxis.

And given the active citation and negotiations at work in Fani-Kayode's photographs, they cannot be understood without a detailed reading of different stages and priorities within the histories of queer activism and image making. As a result, this chapter is divided into two movements: one locates Fani-Kayode in a more canonical lineage of homoerotic or gay art production that persisted well into the 1980s; the other emphasizes the specific challenges and cultural strategies of queer communities constituted along more intersectional lines. Fani-Kayode was a relay point between these histories, much in the same way that his art drew together heterogeneous modes of diaspora and black strategies. What follows can be best understood as parts of a continuum in which Fani-Kayode contested histories of representation and interlaced them with larger questions of race and nation.

The passage by Lord cited earlier is brief, a caption above a reproduction of an image from *Black Male/White Male*. She does not specify precisely what "queer diasporic modernity" might look like, but her aim in *Art and Queer Culture* is to create jumping-off points within a canon that works against the grain of the canonical. Here, Fani-Kayode emerges in a history of Western art that includes Brassäi and Berenice Abbot, Pablo Picasso and Andy Warhol. His entry faces a picture of Cookie Mueller taken by Nan Goldin and displayed as part of her 1985 slideshow of the New York demimonde, *The Ballad of Sexual Dependency*. Similarly, two of Fani-Kayode's black-and-whites (*Ebo Òrìsà* and *Bronze Head*) appear in *This Will Have Been*, adjacent to several Robert Mapplethorpe photographs, including the pedestaled black body of *Ajitto* (1981) and the controversial *Man in a Polyester Suit* (1980). They shared a wall with works by Félix González-Torres and David Wojnarowicz—the former's two clocks gradually losing time with each other, and the latter's epic appropriation of fearsome buffalos cascading from a cliff set the interpretive stage for Fani-Kayode's work: queer pictures, AIDS pictures, records of a generation of artists lost to a plague (Mueller's fate, too). The specific method by which Fani-Kayode used his practice to engage with HIV during the late 1980s warrants its own discussion, which follows in the final chapter of this book. For now, it is worth noting that when compared to the documentary vérité of Goldin's promiscuous camera or the dense allegory of loss in Wojnarowicz and González-Torres, Fani-Kayode's photographs do not seem overtly political.

As I note elsewhere, this potential distinction is made sharply in the Black Audio Film Collective's *Twilight City*. When Fani-Kayode appears for the second time in that film, he enacts a shadowy ritual between two glistening men, as choreographed and subtle as a Japanese tea ceremony. Importantly, this interlude is juxtaposed with scenes of crowds marching in demonstration against "Clause 2A," a 1988 law in the United Kingdom that criminalized public education on homosexuality. This, and the broader climate of homophobia that suffused British life during the Thatcher era, is described in the film through interviews with committed practitioners such as Savariti Hensman of the Black and Gay Lesbian Centre, and the activist Femi Otitoju. They argue that 2A and the 1986 law (section 28) from which it was drawn institutionalized discrimination and allowed people to be fired from jobs, derailing lives and ending careers in teaching and the care of others.

Exposure 2 of this book argued that in spite of the priority that is often given to realist or openly activist modes of political address, in the context of *Twilight City*, Fani-Kayode's tableaux nonetheless did critical work. In the sequence outlined earlier, his intervention serves as a counterpoint. Amid descriptions of policy, rumination on Christian conservatism, and footage of public demonstration, Fani-Kayode's alchemy happens in an adumbral noplace, beyond the diurnal grind of legislative politics. He offers a glimpse into a different world, a zone of communion and eroticism that animates the urban twilight in spite of the quotidian indignities (and, for many, hopelessness) of waking life. And while a great deal of art-critical attention has been paid to the activities of New York–based ACT UP (and the closely related collective Gran Fury),[4] the British context (and Fani-Kayode's role in it) is perhaps less discussed, in no small part due to the Conservative government's overt suppression of queer activism.

Indeed, active censorship of education and literature on nonheterosexual desire and AIDS itself was complemented for much of the 1980s in England by a gamut of public discourse—television, advertisements, newspapers—that solidified a correlation between homosexuality, deviance, and disease. As the historian and theorist Simon Watney argued in 1987, the urban American model of "gay liberation" and its related politics of identity was unique, abetted by First Amendment protections in a country that emphasized individual rights over class distinction. This configuration gave rise to an increasingly broad and aboveground discourse of gay rights—especially relative to the British and European model, which led to an altogether different set of contradictions. On the one hand, decency laws in the latter meant that in the early years of the epidemic American publications on gay men's health were literally smuggled across the Atlantic via diplomatic and clandestine channels.

As Watney argued at the time,

> one of the most unfortunate aspects of the media coverage of AIDS in Britain has been the gigantic opportunity it has afforded most commentators to treat the words "homosexual" and "gay" as if they were synonyms, as if gay liberation and the entire sexual politics movement of the 1970s had simply never happened. . . . In any case, British gay politics has lacked that powerful ideal and model of civil rights which is so centrally inscribed in the American constitution.[5]

Conversely, a deep-seated British tendency toward collectivity fostered, in Watney's account, a network of nonprofit organizations, cooperatives, and subcultural modes of address—especially music, poetry, and theater—that formed a counterpublic in which advocacy and collaboration occurred in spite of more mainstream antagonisms. It was at precisely this level that Fani-Kayode's photographs intersected with queer activism.

While Fani-Kayode was notably wary of being co-opted by movement politics in general (Hirst warned in 1990 that he was "not interested in being seen as a 'gay' or 'black' artist, and especially not a 'black gay' artist"), he was also aware of the tactical value of collectivity and the radical potential of a deeper history of homoerotic representation that he might elaborate and complicate. In "Traces of Ecstasy," Fani-Kayode conceded that "since I have concentrated much of my work on male eroticism, I have also experienced homophobic reactions to it, both from the White and Black communities. Although this is disappointing on a purely human level, perhaps it also produces a kind of conflict through which to struggle to new visions."[6] He nonetheless recognized that his artistic investigations were staged on an uneven playing field and, as such, he was "active in various groups, which are organised around race and sexuality." For Fani-Kayode, such association provided "confidence and insight," and had "the very concrete effect of providing the means for otherwise isolated and powerless artists to show their work and insist on being taken seriously."[7]

But Fani-Kayode was also aware of the cost of the patronage of what he considered to be interest groups that laid claim to his practice. He archly noted that while his work's then-marginal status meant that he would rely on the support of "the homosexual bourgeoisie," that supportiveness was not because "it is especially noted for its championing of Black artists, but because Black ass sells almost as well as Black dick."[8] This charge of racial fetishism is significant in understanding the interplay (described in detail below) between Fani-Kayode's photographs and those of Robert Mapplethorpe (1946–1989). It also conveys the awareness with which Fani-Kayode balanced the various constituencies that would bring his work to light. For all that, even a cursory perusal of any of Fani-Kayode's series would suggest that they engage with "male eroticism." There are, in fact, at least two trajectories through which one could read Fani-Kayode's as "gay art": his citation and elaboration of a history male nude portraiture, and his rehearsal and riffing on theatrical and Camp modes.[9]

Black Jesus

In 1990, Alex Hirst produced a 41½ × 40 cm gum bichromate print in rich greens and blues titled *Ecce Homo*. As the title suggests, the photograph depicts a moment from the story of the passion of Christ, before his crowning with thorns and ultimate crucifixion. *Ecce Homo* (behold the man) is a portrait that builds on iconography developed through devotional scenes in the Byzantine church and, later, through sixteenth- and seventeenth-century painting. Typically, a solemn Jesus—bearing a staff and loosely robed—looks downward, at once resigned and serene, his hands bound. While Titian's version created around 1576 is literal, centered on the pictures' narrative import, in the hands of Caravaggio (1605) the moment exudes both tension and tranquility, a study in the power of light and shadow. Hirst's version, likely from a Fani-Kayode negative, removes context and garb altogether, centering on a black figure with a downcast gaze, hands crossed over genitals. He occupies the frame vertically and splits it horizontally: to his left, blackness; to his right, ethereal light. Like Fani-Kayode and Hirst's other pictorialist prints, *Ecce Homo* uses outmoded technology to create a bridge to earlier moments—in this case religious history, Baroque painting, and late nineteenth-century photography.

Such a confluence of nude black portraiture and gauzy gum bichromate also confirms a link postulated by Kobena Mercer between Fani-Kayode and the Boston-area photographer F. Holland Day (1864–1933), a crucial touchstone in a queer counterhistory of photography that Fani-Kayode and Hirst, here, bring into sharp relief.[10] The scion of a wealthy family, Day was widely known as a commercial portraitist but also as a collector of Christian and occult ephemera, as a publisher who brought queer literature (such as Oscar Wilde) to a wider audience, and for his friendliness with the black community in both Boston (where he kept a studio) and his small town of Norwood.[11] Once one begins to look through Day's portfolio, the clear connections with Fani-Kayode become nearly impossible to miss.[12]

Indeed, Day came to prominence in the pages of Alfred Stieglitz's *Camera Notes* in 1897 with the cameo-style reproduction of his portrait of a man, enthroned and muscular, draped in striped cloth and holding what appears to be a roughly hewn staff—*An Ethiopian Chief* (1897; figure 3.2)—whom many assumed to be Day's valet, Alfred Tanneyhill. This figure seems to have been shot in multiple combinations (including robed in a leopard skin), and is echoed in 1897's *The Smoker*, in which the black sitter gazes coolly beyond the frame, long pipe languidly in hand. Eight years later, Day produced a series of ethereal portraits of anonymous black subjects (this time clothed women) using the gum process.[13] Fani-Kayode did not share with Day the willful misrecognition of African forms common to the late nineteenth century.[14] Nevertheless, beyond adapting Day's pictorialism, Fani-Kayode seems to have borrowed elements from Day's pictures throughout his *Black Male/White Male* portfolio—from the striated gown worn by the meditative "chief" figure in *Under the Surplice* (1987; figure 3.3), to the incongruous leopard skin that appears in the playful portrait *Which Doctor? Herr Doktor Scheidegger*. Elsewhere he poses his models with ornate cruciforms and staffs, held in suggestive ways throughout the photographs that he culled for his book.

Day is well known among historians of early modernist "amateur" photography, and his works are held, for example, in the Metropolitan Museum of Art. But, to reference his oeuvre so overtly between 1983 and 1989 would have been idiosyncratic, and certainly not accidental. One possible explanation is that Fani-Kayode was reactivating a lineage in which he was signaling himself as a part, doing photo-historical work and also directing the reception and interpretation of his portraits. Placing his and Day's photographs side by side, the potentially suppressed homoerotic dimensions of the latter's images become clearer in light of Fani-Kayode's, as do the theatrical and transcultural elements in Fani-Kayode's photographs in light of Day's. *Ecce Homo*, distinct in its melancholic tones, further solidifies this connection. For his part, Day used his photographic practice to complicate the iconology of both Greco-Roman forms and moments from Christian narrative amid an era marked by religious skepticism and the gradual medicalization of homosexuality as deviance.[15] Many of these scenes, including enactments of the crucifixion itself, were staged in the Massachusetts countryside and faced critical backlash against what the historian Kristin Schwain has called their "decadence," a term that became a "burdened euphemism for multiple infractions against public taste and served as a surrogate for the homosexual."[16]

To Day's "perversion" of the passion, Fani-Kayode and Hirst add another layer of transgression, substituting a nude black man for the bearded and robed white figure retained in Day's composition. Broadly speaking, even the most pictorial Fani-Kayode photograph is not a note-for-note restaging of Day, but the two men shared an overlapping interest in a long-standing (if repressed) history of the homoerotic male nude and, in particular, in creating textured, luminous scenes of young men sporting religiously charged accou-

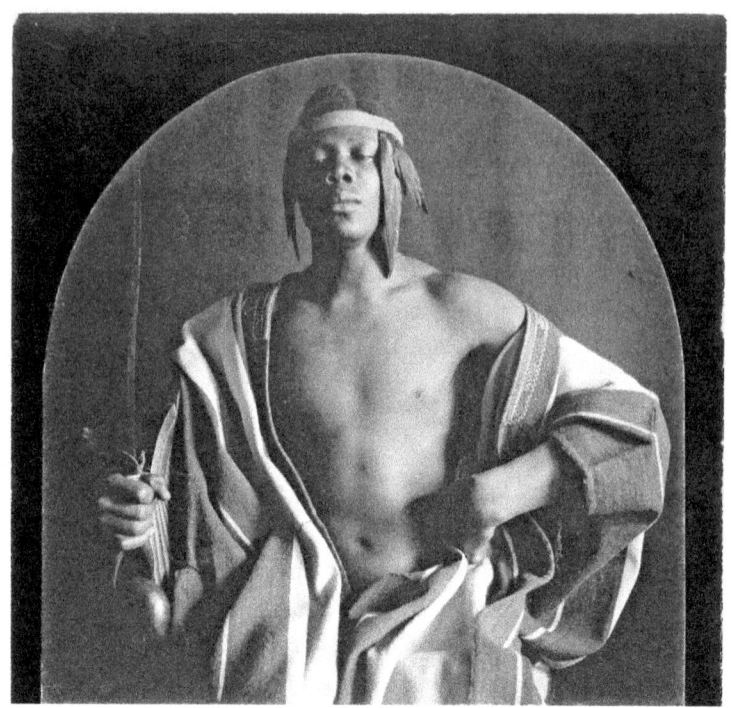

Figure 3.2 F. Holland Day, *An Ethiopian Chief* (ca. 1897).

trements. The latter is pronounced in, for example, the final pages of *Black Male/White Male*, in which an image of a shirtless model seemingly shearing off his member is followed by a succession of substitutions for the phallus: a bellowed camera in *Snap Shot* (figure 5.8), tassels in *Untitled*, raffia in another *Untitled* and, finally, an ornate statuette of Christ on the cross, wreathed in roses, and held between clasped hands by a nude draped in sheer fabric (*Crucifix*). In *Offering* (figure 3.4), a set of oversized shears that appears throughout his contact sheets is pressed beneath a waistband, implying a connection to Attis—the Greek consort and patron of eunuch priests. His self-castration is a story of gender ambivalence, of arrested heterosexual coupling, and, ultimately, resurrection.

Such queering (or at least sexualizing) of Christian iconography was particularly significant in the context of eighties London. For one, religious symbols had reentered mainstream art as precisely that—especially in the landscape of large-scale painting. Day's shimmering tableaux vivant were largely replaced

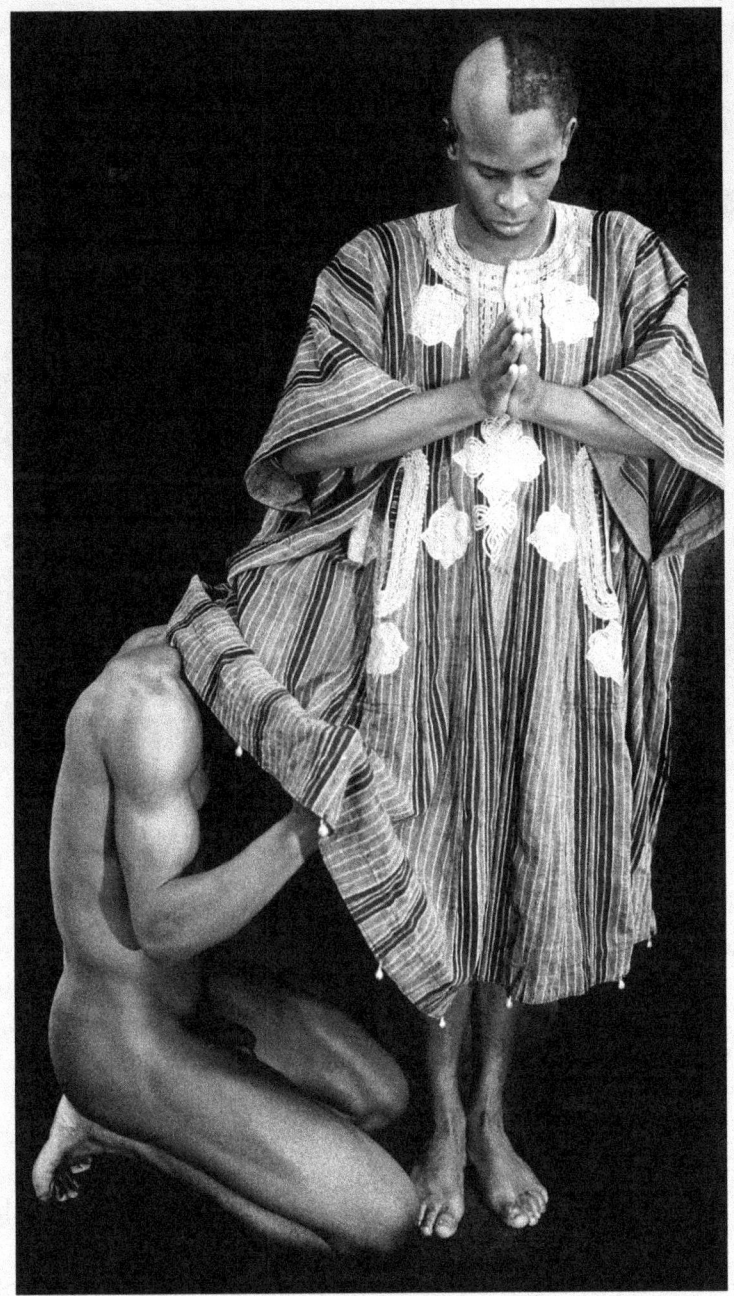

Figure 3.3 Rotimi Fani-Kayode, *Under the Surplice* (1987).
© Rotimi Fani-Kayode / Autograph ABP. Courtesy of Autograph ABP.

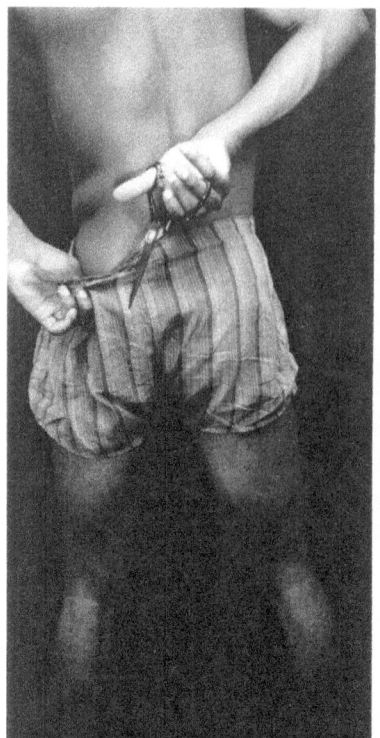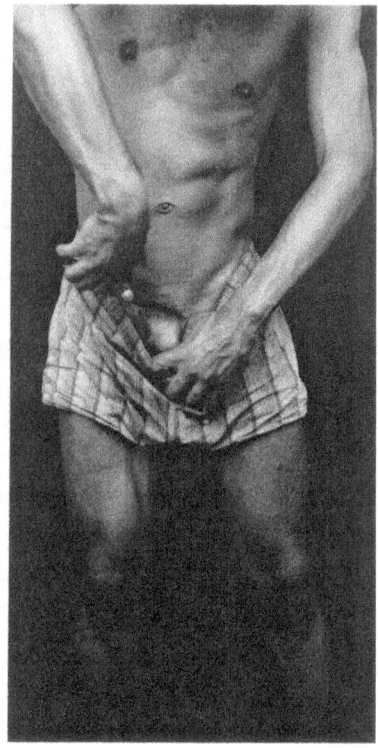

Figure 3.4 Rotimi Fani-Kayode, *Offering* (1987). © Rotimi Fani-Kayode / Autograph ABP. Courtesy of Autograph ABP.

by the flattening effects of the deracinated signifier. Second, it was in the British context that figuration—especially its homoerotic variants—had largely survived the disruptions of modernism. Francis Bacon's portraiture shifted, after 1964, to include friends and his lover George Dyer. Earlier still, it was in late Victorian England that Day found both an intellectual framework *and* pitched condemnation for his "decadent" reenactments. As Schwain elaborates, when Wilde was convicted in 1895 for indecency, he and other writers (such as Walter Pater) "celebrated male beauty and Greek love and sought to furnish cultural legitimacy for same-sex relationships through an amalgamation of paganism, Neoplatonism, and Christianity. In these circles, Christ could serve as a typological model for asserting individuality against institutional authority."[17] Given that he was a student of Christianity and the classics, such subtext would not have been lost on Fani-Kayode.

Fani-Kayode was hardly the first artist of the postwar period to align classical forms, male eroticism, and black-and-white photography. Indeed, a collection of photographs and essays edited by the critic Emmanuel Cooper, which was going to press during the last months of Fani-Kayode's life, laid out a constellation of homoerotic photographs. *Fully Exposed*, published in 1990 and blurbed by London papers *Capital Gay* and *The Observer*, constitutes a visual history of the male nude from 1860 to the late 1980s and stakes out its various vectors and repressions, especially in the context of fine art.[18] Cooper concludes that while the female form was long regarded as the epitome of tradition and beauty, the male body was only accepted at its extremes: clothed or otherwise in a position of mastery for fine art, or in nonart contexts as scientific specimen or, more likely, pornography. Photography in particular was dangerous terrain, seen as it was for much of its history as literal documentation.

As late as the 1970s, the primary outlets for the photographic male nude—especially the undraped or fully naked figure—were the pages of muscle and fetish magazines, in which the "beefcake" archetype was solidified and images of leather and bondage culture circulated. In other words, the nude was largely the province of alternative publications with a substantial gay viewership. To wit: the very Supreme Court decision to which Simon Watney points as a foundation for the American "civil rights" model of gay liberation was won by the publication *One, Inc.* in response to obscenity charges by the United States Post Office. That 1958 case established First Amendment protections for the material and thus created an open channel for the interstate distribution of openly homoerotic material. It was an early victory for groups such as Robert Mizer's Los Angeles–based Athletic Model Guild (AMG), through which he photographed men wrestling, in bodybuilding poses, or with the Greco-Roman undertones of turn-of-the-century European nudes (for example, those by Baron Wilhem von Gloeden).

The AMG and related groups evolved in the decades after World War II and gradually removed the hand-painted dots that obscured men's genitals—for many critics, a sure sign of the migration from art to pornography.[19] One rather immediate connection between Fani-Kayode and this history sets the tone for the discussion below. As Richard Meyer has shown, Mizer's *Physique Pictorial* used illustrations by the celebrated Tom of Finland (1920–1991)

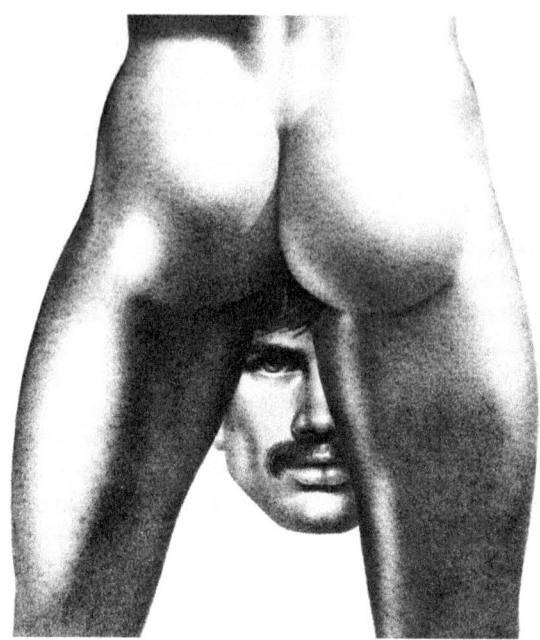

Figure 3.5 Tom of Finland, untitled illustration (ca. 1970s).

that, he argues, visualized an "extravagant homoeroticism" through depictions of musclebound bikers rife with undertones of S/M.[20] Tom of Finland later would be celebrated in his home country with a series of commemorative stamps, one of which shows the nude thighs and buttocks of a man from behind. Between his legs is a disembodied, mustachioed face, gazing back at the viewer (figure 3.5). The image is as surreal as it is suggestive of phallic domination.[21] The illustration is strikingly similar to one of Fani-Kayode's pictures considered above—*Bronze Head* (figure 3.6), in which the flow of power and meaning in the Tom of Finland piece is subjected to a series of knowing substitutions and inversions. For instance, the Fani-Kayode picture suggests both feminine birth and male homoeroticism, and it is as much scatalogical as the Tom of Finland is fellatial. Ultimately, *Bronze Head* works in the mode of surreal reversals rather than the more literal—if humorous—register of the physique illustration.

Cooper's survey shows a wider evolution of the male nude, from the pictorialism of the late Victorian era to the highly bronzed, strikingly sculptural poses produced in England and Germany during the interwar period and the

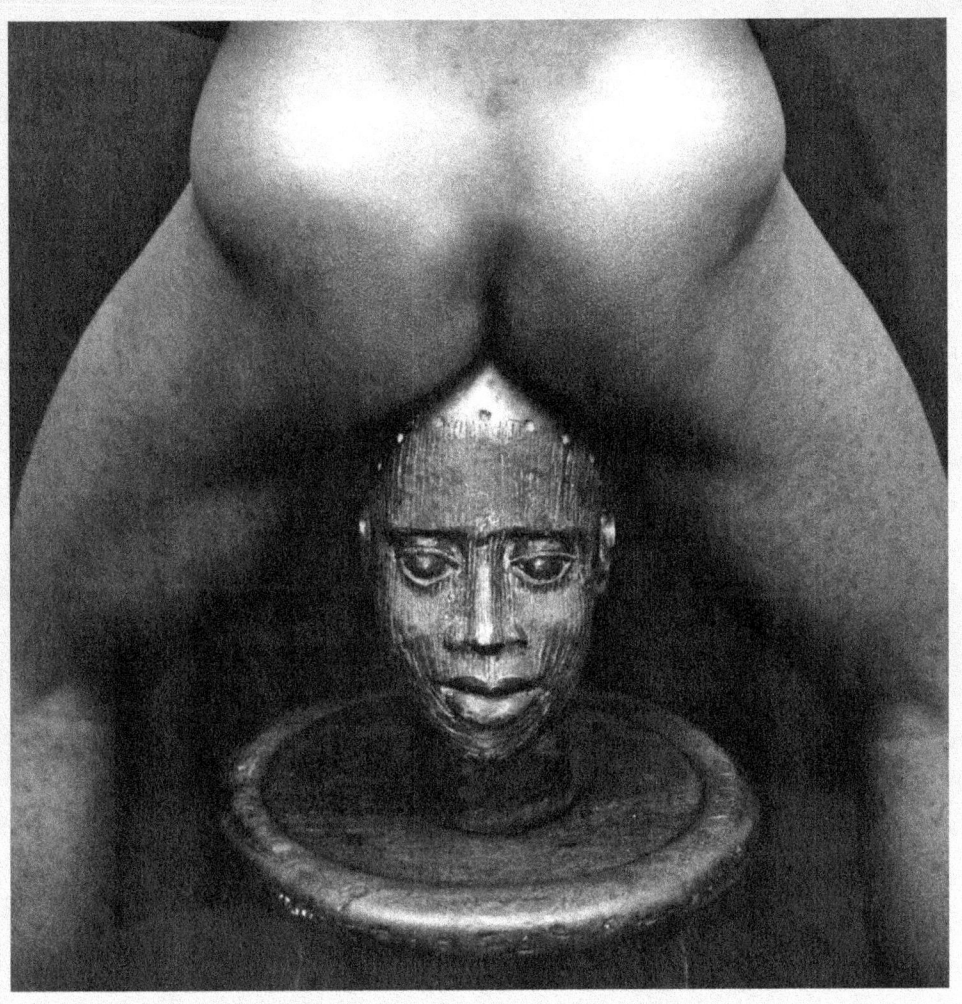

Figure 3.6 Rotimi Fani-Kayode, *Bronze Head* (1987). © Rotimi Fani-Kayode /
Autograph ABP. Courtesy of Autograph ABP.

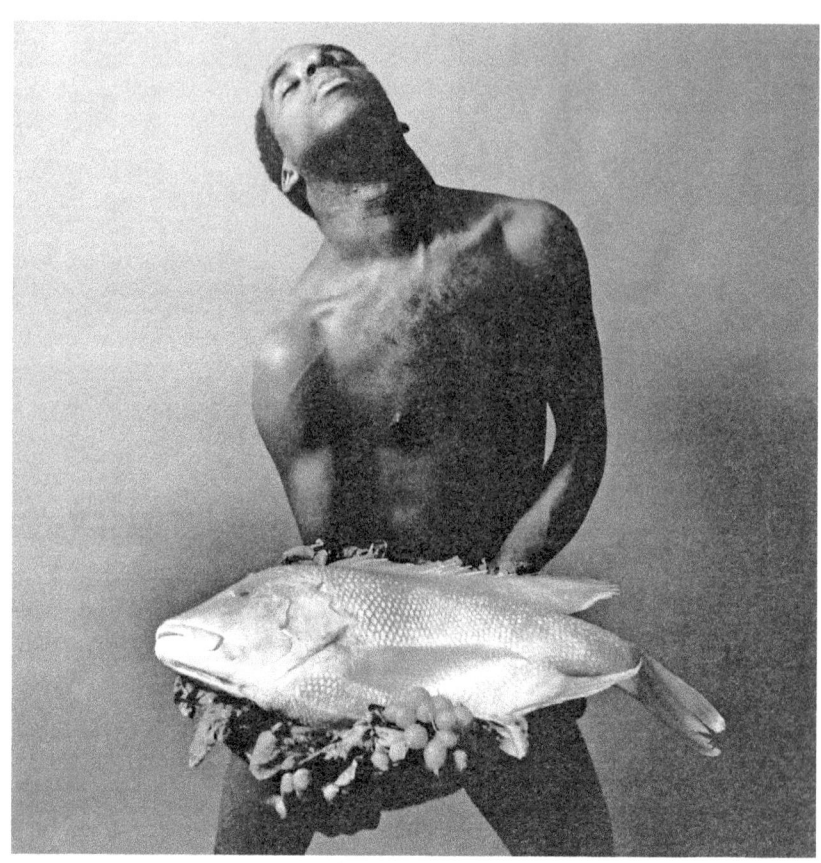

Figure 3.7 Rotimi Fani-Kayode, *Fish Vendor* (1988–1989).
© Rotimi Fani-Kayode / Autograph ABP. Courtesy of Autograph ABP.

allegorical, dreamlike tableaux of George Platt Lynes and Minor White; the latter's forties-era homoerotic works provide near-exact precedents for Fani-Kayode's *White Feet* and *Cargo of Middle Passage*. A Fani-Kayode photograph appears here, too. It is *Fish Vendor* (figure 3.7), in which the subject cocks his head back and stands slightly off balance, hands locked around a massive fish that, in turn, covers his midsection. Significantly, this is one of the few of his pictures where the phallus is seen rather than obscured and, as Cooper argues, taken in the context of eighties nude male erotica, *Fish Vendor* injects a counterpoint of humor and wit into a genre geared toward more aggressive staging and overt voyeurism.[22] One might add that the piece's title, and its playful near-occlusion of the figure's genitals, build on Fani-Kayode's pattern of castration or metonymy of the phallus. Black dick is for sale here, but it is also withheld.

Aside from serving as one of the last projects in which Fani-Kayode was included before his death, *Fully Exposed* is also a remarkable annotation when placed alongside the several collections of Fani-Kayode's and Hirst's photographs. Indeed, it is something of a Rosetta Stone of influences and coded references. For example, two pictures from his 1987 collection, titled *Punishment and Reward*, frame a body from behind. This model wields a wooden staff, at once shoring up the geometries of the composition and suggesting a play of phallic domination—a gift and a spanking. The staff appears again—along with a black leather cap—elsewhere in the portfolio, in *Errol, at the Oval* (figure 3.8). Fani-Kayode ventured further into this terrain in 1989, especially with an untitled piece from the *Bodies of Experience* series (figure 3.9), a large-format square portrait of a figure looking tentatively upward. His face is masked in studded black leather, his mouth receptive to whatever he might receive from beyond the frame to the left—a suspended black sap or dildo. The associations here could not be more overt: the photos refer to the S/M interplay of punishment and submission, domination and withholding that effloresced in gay clubs and was visualized in fetish magazines.

Significantly, even at its most "hardcore," there seems to be a sense of distance at work here—a knowing complication or humorous remove, especially in the color prints from 1989, which juxtapose S/M and various suggestions of sexual consumption and oral sex with calm contemplation and sacred ritual. These pictures provide a clue that while Fani-Kayode was certainly aware of and borrowing from the motifs of beefcake and fetish pictures, he was not restaging or representing them outright. Cooper's text is correct that Fani-Kayode's pictures are subtle rather than overt, marked more by shared humor than by scopic domination, as evinced even in the brief comparison with the Tom of Finland illustration. And *Fully Exposed* provides other starting points, beyond the physique photography of the 1960s and 1970s.

In particular, there are marked similarities between Fani-Kayode's black-and-whites and the "new realist" photography of the 1930s, by artists who emerged from (or were schooled in) French surrealism. For one, the American George Platt Lynes (1907–1955) worked with male subjects but used props and careful lighting to deemphasize the raw physicality of the sitter, instead creating narrative tension and drawing emotional depth from erotic contexts. Like Fani-

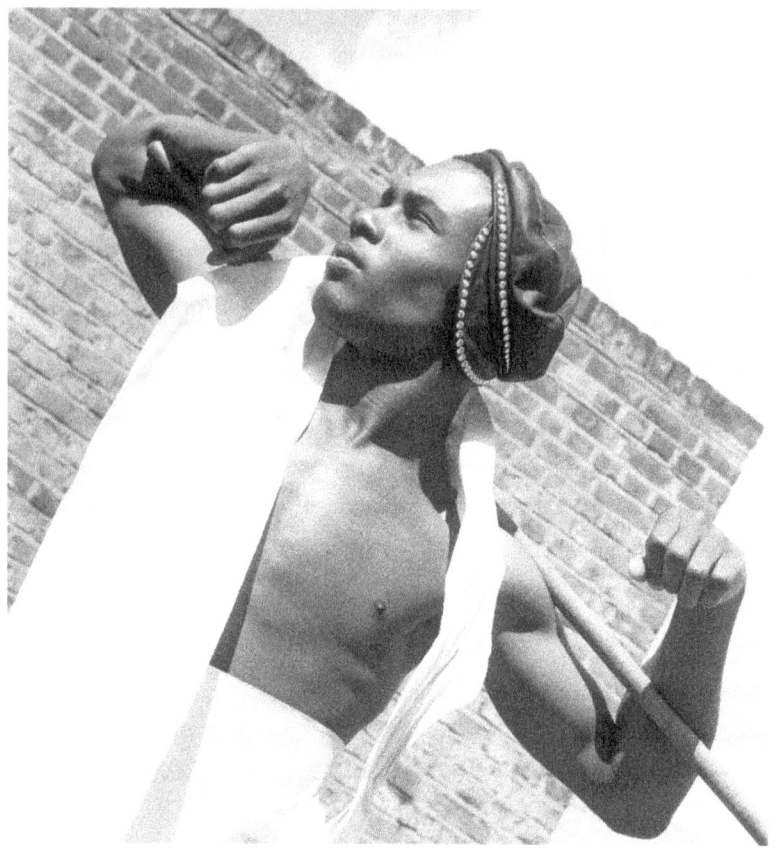

Figure 3.8 Rotimi Fani-Kayode, *Errol, at the Oval* (1985). © Rotimi Fani Kayode / Autograph ABP. Courtesy of Autograph ABP.

Kayode, Platt Lynes balanced desire and withholding in much of his portraiture. And while the s/m subtext is clear in many of the photographs, his method is textured rather than graphic. As Cooper argues, some of those works "have similarities with the beefcake nudes taken by contemporaries like Bruce of Los Angeles, but Platt Lynes rarely aimed for a 'raunchy' statement of sexuality, preferring instead a quieter but deeper erotic expression."[23]

While Platt Lynes's primary medium was widely circulated fashion photography, male nudes were his hidden work, and they display a reserve suited to the tenuous social status of male eroticism in the 1930s and 1940s. As such, his practice is a valuable touchstone for Fani-Kayode, who himself had to negoti-

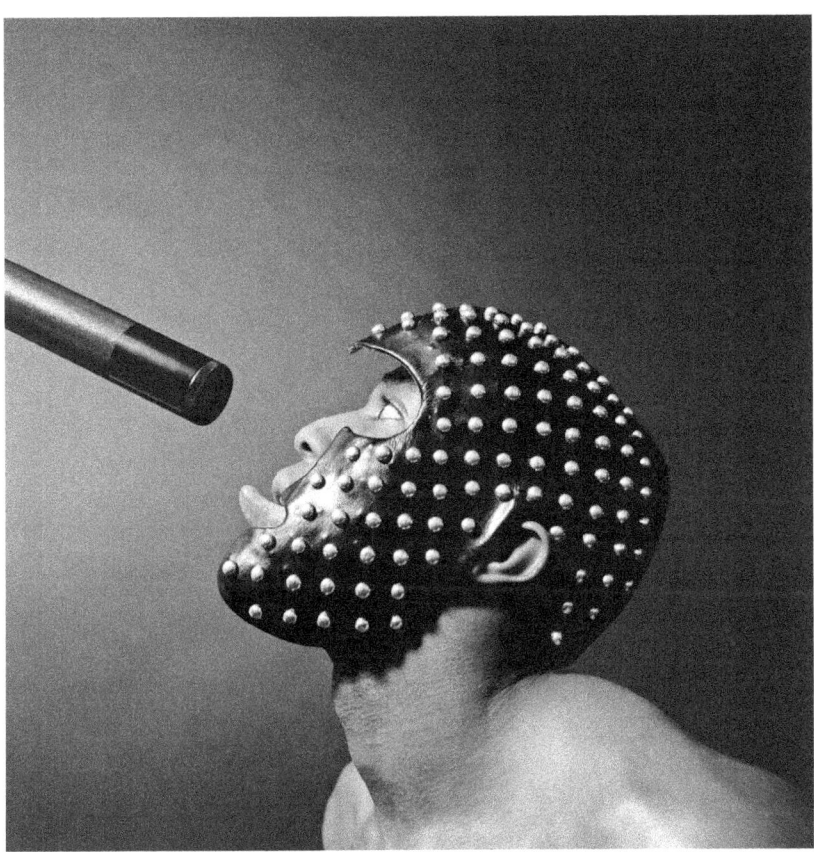

Figure 3.9 Rotimi Fani-Kayode, *Untitled (Bodies of Experience)* (1989).
© Rotimi Fani-Kayode / Autograph ABP. Courtesy of Autograph ABP.

ate the ambivalent terrain of repressive societies, in Lagos and London alike. A work such as *Escape from the Amniotic Sac* (ca. 1987–1988; figure 3.10), which depicts a embryonic form atop a tree stump, breaking free of a plastic cocoon, can be understood in terms of surrealist imagery, as a dreamlike, fantasy of maternal return. It also has a clear precedent in Platt Lynes's *Two Nudes* (1940; figure 3.11). The latter portrays a standing figure who looks on as another man leans against a wall, similarly veiled. In this case the second figure is a subject of desire, certainly, but desire denied, occluded as he is, in a protective membrane. The humorous and feminine contours staked out in Fani-Kayode's version are not present here, but the compositional similarities to this and to

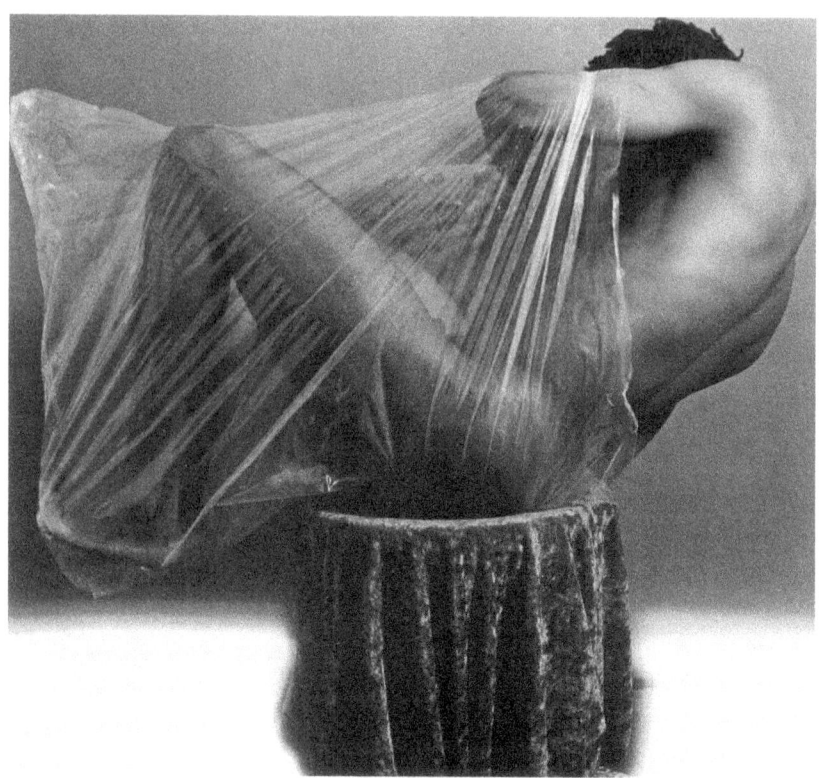

Figure 3.10 Rotimi Fani-Kayode, *Escape from Amniotic Sac* (ca. 1987–1988).
© Rotimi Fani-Kayode / Autograph ABP. Courtesy of Autograph ABP.

portraits by contemporaries such as Minor White and Raymond Voinquel are unmistakable.

PERVERSATILITY

Robert Mapplethorpe is included in the pages of Cooper's survey, too—unsurprising given that by the end of the 1970s, his work exemplified the crossover between the avant-garde and the erotic glossy. There are no flowers or women bodybuilders here, but there is indeed a sculpted black nude who could have emerged from the pages of a fitness magazine (*Standing Male Nude*, 1980). On the facing page are two flabbier, hirsute white men, one clad in black leather, the other suspended from an elaborate hoist with arms and legs shackled. *Dominick and Elliott* (1979; figure 3.12), taken five years after the

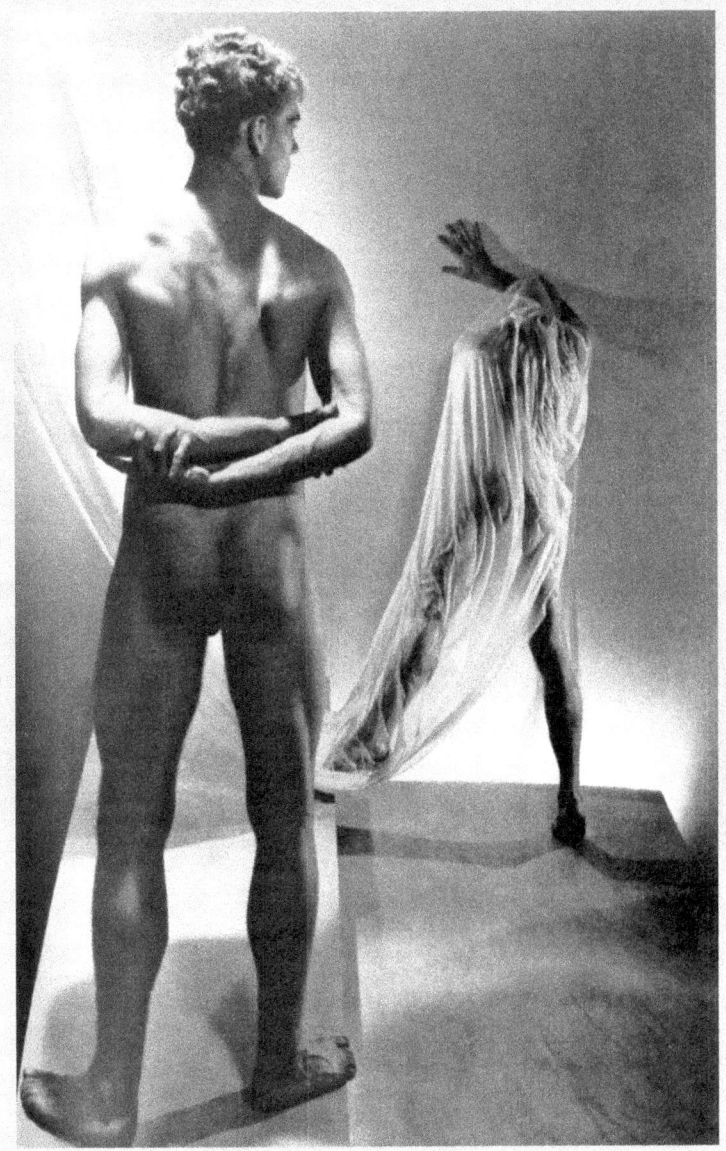

Figure 3.11 George Platt Lynes, *Two Nudes* (1940). © Joshua Lynes.

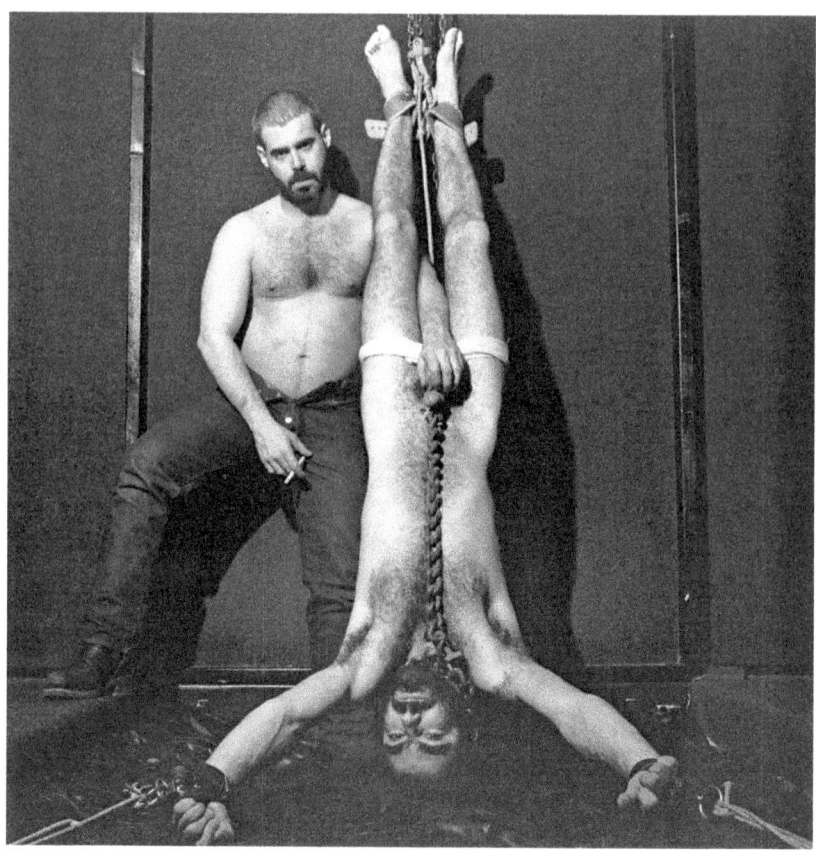

Figure 3.12 Robert Mapplethorpe, *Dominick and Elliot* (1979).
© Robert Mapplethorpe Foundation. Courtesy Art + Commerce.

police raid on the Stonewall Inn in the West Village, is a confident recasting of portraiture that not only foregrounds male eroticism but does so in a plainly sexualized way—the bearish man on the left's tight grip on the testicles of the inverted cruciform of the bound sub is nothing if not a classicizing translation of genre photographs celebrating rough sex and urban S/M practices.

For Fani-Kayode and many of his contemporaries, Mapplethorpe's photographs of black men seemed to encapsulate an entire regime of racial fetishism, of the relay of visual pleasure, castration anxiety, and scopic dominance enacted time and again using the hypersexualized bodies (and totemized body parts) of black men. In contrast, Kobena Mercer's writing sought to position

Fani-Kayode's photographs in critical relation to Mapplethorpe's, first as a kind of antidote and, later, as an example of gay black photography that could coexist with Mapplethorpe's in a larger resistance to the homophobic discursive and legislative practices then common on both sides of the Atlantic. For his part, Fani-Kayode seems to have resisted such comparisons. According to Hirst, perhaps "inevitably, the black and white photographs of this period have been compared with those of Mapplethorpe. Timi liked Mapplethorpe's work, but saw no significant connection between that and his own, except in the purely superficial sense that they both worked with black male models."[24]

Nevertheless, a comparison between the two is telling insofar as it reveals at least two lineages of picturing "male eroticism." Viewing *Dominick and Elliott* in the same setting as *Fish Vendor* drives home the contrasts in their respective methods and gives credence to Mercer's initial reading of racial fetishism. In short, Mapplethorpe's photographs come off as *harder*. This is evinced by the pictures themselves, especially their high contrast (in both lighting and bronzed bodies) and the statuesque—even iconic—poses therein. But, then, many of Mapplethorpe's photographs are also simply more *hardcore*. They map not merely the erotic but forms of sex characterized by domination and control that are translated into a potentially violent mode of looking. This is, according to some critics, a scopophilia that is phallocentric, oriented toward hardbodies or—in the case of many of Mapplethorpe's pictures from the 1970s—active penetration, binding, or sculpting.

Describing at precisely this moment a gaze dominant in cinema, the critic Laura Mulvey argued in 1975 that such looking produced "obsessive voyeurs and Peeping Toms, whose only sexual satisfaction came from watching, in an active controlling sense, an objectified other."[25] This hardcore quality of Mapplethorpe's photographs apparently squared with his lived experience. Firsthand accounts recall Mapplethorpe's affinity for seeking out intense clandestine encounters, from the dungeon to the uptown orgy. Mapplethorpe intimate Jack Fritscher, for one, recalls LSD-fueled evenings spent in search of expression for what the former called his "perversatility," including parties that included ritualistic hazing, submissive servants, and extreme scatology.[26] Fritscher was an editor of the San Francisco-based, post-Stonewall magazine *Drummer*, and he was an early proponent of Mapplethorpe and other erotic photographers such as Arthur Tress, whose picture of a man pissing into a boot follows *Dominick and Elliott* in the Cooper survey. His memoir of his time with Mapplethorpe confirms, on the whole, Mapplethorpe's contention, in a 1983 interview with Cooper that, "if I photograph it, I've done it."[27] For all that, Mapplethorpe's photographs are notable for their clear staging and, ultimately, framing. As the historian Richard Meyer argues, there is little vérité in these pictures, and much of their frisson emerges in the tension between the convention of studio photography and the authenticity of the subjects, who were at once drawn from the sexual terrain through which Mapplethorpe cruised, but also actively performing or amplifying that S/M practice for the camera.[28]

Ultimately, Meyer and Cooper helped to position Mapplethorpe in a visual history of voyeurism and gay liberation, a dialectic of censorship and its resistance played out in the circulation of openly graphic photography. In this light, one can trace Mapplethorpe's politics and photographic language along explicitly American lines, from the Western Photography Guild and *Physique Pictorial* to Robert Mizer and Bruce of Los Angeles and their liberation-era successors in the 1970s and 1980s from *Drummer* to *Gay Power*. There is an intensity to these images, and they rely on, as Simon Watney suggests, American protections on freedom of speech and a model of individual freedoms so beautifully represented in Mapplethorpe's nudes. He takes the viewer into a zone of extremity and removes the censor's obscuring dot, making the pornographic beautiful—no different, in his account, than an erect calla lily.[29]

In contrast, Fani-Kayode's photographs are typified by an ambivalence—a refusal of fixation. During his black-and-white phase, Fani-Kayode's tableaux certainly suggest eroticism but never openly depict a sexual act; dominance is transmuted into shared ritual and entwined bodies symbolizing unity or, in his words, *communion*—an act with sanctified connotation. And while Mulvey's analysis of scopic pleasure is, in her estimation, specific to film, there are at least two ways in which it aptly describes Mapplethorpe's work but not Fani-Kayode's. The visual pleasure that she describes is, for one, unidirectional, with the feminine figure serving as the passive form or raw material for the gaze. Second, the anxiety that is operative in many films is the Freudian narrative of castration (exemplified by a woman's body) that is, in turn, compulsively redirected through acts of mastery or domination. Mercer's original critique of Mapplethorpe broadens this analysis to suggest that the black body—long a site of fantasy, desire, and fear—stirs similar castration anxiety for the white photographer (and viewer). Such anxiety is subsequently displaced not through mastery of women's bodies but through fixation on, in Fani-Kayode's words, "Black dick."

Tellingly, in one of the very few instances when a black member is pictured by Fani-Kayode, the phallus is not black at all, but gold. In *Gold Phallus* (1989; figure 3.13), a model (the photographer Robert Taylor) rests on one knee in a warmly lit space. His face is downcast and he seems to be contemplating his flaccid penis, which mirrors the curved nose of a beaked Carnival mask. The phallus glows like a precious stone that scarcely belongs to the sitter. The image is at once humorous (an untitled piece from this series has the figure's body painted so that the phallus appears as a lengthy proboscis) and an obvious invocation Lacan's conception of the phallic as a source of power and fear, an embodiment of paternal Law.[30] In other words, in *Gold Phallus*, the "Black dick" never appears, and certainly not as an object of pleasurable delectation. Instead it is made a source of ambivalence—a detachable object, an obvious source of consternation, a fetish that has its value brazenly caked to its radiant surface. Castration, here, is not a repressed anxiety temporarily displaced in an act of desirous looking but, instead, the very subject of a photograph that toys with its expectant viewer.

By now, such plays on castration should be familiar motifs in Fani-Kayode's work—on display in *Offering* and *Snap Shot* as moments in which ritual excision is acted out or at least affected through metonymic substitution. In the case of *Snap Shot*, this is communicated by the form of the camera, with its dual significance—as a mode of scopic power neutered through its literal collision with phallic anxiety, and as a receptive orifice (the open aperture) rather than erect presence. This motif plays out again and again in the pages of *Black Male/White Male*. The men in *Black Robert* and *Black Sogi* arch backward in a yogic wheel pose and reclining odalisque form, respectively. Each one is rotated or manipulated just so, the pubic area revealing only patches of hair. There is clear citation of Platt Lynes here, but with an added ambivalence—gone are the luminous but frank portrayals of aroused white men. Instead, in Fani-Kayode's pictures, black and white are intermixed and gender oscillates. Earlier in the book, *White Michael* goes one step further: the phallus is not merely tucked away, but its limp form is cupped away by a well-placed hand, creating an amorphous, scrotal blob of tissue. As a figural study, the photograph explores bodily terrain bordering on the grotesque, but its symbolic resonance is stronger still as soft *informe*, a decomposition of Mapplethorpe's sturdy architectonic lines, burly leathermen, and chiseled, well-endowed black bodies.

Which is to say, while Fani-Kayode's are with one exception portraits of

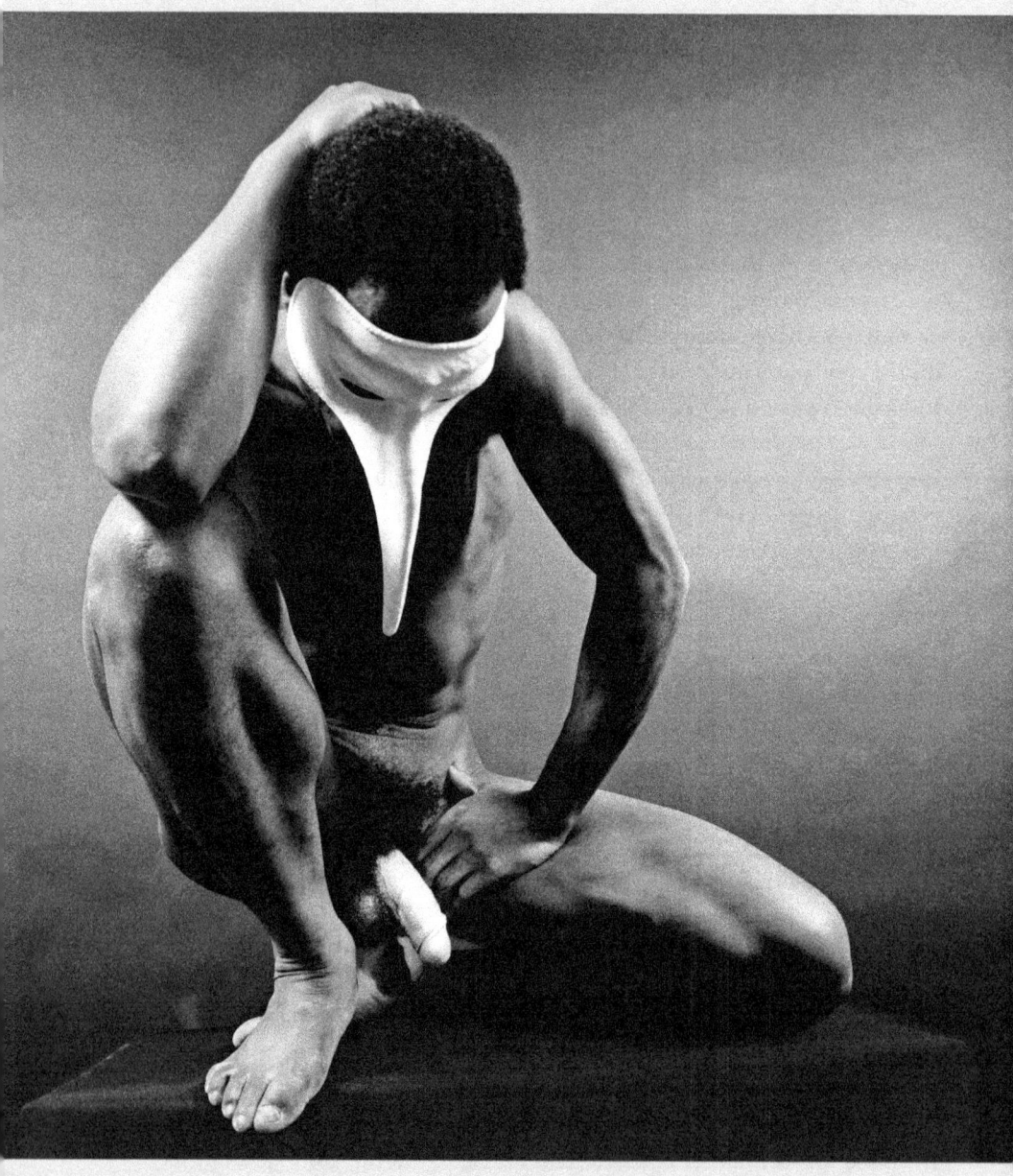

Figure 3.13 Rotimi Fani-Kayode, *Gold Phallus* (1989). © Rotimi Fani-Kayode /
Autograph ABP. Courtesy of Autograph ABP.

men alone,[31] they contrast with Mapplethorpe's insofar as they admit the feminine, even if only in the play of drag or their ambivalent compositional suggestion. Hirst is clear on this point in his introduction to *Black Male/White Male*. Describing the space enacted by the photographs therein, he defines: "Male: in which the female-fantasy is ever present, even in remaining unseen. No threat in these images of males, but certainly a delicious vulnerability, learned from our mothers and sisters. . . . I don't feel that I've swaggered into one of those gloomy men-only places where tired infibulators can relax and get away from their responsibilities."[32] For Fani-Kayode and Hirst, it seems, photographs simultaneously document and generate spaces that are consciously nonthreatening. Here, women are mimed as a sort of homage to an (albeit essentialized) form of femininity located in bodies that briefly embrace their "lack" of a phallus, rather than work to defer anxieties of such a loss. Hirst goes beyond a psychoanalytic register to literally call out to men-only social spaces (perhaps gay bars and clubs) in which women are not welcome, even symbolically. These places are "gloomy," frequented by weary infibulators—that is, the practitioners of female genital mutilation, especially in rural Africa— who can finally rest for a moment. They no longer need to be vigilant in these men-only haunts, there is no one to whom they need to deny feminine pleasure. By contrast, an openness among the men of *Black Male/White Male* to women's bodies and "vulnerability" (lessons learned from mothers and sisters) takes on an element of veneration, a mimicry of mysterious but welcome forces.

This comparison is not to suggest an active misogyny in Mapplethorpe's photographs, but it does underscore a certain phallocentrism in his work (even his flowers are erect, and many of his women are examples of bodies pushed to the outer limits, to near-masculine proportions). Mapplethorpe's photographs, like many of the beefcake and physique pictures that prefigure his own, foreground the phallus, even (or perhaps especially) in its censoring through carefully placed dots. Fani-Kayode, in turn, not only defers or obscures that site of masculinity but playfully works the psychic space of castration: highlighting the phallus as fetish, cutting it away through careful substitution, or converting his sitters into feminized eunuchs. The story of Attis appears again and again, but laden with new iconological resonance.[33] Beyond Fani-Kayode's gender neutering, the feminine (and the surreal) appear in the Platt Lyons–esque *Escape from the Amniotic Sac*, which not only restages birth and separation from the mother but also celebrates a form of abjection—the interiority of reproductive viscera made external, elevated as sculptural form.[34] It is unclear whether this is a surrealist-style fantasy of maternal return or its precise opposite, but it does explore rather than suppress difference in a space of relation and totality rather than the separation manifest by Mapplethorpe's men-only rooms. And as we shall see below, the quality of those rooms themselves matters a great deal.

In an analysis discussed earlier, Richard Meyer noted that Mapplethorpe's are explicitly studio portraits, which gain a shock value from the convergence of the traditional with the then marginal. Accordingly, pictures such as *Joe* do not hide the infrastructure of the studio itself—all the better to subject the sitters to a penetrating, investigative gaze. Fritscher recalls that in his session with Mapplethorpe, he complained about the picture's lack of resemblance. Mapplethorpe responded, "Of course it's not your face. It's your look. I shoot through faces. You're dirty."[35] For all of its entanglements with racial fetishism and scopic power more broadly, there was an incontrovertible visual pleasure at work in the high finish of Mapplethorpe's oeuvre.

While Isaac Julien and Kobena Mercer trenchantly staked out the dangers inherent in such work, they also admitted an attraction to it, arguing that an "ambivalent mixture of attraction and repulsion goes for images of black gay men in porn generally, but the inscribed or preferred meanings of these images are not fixed; they can, at times, be pried apart into alternative readings"[36] in the hands of a savvy (and, thus, reciprocally appropriating) black viewership. What's more, in spite of their restaging of racial stereotype, Mapplethorpe's and other pornographically coded images could work on a positive level, confirming that "'black gays exist.'" In other words, Mapplethorpe's blunt insistence on figuring gay men might amount to a kind of liberation politics in the context of Thatcher-era censorship.

But, then, there were alternative modes of using homoerotically charged imagery to create spaces of visibility. Fani-Kayode's black-and-whites are one such approach. He builds on a tradition of the male nude that is less "hardcore" than ethereal, wherein ambiguity prevails in a dance of desire and withholding; where castration anxiety is rendered not as something to be vigilantly denied but a site of humorous embrace and transfiguration. And while these fantasies, too, were staged in Fani-Kayode's studio, his is an enclosure that seems to lose its contours, evanescing into an abyssal no-place. In contrast to Mapplethorpe's rough downtown loft, Fani-Kayode cultivated a shadowy redoubt where magical rites could unfold behind closed doors.[37] In so doing, he filtered an alternative homoerotic canon through what Julian and Mercer called a "multiplicity of identities" in which "political aspirations for freedom" find "cultural forms of expression."

With his over-the-top *Fish Vendor*, Fani-Kayode was arguably unique in his ability to reclaim, in Julien and Mercer's terms, "the camp and crazy 'carnivalesque' excesses of Little Richard—the original Queen of Rock'n'Roll." Such a reclamation, for them, is transgressive insofar as it historically "parodied the stereotypes of black masculinity to 'theatricalize' and send up the whole charade of gender roles," in turn drawing "critical attention to the cultural constructedness of sexual identity."[38] At the risk of belaboring the Fani-Kayode–Mapplethorpe contrast, a pair of photographs draws the differences in lineage and approach in their practices into sharp relief. One is Mapplethorpe's *Self Portrait with Whip* (1978), in which he occupies the center of the frame, clad in leather vest and chaps, leaning upon a draped support, in something of a perversatile update of David Octavius Hill, the early Victorian Scottish photographer known for his prop-laden, staged portraiture. Mapplethorpe gazes out at the viewer with intensity and defiance, face resting on his left hand while his right holds aloft a bullwhip emanating from his exposed anus.

The other photograph draws on similar iconography, but Fani-Kayode's 1987 *Farewell to Meat* (figure 3.14) implies castration and a sad goodbye. A white figure floats in an inky haze and holds a whip in a gloved hand. But he is crouched, legs tightly clasped, and covered by what appears to be mosquito netting. Unlike in Mapplethorpe's portrait, it is unclear who the model is. He seems to be acting out a dreamlike vignette, his eyes covered by a beaked mask as he squawks into the distance, as if watching something recede. His whip is limp (it does not penetrate) and this is not a portrait but, apparently, evidence of a decadent game. And so, Julien and Mercer are certainly correct that Mapplethorpe consistently produced "out and proud" photographs that visualized—and insisted on the presence of—even the more extreme elements of seventies and eighties gay life. But Fani-Kayode, in turn, enacted that period's topographies and vocabularies of subversion and carnivalesque. As a counterpoint to Mapplethorpe's robust leatherman, *Farewell to Meat* tends toward the comically excessive, to theatricality and jest. In short, beyond its clear interventions into the terrain of formalism and representation, this picture bluntly *camps* the male nude tradition.

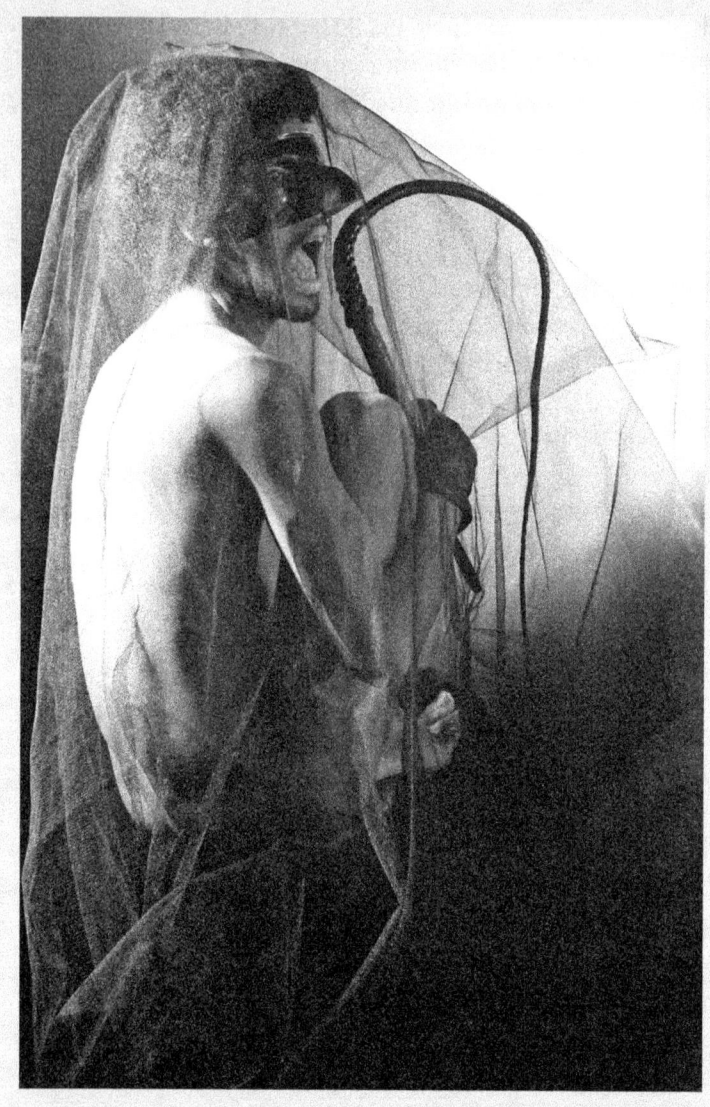

Figure 3.14 Rotimi Fani-Kayode, *Farewell to Meat* (ca. 1987). © Rotimi Fani-Kayode / Autograph ABP. Courtesy of Autograph ABP.

A second way of framing Fani-Kayode's work as "gay art," then, is to consider the various ways in which his photographs depict, document, or build on the existing cultural codes associated with Camp. For, as Susan Sontag famously argued in 1964, "the history of Camp taste is part of the history of snob taste. But since no authentic aristocrats in the old sense exist today to sponsor special tastes, who is the bearer of this taste? Answer: an improvised self-elected class, mainly homosexuals, who constitute themselves as aristocrats of taste."[39] But here, one is already on dangerous ground, as Sontag has been criticized for her reductionism here (Camp is forged, she argues, by Jewish moral seriousness and homosexual aestheticism and irony) and, by her own estimation, because Camp is difficult to quantify as it is primarily a sensibility and a calculus of affinities. Sontag elects to define Camp through a cluster of references, aphorisms, and assertions. Ultimately, she seems to argue, you know Camp when you see it. To which, one might add another problem: that in the intervening fifty years since Sontag penned her essay, "campiness" as an adjective has gradually lost its meaning, even as millennial hipsterism has co-opted its urbane aestheticism and irony (that is, its connection to dandyism).[40] And, writing in 1983, *Square Peg* editors Alex Hirst and Seymour Kelly noted that gay identity in London was increasingly defined in terms of a post-Camp multiplicity of affinities. They noted that "what makes us, as gay men, different from straights isn't our camp sensibility, it's the fact that we're men who like cocks and arses, chickens and clones, butch and femme, bondage and discipline. . . . What we always end up doing is avoiding that sin . . . because even gay people tell us it's right off if we don't."[41]

With such a disclaimer in mind, it is still clear that, in practice, Camp served as a lingua franca of cultural subtext and knowledge for many urban gay men, especially in the decades leading up to the 1980s. It animated many of Fani-Kayode's photographs. And in its arch and decadent sensibilities, Camp indexes a subtle boundary, one that clarifies Watney's distinction between a politicized civil rights approach in the United States and the counterpublic collectivity of the British model that obtained until after Fani-Kayode's death.[42] As the journalist Bryan Lowder has recently argued, "in the hours after Judy Garland's funeral in June of 1969, many gay men seemed content to march down to Christopher Street and trade in their camp credentials for the dour political militancy of the post-Stonewall era." Citing the theorist David

Halperin, he suggests that "the whole project of the assimilation-directed gay civil rights movement of the past few decades is largely predicated on the suppression of queer quirks like camp."[43] Nevertheless, considering Fani-Kayode's photographs as instances that ramify a Camp sensibility adds, at the minimum, a cultural context for understanding his work, especially given that he inhabited a sociopolitical landscape that, as the filmmaker Derek Jarman (1942–1994) argued, was one in which people were forced by Thatcherite politics "back into the closet."[44] Which is to say, Fani-Kayode and Jarman, who both explicitly drew on the aggressive and critical vernacular of punk, used an array of coded languages of sub- and counterculture within the mainstream as strategies of negation, appropriation, and making visible.

Where to start, then? For one, Sontag concretizes Camp as "art that proposes itself seriously, but cannot be taken altogether seriously because it is 'too much.' *Titus Andronicus* and *Strange Interlude* are almost Camp, or could be played as Camp."[45] This appraisal aptly describes many of Fani-Kayode's photographs, which are assiduously staged, composed, lit, and processed. And while replete with the stern iconographies of Western and Yoruban spiritual tradition, they nonetheless often overshoot their mark, achieving a tone of reverie and humor. *Farewell to Meat* is one such example, as are *Fish Vendor* and virtually all of the photographs from the 1989 series *Nothing to Lose (Bodies of Experience)*. The latter are large-format C-prints rendered with saturated color, hagiographic framing, and the illusionistic scale of painting. As material objects, they are nothing if not excessive in what they depict and in their physical execution, but, significantly, these scenes jettison the biblical gravity of their seventeenth- and eighteenth-century precursors. They substitute overtly comedic, theatrical, or over-the-top gestures such as games of hide-and-seek and the simulated consumption (or, in fact, fellation) of lilies and limes.[46]

In other words, Fani-Kayode's late series balance a seriousness of purpose with sly undertones and an atmosphere of jubilation and bacchanal. In a sense, one is confronted here with a kind of straight documentation of carnivalesque in process—not played out in an annual parade but on the nocturnal stage of Fani-Kayode's studio. The performative quality at work here is presaged, to an extent, by Sontag. Writing in a pre-Stonewall America, she argues that "Camp taste is much more than homosexual taste. Obviously, its metaphor of life as theater is peculiarly suited as a justification and projection of a certain aspect of the situation of homosexuals."[47] She seems to reference here the complex back-and-forth of being closeted, of performing one identity while obscuring another. But Sontag could just as well be talking about the underground sites of inversion of mainstream "good taste" (another aspect of Camp) prominent in cities like DC, New York, and London during the 1970s and 1980s, such as the Alternative Miss World (founded 1972), urban "balls," and some theater (musical and otherwise). Which is to say, thinking Fani-Kayode in terms of Camp suggests a range of inflection points with sites in which identity is always already a temporary and performative identification.

Certainly Fani-Kayode was involved with such physical sites of performance: for one, the queer-leaning experimental theater Ovalhouse, which was for a time the locus for his development and exhibition. And concurrently, figures such as Jarman and the sculptor Andrew Logan used their own studio-homes as places to gather for screenings, happenings, and parties. Jarman, having moved on from his studies at the Slade and his bedsit in Sloane Square, relocated to a space near Blackfriars, a raw loft that took on the aspect of permanent stage to a rotating cast; Jarman had himself apprenticed as a set builder. Starting in 1969, inspired by films by Andy Warhol and Kenneth Anger, he began to host film-viewing parties and to work with a Super 8mm camera. He would go on to produce throughout the 1970s what he estimated were the only independent features to be made in the relatively small, conservative British film industry.[48] Logan, working out of a loft in Butler's Wharf, launched his drag-infused version of Miss World and, at his Valentine's Ball of 1976, brought the Sex Pistols to play, bringing them to the attention of the art and fashion worlds in London, as well as the local newspapers.

Jarman in turn explored these concentric London undergrounds and the unlikely confluences of punk rock and homoeroticism in his 1978 film *Jubilee*, which, in its own excesses and fascination with working-class and trash cultures, upended categories of high and low and reverberated in the key of the American Camp auteur John Waters. While his contemporaries have made it clear that Fani-Kayode had seen Jarman's films (and was plainly modeling his *tableaux vivants* on their cinematic precedent), less known was that they both drew from the queer terrain of Brixton. Writing in 1992, Jarman recalled his warehouse burning down in 1979, leading to his move to London's Soho in order to build a new life. At this time, he was increasingly aware of the "gay communes. In Railton Road, Brixton—the whole street had been squatted.

Now we had, or were about to have, lesbian and gay film festivals, gay olympics and academic chairs. I cut my hair short, took off my earrings, put on a leather jacket and, armed with KY and poppers, took off into the night."[49]

There are traces of such overlaps to be found in Fani-Kayode marginalia as well; recall from the discussion of punk earlier the figures dressed in a fusion of period costume: leather jackets, dyed Mohawks, ghoulish face paint, heavy sunglasses, thick eyeliner, and purple lipstick. These candid shots invoke a perennial nightlife in which the proscenium extended beyond the studio or the theater proper and into the city streets (recall figures 2.4–2.7). In Sontag's terms, these Polaroids provide fragments of a larger "aestheticization of life." There is no available evidence that Jarman and Fani-Kayode were close, but it is difficult to see Fani-Kayode's plague saints and red-robed lovers the same way after viewing the films that Jarman made leading up to 1989.[50] Each of these films, in their way, queered or revealed the latent queerness in earlier moments of "high" culture—from late Renaissance painting to Shakespeare, including *The Tempest* and 1985's *The Angelic Conversation*, a monochromatic montage of spoken sonnets, shirtless men, and lingering desire.

The latter would find something of a counterpart in Julien's *Looking for Langston*, which reprised the hazy atmospherics, nonlinear narrative, and superimposition of temporalities for a phantasmagoric exploration of the Harlem Renaissance. Both films are populated by angelic characters—melancholic loners in the mold of Morrissey in Jarman's, winged black seraphim haunting a park in Julien's. Fani-Kayode's own angel, pictured in *White Angel I* and *White Angel II* (figure 3.15) would be right at home. He is an apparitional form in powdery white and diaphanous leggings, complete with flowing black wings (a wig perhaps, or horsehair). His penis is exposed but is by no means the focus: this angel stares confidently upon us or to the heavens with his head cocked back—an elegant pose granted levity by the absurd costuming. He could be on stage, or voguing for the camera.[51]

Similarly, one could easily view the double-printed "twins" in crouched performance on archaic flutes and panpipes in *Every Mother's Son / Child of Suffering* (1989; figure 3.16) as examples of both surrealist revival or a play on the Yoruban veneration of twins. In light of Jarman's 1976 film *Sebastiane*, one is taken back to a classical (particularly Roman) context in which homosexual communion is revealed as commonplace. Here, Dionysian transgression (epitomized by the Pan/Robin Goodfellow–type characters) underscores a society less bound by the repressive strictures of modernity. In the end, both Jarman

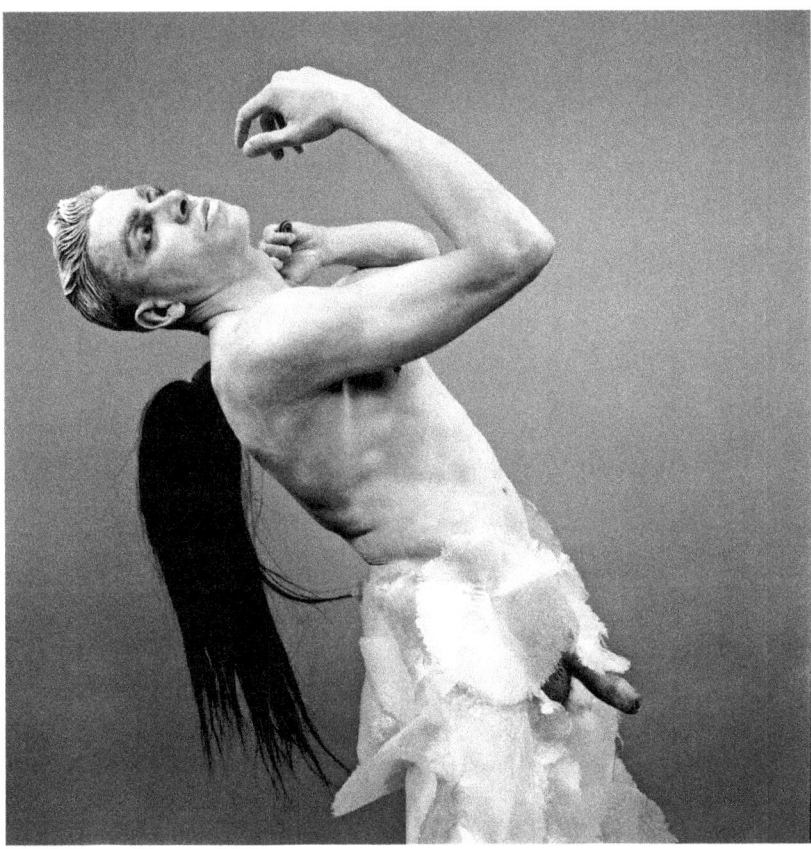

Figure 3.15 Rotimi Fani-Kayode, *White Angel II* (undated, ca. 1988). © Rotimi Fani-Kayode / Autograph ABP. Courtesy of Autograph ABP.

and Fani-Kayode combine theatrical tropes, Camp excess, and anachronism to superimpose a viable, alternative past on a dim present. In their hands, a reactivation of counterhistories of Western life worked to awaken long-repressed connections between temporalities. Such reconnections served as sites of dissent, as a way of denaturalizing contemporary knowledge-power structures. At their best, then, such practices did a sort of resistant political work on history itself, by queering it. This was very much a complement to Michel Foucault's larger project in the 1980s of using genealogical methods to unsettle epistemological systems constitutive of "sexuality" and the statist biopolitics so widely deployed against queer subjects in post-Victorian Europe.

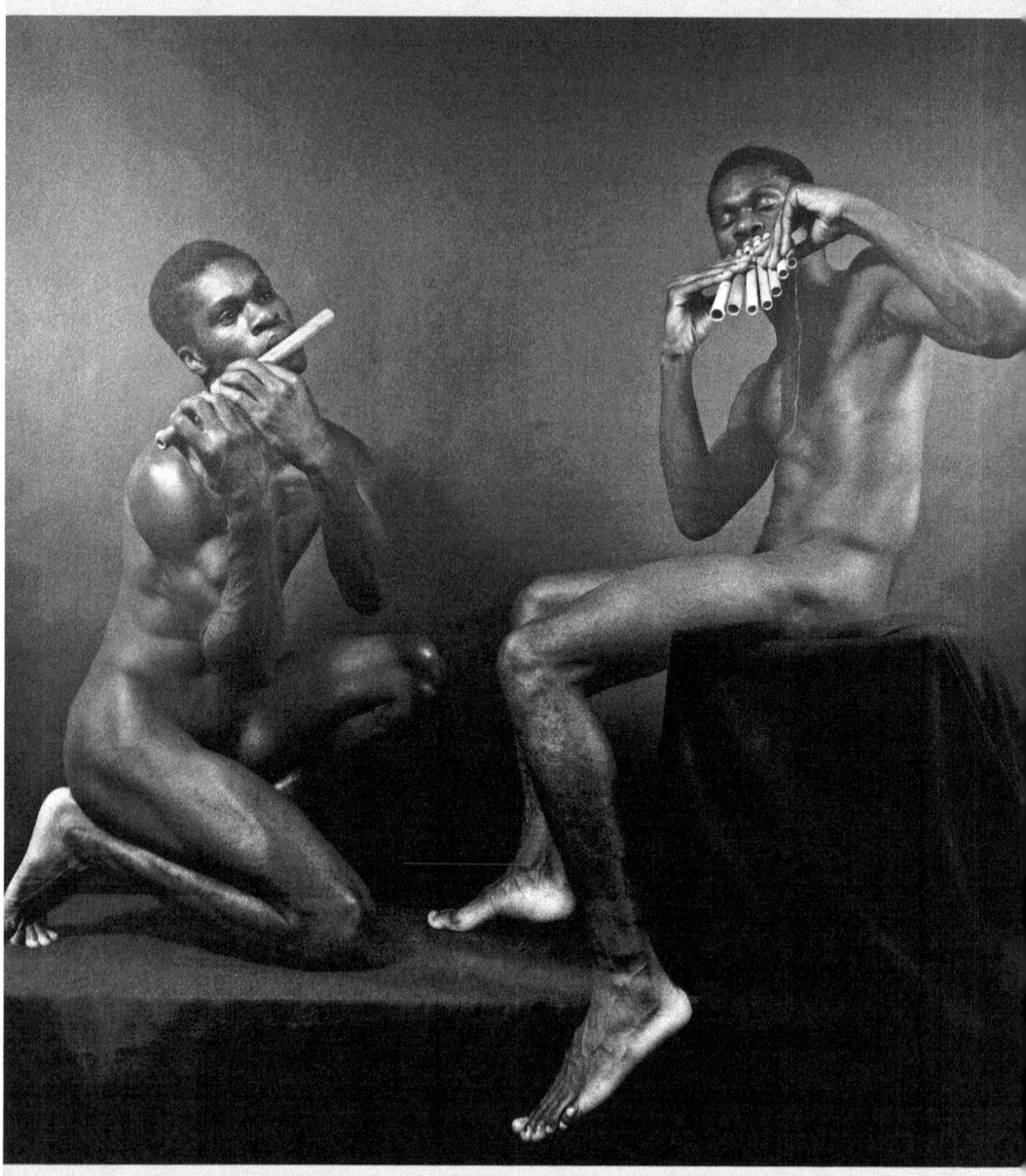

Figure 3.16 Rotimi Fani-Kayode, *Every Mother's Son / Child of Suffering* (1989).
© Rotimi Fani-Kayode / Autograph ABP. Courtesy of Autograph ABP.

And so, there is one final element of Camp worth noting here—its ongoing fascination with antique technologies, its activations of persistent countercultural impulses within modernism. Sontag herself locates the origins of Camp in the late eighteenth century: with the advent of Romanticism and an aesthetic that blended gothic motifs, ruins, and chinoiserie; with the persistence of "mannerist artists like Pontormo, Rosso, and Caravaggio"; and, by the late nineteenth century, "what had been distributed throughout all of high culture now becomes a special taste; it takes on overtones of the acute, the esoteric, the perverse."[52] Sontag links this "special taste" to Oscar Wilde, Tennyson, and Ruskin. This is the precise British public with which F. Holland Day and Europeans such as Wilde and von Gloeden created a transatlantic exchange of homoerotic visual culture that leaned heavily on an appropriated arcadian lineage.[53] Fani-Kayode's panpipers and grape eaters, as well as his *Ecce Homo*, refer in their tone and iconography to these models who, for their part, pioneered a queer photographic fusion of Neoclassicism, orientalism, and pictorialism.

What survived in Camp more broadly, then, was a secret history, with its own turning points, aesthetics, and key figures. And it is important to insist on the camp dimensions of Fani-Kayode's photographs for several reasons: For one, this lens provides a great deal of iconological power in understanding the work itself. But perhaps even more important, it helps to situate Fani-Kayode in a specific lineage of modern practitioners—not modernists, but counterpublic figures who worked to upend the social order through a range of forms, whether sartorial, theatrical, poetic, or pictorial. That lineage is historicized in the seminal survey *Camp*, in which Mark Booth begins his chronology in Roman decadence but creates a more literal genealogy of practitioners ranging from the Romantic poets to Duchamp and Warhol.[54] Both Booth and Sontag highlight the enduring archetype of the dandy, a figure who intersects with modernity as a guardian of aristocratic elegance and taste, an anachronistic (which is to say, uncanny) relic of a fading past.

In this vein, Charles Baudelaire wrote an early treatise on the dandy, implicating him in the early sediment of modernism proper in contrast to the flaneur. The dandy is not the diurnal man of crowds but a denizen of the night, with its secret societies, freedom from the law, and perpetual pursuit of pleasure.[55] Connecting this to the British context of the 1980s, Tilda Swinton recalled of Jarman's circle that their projects were not always in a good taste, had "the whiff of school play," and the group's sensibility was louche and preindustrial—

they were looking for a "dusty magic, an antidote to the mirror ball of the market. . . . This is what Caravaggio knew, painting prostitutes as Madonnas and rent boys as saints, no . . . and saints as rent boys, there's the rub."[56]

There is a utopian quality to this history. It comprises a thinly veiled landscape of transgressive figures—of which Camp partakes—that keeps a certain spirit alive. To wit, such figures reappear under different names in every era as a reminder of what was, and what could be. Their actions and their interventions work in the future anterior, their presence shows the world through the looking glass, suggesting "this will have been"[57]—a politics not of legislation but of provocation, one necessary to short-circuiting the closures of modern life. Fani-Kayode, Julien, and Jarman were manifestations of this spirit in their time, and their aims were not merely hedonistic but visionary and revisionary: they gave the lie to Sontag's conclusion that Camp is necessarily "disengaged, depoliticized—or at least apolitical."[58]

PART II: CHOCOLATE CITY

Back East

Fani-Kayode made his British debut, as it were, on the cover of a 1983 issue of the queer political journal *Square Peg*. But he came to wider prominence with two 1987 publications by Gay Men's Press—his own monograph and an anthology of "gay verse" called *Tongues Untied*, featuring work by five writers, including Craig G. Harris and Essex Hemphill, both based in Washington, DC. The cover of the latter (figure 3.17) featured an image from *Black Male/White Male*, a naked figure clambering up a set of stone steps, presumably on the shores of the beach at Brighton. Consider also *Tongues Untied (Dennis Carney and Essex Hemphill)* (1987; figure 3.18). The title of each refers to Michael Harper's poem "Tongue-Tied in Black and White," which "expounds on how the mores and language of a dominant culture can stifle the creativity of people within that culture."[59] In retrospect, this small book was remarkable as a confluence of transatlantic voices that gave clear articulation to specifically black gay subjectivity and experience.

And so, on one level, Fani-Kayode's photographs seem to elaborate a deep and increasingly canonical tradition of gay image making, tied by the 1980s to a liberation politics centered on the United States and driven by a confluence of underground periodicals and books, by rallying, lobbying, or protesting. His photographs clearly draw on the codes and contexts of then-extant and widely recognized expressions of gay masculinity and its histories. Nonetheless, it would be impossible to understand his pictures and their ambitions without looking to the specificity of Fani-Kayode's imbrication within a global dialogue of *black* gay masculinity and its politics. It is here that Fani-Kayode can be seen as an important point of stress and renegotiation of what it means not only to be black or gay, but to be both.

It is worth recalling here Mercer and Julien's powerful analysis of Mapplethorpe's work contra Fani-Kayode's, with the latter putting pressure on the very "constructedness of sexuality" and working against knowing and unknowing racial fetishism (read: racism) within the gay mainstream. Even so, as the first chapter of this book argues, the very struggle for political rights by black Americans and postcolonial Britons at times failed to incorporate Fani-Kayode and his models, interlocutors, friends, and colleagues. This exclusion often stemmed from traditionalist or heterosexist machismo within some formulations of black radicalism in the Americas and the diaspora.

If the "queer of color's" predicament was a form of double marginalization during the heyday of gay liberation (especially in England), Mercer and Julien's observations productively echo both Stuart Hall's insistence on the addition of race to class critique. They are also usefully aligned with the British theorist Hazel Carby's articulation of intersectional forms of subjectivity and the resulting complications within more universalizing formulations of identity politics. In her landmark essay "White Woman Listen!," Carby reflects on the particular imbrication of gender and postcolonial British identity, arguing that it "is not just our herstory before we came to Britain that has been ignored by white feminists, our experiences and struggles have also been ignored. These struggles and experiences, because they have been structured by racism, have been different to those of white women."[60]

While Fani-Kayode's pictures seem to transgress the boundaries of biological forms of gendering (through iterations of drag, the performance of femininity),[61] in Carby's formulation, men's power, too, cannot be understood as uniform because "black males have not enjoyed the benefits of white patriarchy."[62] Accordingly, discourses around the specificity of black gay subjectivity and politics emerged in cities throughout the United States in the late 1970s, and Fani-Kayode was active in related artistic and critical communities in South London, which in turn served as a magnet for men from the formerly industrial Midlands. His contemporary, the photographer Ajamu,

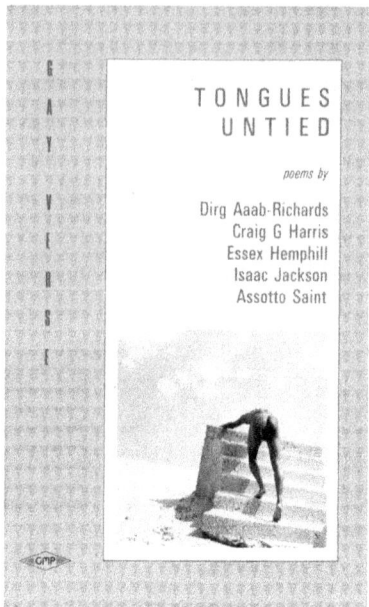

Figure 3.17 Cover of *Tongues Untied* (1987).

was born near Leeds, and recalls moving to London in 1988 because it was a hub of queer activity. He recalls meeting Fani-Kayode, who suggested he join the Brixton Art Collective; his photographs are in many ways of a piece with Fani-Kayode's own, depicting subjects who play with the performance of sexuality and gender identity, and doing so with exceptionally strong studio technique and high finish. Early on, Ajamu's work recorded black gay men at a range of pride gatherings, working to push back against the pervasive invisibility of such subjects at the time. Such a documentary approach is reflected, for example, in the 1989 piece *Cardy Revere at Gay Pride* (figure 3.19), which captures, in wide aperture, a figure posing amid a festive backdrop, propped on his bike and donning a heavy belt and messenger bag. Of this period, Ajamu recalls:

> For some of us artists/activists the seeds were sown in the 80s when we were in our early 20s. . . . The Greater London Council funded an array of groups, Black, Gay, Black and Gay, disabled. Many of us looked towards the USA as well—*In the Life*, first Black Gay Anthology, *Tongues Untied*, Marlon Riggs. Labour authorities were questioning equalities in housing, the Friday group and many activists who were involved in anti-racist groups left due

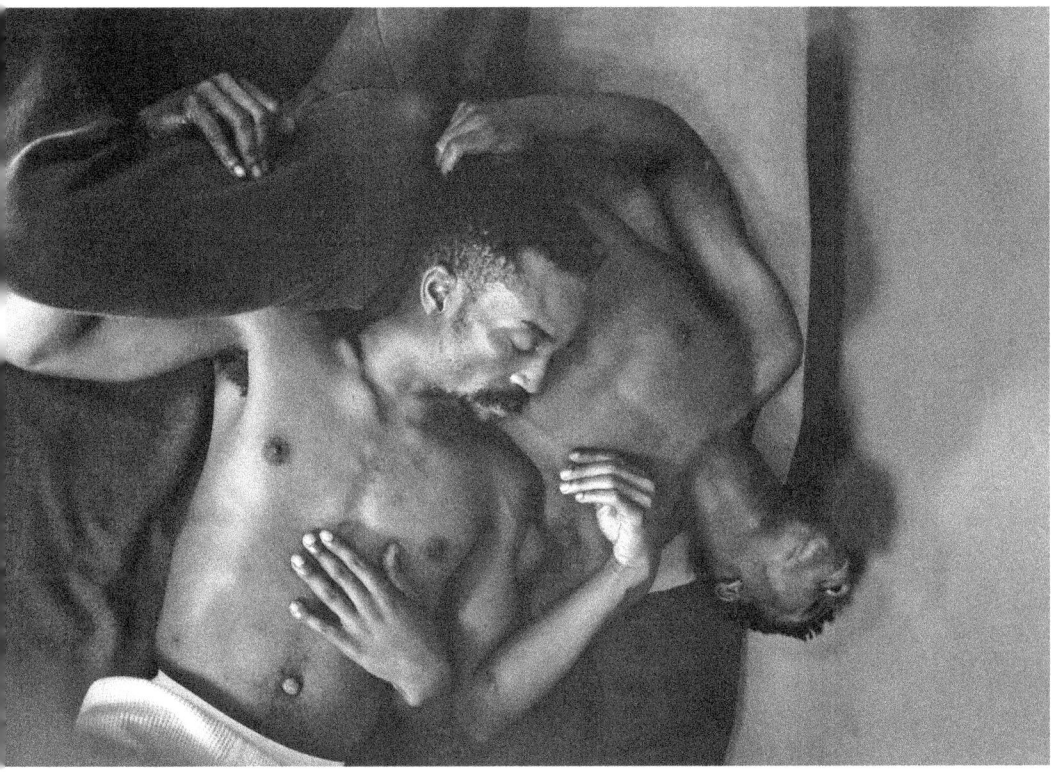

Figure 3.18 Rotimi Fani-Kayode, *Tongues Untied* (*Dennis Carney and Essex Hemphill*) (1987). © Rotimi Fani-Kayode / Autograph ABP. Courtesy of Autograph ABP.

to its racism, and left gay groups due to its racism or black groups due to homophobia . . . so for me the 90s were more about black and queer artists coming of age which set the tone for that period.[63]

This passage is telling in many ways, perhaps foremost in its description of the many overlapping interests and intersections among then-marginal groups that, in turn, were marked by dissent, departure, and reorganization. This suggests a period of intense activism, but also of debate around lines of identification that, Ajamu suggests, became more clearly articulated in the decade that followed. He also reiterates the importance of the United States as a model for the British context and, more to the point, the presence of a transatlantic dialogue with black gay artists associated with the DC, Philadelphia, and New York circles in which Fani-Kayode was deeply immersed during his time

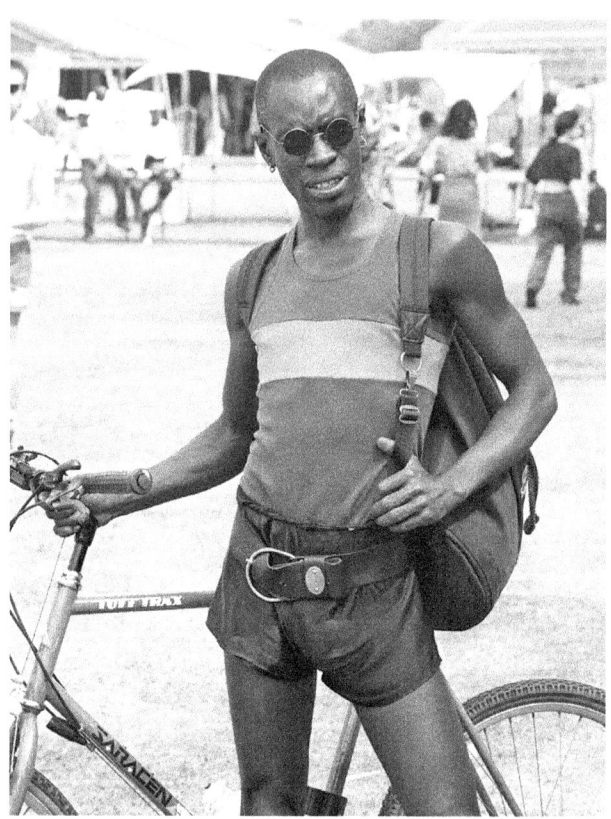

Figure 3.19 Ajamu, *Cardy Revere at Gay Pride* (1989).
© Ajamu. Courtesy of the artist.

in the United States. Marlon Riggs is an especially significant point of reference here as he, too, was a black gay activist and intellectual who died from AIDS-related complications in 1994. His film *Tongues Untied* (1989) was a touchstone in both the United States and England on its release. In just under an hour, it uses vocabularies of humorous sketch, documentary interview, aestheticized tableaux, and sonic montage / call-and-response to produce a critical document of concerns emerging from the living rooms, salons, and gallery spaces in which black gay counterpublics were constituted throughout the late 1970s and 1980s.

The title *Tongues Untied* references an ambition of the project to literally give voice to men who were silenced by various "mainstream" publics. In one striking example, an early section in the film shows Riggs recalling, à la Fanon, his progressive social indexing in the slurs of others: a "punk" or sissy as a child, a "homo" or "faggot" to other black people in Georgia, an "uncle Tom" to those who perceived him as occupying a higher social class (he would go to Harvard), and a "coon" to the "redneck" whites around him. Here, Riggs is, blow by blow, reduced to a set of reductive stereotypes, multiply rejected, and multiply an outsider—too rich, too gay, too black. The film opens with the cyclical vocal refrain "brother to brother to brother to brother . . . ," an echo of the title of Joseph Beam's anthology *Brother to Brother*, completed by the poet Essex Hemphill following Beam's death in 1988. Beam was also editor of the "first black gay anthology," *In the Life*, that Ajamu mentions alongside *Tongues Untied*. Beam, Riggs, and Hemphill were, together, part of a larger circle of black gay intellectuals based in DC.[64] The AIDS activist Ron Simmons recalls a visit to Washington in 1980 when Gary Martin "hosted a discussion group for black gay men at Sidney [Brinkley]'s house. It was the first time I experienced being with a group of men taking part in mature, serious conversation about being black and gay." Sidney Brinkley was the publisher of the DC gay magazine *Blacklight*, and Simmons, as his photographer, would meet Hemphill and join a cohort of black socialites, a clique of "talented black gay men and lesbians. . . . Every weekend there was something to attend: an exhibition, a reading, a music performance, a play or a house party. They were the DC black gay renaissance."[65]

This group was deeply influential back in London, in no small measure because they created a space of debate and representation for intersectional subjectivity and experience that was, by and large, not available in the cultural climate of eighties England. Some exceptions, of course, were Fani-Kayode's and Ajamu's photographs and the work of filmmakers such as Isaac Julien and Hanif Kureishi. The former's *Looking for Langston*, however—which has been widely discussed and has assumed a canonical status in thinking about this period—draws from the American context in fairly direct ways. As the film theorist Manthia Diawara has compellingly argued, the film resists gay essentialism by using "Langston Hughes and the black tradition as enabling texts for black gays to tell their stories."[66] To wit, *Looking for Langston*'s underlying conceit is an explicit imaginative extension of the work of the Harlem Renaissance poet Langston Hughes, realizing homoerotic dimensions of his writing and his social landscape that remained sub-rosa in response to homophobia in both the black community and American society more broadly.

Three poetic voices intersperse the film in text and narration: Bruce Nugent, the "out" contemporary of Hughes's (who died in 1987); the critic James Baldwin (whose sexuality was long a site of contention and debate within the black radical tradition) read, here, by Toni Morrison; and Essex Hemphill. Quieter passages in the film are, in turn, set to balladic songs such as "Blues for Langston" and "Beautiful Black Men" by Blackberri, the San Francisco–based musician and founder (in 1993) of the Queer Cultural Center.

For all of its formal and narrative complexity, Julien's project is, at root, of a piece with the DC group's larger interest in giving visibility to, in Beam's terms, "black men loving black men." Beam argued in an essay from *In the Life* "that such an articulation is the revolutionary act of the eighties . . . which is not rooted in any particular political or class affiliation, but *in our mutual survival.*"[67] Fani-Kayode can be seen as working to serve such a project in several ways. On the one hand, his photographs of black "men loving men" is, in simplest terms, a mode of giving visibility, in positive terms, to black homoeroticism. On the other, both the wide range of signification, disidentification, and transnational syncretisms brought to bear in the photographs are indicative of a multivalence that is "not rooted in any particular political or class affiliation" and staged, by his own reckoning, as an act of survival. More overtly still, one can find traces of the DC and San Francisco scenes in *Black Male/White Male* in particular. The title page of the book features a portrait of Blackberri, with his iconically natty hair and heavy jewelry evident even though his face is occluded by a wooden mask. Similarly, Fani-Kayode's physical movements through the pathways of urban gay life place him precisely at the confluence that Simmons describes in 1979–1980, as Fani-Kayode made his way from Georgetown to New York.

Indeed, it would be the landscape of late-night parties—dancing, drugs, hustlers, sex in public—that inaugurated Fani-Kayode's migration from being the "respectable sort" that his family wanted him to be to another world, hidden in plain sight. Significantly, this happened in the US at the apex of urban white flight, nearly ten years into the aftermath of widespread urban rioting that including the H Street corridor and the area east of 16th Street in DC. According to Hirst, when Fani-Kayode "went to study in Washington, he came across a city where the majority is black, even though it is the capital of the most powerful Western nation. This made a great impression on him. He retained a fondness for his time there and often spoke of the 'Chocolate City.'

It was there that he met his first male lover, Stedman Scribner, and discovered the wild side of urban America."[68]

Ultimately, Fani-Kayode's pictures stage and commemorate the flows of people, poetry, music, and art across the Atlantic: these photographs articulated (and are artifacts of) the formation of a specific queer consciousness within the black diaspora. For example, he dedicated *Black Male/White Male* to "Toni, the spirit of the Clubhouse, Washington, D.C.," an underground disco in that city. And the first photograph in the layout of plates is an entangled pair, Dennis Carney (the British gay rights activist) and Essex Hemphill (figure 3.18). The latter wrote long verse on his experiences in Washington, such as the opening stanza to his celebrated "The Tomb of Sorrow": "Gunshots ring out above our heads / as we sit beneath your favorite tree / in this park called Meridian Hill / called Malcolm X, that you call / the 'Tomb of Sorrow.'" And, later, "Gunshots ring out above our heads / as we cock dance / beneath your favorite tree. / There are no invectives to use against us. / We are exhausted / from dreaming wet dream, / afraid of the passion/that briefly consoles us." Here he writes of a park in the Columbia Heights neighborhood, notorious for its high walls and steep approach. It is a private space within the city, once a locus of weekly African drum circles.

Elsewhere, in his 1992 poem "American Wedding," Hemphill writes of an America that rejects him but thinks too little of him and his peers to realize that a revolution is at hand—not necessarily in the streets or the courtroom but, as David Wojnarowicz would call it, "in the shadow of the American dream." Hemphill does not demand equal rights but suggests, instead, their queering: "In America / I place my ring / on your cock / where it belongs . . . / They don't know / we are becoming powerful. / Every time we kiss / we confirm the new world coming." Hemphill and contemporaries such as Adrian Stanford in Philadelphia (who, like Fani-Kayode and Joseph Beam, died before 1990) worked to develop a poetry that built on the black sonic tradition and the contemporary textures of urban gay life. In this sense, his practice and that of the poets around him sought to create an alternative discourse of resistance that worked in parallel to mainline (and, at times, reactionary) gay liberation in the late 1980s.[69] Instead, Stanford writes of Philadelphia in an incantatory, expansive mode: "i am pinioned in your arms, silent and hard breathing. / each breath creating galaxies; where unnamed / children call me god—and shout in their private gloom, as i do: fuck me now." ("In the darkness, fuck me now"). Or in his remembrance of then-gay epicenter near Washington Square, that "black sarah ruled / and we of lesser divinity paid homage to her / with our pansy smiles. / we breathed magnolia air, dreaming other vision / through the velvet of our mascara lashes."[70]

In his rhapsodic manifesto "Hey, brother, what's hap'nin?," Cary Alan Johnson is more explicit in his demands for urban cred: "I'm looking for a real brother who knows the streets, don't take no shit, kicks ass when he has to, kills white boys for fun, eats bullets for breakfast, drives a mustang, done been to jail." And while there is more than a hint of irony in his demands, Johnson's piece alludes to the heterogeneous, even fragmented, character of the gay landscape of the 1970s and 1980s. The community was divided, at times, on explicitly racial lines, a division already manifest in Mapplethorpe's fetishism. The latter, not content with the S/M of places like New York's Mineshaft, would need to go in search of black men—the ultimate in exoticism.

That Fani-Kayode came of age in Washington and New York (and Interstate 95 connects them, through Philadelphia) and features Hemphill in several of his early photographs adds specificity to the reservations he alludes to vis-à-vis the "gay bourgeoisie" and its desire for "Black ass" and "Black dick." Just as Fani-Kayode was likely influenced by the refined London loft parties of the Andrew Logans and Derek Jarmans of the world, he also drew on his time in black America. They were critical years, on the streets of cities suffused with punk insouciance and by the sonic byways of jazz and funk, where drag queens walked the runway and vogued: the scene was heterogeneous to be sure but, also, to borrow Kobena Mercer's phrase from later in the decade, was recognizably "freaky deaky."

And while this constellation of American queer circles served as a beacon for Fani-Kayode and others in England, the particular welter of class and ethnicity that characterized postcolonial London meant that the flows of "diasporic queerness" were not a one-way street. Indeed, for all of the ways that *Looking for Langston* drew on American histories and voices to give expression to same-sex-loving men in the British context, Julien's film was reciprocally influential back in DC. Simmons recalls Marlon Riggs leaving a copy of the film at his home for Hemphill: "I was going to wait until Essex and I could see the film together but curiosity got the best of me. . . . I was mesmerized and captivated throughout the entire film. It was the most beautiful and poetic film about black gay men I had ever seen. Essex's poetry told the stories [Hughes] hinted at but I believe was afraid to say."[71] Hemphill, in turn, traveled to London in 1986 and was so taken that he considered moving there. This was likely the interlude during which Fani-Kayode took his portrait, nude and interlaced with other activists such as Carney. Hemphill explained in a letter to Beam from London that

> this city is having a tremendous impact on me. In turn I am impacting on its sensibility. . . . I could live here for awhile. A year or two at maximum, using this as a base to invade other European cities. London truly connects one to other places. What appeals to me most is the sheer diversity of people. Indian, West Indian, African, Germans, Italians, Russians—I have met a smorgasbord of ethnically and culturally diverse people individuals who are all impacting in a positive way on my life. . . . I have learned I belong to the world and not to any one movement.[72]

As previous chapters have briefly sketched, South London was, indeed, a cosmopolitan hub in those years, and Hemphill would have encountered the work of queer artists such as Kureishi and Julien, would have likely seen the multimedia projects of Mona Hatoum and Sonia Boyce, Keith Piper, and Sokari Douglas, among others. He was certainly spending time with Fani-Kayode and would have encountered not just gay art or black gay art, but also mediations of queer subjectivity from a broader diasporic matrix. For example, the photographer Sunil Gupta (with whom Fani-Kayode showed in group exhibitions) was Indian born, raised in Montreal, and lived in New York, but relocated to London in 1978. He remembers that the big shift in leaving New York was an "involvement in the larger politics. . . . I joined antiracism committees inside the Town Hall where policies were being made."[73] While much of Gupta's work from the time pictures gay men in India, London helped him to connect queer representations with political activism, including the 1980–1981 series *London Gay Switchboard*, about a local helpline. He recalls making the "accidental shift," by joining a black-Asian student group in 1983, "turning [his] back on the commercial art world and focusing on grass-roots politics." In London, his first encounter with South Asians of the diaspora "was through the black gay group. It became a Sunday afternoon tea and sympathy session for closet gay South Asian guys."[74]

And so, for both Hemphill and Fani-Kayode, London functioned as a counterpoint to American gay circles, as a site of potential in which progressive elements within local government (contra the national regime) provided openings in which politics of race—figured in cosmopolitan and diasporic terms—intersected with gay and lesbian activism, antipoverty interventions, and aid for the disabled. The United States, in turn, provided a model for more militant and overt discourses of self-identification and representation, even at points of divergence, as when the specificity of black gay subjectivity deferred from mainline post-Stonewall conceptions of gay liberation. Taken together, the formations of postcolonial queerness in England and the black gay communities in Washington, DC, the Bay Area, and New York generated nodes of theory, art, literature, and mass publicity that operated in dialecti-cal relation to each other, and in critical relation to more univocal narratives of gay identity. Fani-Kayode was at the heart of this dialogue of queerness formed by subjects of the black and Asian diaspora—as documentarian, as activist, and as a maker of sites in which points of relation between intersect-ing subjectivities could be envisioned and materialized on the pictorial plane.

Queers of Color / Queer Space

Joseph Beam contended that, faced with an array of social forces that opposed the very existence of black gay subjectivity, the act of men of color loving men of color (and, in turn, artists like Fani-Kayode documenting or depicting such) constituted an act of insistent revision and refusal—an act of politics. And as Gupta notes, in eighties London, he too found a niche, "not within the ethnicity of South Asian but, in the post-colonial black arts movement . . . white gay men and black Rastafarians, and an emerging black gay scene. Cross dressing was political rather than simply partying."[75] Gupta describes a Lon-don in which there was an inherent power in performing queerness in public, and where intersectional forms of minoritarian subjectivity could be physi-cally enacted. But there may be a few implicit problems to this formulation.

For one, Fani-Kayode and those around him enacted what Nancy Fraser would call "subaltern counterpublics"—publics within an allegedly neutral public sphere that operate from a position of relative marginalization. These counterpublics worked collectively within what then might be called gay and lesbian liberation, against a larger set of societal norms that sought to actively repress or closet queer subjectivity and its representation. Given the legisla-tive and discursive scale of such a project, how might Fani-Kayode's photo-graphs contribute, as highly aestheticized meditations of the nude that riff and signify on various histories of art and visual culture? Which is to raise a second issue that should be clear at this point: that those very photographs are indicative not of a univocal gay collectivity but of an array of constituencies that overlapped or dissented in various ratios. The matter is complicated insofar as Fani-Kayode's photographs do not purport to represent one of these counterpublics, but instead draw them together. Much as he found points of inflection and relation between seemingly disparate forms of the black radical and diaspora traditions and various musical, visual, and literary histories, his work also charts the formation and performance of gay subjectivities that confound dyads of gay/straight, male/female, black/white, colonizer/colonized, and so on.

This braiding of intersectional subjectivity and diasporic practice is, ultimately, a precursor to a gamut of practices and discourses that began to crystallize more fully in the decades after Fani-Kayode's death. In drawing together seemingly antagonistic genres such as the (white) muscle magazine, nineteenth-century homoeroticism, Camp, punk, and black and postcolonial modes of gay expression, his photographs laid the groundwork for some of the theoretical terrain already staked out in the previous chapter—what José Esteban Muñoz dubbed *disidentification*, a

> third mode of dealing with dominant ideology, one that neither opts
> to assimilate within such a structure nor strictly opposes it; rather
> disidentification is a strategy that works on and against dominant ideology.
> Instead of buckling under the pressures of dominant ideology (identification,
> assimilation) or attempting to break free of its inescapable sphere . . . this
> "working on and against" is a strategy that tries to transform a cultural logic
> from within.[76]

Muñoz's formulation emerges from his analysis of "queers of color." He argues that such a formulation productively reconciles many of the seeming contradictions actively debated during the 1970s and 1980s—notably Mercer's concerns about Mapplethorpe's racial fetishism versus the necessity of working en bloc with white gays,[77] and of balancing the utility of essentialist identity politics with individual expression. Disidentification, in the simplest terms, recognizes the dynamic and intersecting forces through which subjectivity is provisionally constituted and performed, and the utility of strategies of identification, appropriation, signifying, and ambivalence within larger publics—whether British homophobia or the priorities of mainstream post-Stonewall forms of gay collectivity. And as Michael Warner argues, the performance of counterpublic address is its own form of politics, one of imaginative world building—especially once discourses (in this case photographs and text) enter wider circulation.[78]

With that in mind, this chapter concludes by discussing the spatial dimensions, the *publicness* of Fani-Kayode's photographs. Looking back, it seems that the ultimate power of his art in terms of gay politics in the 1980s was to use strategies of disidentification to draw together counterpublics constituted from a long tradition of gay visual culture. That art, in turn, proposed new subjectivities and topographies that constituted a then-nascent counterpublic of what, in subsequent years, would be theorized as queerness. As Fani-Kayode's photographs circulated in networks of extant gay sites of gathering and exchange, he worked to envision new zones of queer possibility, rooted in his experiences in the diaspora and in his movements through the Atlantic world. Such a shift, it should be clear, is of a piece with Fani-Kayode's larger interest in transgressing frontiers, blurring temporalities, and suggesting identity as a process of relation rather than difference. As Warner himself argued, queerness even complicates geographic rootedness: it emerges locally but operates as a system for revising and resisting boundaries inscribed by dominant ideologies.[79]

At the same time, such counterpublics were forged—like diasporic practices more generally—by linking disparate locales through travel by people, of course, but also by material culture in the form of music and literature, art and pulp. The last chapter described the significance of heterotopic "underground" sites that created meaningful spaces of dissent and subcultural organization and self-articulation. Carnival, the rock club, the bathhouse, the disco—these were all physical places of celebration and conviviality but also nodes of resistance to a dominant public sphere. They worked in parallel to or in conjunction with community centers, storefront galleries, and locally generated publications such as Rasheed Araeen's *Black Phoenix* or *Square Peg*, of which Hirst was a fixture on the editorial team. The latter's masthead noted that *Square Peg* was "a collective but individual articles do not necessarily represent a collective point of view." It featured contributions from men and women, young writers, visual artists, MPs, and a range of people in between. Its pages thus served as a site for discourse on outward-facing issues and also intraqueer debates around questions of political tactics, aesthetics, sexism, race, and racism.

Importantly, it was through such channels—gay newsletters, journals, bookstores, and group shows—that Fani-Kayode found reception and a public in the first place. Autograph ABP was not founded until the closing years of the decade, and his work was only drawn into more explicitly contemporary African or black diasporic fields of scholarship and curation during the 1990s, with Mark Sealy's group exhibition at *Les Rencontres d'Arles* in 1993 and Okwui Enwezor, Claire Bell, and Octavio Zaya's *In/sight* exhibition at the Solomon R. Guggenheim Museum in 1996. Indeed, Fani-Kayode's portfolios of large-scale color works—his writing with light—were first shown at a small gallery in Brighton, where he briefly lived in 1983, but also circulated in print within a few months in the pages of *Square Peg*.

In 1984 Hirst connected Fani-Kayode with a group show of gay and lesbian art at the Brixton Art Gallery, and during the next several years Fani-Kayode showed in gay and lesbian–focused shows, such as *Misfits* at Ovalhouse and at the Submarine Gallery.[80] Taken together, these are the sort of physical and discursive locations that, as Simon Watney argues, provided the very substrate of a British approach to queer collectivity. And it was in gay journals and newspapers that Fani-Kayode's shows were noted, portfolios described, and eulogies written. London's *Capital Gay* offered one of the few exhibition reviews of printed works from *Black Male/White Male* in 1988, "in which a black perspective on the eroticisation of black men elicits a new vocabulary of stimuli and responses, contrasting with the works of white photographers such as Robert Mapplethorpe."[81] The book itself was translated into German and evidently made its way to Europe and, indeed, all the way to Australia, where the gay publications *Campaign* and *OutRage* featured it as part of their book clubs in 1989.[82]

If Fani-Kayode relied on local and global networks of gay and lesbian discourse and space—a counterpublicity—there was also something quite plainly spatial about the photographs themselves. This is evident in his use of neighborhoods, studios, apartments, and foreign cityscapes. *Black Male/White Male*, as a book, was in Hirst's estimation, "a one-sided discourse, a tale of desire: Africa—Europe—America: fantasy-continents in which these images find some of their contexts, not least of which belong to the triangle of trade in finished goods, raw materials, and slaves."[83] And in traveling the currents of the Black Atlantic, both Fani-Kayode and his photographs alighted on and metonymically rendered more abstract physical zones. Hirst remarks in the introduction: "America is a series of interiors in Manhattan, cool in spite of the heat-induced frenzy on the street. There's a hint of air conditioned paranoia here. Bleached hair with roots that need retouching. Juju in the Jungle (from Adam Clayton Powell make a left at 125th). Within megatons of glass and steel, delicate boys on angel dust explore their allergies. Africa occasionally peers into the bathhouse cubicle where Europe lies ready-greased but asleep."[84] This passage is explicit in its references to black gay men, but also black and white desire—from delicate young men with bleached hair and dark roots to greased inamorati laying in wait in urban bathhouses. It locates the images, if only temporarily, at an intersection in Harlem, in apartment studio spaces away from the particular fugue state of summer in the city. Africa and Europe appear synecdochically as black and white men.

Crucially, in the pages of the book, it is Africa that is possessed of scopic power, gazing upon the quietly dormant Europe. Hirst describes a new kind of cartographic exploration that reinforces the heterotopic and diasporic logics that underscore the pictures: America is a series of hidden interiors and intimate encounters; a sense of movement among the nodes of the Black Atlantic prevails; and desire—for substances, bodies, and easy intimate afternoons in the cool—is explicit. Considering *Black Male/White Male* holistically, one might return to the contrast between Mapplethorpe's studio and Fani-Kayode's as they appear in their respective portfolios from 1986 to 1987.[85] As Hirst's evocation of air-conditioned apartments in Harlem suggests, the location of these pictures is for the most part the transcendent placelessness of anonymous apartment studios—the terrain of the picture itself is delinked from temporal or environmental markers. That atemporality is amplified by the date *range* that orients the pictures across a five-year span. Such anonymity, such a suspension of specific placing, at once heightens the insularity and intimacy of many of the pictures and shifts *Black Male/White Male* away from the realm of documentation and into a more ambiguous space. Here, one confronts a deterritorialized zone of possibility that could be anywhere or nowhere in the course of Fani-Kayode's migrations. The images in turn mediate an archive—one that visualizes diasporic queerness and postulates such mediations as sites for revision and possibility.[86]

In looking at Fani-Kayode's haunted shorelines, gritty streets, and languid models, or reading Hirst's textual evocations, one cannot help but recall here the diaries of David Wojnarowicz. He was another artist who documented his travels through the hidden redoubts of the East Coast underground. He was noted for posing as a latter-day Arthur Rimbaud, and his notes are a reverie of physical and psychic location. Writing in 1979, for example, Wojnarowicz recounted his secret beach on the West Side Highway and its piers, where abandoned warehouses became the raw material for artists such as Gordon Matta-Clark, and where there were worlds through the looking glass, where men had sex among the wreckage or tripped on psychedelics in leisure on the docks.[87] This is the terrain described in Douglas Crimp's memoirs of a New York in transition, in the years after Stonewall, and during a period of ruination and possibility. These are the piers documented by Alvin Baltrop (figure 3.20), who, like Fani-Kayode, lucidly captured encounters between men, black and white alike. This is the downtown of Fani-Kayode's early adulthood, depicted by Wojnarowicz's friend Peter Hujar: its husks of buildings and long nights creating a parallel landscape—a mirror world, a place within and beyond all places—in which desire might be liberated, the world reenchanted.[88]

If the above begins to read as metaphysical, veering on the Romantic, all the better. If the hegemonic discourses of modernism worked to repress other modes of perception within the field of the visual, many of its counterdiscourses in the 1970s and 1980s only complicated matters further, moving away from premodernist knowledges and techniques and toward a return to the self not as physical, desiring body in place but as culturally mediated sign. As we have seen, this register—of signification and productive irony—is called upon in aspects of Fani-Kayode's practice. But the second half of this book takes his own claims about his practice, as well as the psychic and (im)material landscapers where he worked, more seriously. These layers of his photography, what he alternately defined as seeking truth or channeling techniques of ecstasy, can be understood better not through histories of homoerotic images but through those spaces in Lower Manhattan where a new beachhead was established and then evanesced; in the parlors of DC; or the after-hours lofts and clubs of the midnight city.

Such places rely on the provisionality, the utopianism, the hedonism, and the resistant elements that have long defined the various countercultures of modernity—Romanticism, for one, and its inheritors in Black Atlantic surrealisms. All of these elements are taken up in the pages ahead. It is worth concluding here, however, that many of the ambivalences of many variants of Romanticism and also of Fani-Kayode and Hirst's work also radiate through Wojnarowicz's writing and Hujar's photographs. In each, there is a poignant sense of temporariness, that the artist has found a place between places, between times, in which the membrane between a lost past and a better future

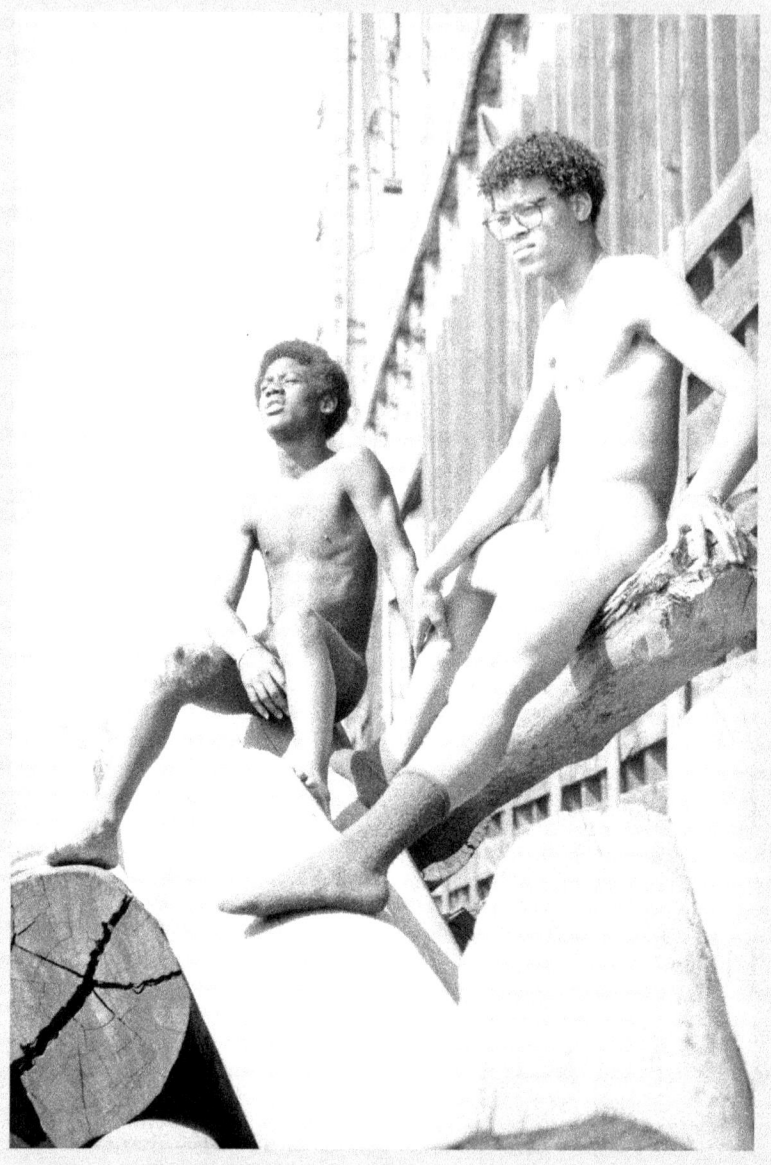

Figure 3.20 Alvin Baltrop, *The Piers (River Rats)* (1972–1975). © The Alvin Baltrop Trust. Courtesy of the Alvin Baltrop Trust and Third Streaming.

are drawn into focus and, for some brief moments, enacted and documented through pictures and through writing. Hujar, Baltrop, Crimp, and others found possibility in ruins and decay, but that possibility was always tempered by something else—a sense of foreboding and fragility that lent a particular intensity to each click of the shutter.

It is obvious in retrospect that Fani-Kayode's artistic life correlated exactly with another timeline: the escalating AIDS crisis. *Black Male/White Male* was published in 1988, by which time HIV/AIDS had devastated the lives of many of those very people who populated the studios and lofts, those who provided that underlying spirit of the dance club and bathhouse.[89] On the one hand the situation in London was always comparatively more underground, more improvised, and necessarily subtler than its American counterpart. On the other, the recognition that HIV/AIDS could spread beyond the gay metropolis as the 1980s progressed meant that, even in the US, gay men faced the manifold challenges of an epidemic, intracommunity discord and debate, a virulently conservative government, and a reactive media through which negligence and fear-mongering merged. This confluence decidedly altered the trajectory of queer publics and politics by mid-decade.[90]

As Fani-Kayode and Hirst wrote in 1989, "HIV has forced us to deal with dark ambiguities. Where better to look for clues than in the secret chambers of African shrines, the sumptuous ruins of Coptic and Eurasian temples, and the boarded-up fuck-rooms of the American dream?"[91] And with this turn toward more metaphysical territory and the day-to-day specter of the AIDS crisis, it is time to look to the strange materiality and premodernist recuperations of the photographs themselves, and to the provocative manner in which Fani-Kayode revivified temporal strategies and seemingly obsolete arthistorical technologies to propose new responses to the existential perils of the late 1980s. Or, as Jarman would have it, "All art is concerned with death: Goya, to those renaissance artists in their dissecting rooms; Rembrandt getting older in his self-portraits; Monet's water lilies—which became the memorial for the first World War; the poetry of Wilfred Owen and Donne—*Death Be Not Proud*. That's why I love Wilfred Owen—I feel sympathy, it's just a different war."[92]

THE QUEEN IS DEAD

Searching for sea shells, waves lap my wellington boots, carrying
lost souls of brothers and sisters released over the ship side. . . .
You don't want me in your green and pleasant land.

Ingrid Pollard, *Rencontres au noir: Black British Photography*

Take me out tonight / Where there's music and there's people
/ And they're young and alive / Driving in your car / I never, never want
to go home / Because I haven't got one anymore.

Morrissey, "There Is a Light That Never Goes Out"

Romanticism in its many senses is everywhere in Rotimi Fani-Kayode's photographs. It is a dominant mood between his subjects and is ambient in the
tone and texture of the black-and-white pieces made in the years before 1988.
Such Romantic atmospherics become even more pronounced in the alternative process experiments conducted with and by Alex Hirst between 1987 and
1992. Indeed, for all of the homoeroticism that suffuses these portfolios, sex
is only ever implied, gestured at through playful substitution, or the sense
that one has caught the sitters in a moment of intimacy or secret communication, *in media res*. Sometimes Fani-Kayode pictures them just on the cusp of
something, enjoying an intensity of desire, or a lingering afterglow. In *Technique of Ecstasy No. 4*, for instance, calm radiates throughout the image. The
figures are naked, one black and one white, one face down on the floor, the
other sitting atop his thighs. They occupy a languid in-betweenness, perhaps
recovering from what Georges Bataille, following a centuries-old tradition,
called "the little death" of ecstasy. Fani-Kayode captures here a sense of ease,
of luxuriation, or even relief. Another picture, a more broadly cropped black-

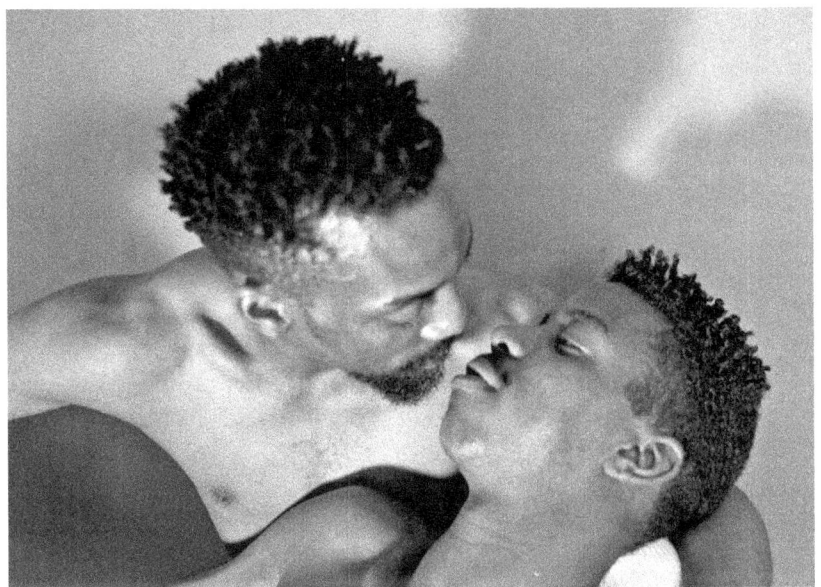

Figure 4.1 Rotimi Fani-Kayode, *Kiss* (undated, ca. 1987). © Rotimi Fani-Kayode / Autograph ABP. Courtesy of Autograph ABP.

and-white called *Kiss* (figure 4.1) shows two figures in repose, gazing into each others' eyes, their shadows playing off the walls. Here the stoppage of time, the transportation enacted in an ineffable moment of communion, is indexed in silver gelatin.

In contrast to a great deal of then-contemporary homoerotic imagery, there is neither a rush of anxiety nor an air of prurience in these images. Fani-Kayode's images recall instead moments drawn from a more subtly erotic Victorian lineage—in them, his figures partake in scenes of delectation, of literal romancing. At the same time, Fani-Kayode's precise execution means that the scenes, too, are somehow elevated, aesthetically romanticized. Similarly, alternate process prints such as *Tulip Boy* and the slate of platinum and gum bichromate prints produced in 1988–1989 all enact a rusticated aura—a haze of antique materiality and vaporous finish. And in a different technical mode, the *Black Male/White Male* book shows an image called *Torso* (figure 4.2), which is printed slightly out of focus; it foreshadows those later technical experiments. The figure here wears a brocaded belt and is shot from behind, his arms extended in a pose that mirrors both crucifixion and a bull's head (arms

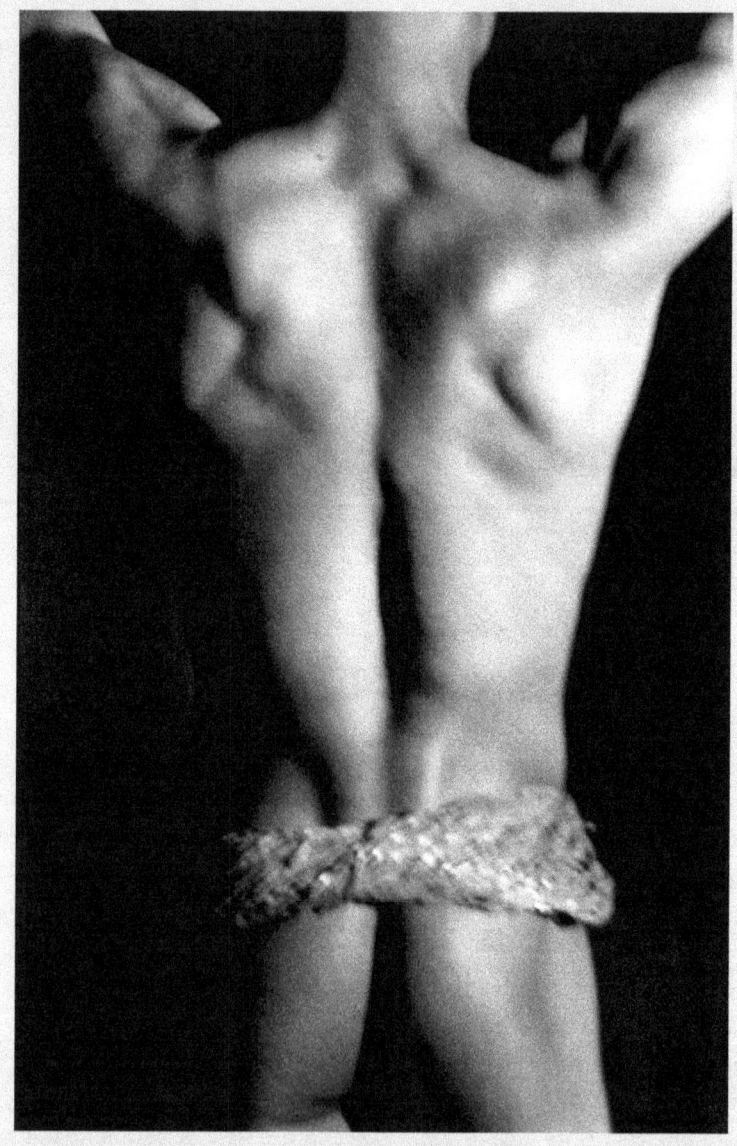

Figure 4.2 Rotimi Fani-Kayode, *Torso* (ca. 1984). © Rotimi Fani-Kayode /
Autograph ABP. Courtesy of Autograph ABP.

for horns)—a pose that in the hands of Man Ray was recoded forever to evoke that mythic, labyrinth-bound beast, the Minotaur.[1] Taken together, these pictures connect Fani-Kayode and Alex Hirst to deeper horizons still: of the post-Enlightenment cultural movement known as the Romantic, which was exemplified in the art, literature, and music of the early nineteenth century.

The succinct tracing of the exotic and erotic in *Torso*'s figure—his muscled black body, the "near-eastern" resonances of the belt—call to mind French Romantic and orientalist genres of painting that depicted opulence and sexual excesses, in the canvases of Delacroix for instance, or in scenes staged in photographic clarity by Ingres or Léon Belly.[2] Even the implication of languid hookah sessions or the distorting pleasures of hashish or opium are called forth in Fani-Kayode's sharply focused medium-format picture *Pipe* (1989; figure 4.3), in which the model draws from a long, ivory-toned stem. No smoke is seen, and the subject's eyes are closed in deep focus. He is transported, intoxicated. The symbolist evocation of the pipe as serpent in Paul Gauguin's own self-portrait of 1888 could not have been far from Fani-Kayode's mind here,[3] nor René Magritte's droll observation in his own depiction of a pipe that *ceci n'est pas une pipe*.[4] Whether one takes this as a moment of fellatio as metonymy or as a mere act of smoking, the lush tonal depth of the picture and the figure's otherworldly countenance suggest layers of poetic reference, of Samuel Taylor Coleridge's closing couplets: "Weave a circle round him thrice, / And close your eyes with holy dread / For he on honey-dew hath fed, / And drunk the milk of Paradise."[5]

Traces of the gothic are evident elsewhere in *Black Male/White Male*. In another photograph, a sitter called *Philip* (figure 4.4) contemplates a single lit candle. He sits in a kind of reclined contrapposto—at ease amid a diffuse background. His face is caked in white, conjuring the theatrical, evidently, but also the metaphysical netherworlds of the departed. Philip's pallor here is reminiscent of Kongo *minkisi* figures, with ghostly white visages that mark them as denizens of a subaquatic spiritual realm,[6] and also of the Japanese masquerade tradition of Noh, in which painted shell masks convey a range of emotional or archetypical functions. His object of attention—that burning candle—is a throwback to premodern lighting and an invocation a common transcultural mode of spiritual activation and veneration, from crossroads in Bahia to altars in Catholic churches.

But even beyond the studio, other moments suggest the Romantic as a more ambient quality within Fani-Kayode's life. One unpublished 8″ × 10″

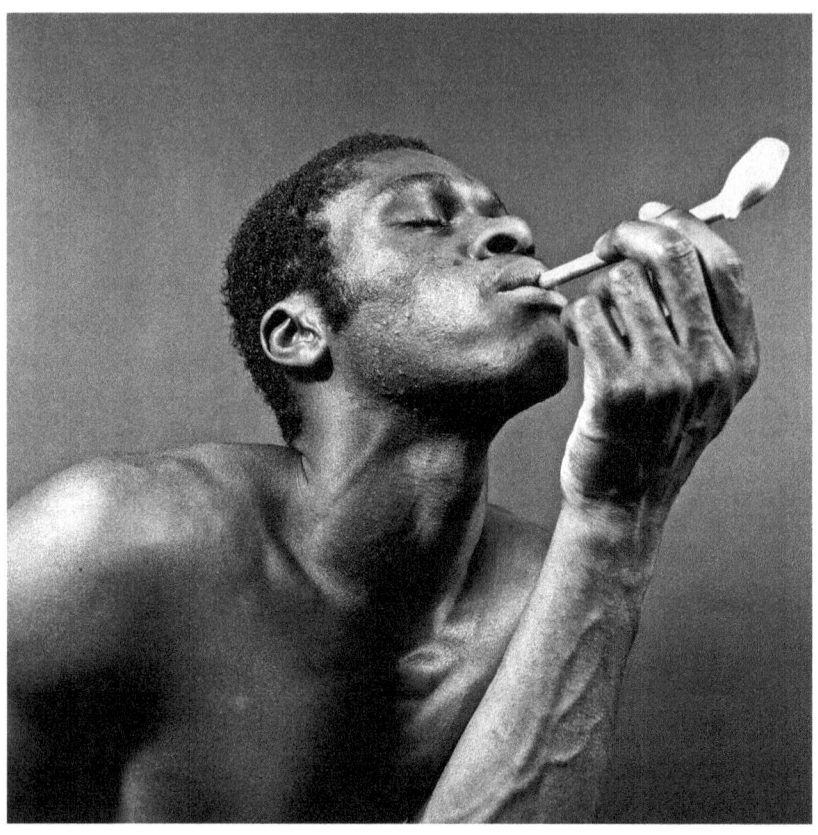

Figure 4.3 Rotimi Fani-Kayode, *Pipe* (1989). © Rotimi Fani-Kayode / Autograph ABP. Courtesy of Autograph ABP.

print (figure 4.5) shows his partner, Alex Hirst, sitting casually in a massive doorway. Geographically, this could be easily be London, the Vatican, or somewhere in between, but the building's age is marked by its weathered stone, heavy construction, and distressed wooden door. Hirst is caught in a candid moment—crew cut and thin mustache, gazing to his left, beyond the frame. His cropped white shirt features a ghoulish form, hairless and skeletal. Despite its contemporaneity, the setting of the aged building paired with the preoccupied young man, seemingly pausing in his course through the streets, calls to mind the memento mori. In a sense, the scene is reminiscent of Nicolas Poussin's 1638 *Et in Arcadia ego*, in which wandering youth are confronted with a stark reminder of death in the foreboding inscription

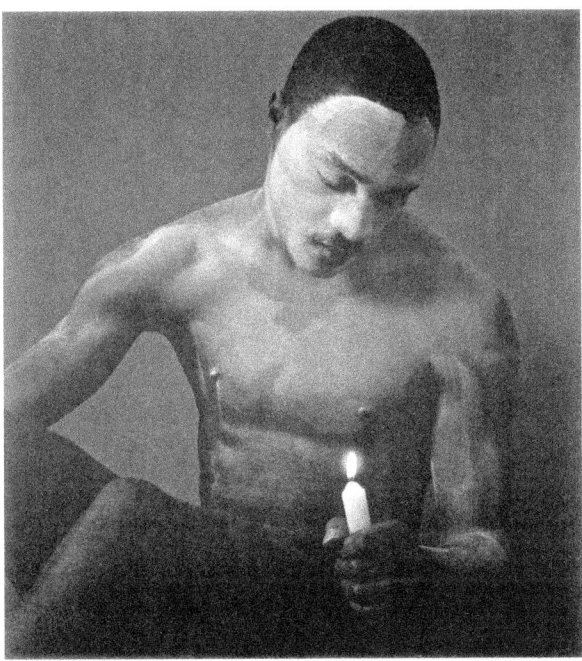

Figure 4.4 Rotimi Fani-Kayode, *Philip* (1987–1988).
© Rotimi Fani-Kayode / Autograph ABP. Courtesy of Autograph ABP.

on a grave marker. One might similarly be reminded, in paging through Fani-Kayode's pictures of transsexual priests amid infinite pools of black, of the great Romantic painter Caspar David Friedrich, whose forays into gothic nostalgia portray moonlit monasteries and graveyards, or the sublime mystery of a monk dwarfed by the sea.

For his part, Alex Hirst closed his reflections on this body of work from 1988–1989 by citing the death of the body as the great source of inspiration, as evidence of life's chaos and mystery. Of doctors and metaphysicists, he notes that they "promise us enlightenment, ecstasy and reintegration with the cosmic purpose. And why not? They beguile us with the notion that love expresses the joyous and tragic sense that the self is not alone. They have hinted that diversity is a necessary aspect of all images of affinity, and that otherness is a variation of sameness. They testify that our ancestors are everywhere. Art and science are ritual."[7] While much of this, and the text from which it is drawn, is plainly Romantic (that is, nostalgic, irrational) in its tone, this last

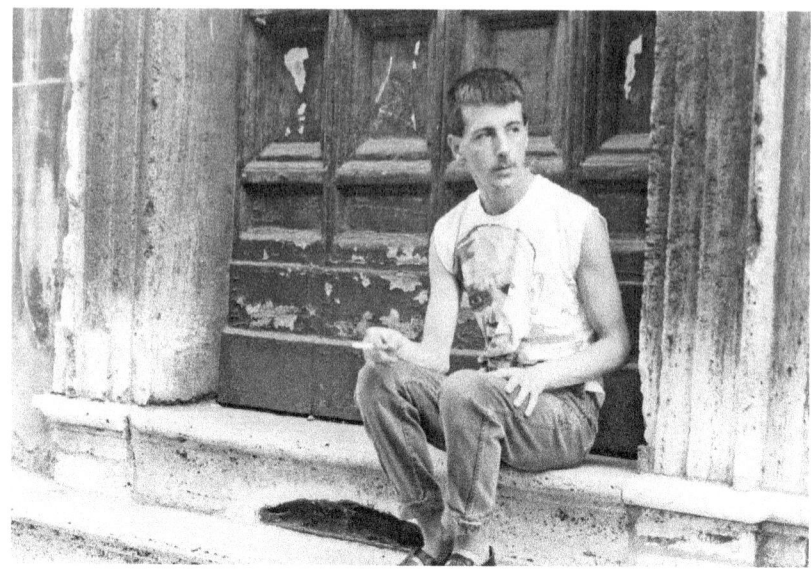

Figure 4.5 Rotimi Fani-Kayode, *Untitled* (*Alex Hirst*) (undated).
© Rotimi Fani-Kayode / Autograph ABP. Courtesy of Autograph ABP.

line is crucial: Hirst proclaims that perhaps even the most measured, the most scientific modes of inquiry are at root not opposed to the metaphysical but are, instead, of a piece with it. But why such a declaration? Why a return to Romanticism on the far side of a modernism that overtly prioritized and valued the rational, the progressive, and the concrete over and against the more visionary and transient concerns that animated the counter-Enlightenment gloom of the early nineteenth century?

STYLE AND DECAY

Romanticism is a term that returns to the critical lexicon time and time again, typically to describe the presence of sincerity or mysticism (forms of belief) in contemporary art. Some veins of the New York vanguard of the 1980s have been called Romantic, with their seeming legions of young people from the suburbs and the middle west alighting on the city, cultivating neobohemias in the blighted shadows of the American dream. Such a formulation suggests both a youthful optimism or a starry-eyed revivalism of a lost past. In the case of the early eighties downtown New York scene that was ascendent during Fani-Kayode's several years there, one could look to the recollections of Ann Magnuson, the tabloid *People*'s "funny girl of the avant-garde" in 1985. She described life in the East Village and Lower East Side as "having just enough to get by and never wanting more. Living for the moment. Doing nothing, trying everything. Hanging out with your artist friends with no timetable, no pressure, no agendas.... Pretending you weren't a debauchee as long as you got home before sunrise.... Not giving a fuck about the *New York Times* or anything above 14th Street."[8] Magnuson's words capture a yearning for a certain kind of artistic life—one that draws on the Parisian or Berliner demimondes of yore. But beyond the more youthful (or cynical) forms of *romanticizing* one's own life that she describes, one might also consider Romanticism *as such* a discrete set of stylistic or iconographic conventions, and a more generalized resistance to linear or positivist accounts of time, experience, and meaning. Romanticism as an outlook and method manifested in eighties New York through experiments with repetition and duration that emerged initially in West Coast performance and film, afterhours "clubism,"[9] and investigations of "sublime time" in the after-midnight East Village landscape. Here, the history of the avant-garde and its spirit of rupture was self-consciously reignited as a viable method rather than a lost artifact.[10]

Across the Atlantic and during roughly the same moment—from 1979 to 1982—Neoromanticism had emerged as a defined style, particularly in the realms of music and fashion, which were notable for their fusion of rococo dress, non-European rhythmic patterns, and postpunk synthesizers. Consider, for instance, Adam and the Ants (1977–1982), who presented themselves as latter day buccaneers (albeit with garish makeup) but also drew on "world music" such as Burundi drums.[11] These several years also marked the emergence of The Cure into the mainstream; their records channeled early nineteenth-century literature and travelogue, with a synthesis of pathos and exoticism. 1979's "Fire in Cairo" ("The dying sun / Night-time follows / Silence and black / Mirror pool mirrors / The lonely place / Where I meet you / And burn / Like fire / Burn like fire in Cairo) conjures, by turn, mystery and eroticism, the sonic equivalent of a stanza of Coleridge or the orientalist tableaux of Jean Gérôme.

Similarly, Malcolm McLaren's project Bow Wow Wow—famed for their hit "I Want Candy"—embodied a stylistic catholicism that gleefully blended Native American caricature, punk hair, modernist gesture, and late eighteenth-century excess. The cover of their 1982 EP *The Last of the Mohicans* (which included the track "Louis Quatorze") featured members of the band dressed with dandyish flair, with singer Annabella Lwin crouched and nude. The scene is a Neoromantic riff on Édouard Manet's 1863 *Le dejeuner sur l'herbe*, which marked Manet's upending of the propriety of the French academic system and its annual Salon. Just as the Manet was scandalous for its vulgar, realist appropriation of canonical European painting, the album cover was shocking in its own ways—the pubescence of the unclothed singer and the calculation of McLaren, who sold his own line with Vivienne Westwood of "Neoromantic" clothes.[12]

The *Evening Standard* editor David Johnson recalls the galvanic force that the New Romantic mode would have on British urban life during the transitional period between the so-called Winter of Discontent that typified the years of austerity and privation during the late 1970s and the Thatcherite boom years of the latter half of the 1980s. Johnson locates the roots of New Romanticism in a scene that coalesced in 1979 around London's Covent Garden area at the archly named club Blitz. This party in a "shabby wine bar" became a weekly site where "precocious 19-year-olds presented an eye-popping collage, posing away in wondrous ensembles, emphatic makeup, and in-flight haircuts that made you feel normality was a sin . . . lads in breeches and frilly shirts, white stockings and pumps, girls as Left Bank whores or stiletto-heeled vamps dressed for cocktails in a Berlin cabaret, wicked witches, kohl-eyed ghouls, futuristic man machines."[13] The "Blitz kids" that set the contours of a Neoromantic revival during the ensuing several years relied on forms of pastiche and nostalgic mimicry, to be sure, but its ranks—drawn from art schools and a broad and disillusioned lower-middle class—also responded to the dual currents of the corporatization of popular music and the persistent unemployment the pervaded postwar British life.

While the growing pains of neoliberalism were felt in much of the world during those crucial years in the late 1970s, the fallout of deindustrialization and the end of empire marked a definitive blow the British psyche, leading to an atmosphere of lapsarian decay, especially outside of London. While such a sensibility may be difficult to measure, it was crystallized in the gothic tones of the era's youth culture. To take one example, the iconically downcast Smiths singer Morrissey, who penned songs such as "Cemetery Gates" and "Vicar in a Tutu," vividly recounted the 1970s of his childhood. He recalls living in "forgotten Victorian knife-plunging Manchester, where everything lies wherever it was left over one hundred years ago. . . . Past places of dread, we walk in the center of the road, looking up at the torn wallpapers of browny black and purples as the mournful remains of derelict shoulder-to-shoulder houses, the safety now replaced by trepidation."[14] Similarly, the photographer Craigie Horsfield worked contemporaneously with Fani-Kayode, snapping nude pictures of his wife in the East End of London, a place of working-class destitution that seems to have never recovered from the war.[15] His process was to delay the printing of his negatives, soaring them away like a time capsule, to enhance their uncanny effect as missives from another time. According to Johnson, amid this backdrop, bands that emerged from Blitz, such as Spandau Ballet, thus took on a specifically Baudelairian cast, serving not to forge new revolutionary pathways but "to trap the present . . . express the aspirations of society as it is, not as others would wish."[16]

As a first wave of New Romantic stylistic and sonic cues, the members of Spandau Ballet were known as the "Angel Boys"; in this light, one might think back to Rotimi Fani-Kayode's own *White Angel* pictures, which decidedly enact a homoerotic Camp but also echo rather explicitly the gender fluidity and rococo pomp of Neoromanticism—forged in post-Labour London but by then a diffused and widely imitated aesthetic of its own. Considering the specific London-based queer codes through which Fani-Kayode developed his own aesthetic—namely, the Neoclassically infused, high-minded theatricality that typified the work of Derek Jarman—his photographs undoubtedly responded to the particular confluence of goth and glam, ethereal and effete staked out by the Blitz kids while he studied in New York.

The photographer Graham Smith, a key documentarian of the turn-of-the-decade underground, for example, frames Blitz's promoter, Steve Strange (with rosy cheeks and stovepipe hat), riding a Ferris wheel with Spandau Ballet's Martin Kemp, amid shirtless onlookers at Andrew Logan's Alternative Miss World pageant in 1981. Another picture from 1980—*Myra and Michele Clapton at Stephen Linard's Neo Gothic Fashion Show at St. Martins* (figure 4.6)—shows two vampiric figures, heads shaved and cigarettes dangling from their mouths. They don elaborate eyeliner and oversized earrings and, draped in corded monastic vestments, they are dead ringers for the central figure in Fani-Kayode's *Under the Surplice* (figure 3.3). The figure on the left's headgear, fashioned of cruciformed lace, foreshadows a similar halo situated above a red-cassocked initiate, executed in vibrant color for a series in 1989 that would later be dubbed *Communion*.

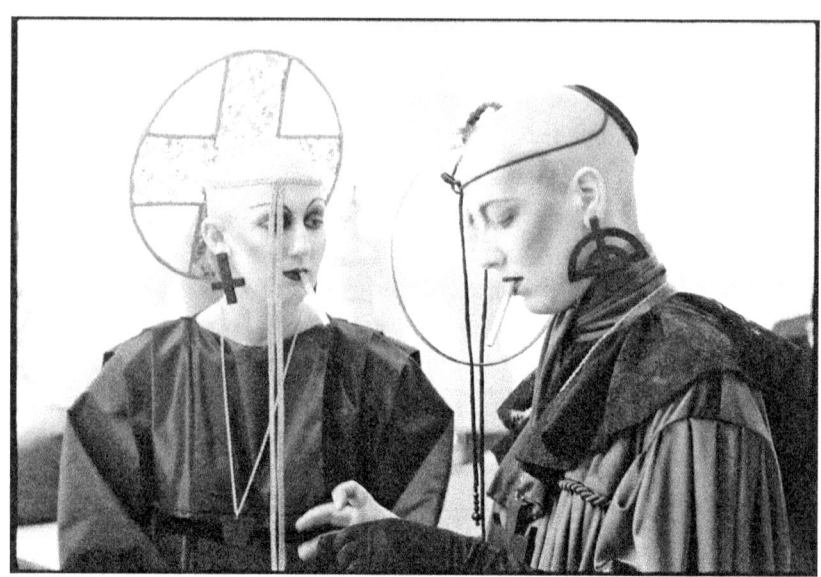

Figure 4.6 Graham Smith, *Myra and Michele Clapton at Stephen Linard's Neo-Gothic Fashion Show at St. Martins* (1980). © Graham Smith. Courtesy of the artist.

These are stylistic connections, to be sure, the celebratory excesses of urban youth culture. But for all of the faddishness and pastiche implied in "Neo-romanticism," the resurgence of the Romantic had its roots in deeper currents within British cultural practice, indeed had been a leitmotif within its art and literature for some time. One might think back to the mysticism of William Blake and the moody detective serials of Arthur Conan Doyle; to the seventies rock band Black Sabbath or the Mancunian photographer Martin Parr. Both Sabbath and Parr emerged from the Midlands of Birmingham and Manchester, respectively—cities in rapid postindustrial decline. Accordingly, Black Sabbath (founded 1968) pioneered a dark and brooding blues music that set the stage for the emergence of heavy metal. Parr, for his part, took seemingly quotidian documentary photographs—snapshots—that revealed cities in states of dereliction seen in the housing blocks, factories, and boarded-up pubs in his *England, Liverpool* (1983–1986). This larger series is at once starkly prosaic in its framing of contemporary ruins and rendered otherworldly though jarring angles and careful use of flash and ambient lighting.[17]

Running parallel to this history is the painting of two of England's most celebrated artists, the portraitists Lucien Freud and Francis Bacon. Outliers from the abstract formalist imperatives of postwar modernism, each blended expressive brushstroke and dark palettes to generate a haunting figuration indebted to the lineage of Romanticism. Bacon's *Triptych—August 1972*, for example, is a three-panel study in the decomposition of a bruised and disfigured body. It is at once homoerotic and elegiac, a scene of struggle and transfiguration set against a black void, apparently made in response to the suicide of Bacon's lover, George Dyer.[18] Bacon also provided an example not of a break but of the continuity in British art of the dark registers of classical and Baroque motifs—Cimabue's thirteenth-century crucifixes or Diego Velasquez's portrait of Pope Innocent X (1650).[19] Ultimately, such British variations of Romanticism would have been ambient for Fani-Kayode, living in England during his adolescence in the early years of the 1970s, and returning for good in 1983. The Bacon triptych, in particular, was acquired by the Tate Britain in 1980; this and other Bacons likely hung in the gallery, just across the Thames from Fani-Kayode's studio in South London. He would have been well-acquainted with such dark figuration and, in his refusal of abstract or conceptual approaches in favor of portraiture and aesthetics, or his distortions and appropriations of the Baroque, he was not only Bacon's contemporary but a kind of kindred spirit.

During the last several years of his life, Fani-Kayode increasingly turned away from the more frenetic or erotic registers of his early work and began to connect the balance of spiritual gravity and performative activation typical of Yoruban art with a host of transcultural equivalents. To this end, alongside the black leather-clad nocturnal denizens or nude lovers, he began to depict figures in the guise of initiates: priest, ritual practitioners, followers of secret societies. His depictions of "black friars" in 1988 and 1989, for instance, draw together the imagery found in Graham's depictions of the Blitz kids and Bacon's purple-clad popes. *Grapes* (1989; figure 4.7) shows a figure from the side, his face hidden by a cascade of tight dreadlocks which are, in turn, covered by draped purple fabric.

This regal priest, not Rastafarian per se, but presumably not Christian, signifies royalty both in his garb and in the veiling of his features: in Yoruban tradition, a king wears a conical crown with beaded strands, protecting his subjects from the intensity of his gaze, from the resonant spiritual energy that relays between multiple worlds. But then, he also looks on a bundle of the picture's titular white grapes, a call to a classical lineage of the Dionysian, the rites of spiritual communion alluded to in Caravaggio's 1595 *Bacchus* (figure 4.8).

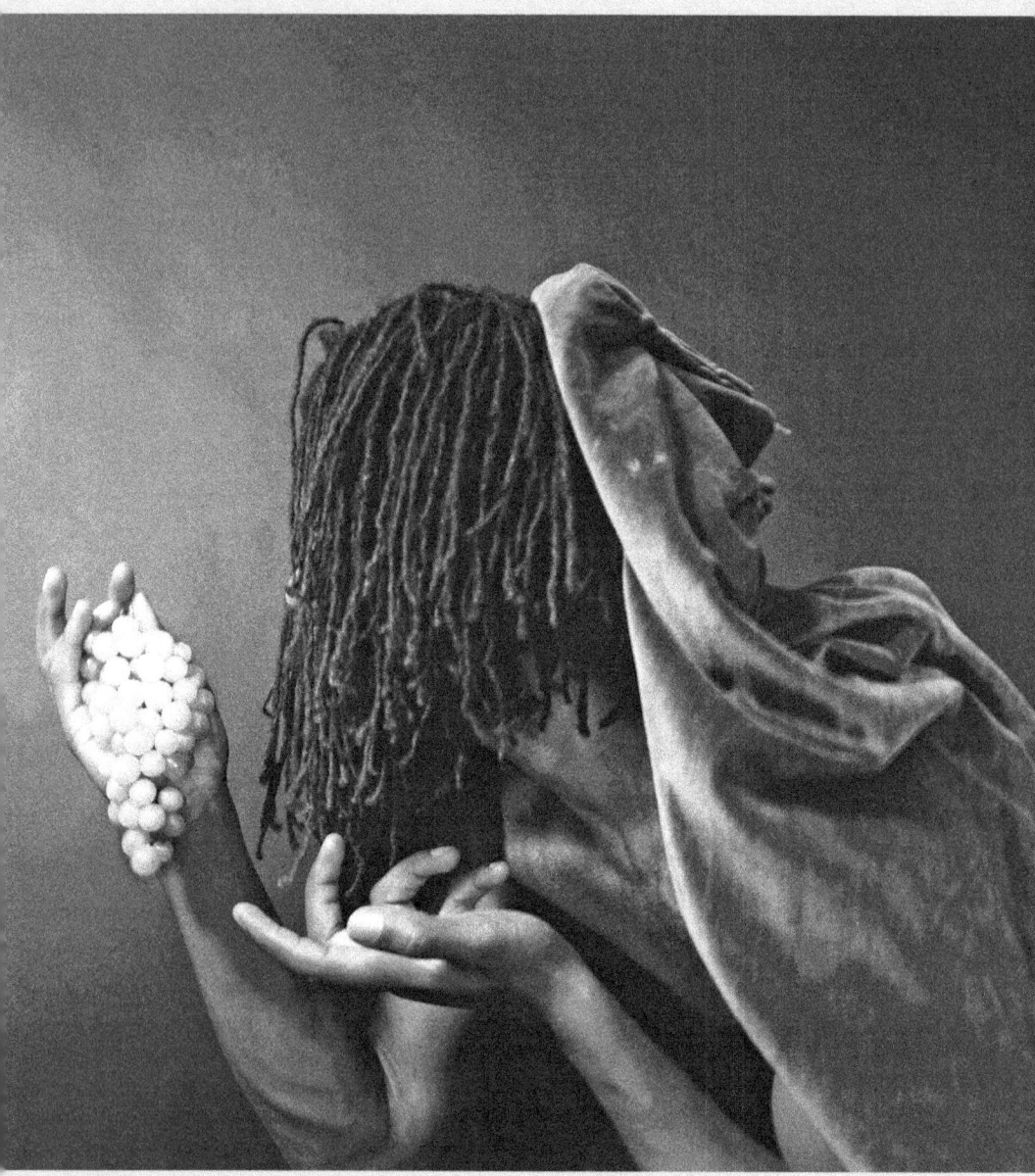

Figure 4.7 Rotimi Fani-Kayode, *Grapes* (1989). © Rotimi Fani-Kayode /
Autograph ABP. Courtesy of Autograph ABP.

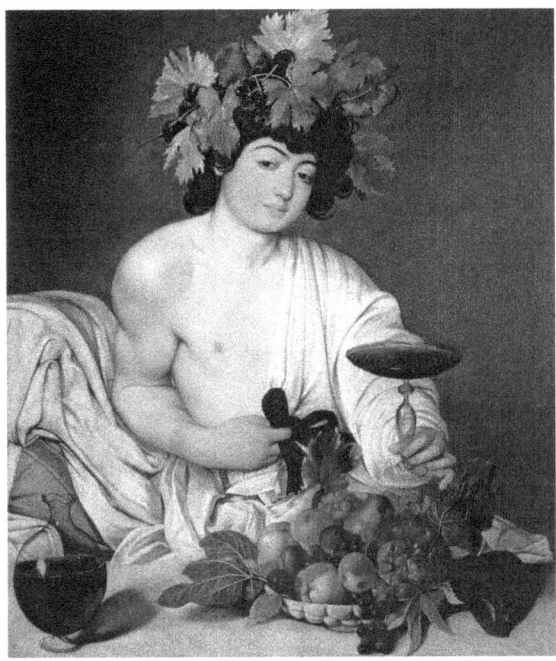

Figure 4.8 Michelangelo Merisi da Caravaggio, *Bacchus* (1595).

The fulsome wine vessel in that painting was a recurrent prop in other Fani-Kayode pictures from this period, which balance a bird mask atop a similar jar, connecting two strategies that blur the supernatural and the imminent—divine knowledge and ritualistic bacchanal. Caravaggio had rendered himself as the *Bacchino malato* a year earlier, countenancing a similar stem of grapes. And Cindy Sherman famously updated that self-portrait in her own *Untiled #224* of 1990. But while Sherman shared with Fani-Kayode an interest in confounding the stability of a sitter's identity in the play of humorous performance and masquerade, they seem to have their eyes set on different targets. Where Sherman genealogically contests the primacy of Neoclassical aesthetics that had reappeared as a sign of genius in the 1980s, there is a sense in *Grapes* of alighting on the black friar *in media res*. Fani-Kayode was not invoking signifiers of the Dionysian or of Romantic priests among sepulchers. He was trying to reactivate a long-buried technology.

Romanticism is a pliable and evocative rubric, put to various uses by the avant-garde scenes of New York and London during the long 1980s. But Romanticism also helps to specify the motifs and methods that unify Rotimi Fani-Kayode's entire oeuvre. In the most obvious terms, he pictures literal romances—embracing nudes, subtle homoeroticism, lush tableaux, and haunted rooms. But he also employs a more generalized romanticism—that of elective affiliation or longing from afar. Fani-Kayode, like so many others young artists and writers of the time, located himself in the ruins of industrial capitalism, reliving or rekindling the sentiment of earlier bohemias and avant-gardes.

Such connections carry with them a hint of the pejorative, of inauthentic distance or innocent exuberance. And it is true that Fani-Kayode began his career during the advent of New Romanticism as a self-conscious style. Kobena Mercer has gone as far as to define his "singular" output as "Neo-Romantic, Afro-Atlantic."[20] This formulation leaves Fani-Kayode and many of those working concurrently with him suspended in a purgatory of undefined belatedness or anachronism. I would argue instead that Romanticism has long constituted a persistent and dissonant counterpoint within modernity and its various cultural formations. Fani-Kayode activated this lineage to develop his "technique of ecstasy." It also provided him with temporal method that both complemented and resisted the then-pervasive binaries of artistic modernism/postmodernism. This is what Hirst called their "transhistorical" method.

One of the very challenges of theorizing Romanticism is that it has never fully been codified, operating instead as a roving, oppositional force to many of the imperatives of the early 1800s. As the intellectual historian Isaiah Berlin has famously argued, on the one hand Romanticism has clear forebears and progenitors in the nineteenth century, and it was quite evidently constituted as a reaction to the Enlightenment project (i.e., Euro-American modernity). But it was, on the other hand, necessarily *not* a unified movement. As such, Berlin cites nearly a hundred instances of Romanticist preoccupations, a mosaic that includes: "the primitive . . . youth, life . . . fever, disease, decadence . . . Death itself . . . the white radiance of eternity . . . dissolution in the eternal all-containing spirit. It is the strange, the exotic, the grotesque, the mysterious, the supernatural, ruins, moonlight . . . the ancient, the historic . . . joy in the passing instant, a sense of timelessness. . . . It is nostalgia, it is reverie, it is intoxicating dreams, it is sweet melancholy and bitter melancholy."[21]

The Romantics are remembered as wandering young men, deracinated by the increasing cosmopolitanism of their age.[22] They believed, according to the art historian Marsha Morton, that knowledge and understanding "were acquired not from a mastery of facts, but through imagination and revelation, and they chose to convey meaning through symbols, allegories, and hieroglyphs, referents that are indirect and endlessly suggestive."[23] The subject matter, for these followers of Albrecht Dürer and Friedrich Schlegel, was distant from everyday life—gloomy, and "stamped with the remains of past cultures"—in short, gothic. In its then-contemporary theorization by Schlegel, Romanticism was a state of "eternally becoming . . . exhausted by no theory. . . . It alone is infinite just as it alone is free."[24]

In the early moments of Romanticism, then, one finds an antipode to modernity and a conflict within the roots of modernism itself. The modernist strain that adapted the atheistic rationalism that Romanticism rejects—and that is (ironically) consolidated in postmodernism's sterilized posthistoricism[25]—is thus called into question. In Romanticism, one sees the tensions between the Enlightenment project and its darker, oft-repressed others: the unconscious, metaphysics, unshakable forces that blur past and present.[26] The spirit that undergirded Romanticism was, therefore, an incarnation of a counterculture of modernity—and as a twin shadow within modernism, its underlying *pulse* would resonate in different guises for decades to come. American detective fiction, the poetry of Arthur Rimbaud or Isidore Ducasse, the primitivist fantasias of postimpressionism, occultist Victorian mysticism, and the transatlantic exchange that was "pictorialist" photography in the 1890s all constitute such moments.[27]

It was against this backdrop that, in 1987, Alex Hirst drafted the opening passage of Fani-Kayode's collection *Black Male/White Male*. Here he provides a trove of poetic references that help clarify Fani-Kayode's intent for the pictures that follow. Of *Black Male/White Male*, he says that we "may perceive in it a certain tragic freedom in the grand manner, where the pre-modern collides with the post-modern for a few moments of bewildering intimacy."[28] Hirst's disclaimer certainly describes the "collisions" at the heart of the book, but he is also describing the larger arc of Fani-Kayode's practice, a photographer not bound by a single temporality or identity. He was an artist who reached back to traditions that had lost either their viability or their cachet over the decades,[29] and who was freed by a postmodernist catholicism around image making that defined the art world of his adult life.

In this brief passage, Hirst also recasts a relationship to time itself: if modernism (and modernity in general) works dialectically, in the direction of progress, then his and Fani-Kayode's orienting the viewer back to the past is already an act of transgression—to do so as a "collision" of traditions and chronologies in one room or one frame upends the very linearity that had largely defined life since the Enlightenment. And this is where Fani-Kayode might have picked up the psychic dissonances that prefigured Romanticism, not as an arch reference but as a genuine method, an iteration of a spirit that kept returning as the avant-garde, time and time again. Writing of the New Romantics, Johnson recalled that Steve Strange wanted club nights not to be places of passive consumption but places of transformation where participants could, in David Bowie's words, be "heroes for one day," and where the weekly gatherings were "shrouded in ritual."[30] That is, New Romanticism signaled an exhaustion with the left-politics of the day and also with mediated or staid modes of self-expression. They thus turned back to forms of ritual or of utopian communion, and to the sartorial gestures of the dandy or after-hours occultism, seeking worlds beyond the humdrum towns of quotidian British life.

That the earlier Romantics themselves (and later, many surrealists) centered their energies on motifs of the gothic was, indeed, prescient: their paintings and poems elaborated metaphors of haunting and suggested the return of what cannot be fully repressed. In this sense, the photograph can function much like the tell-tale heart of the 1843 Edgar Allan Poe story of the same name, where hidden aspects of individual or collective histories always return, unbidden, seeking acknowledgement or resolution.[31] Hirst and Fani-Kayode would in turn come to describe their own practice in relation to the landscape of the 1980s as offering some "points of faith and light among the many blind alleys of this century's cynical and doomed Byzantium."[32]

To specify the modes, motifs, and methods that reemerged in the work of Fani-Kayode and his contemporaries, then, one could point to three common threads—all of which echo Romantic currents and many episodes in between. The first is the power of the object itself: to conjure the past, to exude aura, to operate beyond the material or the semiotic. A second is a return of gothic or supernatural modes. Of course, those familiar with the study of African art will already recognize the uneasy relationship between the ghostly as a meta-phor or aesthetic, and as an actual field of metaphysical belief, as well as the ways in which diaspora traditions are coupled with these modes.[33] Vital histories and literature of the Atlantic slave trade frequently invoke haunting, of a past barely concealed but still unreconciled, and the historian David Marriot goes so far as to argue that black life can be interpreted "as the work of death, a work born of fidelity to death, but without transcendence." Writing of both visual culture and political violence, he cites the theorist Achille Mbembe: "the dead are not even corpses, but 'simple relics of an unburied pain, empty, meaningless corporealities, strange deposits plunged into cruel stupor.'"[34]

In looking back across the Atlantic to the African continent, there are many examples of art being used to access spiritual realms and liminal states,[35] with photography specifically employed as a tool to create metonymic images—much as in Victorian Europe it was thought to record the supernatural, beyond our field of vision.[36] But the gothic and auratic were also present in the popular culture of London, too, exemplified by Salman Rushdie's pantheon of spirits and demons, or Haruki Murakami's refinement of the metaphysical noir. Sonically and sartorially, of course, punk music and the postpunk and metal subcultures that typified the urban demimonde of the eighties came to be synonymous with the contemporary gothic. Think black motorcycle jackets, safety-pinned denim, and youthful bands such as Siouxsie and the Banshees, Sisters of Mercy, Bauhaus, The Birthday Party, Depeche Mode, and many others, all of whose dark iconography mirrored a sense in their often-elegiac music of living out of place, in decadent end times. Mercer himself even nods in this direction: in a signal essay on Fani-Kayode, he titles a sub-heading "Communion: Love Will Tear Us Apart," a nod to the famed 1980 song by Joy Division also inscribed on the tombstone of the band's front man, Ian Curtis, who died at 23.

And if the auratic object and the return of the gothic constitute two well-springs for Fani-Kayode, one can add a third inheritance—a nonlinear conception of time. For surrealism, nonlinear frames were the province of the dreamlife and altered states; in diaspora studies it is sometimes called spectral time.[37] For the Romantics, temporal slippage constituted much of the appeal of the gothic, not as motif of style, but as a means of countering the positivist and progressive flows of Enlightenment subjectivity.[38] For them, the gothic functioned in two ways: as a form of uncanniness, an acknowledgment that time rarely flows in one direction, that the past is always present, ready to rupture into—to haunt—our quotidian lives;[39] and in the more mnemonic and personal register of nostalgia.

Writing of Novalis, Berlin argued that such Romantic nostalgia "is due to the fact that, since the infinite cannot be exhausted, and since we are seeking to embrace it, nothing that will do will ever satisfy us. . . . Stories which are symbolic or allegorical or contain all kinds of mystical or veiled references, esoteric imagery . . . are all attempts to go back, to go home to what is pulling and drawing him."[40] Romanticism, then, is a kind of quest for what might never be attained, and the artist's attempt to return self and viewer to another place or time. For the Romantics, consolation might be found in misty mountains or pre-Renaissance churches; for Fani-Kayode and his peers it was allegory, the exile's half-remembrances of home, or the nocturnal ruins of the postindustrial city that would have to suffice.

In this light, it is easier to understand, for example, the emergence in the New York downtown or London and Manchester scenes of artists and musicians who took their cues less from contemporary visions of an emergent "cool," hypermediated, or cybernetic world but, instead, dug deep into to the sedimentary layers of the early modernist and counterformalist traditions.[41] Hence Patti Smith, riffing on nineteenth-century poetry; David Wojnarowicz taking portraits of himself after dark, posed as a latter-day Rimbaud; the poet-critic Rene Ricard writing his incandescent paean to a young Jean-Michel Basquiat in a 1981 piece for *Artforum*, which invoked a rogue's gallery of self-made or marginal geniuses, from Caravaggio to the graffitistes of the South Bronx, and the "radiant child" cocooned within each.[42]

This is the return of the roving flaneur, or his prototype in the suffering solitary hero; this is what Berlin identified as an unbridled passion and self-immolating energy that counterbalanced the anesthetizing rationality of modern life but was tempered by the wistful certainty that tomorrow will never come. This is what Alex Hirst meant when he spoke of the "tragic freedom" that viewers would recognize in Fani-Kayode's pictures: not contemporaneity so much as an awareness that time was fleeting; that, in their words, every moment counted.

Each of these Romantic inheritances—the gothic, auratic, and uncanny—are all evident in a collaborative film project with Reece Auguiste and the Black Audio Film Collective. Like Fani-Kayode and Hirst, BAFC seemed to recognize that for all of the go-go spirit and neoliberal excess that typified much of the discourse of Britishness at the time, for many, England itself could be conceived as a place of ruination, dogged by lingering spirits—of empire, of industrial life, of a vibrant middle class, of closely knit communal relations. Whether such things existed at all, in the years following a decade of fuel shortages and rationing of the 1970s, skepticism of the Labour governing agenda, and the victory of the Conservatives in 1979, many saw monuments of failed promise as they walked the streets of a Midlands in decline. They saw their forgotten communities threatened by the new imperium of international finance and its relentless procedures of gentrification and dislocation.[43]

Against such a backdrop, Fani-Kayode's somber but beautiful portraits might be read as a form of indulgence, especially in comparison to the grittier, more research-driven productions of the BAFC.[44] And just as *Handsworth Songs* used montage and archive to deconstruct the uprisings of the early 1980s and their attendant discourses, BAFC's 1987 film *Twilight City* centers on London's Docklands, the river on which it rests, and its remaking during the final years of the decade into a plaza of corporate skyscrapers amid the working-class Tower Hamlets.[45] *Twilight City* is an epistolary sequence, a montage, a documentary. BAFC reclaims here two narratives appropriated in Thatcherite discourse, of the gutting of the labor class and the presence—the very Britishness—of postcolonial subjects.

Yet Fani-Kayode is here, too. He was not part of the collective, but he was a friend and fellow traveler. To the group's sonic-filmic montage approach, he provided a recurring lyrical counterpoint—an errant in the mix. In *Twilight City* one sees several of his black-and-white photographs brought to life in brief sequences, of a man drinking milk from a gourd, or long tracking shots of several still images. He is not interviewed alongside Homi Bhabha and Paul Gilroy. Instead, photographs alone are interspersed, as moments of nocturnal mystery periodically rupturing the flow of the film. Fani-Kayode is never introduced by name, but a moving image of one of his figures (a man with a powdered face, holding a flickering candle—Philip, again) appears as the narrator writes to her mother in Dominica, "you say you hope I haven't joined the city's lost souls; those who shuffle in the shadows, always waiting for the darkness to melt the autumn evening light. You ask if the winter evenings still last forever: yes they do. And as the old London dissolves, your lost souls are becoming more visible." Fani-Kayode, too, was a lost soul, a bearer of gothic and Yoruban esoterica, but one who figured other lost souls and the ghosts of empire not yet departed.

In practice, BAFC's method here is diagnostic but also uncanny in its play of history, an approach that Jean Fisher—drawing on Walter Benjamin—has interpreted as dialogic, using temporal collision in order to disrupt narratives of linear progress, to resituate the present in terms of a haunted past, of earlier traumas.[46] The collective's John Akomfrah recalled of Fani-Kayode's role in the film that the latter had wanted to move his practice into new terrain, to expand ongoing investigations into a new lens-based register, working closely with Akomfrah and Reece Auguiste to prepare the scenes. "A lot of what happened during that week in the studio was to use his photographs as a point of departure, because we knew the final piece would end up a mixture of what we had created, which were always kind of acts of homage to his work. The idea was to make sure people could see the coexistence of those two things." And crucially, at a time when both the BAFC and Fani-Kayode had clear ambitions for their work but worked in relative anonymity, "he, as much as us, was interested in seeing how the work could circulate in different ways. . . . If you could make some money, devising scenarios like Derek Jarman, he was happy to go down that route. Jarman was important to him . . . so it was a space that everyone was in conversation on for that film."[47]

Fani-Kayode's larger arc, too, can be framed in similar terms. One clear example in which Fani-Kayode enacts such a "dialectic image" is *Cargo of Middle Passage* (figure 4.9). Understood in the American context, this print might suggest memorial, a pointed rephrasing of an elemental strand of national history. But in the Britain of the 1980s the connections would have been less obvious, but no less powerful. The picture, seen there, would subtly reactivate a history in which the Atlantic trade is not a story of the Americas but one that goes back to the foundation of Britishness itself at the dawn of the eighteenth century: a trade that links the former Gold Coast slave port at Elmina to the entrepôts of Liverpool, London, and Kingston; a trade depicted in the Romantic seascapes of J. M. W. Turner.[48]

Cargo's single subject, reduced to mere commodity, functions metonymically, conjuring the larger system of chattel slavery and its dehumanizing pro-

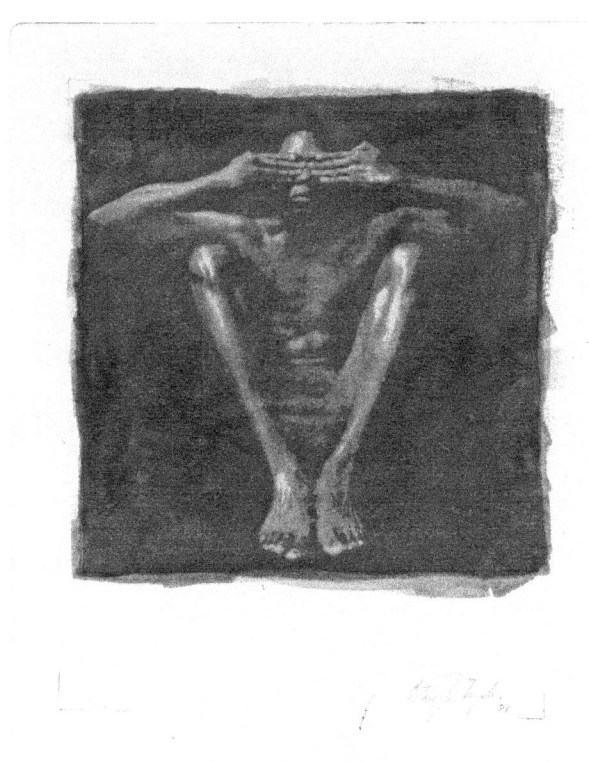

Figure 4.9 Rotimi Fani-Kayode, *Cargo of Middle Passage* (1989).
© Rotimi Fani-Kayode / Autograph ABP. Courtesy of Autograph ABP.

tocols that made such a transformation possible. But this is also an uncanny object: Fani-Kayode uses the antique surfaces of the gum bichromate print to dislodge memories of distant temporal shores, to channel a trauma from the fog of history and awaken it in the present. What *Cargo* lacks in exegesis, it provides in evocative parsimony amplified in no small part by its *aura*, its dense materiality and ethereal tone.

In this light, Fani-Kayode and the BAFC can be seen as working to similar ends using complementary modes, different registers of visuality and encounter. As the Otolith Group's Kodwo Eshun has argued, BAFC's films resuscitated the "'historical presentness' of . . . images and simultaneously mourned their passing; its dual quality of summoning up the archive while laying it to rest imbued [*Handsworth Songs*] with a 'mournful angelic quality.'"[49] Such effects were reliant on variation in the flow of temporality in many of the films, notably in the recurrence of tableaux as counterpoints within the narrative, including when in "*Twilight City*, Auguiste staged the high-contrast black-and-white photography of Rotimi Fani-Kayode's *The Milk Drinker* (1986) and *The Fish Vendors* (1988) as *tableaux vivants*. In a darkened void, male figures posed in a gestural vocabulary nuanced by Christian themes of supplication complicated by the language of homoerotic encounter."[50]

For Eshun, the impact of the tableau—in *Twilight City* and elsewhere—is that it "not only halted narrative; it allowed for a reflexive hiatus in which the camera staged an encounter between the film frame, the limits of photography and the form of history painting."[51] And, so, while their approaches may initially seem disparate both Fani-Kayode and BAFC aimed, in those late years of the 1980s, to challenge the boundaries of nation, most notably through practices that worked to complicate accepted histories while reanimating others, and staging disruptive breaks within their own medium (the reflective hiatus within the filmic, or the visual pulsations and syncretic translations within the photographic).

ROMANCE AND DIASPORA

Ultimately, Romanticism in all of its forms constitutes a kind of longing—for histories more stirring than one's own, for a world that is not disenchanted by modernity, a life in which one is, in Bacon's terms, not outside of tradition but of a piece with one. Living in an age of unfettered capital, the threat of nuclear catastrophe, and the attenuation of the radical politics of earlier decades, some may have seen Romanticism as a form of withdrawal or wishful thinking. But it might also mark a tactical shift, a return to methods that punctuated and short-circuited modernity from its very inception, which in their varied iterations produced provisional locations of revision and revelation. According to Hirst, through Fani-Kayode's pictures the viewer is able to perceive seemingly disparate places and times as contiguous. Here, "Europe is an old dream. Young leather boys stalk through the ruins of its splendour, wielding whips and talking dirty. . . . Effete natives try to grow moustaches. Disillusioned immigrants rock themselves to sleep and dream of uprisings. Goethe writes *Faust*."[52]

For those "disillusioned immigrants" in particular, Romanticism suggests not just temporal dreams but spatial ones, too—memories from the fragile years of early childhood, of distant shores, the homes of one's parents or grandparents. While it is clear that Fani-Kayode did indeed make his way back to Africa after finishing graduate school—he had a show at the B&J Gallery, Lagos, in 1985 and took pictures of Togolese fishermen around this time—for him the Lagos of his childhood was, like Europe or America, a point on an elusive map, deeply held but suspended just beyond a veil, a seemingly impossible psychic passage. More broadly, such physical and temporal distances are the roots of what Paul Gilroy has called "romantic Afrocentrism," of black subjects in the Americas identifying with traditions held on the far side of the Atlantic. And "diasporic time," as Tobias Wofford has argued, relies on anamnesis, a mode of resistance to post-Enlightenment accounts of time that conjoin an imagined or idealized past with a desire to enact a more utopian future.[53]

Perhaps for this reason the historian Steven Nelson has argued that in the writing of Fani-Kayode, Hirst, and Kobena Mercer, "Africa, particularly things Yoruba, are romanticized and given a nostalgic gloss." For Nelson, this "romantic Africa" works on two levels—allowing Fani-Kayode to play out a "Freudian family romance," addressing feelings of exilic loss and abandonment through transgression of typically African forms, and also providing a means of transcending his own marginalization, his liminal position as a black, queer artist working in the 1980s.[54]

This ambivalent distance (this chasm, in Nelson's words) between past and present, here and there, marks Fani-Kayode's practice, too, as diasporic. Diasporic "not as end product, but a tool to be used among other tools," freeing the pictured subjects from the constraints of the body and the immanent world—a mode of "undoing, destabilization, and deconstruction."[55] And so, Romanticism, like the liminality of diaspora itself, supposes a kind of distance, in the parallax of vision, the imaginative unmooring, and the transgressive desire it produces. Which is to say that this confluence of diasporic longing and Romantic longing cannot be written off as the performative intensity of youth. Instead, Fani-Kayode found congruent pathways into different forms of futurity—ways of reenchanting the world in opposition to the tired pathways that had defined modernist painting and photography or their hypermediated successors of the early 1980s.

As Fani-Kayode recalls, his early education in Nigeria was a Christian one, taught in English "as though the language and culture of my own people, the Yoruba, were inadequate or in some way unsuitable." While he rediscovered

Africa from afar, he did so not as a political gesture, an affinity or signification of a past disrupted centuries earlier by the Atlantic trade. For Fani-Kayode, Yoruban cosmology felt close to hand, reverberating just below the surface of an unseen metaphysical membrane: to reaccess this cosmology was validating and allowed him to "see parallels now between my own work and that of the Osogbo artists in Yorubaland, who themselves have resisted the cultural subversions of neocolonialism and who celebrate the rich secret world of our ancestors."[56]

And so, Fani-Kayode certainly relied on neo-avant-garde or critically postmodernist approaches such as appropriation, ironic citation, and an insistence on the multiaccentuality of signs in order to, as Mercer has argued, cut into and resist the "master codes" of art history and hegemonic cultural formations.[57] In this way he contributed to a genealogical form of interrogating a shared history of an always already cosmopolitan modernity. But in the case of some of modernity's countercurrents—such as Romanticism and its successors in global surrealism or the gothic resurgence of the 1980s—a semiotic reading is insufficient. Fani-Kayode was not simply, in Abigail Solomou-Godeau's terms, "playing in the field of the image,"[58] not simply documenting the world or manipulating its myriad signifiers. He was looking beyond the here and now, attempting to find pathways to realities yet to come. As Hirst noted several years after Fani-Kayode's death, "I think there were other concerns there . . . trying to make sense of the connections that exist between west African culture and western of European culture; and also to make sense of the correspondences between ancestral and contemporary values."[59]

A key insight of both psychoanalysis and gothic fiction is that (to paraphrase Faulkner) the past isn't even past, that it pulses on in the form of trauma and memory, fantasy and desire. Fani-Kayode sought that pulse, that echo of the past. He sounded out confluences of ancestral values in the contemporary, seeking to bring out the "spiritual dimension" of his photographs and invoke his own technique of ecstasy that resonated with a range of practices in Europe, the Americas, western Africa, and Japan that had briefly ebbed but awaited reactivation by him and by others. The next two chapters explore these layers of signification and invocation in Fani-Kayode's photographs—not documents but homological equivalents to the Blitz. As Spandau Ballet's Gary Kemp remembered of that moment, "[We] helped make the future the country of the young. And we dance differently there."[60]

MIRROR WORLDS

From the beginning, people have sought to follow the contours
of the shadow, to capture the reflection, to represent things and people.
Thus art and magic were born together. . . . Since the mirror is capable
of furnishing the image of the things one sees, it must also be capable
of giving the image of things that are ordinarily invisible.

Pierre Mabille, 1938

There is a key moment for most of us in this country when you have
this primal scene. You either literally look in the mirror, or it comes to you
as a kind of Joycean epiphany. . . . I do believe in ghosts, I saw them at work
here in the seventies and eighties. People imagine you're talking about a
figure with a hood. I'm not interested in those. I'm interested in phantoms,
Doppelgängers, the way we're ventriloquized by things beyond our control.

John Akomfrah, interviewed by the author, 2017

BLACK MAGIC

Rotimi Fani-Kayode principally shot and processed his photographs in silver
gelatin, only returning to color Cibachrome and alternate process prints in
1988.[1] Such a choice was practical: smaller, medium format or 35 mm setups
that had been in use for most of the century were widely available and economical to produce in the community spaces and makeshift darkrooms to
which he had access. But these technical choices were also inexorably linked
to the emergence of certain genres integral to what had become canonized as
"art photography" by the late 1970s, manifest in the decisive moments and
voyeurism of the urban sleuth, the high tonal range of the modernist formal-

ist, and the gamut of disorienting techniques pioneered by the European and American surrealists of the interwar period.² By now, the history of surrealism rests front and center in accounts of the twentieth-century avant-garde. Yet for all of its influence on the postwar cultures of Europe and the United States, during Fani-Kayode's 1980s, surrealism's legacy remained unsettled.

Even in retrospect, surrealism can be difficult to pin down. It is a wide-ranging sensibility operative across a range of social and creative practices, seeking in its myriad forms to shear fixed boundaries, be they terrestrial or psychic. Surrealism was and is, in short, a kind of transgressive counterculture within modernity. Early surrealists, such as André Breton and Max Ernst, consciously linked up with the Romantic and gothic tradition, from the subjective and dreamlike register of their own work to the disturbing imagery that animated the poetry of earlier writers such as Baudelaire and Lautréament.³ Questions of desire, fantasy, prohibition, and sexuality populated surrealism from its inception. By the 1930s, when Georges Bataille became the circle's intellectual leader with his several publications, other, more disturbing fascinations came to the fore: ethnographic expeditions and primitivist fetishism, occultism and accounts of outright violence in pursuit of the ecstatic or erotic transcendence of the self.⁴ Indebted from its early years (1920–1924) to the psychoanalytic investigations of Sigmund Freud (and, later, Jacques Lacan), surrealism productively mediated dreamscapes and the friction produced in the relay of repression and compulsion. American artist Joseph Cornell went as far as to call European surrealism "black magic."⁵

Accordingly, surrealism cannot simply be designated a style—it is, instead, a codex for a host of concerns that militate against the rational orders so central to the Enlightenment project. In this way, it both prefigured and haunted modernism's realist and formalist guises. By the 1980s, dissident modernists turned to surrealism and its histories, locating it as the unconscious of modernity itself, steadily pulsing away.⁶ That surrealism would persist into that decade (and beyond) is, of course, unsurprising—its time is measured not in linear quanta but in the circular and repetitive meters of trauma and memory. In other words, surrealism shares a temporality with Romanticism, for one, and the haunted modernity evoked in the black radical tradition.⁷ The surreal tarries with the uncanny, the slippage between subjects and objects, and the persistent interpenetration of past and present.

Less abstractly, surrealism as it developed during the interwar period was a tactical treasure trove: in order to make the "real" in surreal, to render the invisible visible or the marvelous manifest, artists pursued new forms of mimesis and representation. With respect to photography—that most ostensibly denotative and objective medium—photographers such as Man Ray, Raoul Ubac, Maurice Tabard, Brassaï, and Hans Bellmer updated Victorian occultism, photography's indexical function, and the gothic currents of Eugène Atget and E. J. Belloq.[8] For the purposes of this chapter, it is worth noting that Bellmer's play of uncanny bondage was electrified by careful hand tinting while Man Ray pioneered the rayograph (a photo without a camera) and solarization, in which tonal values are doubly inverted, casting an ethereal silver halo. Similarly, Tabard pursued multiple exposures that ramified and juxtaposed their subjects to montagelike effect, while Ubac would be noted for his *brûlage*, a heating and distorting of the photographic emulsion. No longer mere pictures, in the hands of the surrealists silver-gelatin prints became strange artifacts in their own right.[9]

It should be clear from examples considered in preceding chapters, then, that Fani-Kayode availed himself of surrealist technological procedures. *Bronze Head* (figure 5.1) and *Ebo Òrìsà* (figure 5.2), for instance, play on the gender ambivalence at work in the sculpture of Alberto Giacometti and—here as elsewhere—the appearance of masks as props in *Black Male/White Male* call to mind the appropriation of "primitive forms" in the photographs of Man Ray and Jacques-André Boiffard, to say nothing of the overtly ethnographic spreads in the pages of *Documents*. The multiple exposures that yield Fani-Kayode's bleached twins and serenading pipers, or the staccato flickers of *One in Three* (figure 5.3) are each indebted technically to Tabard; *Knave of Spades* and *Joining of Equal Forces* elaborate the uncanny cropping and use of mirroring typical to surrealist photography in general, and to Brassaï's blurring of nude subject and part-object.[10] In turn, the latter's *demimondaine* sorties through Paris and Berlin in the earlier years of the 1930s are clear forerunners to Fani-Kayode's explorations of pleasure in the after-hours city. Indeed, *Black Male/White Male* could be persuasively read as, quite simply, a surrealist portfolio. The aim of this chapter is to ask what it would mean to do just that. There were, after all, potential risks implied in Fani-Kayode's undertaking such a project, from charges of anachronistic mannerism to complicity with what was, at a minimum, a network of artists whose handling of race, sex, and, in particular, Africa was compromised.

The art-historical case is in many ways undeniable, at least on the level of technique and affinity, and some scholars have already drawn such connec-

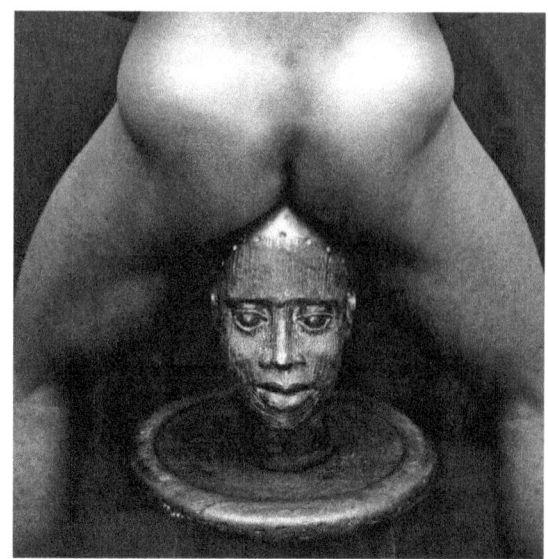

Figure 5.1 Rotimi Fani-Kayode, *Bronze Head* (1987).
© Rotimi Fani-Kayode / Autograph ABP.
Courtesy of Autograph ABP.

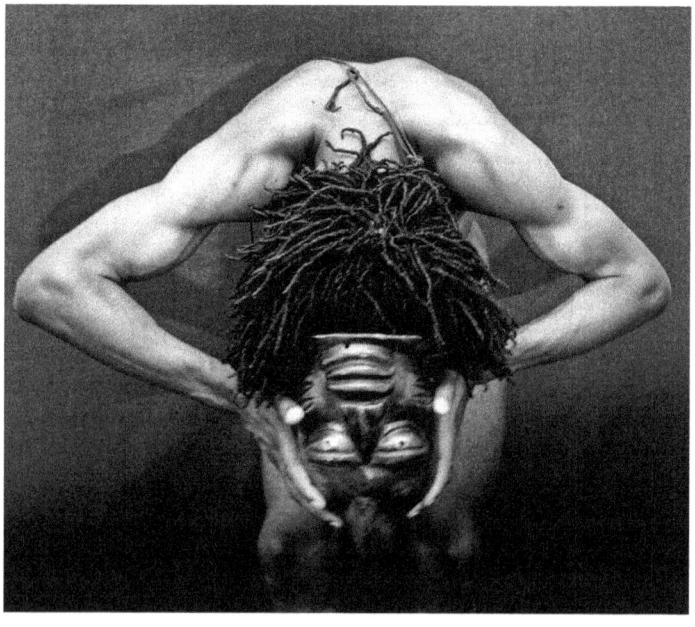

Figure 5.2 Rotimi Fani-Kayode, *Ebo Òrìsà* (1987). © Rotimi Fani-Kayode /
Autograph ABP. Courtesy of Autograph ABP.

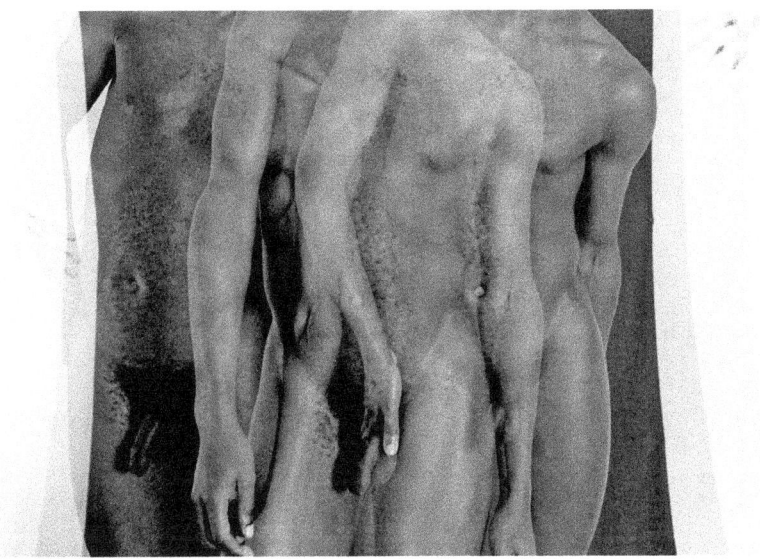

Figure 5.3 Rotimi Fani-Kayode, *One in Three* (ca. 1985). © Rotimi Fani-Kayode / Autograph ABP. Courtesy of Autograph ABP.

tions: Steven Nelson trenchantly connects Fani-Kayode to Bataille, his primitivist fascinations, and his investment in erotic dissolution.[11] Similarly, Clare Grace wrote in 2012, in a brief analysis of *Ebo Òrìsà* and *Bronze Head* (both pictures from *Black Male/White Male*), "given the disparate cultural references in his photographs—from Man Ray to Yoruban sculpture—it is hard to avoid mention of the artist's biography."[12] Grace, writing in the context of the *This Will Have Been* retrospective, importantly positions Fani-Kayode at an intersection of activism and formalism, and she is among the only commenters to make mention of the clear absorption of Man Ray's work into Fani-Kayode's.

Grace does not, however, move beyond affinities to asking why and to what end connections to Man Ray (and, ultimately, other surrealists) operate beyond the level of technical procedure or homage. Indeed, taken at the level of visual similarities, one might argue that Fani-Kayode was simply appropriating the technical dimensions of surrealist photography in order to produce, like Arthur Rothstein's 1954 photo of Eartha Kitt, a visual account of repetition—the beats and breaks that structure the sonics within many diasporic forms cultural production. Indeed, this very image, which Fani-Kayode's multiple

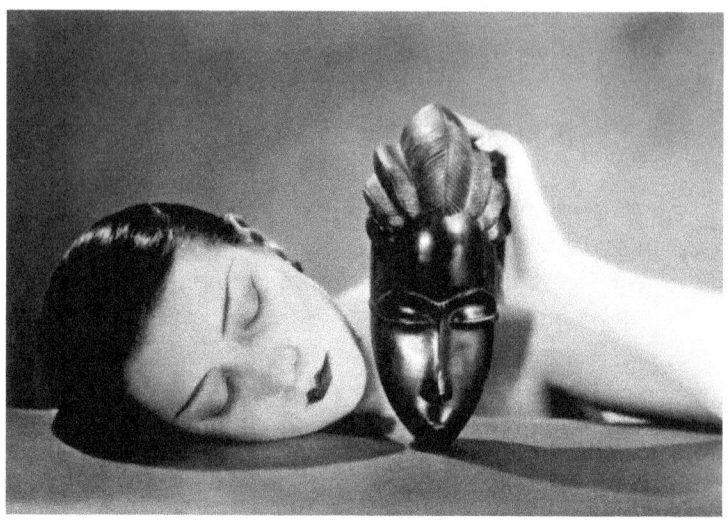

Figure 5.4 Man Ray, *Black and White* (1926). © Man Ray Trust /
Artists Rights Society (ARS), NY / ADAGP, Paris.

exposures of 1985 seem to echo visually, was paired with an essay by theorist James Snead published in 1989 for a New Museum of Contemporary Art catalog. Therein, Snead argued that many black cultural forms are typified by a "return of repetition," one that recognizes circularity and returns, but like the dialectic, permits for shifts in meaning and value in each enunciation. In the terrain of Henry Louis Gates Jr.'s then-contemporary analysis of signifying practice and Fred Moten's theorization of sound and image, Snead argues that in repetitive enunciation, practitioners might, like a jazz drummer, generate productive pauses, redirections, or breaks. He elaborates, "Black music sets up expectations and disturbs them at irregular intervals: that is will do this, however, is itself an expectation."[13]

Of course, given surrealism's pervasiveness by the 1950s in the realm of fashion photography and also in transatlantic articulations of black radical practices, Rothstein's picture cannot be read as a separate polarity or origin point altogether. Similarly, Fani-Kayode's uses of surrealist technique must also be read as signifying in the larger visual field of surrealism—one that, I should add, was always already implicated in a complex psychic zone of relation to material and phantasmic articulations of blackness.[14] And so, the pages ahead argue that Fani-Kayode's uses of surrealism were anything but stylistic or coincidental. His photographs from the years before 1988 seemed to draw on global surrealism in two related ways: on the one hand, repurposing its themes and techniques as a form of signification on deeper currents of modernity and modernism, and, on the other, elaborating the very play of desire, reversal, and fantasy at the core of the surrealist project, broadly construed.

Indeed, beyond a more obvious semiotic play of citation and inversion, by 1988–1989 it became clear that surrealism was a productive vehicle through which Fani-Kayode and many of his contemporaries could meaningfully represent and enact realms more commonly associated with dream life, the supernatural, and Yoruban spiritual practice. Ultimately, it seems that the photographs did not merely envision such spaces but served as documentation and catalyst for the uncanny tableaux of people and objects that Fani-Kayode arrayed before his camera. This latter shift was consistent with earlier surrealists' contention that photographs possessed a strange, auratic materiality. It also suggests that Fani-Kayode tapped into shifts *within* surrealism as it assumed global proportions and opened onto the what some mid-century artists began to formulate as the "superreal." His last works not only explicitly reference the ritualistic dimension in the work of several postwar Japanese artists but also permutations of music, psychedelia, and quotidian intensity that informed many self-consciously inter- (and outer)nationally oriented black artists of the 1960s. As Rebecca Zorach has noted, the "importance of the superreal, I think, is in its refusal to abandon the intensity of life *as lived* in favor of a separate, pure, or even fantastical aesthetic experience." She cites Romare Bearden, who recognized that things were "going on right outside of his studio window 'that neither Dali nor Beckett nor Ionesco would have thought possible.' Rather than denying lived experience in favor of aesthetic pursuits, 'superreal' art adds to it."[15]

Zorach borrows here from the American painter and leader of AfriCOBRA, Jeff Donaldson, who codified the superreal in a 1970 issue of *Black World*. While this formulation suggests a realist approach to an incandescent world, in its fusing of the countercultural and pragmatic, the real and the unreal, it is also of a piece with larger diaspora elaborations of the surrealist project. As the historian Robin D. G. Kelley has argued, "surrealists have consistently opposed capitalism and white supremacy, have promoted internationalism, and have been strongly influenced by Marx and Freud in their efforts to bridge the gap between dream and action."[16] In his move from signifying on modernist history to mapping secret worlds and, ultimately, to picturing the superreal of his daily life and his excursions into the unknown, Fani-Kayode did something new. He mediated many of surrealism's contradictions while also looking beyond, into a photography imbued with near talismanic energy.

WHITE BOUQUET / WHITE FEET

If the technical affinities between Fani-Kayode's photographs and those of Man Ray, Boiffard, Tabard, and Ubac are rather straightforward, his relationship to the deeper project of surrealism, with its many contradictions and enthusiasms, is less so. Initially Fani-Kayode seemed to be productively signifying on surrealism more broadly—appropriating and *détourn*ing, sure, but also breathing new energy into it, using its visionary space to enact places of contingency, desire, and relation. So, while surrealism in its 1920s articulations is rightly critiqued for its primitivist complicities, there are some rather striking parallels in intention between these earlier moments and the experiments that Fani-Kayode undertook sometime around 1983.

To reiterate, surrealism's persistence into the 1980s is understandable: as a counterculture of modernity, surrealism under Breton and Bataille sought to resurrect elements of human culture repressed or wrongly coded by the post-Enlightenment world; and in its postwar iterations, surrealism's transgressive orientation and intermedial tactics made it a productive force within the diaspora, too. Indeed, in a detailed review of several projects from the mid-1990s in which questions of race and surrealism intersected, the literary theorist Brent Hayes Edwards argues that Bataille's relationship to black cultural production was less pernicious than one might gather, and that black artists and anticolonial revolutionaries were able to apply surrealism to a range of transatlantic literary and artistic practices.

Edwards suggests that Bataille's surrealism articulates a "crisis of black modernity," and that the surrealist theorist distinguished the "primitive" from more contemporary forms of black art, such as jazz. Edwards believes this distinction to be an instance of the decategorizing operations of Bataille's heterology. The latter term is significant, as it specifies an alternative but still critical form of materialism: according to Yve-Alain Bois, for Bataille "there is no third term, but rather an 'alternating rhythm' of homology and heterology"; each time society cements itself through homogeneity, "the job of the *informe*, base materialism, and scisson is to decapitate it."[17] For Edwards, cosmopolitan black cultural production was at once both/neither primitive

178 / Exposure Five

and/nor European, and thus worked to undo sites of dyadic thinking central to the nineteenth-century hierarchical projects that constitute both modernism and colonial-era ethnography.[18]

Simply put, for Fani-Kayode to take Man Ray (or Brassäi or Bataille) as a starting point is more straightforward than it might initially seem.[19] In the decades after World War II, surrealism and the black radical tradition—from Africa to the Caribbean to the North Atlantic—were helixed into a heterodox (and self-consciously global) form of praxis. From its earliest inception, according to Kelley, "surrealism may have originated in the West, but it is rooted in a conspiracy against Western civilization. Surrealists frequently looked outside Europe for ideas and inspiration, turning most notably to the 'primitives' under the heel of European colonialism. Indeed, what later became known as the Third World turned out to be the source of the surrealists' politicization during the 1920s."[20]

For all that, one has to tread carefully when considering the European avant-garde alongside the fact of racism and, at the time, colonial power. For example, one of Man Ray's most celebrated photographs—*Black and White* (1926; figure 5.4)—rather overtly plays in double entendre, both in referencing the photographic process and also the two heads that occupy the frame, Kiki de Montparnasse's white visage and the western African (likely Baule/Ivoirian) mask that functions as a stand-in for blackness as such. While *Black and White* can be seen as a sort of celebration of African forms, it also bespeaks a period in which black cultures were both fashionable and served as synecdoche for "primitive" (read: magical, authentic) consciousness within the colonial matrix. In this sense, Man Ray's picture deals in a form of reductivism that is also symptomatic of then-contemporary obsessions with jazz or with the black African as an inherently sexual or rhythmic being.[21] More precisely, *Black and White* can be seen on a few levels as a document of fetishism—in its conflation of subjects and objects (Montparnasse and the mask are pictorially imbued with aspects of each), and in the restaging of the wooden form as a talismanic object. These associations are amplified by a version of the picture that is solarized, producing an ethereal, haloed effect. But fetishism—a central topic in the next chapter—also specifies a more psychic set of relays, the ambivalent play of attraction, misperception, and repulsion that defined so many encounters between the "black and white" populations of the world since the earliest days of modernity.

Fetishism in this register only intensified by 1929 in the pages of Bataille's journals, which would define surrealism for much of the decade to follow. His fascination with shrunken and disembodied heads and his participation in ethnographic exploration confirm an exoticist streak in many sectors of the surrealist enterprise. As Steven Nelson suggests, Bataille's fixations were just that: obsessive, misguided, reductive, and fantastic.[22] Indeed, in its various formulations, surrealism and its offshoots were complexly bound up in thoroughly racialized power relationships and investigations. The Trocadéro, site of the late Victorian ethnographic exhibition, was demolished in 1935 but had, in some ways, already been displaced by the avant-garde in their own work, including the museum without walls that was *Documents*.[23] On the whole, as a project within modernism, surrealism has long been caught up in issues of power, scopophilia, and primitivism—a term that defines both an earnest celebration of "the primitive" and also its ambivalent appropriation in ways that reiterated rather than challenged European superiority.[24]

Fani-Kayode intervened into precisely this terrain with two photographs from the mid-1980s, reproduced on facing pages in *Black Male/White Male* and mentioned in the preceding chapter: *White Bouquet* and *White Feet* (ca. 1986–1987; figures 5.5 and 5.6). These square-format silver gelatin prints explicitly draw on surrealist staging and techniques (the double exposure of the former and the sexualized and gothic tone of the latter) but also reiterate at least two links in a deeper chain of signification within European painting, each staged through the citation of a reclining female nude. Already a Renaissance and orientalist standby, this trope was repurposed in canonical modernist works by Manet (*Olympia*, 1863) and, roughly thirty years later, Paul Gauguin (*The Spirit of the Dead Watching*, 1892). For his part, Fani-Kayode specifically employed aspects of Bataille's *informe* as a decompositional strategy that arrested those paintings' symbolic and formal closure, subjecting both to a process of expansion and deferral. One such tool is *bassesse*—the inversion of subjects from the upright to the horizontal, or around the vertical axis; another is using photographic processing (its chemicals, emulsions, and exposures) to dematerialize the figures through technical means.[25] A third, as Craig Owens has elaborated, drawing on the Derridean notion of the abyss as ground for the infinite deferral of closure, is the visual strategy of *plier*, of folding and mirrored duplication.[26]

For their part, the aforementioned paintings, as notable instances of modernist recodings of received convention, were themselves deeply embedded in emerging debates in the 1980s around questions of vision and power dur-

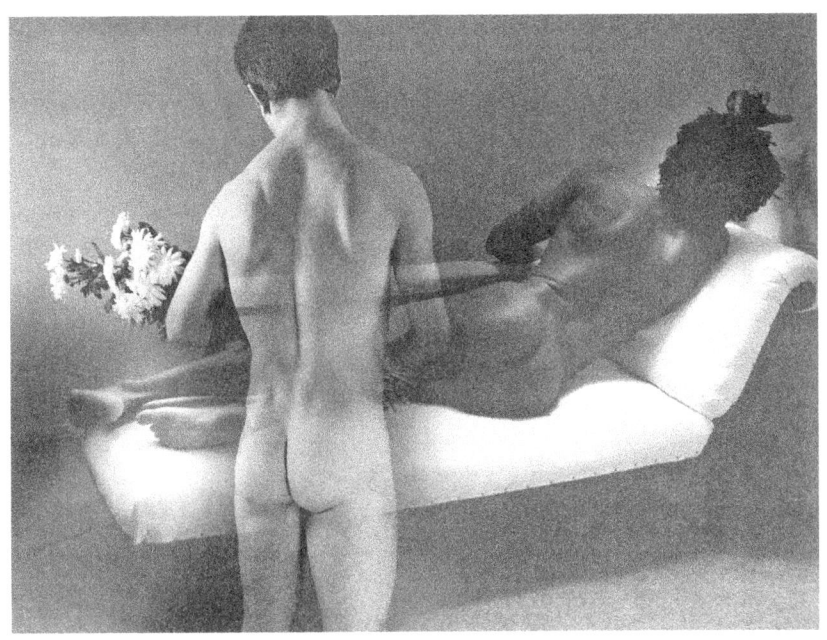

Figure 5.5 Rotimi Fani-Kayode, *White Bouquet* (1987). © Rotimi Fani-Kayode / Autograph ABP. Courtesy of Autograph ABP.

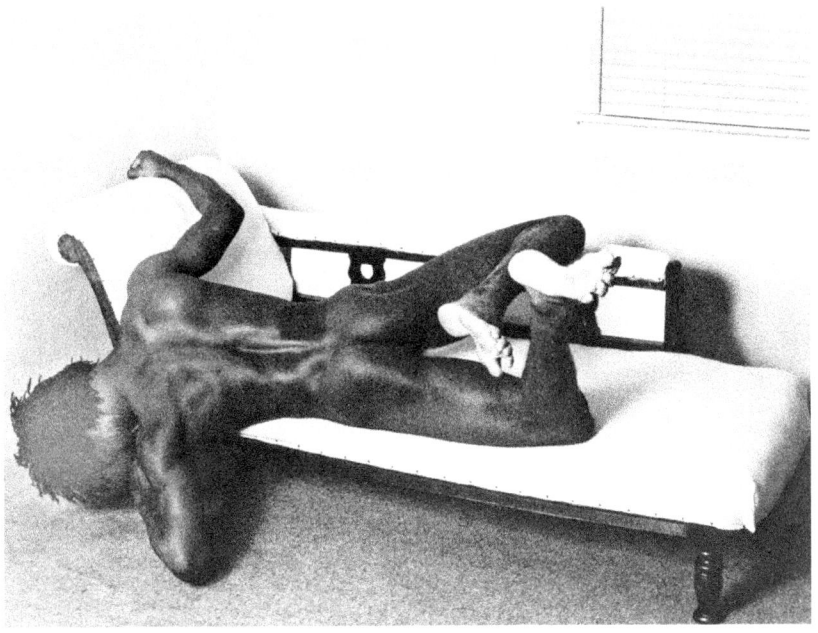

Figure 5.6 Rotimi Fani-Kayode, *White Feet* (1986–1987). © Rotimi Fani-Kayode / Autograph ABP. Courtesy of Autograph ABP.

ing the high-colonial era.[27] And, as Mark Sealy argued in 1995, part of Fani-Kayode's interest in these works was one of reclamation, suggesting that the "canon" was a place in which he, too, could intervene.[28] Relative to other invocations of these works in those years, Fani-Kayode's photographs are powerful instances of signification in which the historical complex of primitivism itself (from Manet to Bataille) is brought into relief. At the same time, those scenes are reconfigured in the pages of *Black Male/White Male* as part of the more immediate project of visualizing an intersectional, queer, and cosmopolitan field of desire and communion.

Perhaps for these reasons, if there is a single image that has received the most sustained attention in the *Black Male/White Male* portfolio, it is surely *White Bouquet*. As Nelson has argued, Fani-Kayode's *White Bouquet* is something of a complement to its "original": it represents Fani-Kayode's interest in "incomplete" bodies, but "both pictures explore in great detail, however, white male desire, and they both insert into more public arenas that which was largely spoken about and represented in private"—namely, prostitution in the case of *Olympia* and black male sexuality in the case of *White Bouquet*.[29] This particular iconographic history was further elaborated first by Gauguin and then again by Brassaï in his unsettling black-and-white nudes of 1932–1933. The latter build on the precedent of *Olympia*, this time by transposing the figure into photography and adding a psychoanalytic dimension to already palpable connections to the Parisian demimonde. Later still, Jean-Michel Basquiat picked up on *Olympia*'s unspoken racial hierarchies in several works from 1982, including *The Maid from Olympia* and *Three Quarters of Olympia Minus the Servant*. In a more playfully appropriative mode, Yasumasa Morimura's painted photograph *Portrait (Futago)* of 1988 (figure 5.7) substituted the artist for the courtesan; and, in 1989, the Guerrilla Girls further decoded the gender and power play of the entire sequence,[30] gorilla-masking an Ingres odalisque and putting her on a striking yellow billboard.

By the 1980s, in other words, *Olympia* had become less of a painting than a locus of symbolic resonance—of signification. Its unmistakable composition was made a shorthand for the myths and elisions of early modernism, and a site for their excavation and rehearsal. For a photographer such as Fani-Kayode, attuned as he was to the larger matrices of the gaze, racial fetishism, and desire that have defined the medium for much of its history, it would have been tempting to integrate *Olympia* into a practice that itself prioritized masquerade and figuration. But in performing his own substitutions and re-

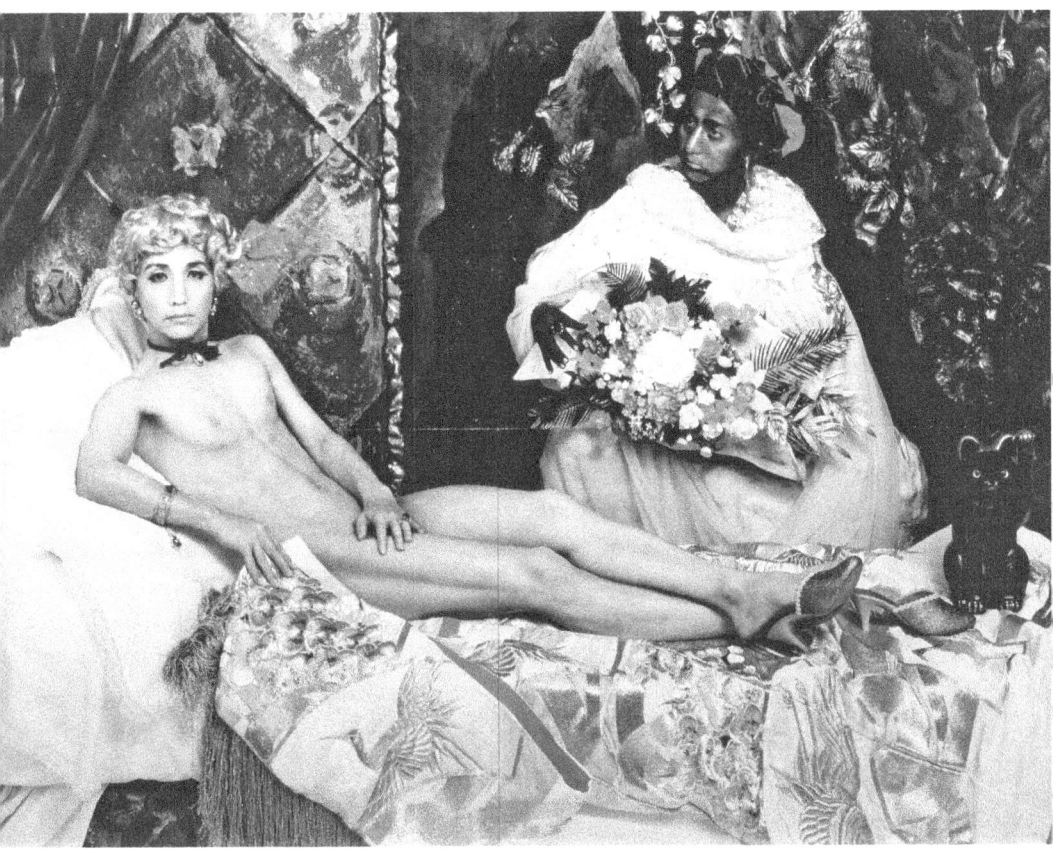

Figure 5.7 Yasumasa Morimura, *Portrait (Futago)* (1988). © Yasumasa Morimura.
Courtesy of the artist and Luhring Augustine, New York.

versals on such a highly charged work, Fani-Kayode would have to account for the specific resonances that Manet's *Olympia* had in emerging feminist and postcolonial critiques.

To this end, Nelson and the art historian Kobena Mercer have thoroughly accounted for the pictorial mechanics of *White Bouquet*. Mercer persuasively notes three acts of *reversal* or inversion at play in *White Bouquet*. Most obviously, Fani-Kayode's photograph rotates the perspective of *Olympia* 180 degrees, forcing the viewer to regard two figures not frontally, as through the door of the Parisian flat, but from behind, as an act of bearing witness. In a second shift, Fani-Kayode substitutes male figures for *Olympia*'s two women, thus eliminating one vector of scopic power in the Manet original: the black maid bearing flowers (likely from the painting's implied spectator, an affluent suitor) becomes the subject of a courtly gesture by the white figure in the foreground. That figure, with his head gently cocked, cradles the flowers in a tender offering to his potential lover, who has turned away in quiet repose. Hence a third reversal, the "liquidation," in Mercer's terms, of *Olympia*'s gesture of outrage and withholding—the transactional quid pro quo of the courtesan is reconfigured as a process of giving. The flowers, for their part, lose their corner-store tawdriness and, in their stunning whiteness, emerge as an offering.[31]

Fani-Kayode thus redirects symbols both abstract (the purity of the white bouquet) and indexical (gender identity). He removes the feminine altogether, such as the accoutrements of jewelry and the black cat, and elides any sense of overtly dominant interrelation. This transcoding reveals heterosexual relations under modern capitalism as fraught (even violent) and implies that Manet's canvas visualizes and reiterates those relations. Nelson argues that *White Bouquet*, in its compositional choices and deft reversals, fundamentally destabilizes the naturalizing reifications and implied voyeurism encoded in several centuries of recumbent nudes. While it shares with *Olympia* an interest in white male desire, it builds on the visualization of that power in Manet's painting by expanding the field of desire it portrays and enacts.

And so, *White Bouquet*, with its "canonical treatment" of its apparently queer subjects, is, according to Nelson, "an exploration of same-sex desire, race, and the possibility of the very fusion of the bodies."[32] For him, this last point is crucial: even though the black body is revalorized here as a solid, gleaming object of desire in its own right, the desiring white body is the viewer's entrée into the scene. At the same time, the white subject is figured as spectral and translucent, anchored only by the corporeality of the man on the pristine divan.[33] As such, one could add to Nelson's reading another level still, a fourth reversal at work. Whereas the black body has long been contingent, marginal, or fetishized in Western art, here it revealed as the one element of the setup that seems to be stable. The figure on the divan is not seen to be "doubly conscious" but, in contrast to the flower bearer, relatively whole. This is an image that centers and concretizes the black body and suggests what historians of colonialism have long known—that whiteness is contingent, defined as *not* black. Such an account inverts Fanon's analysis of the black body as imbued with meaning from without, the body as a self-alienated terrain encoded and produced by discourse and fantasy in relation to (white) subjects for whom it is an Other.[34]

The partial dematerialization at work in *White Bouquet* also opens onto the possibility of not only physical congress but a literal fusion of bodies. While a coming-together of this sort has long been a poetic trope for sex, Fani-Kayode's picture of bodies in varied states of contingency and evanescence generates a space where two might, even briefly, be one. As Nelson argues, this definition of the erotic has a champion in Bataille, himself fascinated with "ethnography and the bodies of non-European women." Bataille's eroticism, predicated on losing one's physical coherence (or experiencing the "little death" of orgasm) is one avenue into a singular self-annihilation and union with another. Arguably, Bataille's version is "pathologically heterosexist," meaning he views the woman's body "merg[ing] into the body of the male" as a threat to the myth of a subject's unity, its wholeness. In contrast, the effect of *White Bouquet*'s oscillations of passivity and power, black and white, stability and contingency is to expand on Bataille's insight while highlighting its biases.[35] While Bataille in particular might not have been an obvious starting point for Fani-Kayode, the pictures in *Black Male/White Male* ask the viewer to start thinking in that direction.[36] Which is to say, *White Bouquet* is a tableau of desire and spectral photography to be sure, but also a carefully staged set piece that tactically employs techniques of heterology, dissipation, and axial reversal that were associated with surrealist photography and film from the 1930s forward.

FLIP FANTASIA

It is at this confluence of the modernist avant-garde, primitivism, and fetishism that surrealist strategies begin to take on critical value in Fani-Kayode's work: his substitutions of male and female or black and white worked in concert with surrealist strategies of multiple exposure, voyeuristic framing, and mirror inversions. They not only restage scenes so familiar as to be a cliché but draw forth their deeper chains of signification. Crucially, unlike peers who also used poststructural or avant-garde strategies to critique the form of the nude, Fani-Kayode's signifying did not so much preserve the original sign but relied instead on surrealist technique to expand, disorient, and ramify it. In his photographs, signs are imported not as static, readymade forms, but as more elastic catalysts of chance and improvisation that retroactively signal and interrogate the latent assumptions of the "originals."

Take, for example, several other uses of *Olympia* that I alluded to earlier. In the years before *Black Male/White Male* was published, Cy Twombly and Jean-Michel Basquiat could simply invoke the title of the 1863 odalisque and produce graphically chaotic canvases that, because they were linked to that earlier instance, produced meaning by inference—that is, of the sign's violent cancellation. By the late 1980s, other photographers adapted *Olympia*, again as a fully formed and stable sign. Morimura, for one, relied on the audience's familiarity with the form of *Olympia* as one with a readily available set of associations, and his version essentially provides a *copy* that is then subjected to a simple transposition of the artist in costume, much like Cindy Sherman's citation of Baroque painting, but without the latter's use of abjection as desublimatory strategy.

Two common strategies connect each of these cases: the recognizable "sign" of *Olympia* is first invoked or faithfully reproduced, and then *acted upon*—in Basquiat's and Twombly's *graffitisme* and in Morimura's knowing substitution. These initial reproductions are notably flat, as each artist deals primarily with surface effects, creating compressed and stable pictorial space. In spite of the camp humor in *Portrait (Futago)*, for example, there is little sense of dynamism or possibility. Indeed, Morimura himself noted that he did not so much want to complicate *Olympia* but to partake in it, even as he reinscribes the core compositional and relational moves of the original.[37] By contrast, *White Bouquet*, with its inversions, reversals, and spectral dissipations does not reproduce the sign but, instead, draws on its source code to create something new. Here, Fani-Kayode initiates a range of humorous slippages that nonetheless draw on and underscore the many layers of citation and connotation encoded in each earlier instance.

In some ways, this logic is of a piece with *Olympia* itself: Michel Foucault has argued that, in developing his paintings as mirror worlds, Manet was able to shift art from depictions of a "real" or idealized world and also disrupt the fallacy of the autonomous art object and the unimplicated viewer.[38] In so doing, he also reflected back seemingly invisible elements of daily life that were hidden in plain sight—the demimonde, sex traffic, black servitude, and the articulation of capital through the body and into the fabric of the social. Foucault (by way of Bataille, in his account) explains *how* Manet enables the viewer to see differently, by preventing the picture from ever fully resolving into a mere snapshot. In short, Manet's mirrors create an instability that resists closure. Perhaps unexpectedly, Fani-Kayode's work in a photographic mode (with its many unresolved or multiplied subjects, axial reversals, and doubled subjects) therefore functions in much the same spirit as the former's mirroring in *Bar at the Folies-Bergère*.

All of which is to suggest that, unlike immediate peers such as Basquiat or Morimura, Fani-Kayode does not simply import canonical images as a *montageur* (working with fully formed, flattened signs); instead (and like Manet) he draws from the technologies and iconographies of the past to destabilize them from within. Rather than bowdlerize or *détourne* Manet's painting, in *White Bouquet* Fani-Kayode builds on his framework, implicating the viewer as an onlooker rather than as a party to the central transaction. By projecting the white figure into the field of vision, putting the bouquet back into his hand, and merging the two feminine figures (the prostitute and the maid) the picture enacts a series of inversions and axial reversals. The final tableau ultimately resists interpretive closure. That Fani-Kayode is black himself, one should note, does not exactly eliminate the scopic pressures in play in looking on a site of homoerotic encounter. As his one-time peers Stuart Hall and David Bailey have rightly argued, merely substituting a black photographer for a white one does not cancel the power of the lens or the gaze—a black subject can desire and fetishize bodies as well as a white one.[39] But by rotating the perspective of the scene and pushing the white suitor into the frame (the viewer, in the Manet version), he replaces confrontation and exchange with an act of witnessing.

Moreover, while Fani-Kayode does the revisionist work of placing the black subject centrally rather than in the marginal position of the maid, he also calls forth the Fanonian schema in which the black subject is, in effect, created in relation to an external white gaze and encumbered with additional layers of meaning—the accumulation of an entire colonial history of discourse and stereotype by which the lived experience of blackness is given a "stable" definition from without. In this way, *White Bouquet* works on a Fanonian level in much the way that Sherman's film stills work from the Lacanian: the subject is revealed as constituted in relation to others, precisely as their Other. The latter is a drama of desire and fantasy in which many of the original surrealists themselves certainly participated. But in using their techniques, Fani-Kayode simultaneously alerts the viewer to another insight of which Bataille, Breton, and company were certainly aware—that difference is forged in contingency, as an ongoing production in the dynamic space of the psyche.

Once surrealist techniques entered Fani-Kayode's photographs—no later than 1985–1986—one can track their uses even in less obvious examples, in photographs that do not rely on double exposure or uncanny substitutions. Throughout *Black Male/White Male*, Fani-Kayode signified on primitivist modes, in turn subverting or queering them. Some obvious examples appeared earlier in this book—as in the subject-object blurring and play of African mask in *Ebo Òrìsà* and *Bronze Head*, for example, or the gender ambivalence of several other reclining sitters, which constitute a direct update of Brassaï's nudes of 1933 (pictures that some historians have argued produce a visual oscillation between masculine genitalia and a (headless) female body in repose).[40] Elsewhere, Fani-Kayode's signifying is even more overt. On *White Bouquet*'s facing page, he revisits *Olympia* once again, through Paul Gauguin's 1892 *Spirit of the Dead Watching*. This was a powerful choice, as Gauguin demonstrated early on the suggestive power of axial reversal. In his storied painting, he too, compositionally shifts the odalisque, flipping his feminine subject across the vertical and positioning her prone, with hands raised in mock surrender. In place of the black servant, he substitutes the eponymous *Manao tupapau*—a frightening local spirit.

This is a telling choice for many reasons. For one, *Spirit of the Dead Watching* is exemplary of unreconstructed primitivism. As Abigail Solomon-Godeau has argued, although Gauguin was himself a radical for his time, drawing the "primitive" into canonical European painting, he did so from a position of tremendous power, and this scene almost certainly reflects the sort of sexual domination Gauguin exercised as a white European during the late Victorian era. Hal Foster further complicates the narrative by arguing that Gauguin's paintings act as a site of fetishism wherein he reconciles his own ambivalent desire by hypostatizing the powerful disorientation presented by actual contact with his fantasized colonial interlocutors in the rather conservative mode of the reclining nude.[41] For example, the prone position rather overtly suggests a shift to anal sexuality (and, for Foster, anal sadism) that Gauguin actively worked to repress in various encounters in Tahiti that awakened his homoerotic desire. The spirit of the dead, in turn, functions as a sort of superego or paternal Law, haunting or cursing the encounter. His own statement confirms the reactionary conservatism of the painting: he oscillates between describing the picture as a depiction of authentic local lore or as a simple European genre painting, a nude tout court.[42]

By contrast, Fani-Kayode's *White Feet* reverses the setup once again along the vertical axis, substituting a black man for the Tahitian woman. The spirit of the dead is nowhere to be found. The scene, in turn, takes on a new set of associations: on the one hand, homoerotic looking is a given here, all the way down to the implication of anal intercourse, citing as it does a turn-of-the-century homoerotic portrait by Guglielmo Plüschow; on the other, the title draws the viewer to the bottoms of the subject's feet, a place on the body where even the dermal determinism that occupies Fanon is called into question. In effect, the composition is drained of the ambivalent and repressive tone of the Gauguin, substituting instead desire tempered by humor. In *White Bouquet*, Fani-Kayode openly depicts the fragility of the white mastery that Gauguin works so fervently to dispel. On the facing page, in *White Feet*, he actualizes the homoeroticism that *Spirit of the Dead Watching* so carefully polices. The mood here draws, too, on aspects of the gothic and the surreal—there are textural traces of E. J. Bellocq's *Storeyville* pictures and Brassaï's ghostly, foreshortened nudes—but the scene registers more as a queer fantasia than patriarchal scopophilia. In this sense, one can see clear convergences between the *Black Male/White Male* portfolio and Isaac Julien's *Looking for Langston*—a film established earlier as part of Fani-Kayode's transatlantic lexicon, but one that, here, quite obviously shares a tonal register of after-hours communion, desirous longing, and hidden nocturnal cabarets.

Significantly, in both *Looking for Langston* and *Black Male/White Male*, the artists take on Mapplethorpe's neoprimitivist cruising. Julian does this by quite literally displaying enlarged Mapplethorpe canvases in the loftlike home of one of the central characters. Fani-Kayode, by contrast, applies surrealist strategies yet again. For Kobena Mercer and Julien,[43] Mapplethorpe's handling of black men was a continuation of earlier (culturally racist and biologically reductionist) tropes—all bronzed and taught muscle, ample phallus, and raw sexual energy—ready to be "shot," captured, and mounted into objectifying fragments by Mapplethorpe's camera. While nineteenth-century uses of the camera as a proxy for an actual gun in photographic safaris of a feminized and passive "dark continent" are by now well established,[44] Mapplethorpe's urban safaris are particularly unsettling in their brazenness and anachronism—especially given Mapplethorpe's relative power as a connected and already iconic photographer.

The contrast between Fani-Kayode's ambivalent-androgynous mode and Mapplethorpe's continuation of a more familiar fetishistic approach is well underscored in one of the later pictures in *Black Male/White Male*. For instance, Fani-Kayode's *Snap Shot* (figure 5.8) derives its remarkable power in part from the abysslike contours of the image itself, and in part from the context of the book, which concedes the physicality of difference but forces the meanings of that difference into constant *deferral*. The black and white here, those irreducible racial and tonal differences that, in effect, make photography possible as a visual language, are no accident. Recall Hirst's larger summation of the project: Fani-Kayode's subject is "Black–white: fantasy-races in which infinite difference reveals infinite affinity. In approaching these images, I have to be as careful as the title of this book."[45] In contrast to the profusion of blackness in *Snap Shot*, the formal idea was executed at least a decade earlier in stark whiteness by Mapplethorpe, during his experimentation with Polaroids from 1970 to 1975. But for all their compositional similarity, the two pictures demonstrate precisely the difference between their two practices, a difference that cannot be reduced to the color of the artist's skin.

Specifically, Mapplethorpe's image, clearly staged against the white brick of a studio space with a camera laid horizontally, several inches above his genitals—which are not obscured by the camera but instead by a white dot—is clearly autobiographical. This is a man locked in the narcissistic web of looking at and solidifying the self with his camera. Gone is the metaphoric and visual abyss of *Snap Shot*, gone are the blurred edges of the sitter's body, and the metonymic collapse of phallus/womb, with its contingent play of power and abjection. In their place, a man in a room, his gender not at all ambivalent but clearly censored—a censorship that his incipient practice will seek to overcome through the recapitulation of the silenced and marginal in the rarefied terrain of classical figuration. Where Fani-Kayode's project enacts ecstatic fusion, *informe*, and *bassesse*, Mapplethorpe's is one of skilled elevation—a making visible and unified, promising more to come.[46]

More broadly, then, Fani-Kayode used surrealist methods to signify on Mapplethorpe's pictures. Where Mapplethorpe made beautiful "gay pictures" and Apollonian (that is, classicist) tableaux of "Other" bodies, Fani-Kayode pressed the Dionysian angle and made queer pictures in which subjectivity (in front of and behind the lens) was called into question alongside the primitivist trope of fixating on black bodies.[47] This is a reminder of Mercer's original incisiveness. The power of his critique of racial fetishism is brought into sharp

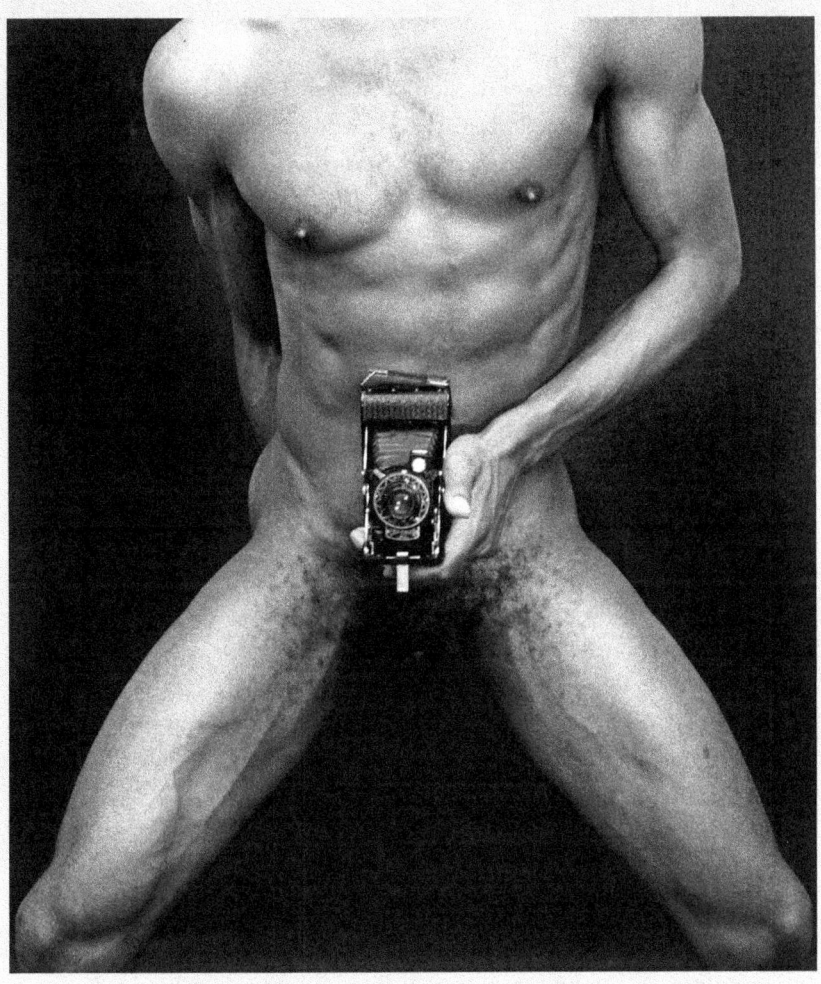

Figure 5.8 Rotimi Fani-Kayode, *Snap Shot* (1987). © Rotimi Fani-Kayode /
Autograph ABP. Courtesy of Autograph ABP.

relief when looking side by side at Mapplethorpe's remarkable control of his medium and the unsettling vision of Fani-Kayode's photographs, when comparing the latter's with the collection of modeled black bodies culled from nearly a decade of Mapplethorpe's practice and assembled in the *Black Book* (1986). While there is an entire chapter's worth of material in these striking visual comparisons alone, one can make shorthand of them by noting, at every turn, Fani-Kayode's citation and then reversal, fraying, softening, blurring, or decomposition of Mapplethorpe's high-gloss, precision images. The fetishistic craving of *Ajitto* and the cold modeling of *Derrick Cross*'s arm are counterbalanced by the diptych *Prohibited*, in which a leg displays power and form but the tones of the image itself are gray and muted. *Prohibited*'s movement is balletic; its wilting white flowers rest on an abstract form in a gesture worthy of Brassäi—the small of a man's back transfigured.

Similarly, the figures *Leigh Lee* (figure 5.9) and *Thomas* are, by Mapplethorpe, sculpted into a pose with vertical clarity, sharply drawn and suggestive of Attic form: perfect geometry, lean musculature against a pedestal. Compare *James* (figure 5.10), another man with bleached hair: his race is, for a moment, complicated, the black of his skin not so resonant and deep, the neat dichotomy of black male or white male unsettled.[48] He is shot from above, in a position of emotional vulnerability. His body is crumpled, caving in around himself in amorphous *informe*. Elsewhere, Mapplethorpe's slick leathermen openly kissing are complemented by a moment of intimacy and quiet human connection in Fani-Kayode's picture of Denis Carney and Essex Hemphill. Athletic, idealized black feet severed from *Marty Gibson* are mirrored (again) by *White Feet*, comically and tragically entangled on the white chaise longue. Mapplethorpe's noble black savage is inverted axially and racially, deflated by campy parody, a white man in a shabby leopard skin, awkwardly squatting without the vertical supports of Mapplethorpe's original. The picture is a rather literal channeling of Bataille's zoomorphism and base materialism. The figure of the "noble warrior," one who conjoins Mapplethorpe with F. Holland Day and Leni Riefenstahl, is humorously flipped and inverted. In his place is a figure comically reduced, a pasty man in a tawdry costume, poised to take a shit. And so on.

While Exposure 3 described the larger cultural political stakes of the contrasts between Mapplethorpe's and Fani-Kayode's photographs, here it becomes clear that surrealist theory and creative strategies were a wellspring from which Fani-Kayode drew as a matter of process. Aside from directly

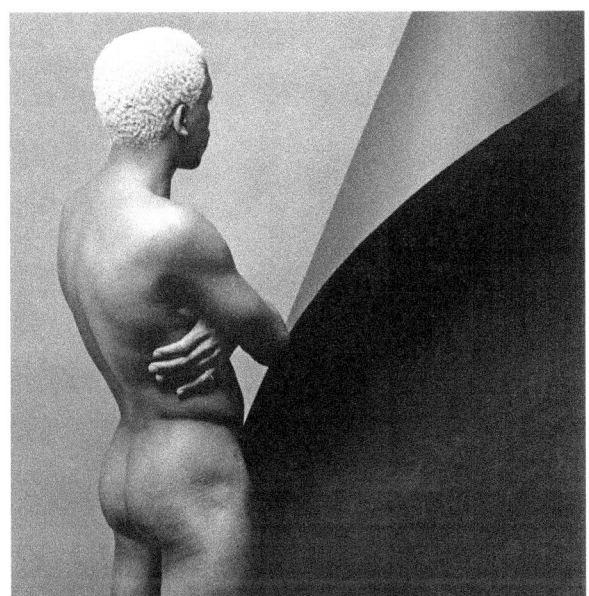

Figure 5.9 Robert Mapplethorpe, *Leigh Lee* (1980). © Robert Mapplethorpe Foundation. Courtesy Art + Commerce.

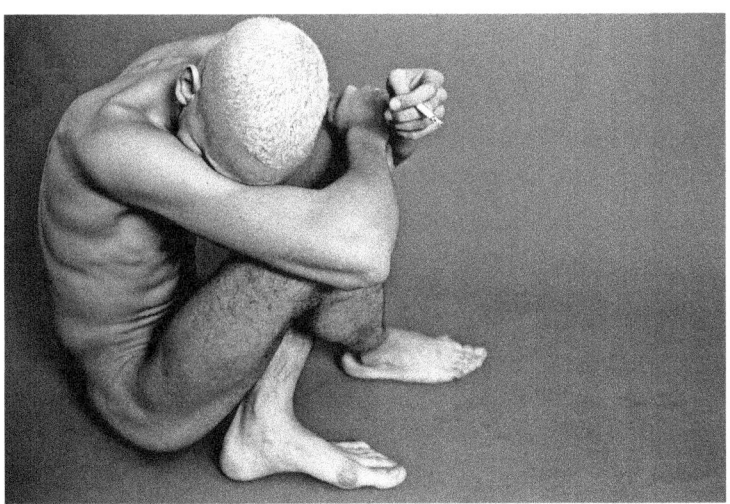

Figure 5.10 Rotimi Fani-Kayode, *James* (ca. 1986). © Rotimi Fani-Kayode / Autograph ABP. Courtesy of Autograph ABP.

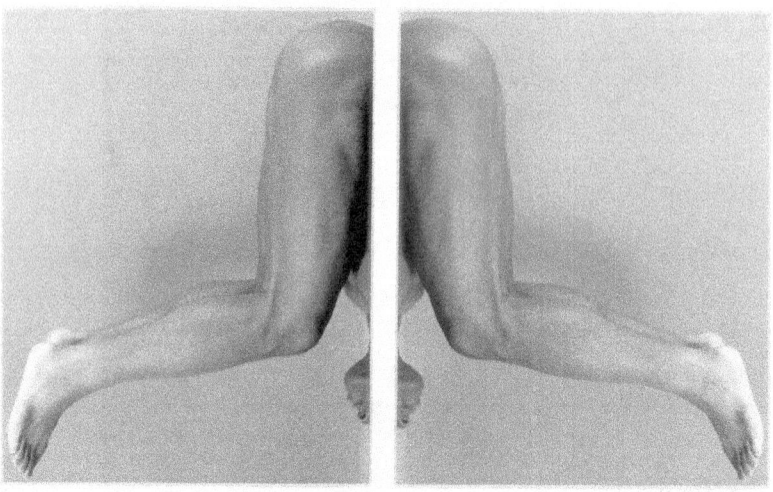

Figure 5.11 Rotimi Fani-Kayode, *Joining of Equal Forces* (1986). © Rotimi Fani-Kayode / Autograph ABP. Courtesy of Autograph ABP.

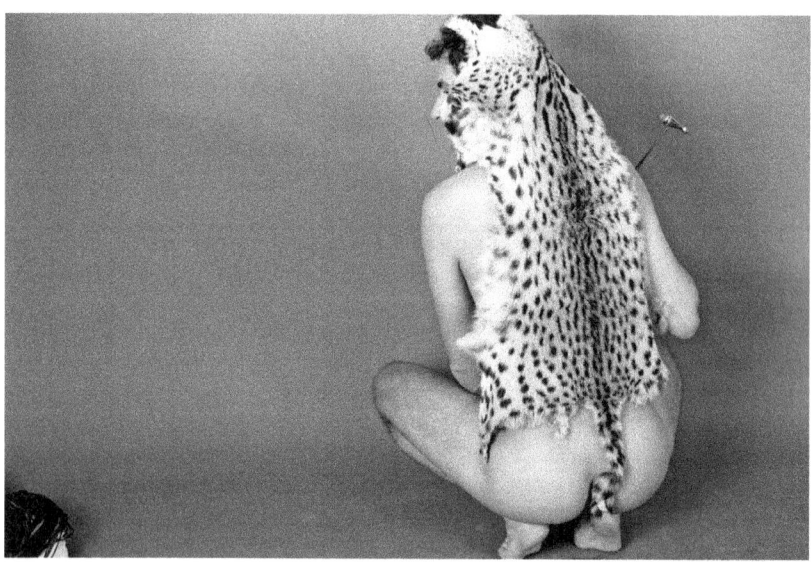

Figure 5.12 Rotimi Fani-Kayode, *Which Doctor? Herr Doktor Scheidegger* (1987). © Rotimi Fani-Kayode / Autograph ABP. Courtesy of Autograph ABP.

adapting the formal approaches initially made available by the interwar avant-garde, he used his own photographs as locations of signification and disidentification. In effect, Fani-Kayode improvised new meanings for a set of practices with a complex primitivist lineage and a tendency toward the fetishistic and heterosexist, while also giving the lie to the very misrecognitions and compulsions at the heart of the European modernist tradition.

It is important to note, however, that such a project was not altogether an act of postmodernist anachronism. Surrealism itself had never fully gone away. Indeed, Yve-Alain Bois and Rosalind Krauss understand surrealism's persistence as a kind of pulse, the incessant beat of the nervous system, the irrepressible throb of eros, the persistent echo of that which cannot be repressed.[49] More specifically, in their recuperation of Bataille, Bois and Krauss point to incursions of the "low" into the field of modernism in general, and their descriptions of flickering neon and the irreducibility of the abject or scatalogical describe on the one hand the eighties-era work of Jenny Holzer, Mike Kelley, and Paul McCarthy but, on the other, the leveling of high and low and margin and center in play for Fani-Kayode. Moreover, as a counterculture within modernity that figured libidinal desire and otherworldly dreamscapes, surrealist approaches reemerged in the 1980s with a vengeance.

For instance, strains of popular culture rather overtly played with tableaux of gothic horror, unreal psychic landscapes, and the uncanny slippages of subject and object. As proof one need look only at films and music videos that gained wide repute—Peter Gabriel's "Sledgehammer," David Lynch's *Blue Velvet*, or David Cronenberg's *The Fly* (all 1986). At precisely the same time, the Virginian Sally Mann built on more formalist photographic approaches to surrealism, elaborating on the slightly earlier work of Francesca Woodman, who was enrolled at the Rhode Island School of Design, and used 1977–1978 to study André Breton and surrealism. She ultimately made nude self-portraits imbued with an ethereal, if not cinematic, effect. The noted *Self-Deceit #1, Rome* (1978), for example, is captured from above in a rusticated no-place. It has Woodman rounding a corner on all fours as if a nocturnal animal, her face at once shielded and mirrored, slightly out of focus. She worked and displayed in alternative spaces in New York from 1979 to 1981 and would have overlapped there with Fani-Kayode prior to her death in January 1981.[50]

While it would be sufficient to stop here with this rather art-historical reading of Fani-Kayode's surrealism, there are a few brief points to make, and they address the ways in which he appears to have taken some of the more arcane and ineffable ambitions of the earlier avant-garde at face value. For one, his continuation of surrealism was not merely a question of affinity or appropriation but, indeed, one of spatial and cosmological ambition. It is unsurprising that he proceeded in this way, as the surrealists moved very much in such a direction themselves. That is, what started with symbolist drawings and Freudian forays into the unconscious ended up, by the late 1930s, a wider field of investigation. That field included journeys to Africa and the Caribbean, retreats in hidden spaces of ritual and sacrifice, or the psychoanalytic ruptures of Lacan, with his emphasis on *jouissance* and the "mirror stage," which postulated that all social subjectivity (the mirror effects of ego and the Law) was akin to an uneasy masquerade played in dynamic relation to outside forces.[51]

For Fani-Kayode, such concerns—which sat in uneasy relation to mainline modernism—were something of a given. He remarked that in African art "the mask does not represent material reality: rather, the artist tries to approach a spiritual reality within it through images suggested by human and animal forms. . . . As an African artist working in a western medium, I try to bring out the spiritual dimension in my pictures so that concepts of 'reality' become ambiguous and are open to reinterpretation. This requires what Yoruba priests and artists call a 'technique of ecstasy.'"[52] So far, this book has taken this phrase "technique of ecstasy" as a jumping-off point for the blend of trans- and countercultural strategies that can enact moments of ecstatic communion, Dionysian carnival, and transgressive release.

Crucially, *signifying* is counted above as such a technique. That is, signification in the hands of many diaspora artists is not merely an act of appropriating a sign readymade, or even improvising new meanings. Instead, signifying connects directly to the very orisha who mediates the invisible spirit world with waking life—Eshu. It is for this reason that Henry Louis Gates Jr. argues that the double voicing and echoes that typify signifying's homonymic doubling demonstrates "that a simultaneous, but negated, parallel discursive (ontological, political) universe exists within the larger white discursive universe, like the matter-and-antimatter fabulations so common to science fiction." Here, Gates invokes a range of textual and allegorical precedents, notably the "signifying monkey," a trickster figure who serves as a narrative echo of Eshu in American oral tradition, as well as Haitian *vévé* ground drawings, marked to invoke the *loa*—in this case, Eshu's equivalent, Legba—at the intersection of two pathways, the confluence of twinned, mirror worlds.[53]

Such an interpretation is particularly resonant in Fani-Kayode's photographs

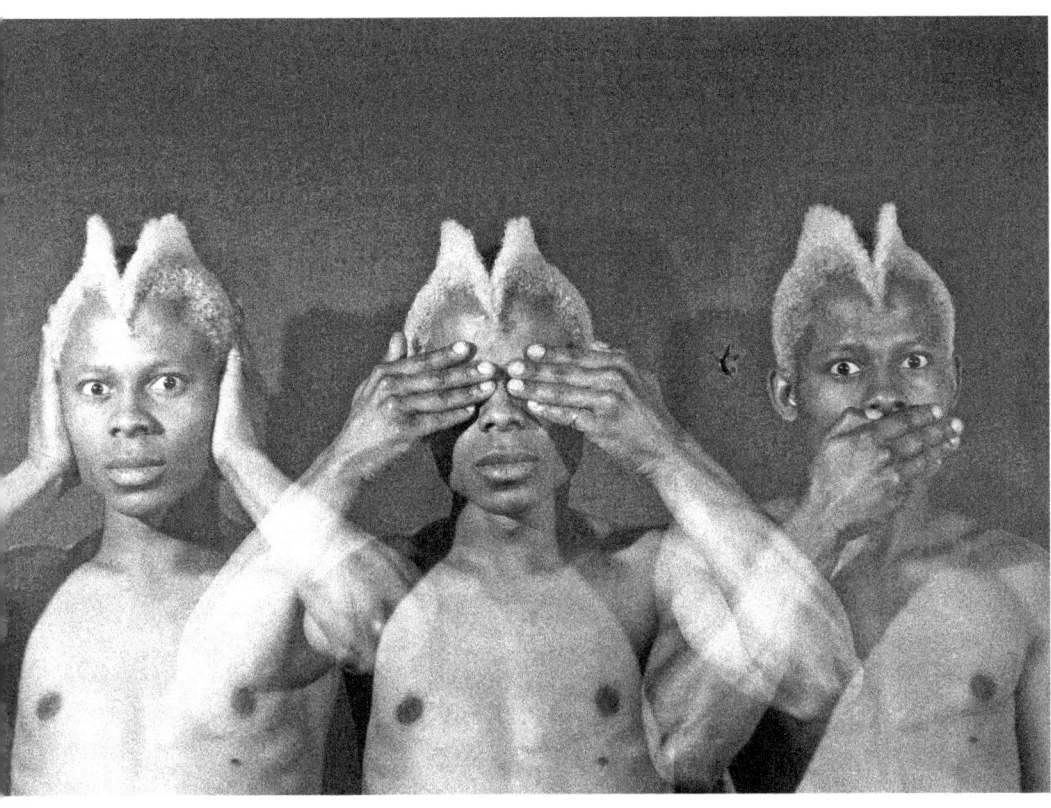

Figure 5.13 Rotimi Fani-Kayode, *Untitled* (*Hear No Evil, See No Evil, Speak No Evil*) (ca. 1985). © Rotimi Fani-Kayode / Autograph ABP. Courtesy of Autograph ABP.

from this period, as it specifies the performative rather denotative work he seeks to do in the field of the image—not to merely replicate an iconographic form but subject it to an ambivalent play of multiplication and subversion. Fani-Kayode's frequent invocations of Eshu can thus be read as drawing on his role not only as emissary of creative energy but also as ruler of the crossroads or, as Gates argues, as the patron of the dual act of interpretation and criticism. Indeed, in a multiply exposed print from 1985 (figure 5.13), Fani-Kayode hints at the porous boundary between the realms of spiritual and profane and also the crucial intersection of speech and vision. Here a figure whose double-lobed hair suggests the twinning of *ibeji*, and the Janus-headed ruler Shango is rendered as triplets, respectively covering ears, eyes, and mouth.

These figures, too, invoke the signifying trickster, but in the transcultural parable of the "three wise monkeys" who hear, see, and speak no evil. In this story, meanings are multiplied, as these figures might variously promote pure thought and speech (good character), the virtue of silence or mystery, or the dangers of remaining silent in the face of evil. As an important enunciative tactic of both criticism and relation, Fani-Kayode is not simply transgressing one sign or depicting a distinct space of difference. To wit, for Gates the play of doubles occurs not at the collision of intrinsically separate realms but at a location that reveals their points of inflection from a new vantage: Eshu's crossroads. As such, parallel "universes, then, is an inappropriate metaphor; perpendicular universes is perhaps a more accurate visual description."[54]

ECTOPLASM

Given the rather overt ways in which Fani-Kayode engaged with canonical moments in European painting, as well as the formalistic intensity of the work presented in *Black Male/White Male*, questions of affinity and appropriation, style and signification necessarily come to the fore. Fani-Kayode's own statements, training, and immediate cultural context all suggest real familiarity both with problems within Western art histories and with the symbolic terrain of the photograph. Nonetheless, there is yet another way to frame Fani-Kayode's relation to the surrealist current in the twentieth century. As an "African artist working in a western medium," it is equally plausible that Fani-Kayode saw in surrealist procedures an approach that most closely resembled an orientation toward cosmology and creative practice that he had nurtured for much of his life. Notably, surrealism's various attempts to connect with "other worlds"—though complicit in the fetishistic or fantastical entanglements of the colonial matrix—made it the most obvious avant-garde technology on which his practice might build.

Like other young artists who took up aspects of the surreal—notably the gothic ambience, self-objectification, and play of mirrors in the work of Woodman—Fani-Kayode's photographs were decidedly out of fashion. In the main, he resisted the acerbic tone and deaestheticized codes of the realist and poststructural approaches to image making then favored by critics.[55] And as elaborated here in discussions of the "technique of ecstasy," it would have been easy to write off his statements about the strange materiality and metaphysical vectors of such work as quixotic. For all that, Fani-Kayode was absolutely clear about the deeper concerns of his work, which extended well beyond the immediacy of quotidian life. He wrote that both "aesthetically and ethically, I seek to translate my rage and my desire into new images that will undermine conventional perceptions and which may reveal hidden worlds."[56] Autograph ABP director Mark Sealy reflected several years later that what "Fani-Kayode was attempting to communicate was of no concern to the then current Eurocentric photographic trends. . . . The ethereal world was as important to Kayode as the tangible world. In his work he is inviting us to play with him in the grey zones between black and white, gay and straight, acceptance and taboo. This work was the beginning of a constructed twilight cross-cultural zone, a kind of Never Never land where 'reality' is a stranger."[57]

In this light, Fani-Kayode can be seen as mining anachronistic techniques not merely to stylize or transgress them but, instead, to reiterate an insight familiar to many surrealists. There are ancient and mysterious forces that persist, resonating in the landscapes of the interior or the topographies beyond everyday sense perception or routine scientific observation. This is why Breton sought out talismanic objects and sought to tap into subreal aspects of the psyche, why Bataille sought out the ethnographic mission and the occult ritual, and why Brassäi became a quintessential nightcrawler, charting the twilight of the urban underground. This last point is one of rather obvious convergence: Exposure Three laid out the ways in which Fani-Kayode drew inspiration from, documented, or recreated elements of heterotypic spaces, those terrestrial locations that exist both within and beyond the quotidian as a form of mirroring. Fani-Kayode's queer heterotopias of the bathhouse, the cabaret or punk club, the loft or warehouse party, or the ritual space of the darkened studio all found their counterparts, however, in earlier surrealist forays.[58] Some clear examples are Boiffard's untitled photograph of 1932–1933 that depicts in soft focus a head wrapped in taut black leather, a length of chain coiled around the neck. That picture evokes a rather intense mode of bondage and domination and desubjectifies its sitter, converting them into a sculptural form reminiscent of Beninese Edo-type shrines to the head. And in 1934, Brassäi captured a shot of a woman in a black, tightly laced corset and black stockings, body elongated, gazing over her right shoulder. (Compare Brassäi's image with figure 5.14, by Fani-Kayode.)

Brassäi was, of course, known for his charting of sexually infused, afterhours locales—most notably in a series of photographs from 1932 of Parisian bars, as in his *Lesbian Couple at Le Monocle* (1932), a portrait from a queer

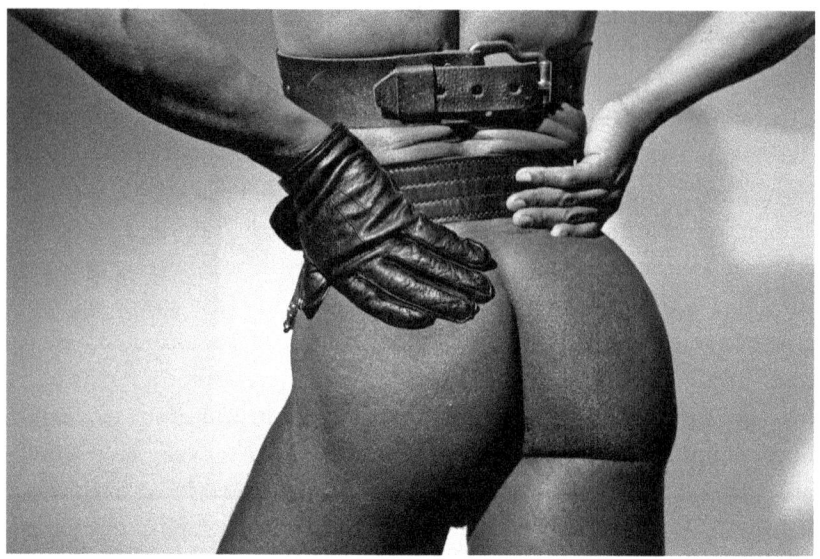

Figure 5.14 Rotimi Fani-Kayode, *Bondage* (ca. 1987). © Rotimi Fani-Kayode / Autograph ABP. Courtesy of Autograph ABP.

bar in Montparnasse. This was a space in which he, the ethnographic eye, was uncharacteristically a minority. The photograph itself was part of a wider portfolio of what he called "faggots, cruisers, chickens, old queens, and famous antique dealers."[59] As Catherine Lord argues of the photograph, Brassaï produced here a site of ambiguity in which a "butch/femme couple sit close together on one side of a cocktail table, looking with interest at the scene unfolding beyond the frame of the photograph."[60] Lord's assessment echoes both Sealy's analysis of the ambiguous grey areas staked out by Fani-Kayode and Judith Butler's more general claim that gender itself is a kind of drag, an imitation "for which there is no original."[61] Brassaï's pictures, which more generally track the "inverted" spaces of nocturnal Paris or Berlin, also map subjectivities that are produced, as it were, through dynamic masquerade or in performative relation to external forces. His photographs serve as a sort of paraphrase of Lacan's mirror phase.

Indeed, Craig Owens pursued this very line of investigation with respect to Brassaï in a piece from 1978. In his essay "Photography *en abyme*," Owens describes Brassaï's *Bal Musette des Quatre-Saisons, Rue de Lappe* (1932), an image constructed of symmetries—two couples are reflected as if mirror images of each other and bounded in turn by a mirror on the rear wall that imbricates the viewer/photographer and the camera, which, in Owens's account, is itself a kind of mirror.[62] In the case of *Rue de Lappe*, the presence of the mirror effects both a visual and a structural folding, and folding in—a recursive process of looking, reflection, and reduplication. Owens believes that this *plier* "suggests the analogical definition of the photograph as a mirror image. . . . Because the mirror image doubles the subjects—which is exactly what the photograph itself does—it functions here as a reduplication, a reduced, internal image of the photograph." Not just reflecting the figures within the image plane, the specific image functions (like photography itself) as a fragment or a miniature (much like the images within *Black Male/White Male* do within Fani-Kayode's larger project). In other words, this mirroring "tells us in a photograph what a photograph is—*en abyme*."[63] It also reminds us of the fragility and contingency of the subject herself—alluded to in Fani-Kayode's *Joining of Equal Forces* and literalized in *One in Three*.

In Owens's terms, the photographic operation, made glaringly obvious by the presence of the mirror in Brassaï's picture, is one of endless "substitution, repetition, and splitting of the self" through doubling/mirroring. The effect is a simultaneous constitution and deconstitution of the subject. The upshot is that the endless possibility of reduplication made available through the photographic process always means that the image is never transparent, never authoritative. It is, rather, implicated in a matrix of looking, of provisional location of its subjects. In much the same way, according to Lacan, this is how the self is constituted, through a process of differentiation from (and through) the reflected gaze of the Other. As a result, the pictured subject is not so much depicted in, but partially *constituted by*, the photograph. Just as for Owens reduplication and mirrors are a through line in Brassaï's work, their implications for the creation of subjectivity and identification register as both object of investigation and formal process in *Black Male/White Male*.

The splintering and mirroring underlying such tactics developed by surrealist photographic procedures is, in Fani-Kayode's book, quite literal. For example, *James in Brixton* (1986; figure 5.15) pictures its eponymous subject with a seductive gaze and unbuttoned, embroidered white shirt. Through a process of reprinting and inversion of the image, of mirroring, it figures him as fragmented form, a doppelgänger of himself. What's more, the image overlays face and sleeve in its top center in a moment of dissipation, rendering neither figure entirely solid, each bleeding into and invading the space of the

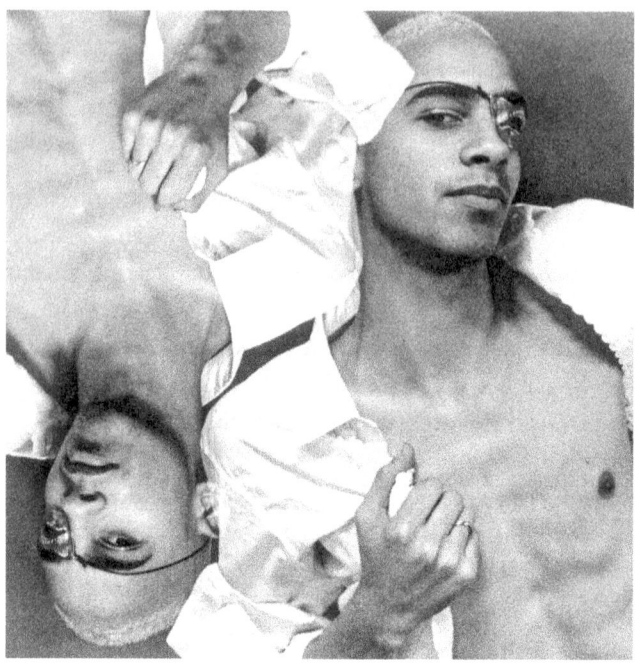

Figure 5.15 Rotimi Fani-Kayode, *James in Brixton* (1986). © Rotimi
Fani-Kayode / Autograph ABP. Courtesy of Autograph ABP.

other. In effect, this gesture ruptures the unity of both the portrait and the
subject therein. Such a disruption of corporeal solidity is also underscored by
the James's metallic eye patch, which invokes Bakhtin and the Carnival tradition of masquerade and, with it, the suspension of dominant social relations
and meanings.[64]

For Freud, of course, the doppelgänger is a moment of the uncanny par ex-
cellence, a self-recurrence that defies temporal and spatial logic, one that (citing Otto Rank) has connections with "reflection in mirrors, with shadows,
guardian spirits, with the belief in the soul and the fear of death."[65] And with
such "belief" the mirror double shifts the viewer beyond the terrestrial world
of the heterotopia and into a more ineffable space of dreams, mysticism, and
the supernatural. By now it would be redundant to reiterate Fani-Kayode's
uses of gothic and Romantic elements in his photographs, but it does seem
clear that he would have located continuities that punctuated these seemingly
discrete moments in European art. One clear point of inflection worth noting

is the recurrence in several of Fani-Kayode's series of otherworldly figures—the shape of the Minotaur or outright depictions of heavenly creatures—that are discussed in detail in earlier chapters. Consider further that angels seemed, in the pages of Bataille's *Documents*, to bridge elements of premodernist belief with primitivist fantasy—as in issue six (1930), which features a study of antique and contemporary images thereof.[66]

Similarly, Maya Deren and Alexander Hammid's 1943 film *Meshes of the Afternoon* develops the uncanny flows of time and dreamlike register of surrealist photography, and features laden symbolism—phones, keys, knives, and a lone flower. The film's female protagonist seems trapped in both the claustrophobic space of her home and the unsettling confines of a dream, haunted by an apparitional figure who bears a mirror for a face; the film concludes with another figure finding the woman dead, the mirror in her home shattered, her initial slumber crossing the threshold into actual mortality. It seems clear, here, that Deren and Hammid are working in continuity with surrealist impulses but also ramifying the latter's ethnographic concerns, a desire to find transcultural approaches to apprehend realities that are just beyond reach, connecting to the quotidian, indeed, through a kind of perpendicular relation. The mirror-faced figure, for example, explicitly invokes the Kongo genre of *minkisi*, objects that exemplify the logic of fetish: inanimate objects imbued with excessive power that mediate multiple worlds (in this case both Europe and Africa *and* the worlds of the living and dead), and figures that, like Brassaï's nudes, oscillate uncannily between animate and inanimate. The famed *nkisi nkondi* is a hunter figure that bears both a knife and a mirror and has the power to pursue the living on behalf of another.

Further, as Robert Farris Thompson has argued, the Kongo cosmological structure, which is structured as complementary mirror worlds of night and day, living and dead, made its way to the Americas through diasporic transmission, most notably to Haiti.[67] This path specifies both the Caribbean tradition to which Fani-Kayode frequently refers, and which he would have encountered in central Brooklyn, not far from the Pratt Institute. Deren, for her part, gained fame for documenting the trance states of Haitian *houngan*s who, in the Voudou tradition, mediate the invisible spirit world of the *loa* through a trance state through which they are temporarily possessed.[68] Such possession is, almost certainly, a version of what Fani-Kayode meant when he described his "technique of ecstasy," the loss of self in communion with other planes of existence. Bataille, too, sought such dissolution through the erotic, and on his various journeys into French West Africa, or the shadowy spaces of his secret society of the Acéphale. It is worth noting, too, that Isaac Julien drew together many of these elements in his *Looking for Langston*. His film is shot with an ethereal (even diaphanous) tonality reminiscent of Deren's *Meshes*, and a nighttime interlude in a park is populated by black angels in metallic armatures. It concludes with a subterranean club dissolving into anachronistic frenzy, as a quiet Harlem watering hole populated by men in tuxedos begins to stomp and groove like an after-hours ball, propelled by the house music typical of the late 1980s.

Nonetheless, in spite of their political, biographical, and formal confluences, Fani-Kayode and Julien seem to part ways here. Where Julien—like many of the surrealists—enacts a space of fantasy and distorted temporality to investigate the psychic space of repression and desire, it is not clear to what extent he believes his films to be doing openly metaphysical (rather than political or imaginative) work. And this is where Bataille and Fani-Kayode *do* have a great deal in common, in their belief in the power of ecstatic communion and their willingness to pursue the genuine dissolution of the self through ritual practice. Bataille spent his life seeking out forms of connection—flattening the valuation of things through *informe*, or moving into unseen realms through ritual practice associated with traditional forms of veneration. In a fairly typical passage that alludes to the power of erotic communion and the uncanny play of subject and object, he would argue that "we escape this empty and sterile movement, this sum of objects and abstract functions that is the world of the intellect, only by entering a very different world where objects are on the same plane as the subject. . . . To make this radical difference between two worlds perceptible, there is no finer example than the domain of the erotic life, where the object is rarely situated on another plane than the subject."[69] But Fani-Kayode had a decisive advantage over Bataille: whereas the latter's position of colonial power always imbricated him in the primitivist encounter, Fani-Kayode had a direct line back to the source material itself. Where the surrealists were fascinated by the power of mirror reversals and uncanny doubles, Fani-Kayode hailed from a place with a cult of twins, those mediators between worlds, in the *ibeji*; where thirties-era avant-gardists sought out psychic expansion through an ethnographic remove, Fani-Kayode could claim an atavistic knowledge, amplified by his encounters with the Caribbean diaspora. A photograph such as *Ebo Òrìsà* can be fairly read as a play of heterological actions—all substitution of masks for heads, literal inversions, and the defamiliarization of the nude. But for Fani-Kayode the *gelede* mask depicted in *Ebo Òrìṣà* refers to a typical Yoruban masquerade, in which spirits are honored and the play of material and otherworldly, self and other, male and female becomes, for a time, ambiguous.

In Fani-Kayode's estimation, it seems, questions of spiritual energy were no mere metaphors or poetic asides. As Sealy argues, much of the meaning of the photographs will remain arcane; while their ambiguities "remain veiled for the uninitiated non-Yoruba audience, when decoded they contribute to the unravelling of the multi-layered symbolism of the work."[70] And yet, the play of masquerade and the physical surfaces of the photographs served, for Fani-Kayode, to create a membrane between the audience and the figures in the frame: "the surface is there to be challenged, but at the same time offer[s] the subject a protective barrier."[71] Sealy's descriptions square with observations about the volatility of divine energy in Yoruban systems—priests of the orishas and readers of Ifá divination must be carefully trained, and kings traditionally wore crowns capped by birds (emissaries between worlds) and fitted with strands of beads that created a protective shield between the energetically imbued visage and the onlooking viewer.[72]

Birds are connected in Yoruban tradition with the spiritual realm in a few ways—aside from royal regalia, they are associated with the herbalist-healer orisha Osanyin and, perhaps more notably, the fearsome goddess of love, Oshun, who flies through the night wielding a large knife and is proficient in the arts of deadly potions and warfare. Alternately, Oshun's magic can be directed into the protection of her initiates, as in the *oshun kole* icon of witch feathers, which is used, in particular, by Afro-Cubans as an amulet against black magic.[73] In a sense, the dualistic Oshun is an apt transcultural reflection of the power of the erotic—the fusion of Eros and Thanatos—a connection likely not lost on Bataille, who published layouts of metallic sculpture adorned with birds (for example, in *Documents* 5 [1929]), as well as images of nineteenth-century bird-topped staffs to Oshun from Yorubaland.[74]

Fani-Kayode was able to neatly draw these associations together in set of 1989 images featuring a collaborator who, again bears the gold-painted phallus and white mask. The bird mask is stitched at the edges, notable for its long proboscis; it recurs in several instances, including the color print *Every Moment Counts II* (figure 5.16). Here Fani-Kayode pictures a mise-en-scène that statically balances forms with sculptural precision, blurring the boundary between object and subject (putting them on the same plane), and situat-

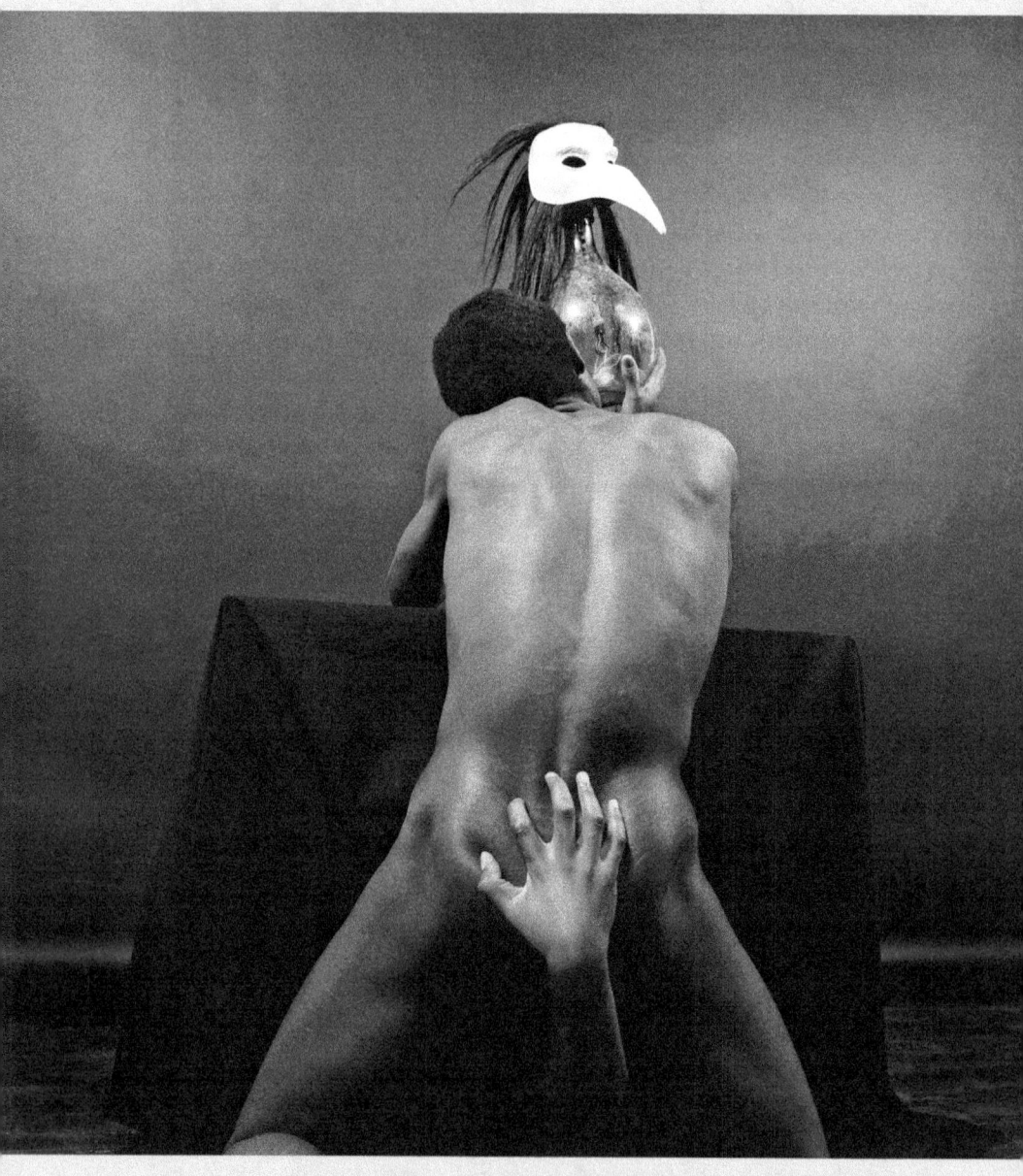

Figure 5.16 Rotimi Fani-Kayode, *Every Moment Counts II* (1989). © Rotimi Fani-Kayode / Autograph ABP. Courtesy of Autograph ABP.

ing them in a moment erotic and spiritual intensity. The figure leans into an abyss from which a disembodied hand reaches through his legs, drawing his pelvis nearer to an implied second man. The central figure, in return, leans in. He seems to kiss the object in his hand, an assemblage of what appears to be a dusty Italian-style wine jug, capped with the mask, which is wreathed in dark feathers. The mask functions here not as ethnographic curio, but as an active agent, conjoining Fani-Kayode's past with the immediacy of his present, seemingly in dual spiritual and sexual communion. The figure's "head" is mounted or substituted by the spirit even as he "receives head." Mercer identifies this mask as *ororo*, a reference that would confirm this association with regal headgear.[75] Although the term *ororo* does not appear frequently in the literature, Robert Farris Thompson also writes of a bird of the mind, *eiye ororo*, which is associated with the head shrine—pure white in color, and representative of God's emissary (perhaps *akoko*), that delivers *àshe* to the minds of mortals.[76] But many viewers would also recognize the mask as Venetian, donned during the transatlantic days of Carnival—erotic and Dionysian dissolution writ large.[77]

Which is to say, by the years 1988–1989, Fani-Kayode arrived at something like a mature style, a singular method that drew together broad swaths of transcultural signifiers and formal strategies to create provisional zones of contact and ambivalence. In many ways, he was aided by surrealist processes, especially early on, as he worked to signify on and disidentify with canonical works of avant-garde art, and to produce Neoromantic and gothic scenes of cinematic beauty and homoerotic intensity. But as the 1980s drew to a close, his relationship to these histories was revealed less and less as one of retrieval or transgression but, instead, as one of continuity with surrealism's deeper ambitions. After all, he had access to the very esoterica that the surrealists themselves sought in the world of dreams or on foreign shores.

Nonetheless, it seems clear that for Fani-Kayode, the last portfolios were not visionary fabulation so much as a careful dialectic between the production of images and the documentation what was actually happening in front of the lens, in the space of his darkened studio. The shift is akin to Deren's move from surrealist cinema in *Meshes* to cinematic documentary in Haiti. To draw on the ramified and expanded surrealist tradition to which Fani-Kayode was apparent heir, his practice progressed from experimentation with surrealist tactics and their explorations of the deep (the subreal) to something more disruptive still—indexing the superreal. He allowed the viewer, in other words, to see behind the curtain and into worlds that overlap with the mundane surfaces of waking life while remaining stubbornly invisible to the uninitiated. To paraphrase Romare Bearden, the texture of life in Brixton and, especially during the long nights in Fani-Kayode's studio was, perhaps, more outerworldly than anything those earlier surrealists could have imagined.

NIGHT MOVES

The Techniques of Ecstasy is the idea that the babalawo (father of secrets
or priest) goes into an ecstatic trance in order to communicate with the god.
Rotimi and I understood the artist to be doing something parallel to that and
also, on a more jokey level, we wanted to show that two black men can
have sex as a means of communicating with the spirits.

Alex Hirst, *The Last Supper*

The work did sit within a particular context but with the added
tradition of Africa. He is Yoruba. He left Nigeria in 1966, but he had a
relationship to Africa that I could not have in Lagos. That was something
that belonged to the past. . . . Lagos was trying to modernize—Fela Kuti,
etc.—Rotimi embraced that Yoruba culture. The difference here is this
expression of traditional ecstasy, the trying to get in touch
with spirituality. African spirituality.

Yinka Shonibare, MBE, in conversation with Mark Sealy, Tiwani Contemporary, 2014

Rotimi Fani-Kayode died at Coppetts Wood on 21 December 1989. The now-
defunct hospital, roughly an hour north of Central London, was known for
its isolation units and for its treatment of infectious and tropical diseases. In
Ruppert Gabriel's interpretive documentary, 1992's *Rage and Desire*,[1] a title
card very clearly notes that Fani-Kayode's cause of death was unexpected heart
failure, subsequent to treatment for meningitis. It also notes that Fani-Kayode
was not HIV positive.

The same year, Alex Hirst displayed his own portfolio of photographs,
some evidently his own, others part of what he considered a posthumous continuation of his collaboration with Fani-Kayode. By 1989 both artists were

well attuned to the fragility and preciousness of life, the imminence of death, and the thin membrane between them. Hirst noted that "being more conscious now of the butterfly-nature and panther-nature of life than I was five or six years ago, I spend as much time as I can re-arranging the elements of the ordinary so as to experience the extra-ordinary."[2] The 1992 touring exhibition was called *The Last Supper*, a fitting title for a survey of a collaboration in which religious imagery had become a conspicuous theme. The exhibition served as a final farewell to Hirst's lost partner, and a harbinger of his own death—presumably from AIDS-related complications—in October 1993.[3] In the accompanying text, Hirst pointedly noted that Fani-Kayode was negative, while he positive, but that their final series, *Bodies of Experience* (1989) and *Ecstatic Antibodies* (which was displayed in 1990), "both deal with issues of AIDS. . . . We were trying say that non-Western medical approaches are as valid as any other. Also, most of the Western drugs come from the rainforest and the people who live there have known these remedies for hundreds, maybe thousands, of years."[4] And so, whatever the cause of Fani-Kayode's death at the age of 34, the last phase of his work seemed in name and content uncannily aware of mortality. Perhaps more significantly, this phase marked his attempts to move beyond the picture as mere screen, producing instead photography as ritual and spiritual procedure. Fani-Kayode did not, like many of his contemporaries, seek to document the AIDS crisis or join in the campaign to make drugs such as AZT available. And in giving up on direct activism or chemical panaceas he used the camera to pursue more arcane or alchemical ones.

In Gabriel's film, Hirst suggests that a fascination with untimely death decisively impacted Fani-Kayode's work starting in 1987. He notes that in the last three years of his life, "the *joie de vivre* of the earlier pictures gave way to a darker, more elegiac vision. That was when he produced the *Abiku* series" (1988).[5] Presumably Hirst is here referring to a range of lush black-and-white portraits emphasizing deep, abyssal space and themes of maternal nurturing. One such picture is *Every Mother's Son / Children of Suffering* (1989; figure 6.1), from a larger series of twin figures with eyes covered by hands or fabric blindfolds. They conjoin Oedipal tragedy, the uncanniness of the doppelgänger and, importantly, the *ibeji* orisha of the twins. Fani-Kayode pictured twins through multiple exposure or double printing starting as early as 1985, with the figure from *Four Twins* (figure 6.2) appearing in multiple works, including a frontal shot from the same sequence that invokes the *ibeji*'s elaborate, crownlike coiffure, mimicked by the precise cropping of the sitter's bleached curls. Other pictures from this period begin to employ a pictorialist method and show a series of crouched figures wrapped in surgical tubing, plastic cord augmented by hand-tinted ectoplasmic green (*Abiku*; figure 6.3).

In Yoruban tradition, *abiku* are children who die before adolescence and the spirits that call them back from the word of the living. Hirst again: "abiku means 'born to die.' . . . Rotimi had discovered that his own name was an abiku name, meaning 'stay by me.'"[6] The hand-tinted prints from this series mark a full-circle return to Fani-Kayode's post-MFA experiments in printmaking and monotypes. Here, figures seem afloat as if in an aqueous substance. The tubing is a simple studio prop, but he transforms it into a strangling noose or wrapped umbilicus—a spectral conduit back to the underworld.

And so, in his last photographs (and in Hirst's in the subsequent years) Fani-Kayode sought to orient his practice toward one of art's long-repressed functions: as a site of communion, encounter, and transcendence. He decisively turned away from the more semiotic and optical fixations that had obtained in the realm of "art photography" for much of the twentieth century, and had reached a zenith in the photographic interventions of many of his contemporaries in the US and Europe. Fani-Kayode embraced chemistries and theories of materiality that had been relegated to quixotic Victorian pursuits, the "primitives" ironically fetishized by modernism, and, of course, strands of surrealist practice in Europe and the Americas.

In one sense, Fani-Kayode possessed something that other surrealists of the twentieth century did not—a lineage that connected him to the traditions and techniques of Yorubaland and its diaspora. But, as we have seen, surrealist procedures were of vital importance to someone who saw himself to be an "African artist working in a western medium." While photography had, of course, been adapted by other noted African artists during Fani-Kayode's life—in the work of Seydou Keïta, Malick Sidibé, and others—it was approaches and modes drawn from global surrealism and from its resurgence in photographic practice in the 1980s that solidified his own approach during that last year of his life.

In a prescient account of photography's alchemical capacity, and reflecting on the disorientation of psychic automatism and the desire awakened in his process, Man Ray wrote in 1933 that seized "in moments of visual detachment during periods of emotional contact, these images are oxidize residues, fixed by light and chemical elements, of living organism." He goes on to describe

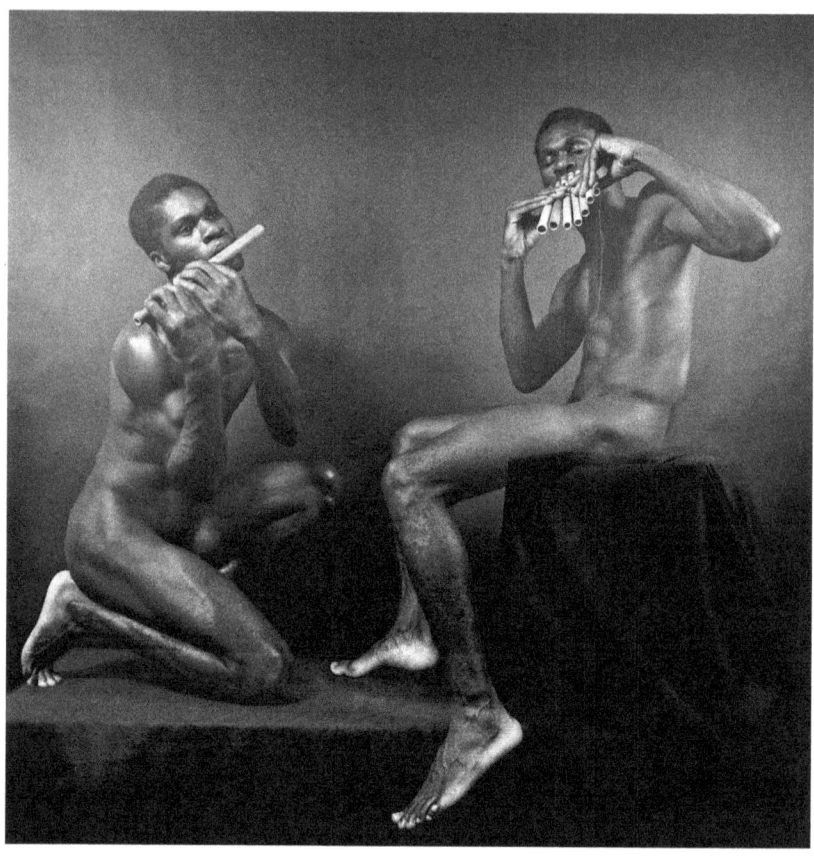

Figure 6.1 Rotimi Fani-Kayode, *Every Mother's Son / Child of Suffering* (1989). © Rotimi Fani-Kayode / Autograph ABP. Courtesy of Autograph ABP.

the photograph as a tragic survivor a transient act of encounter, "like the un-disturbed ashes of an object consumed by flames."[7] Man Ray's conception of photography proposed an art that does not merely represent or signify but that physically indexes people and events, like the grooves in a record. Perhaps more famously, Walter Benjamin, writing concurrently with (and, to a degree, about) surrealism, theorized the singular materiality exuded by an object as its aura.[8] Realism and mechanical reproduction, according to Benjamin, could, in contrast, dispel such potent materiality, and during the subsequent five decades, Marxist and formalist critics generally steered the avant-garde away from considerations of aura, desire, and the superreal more broadly. But out

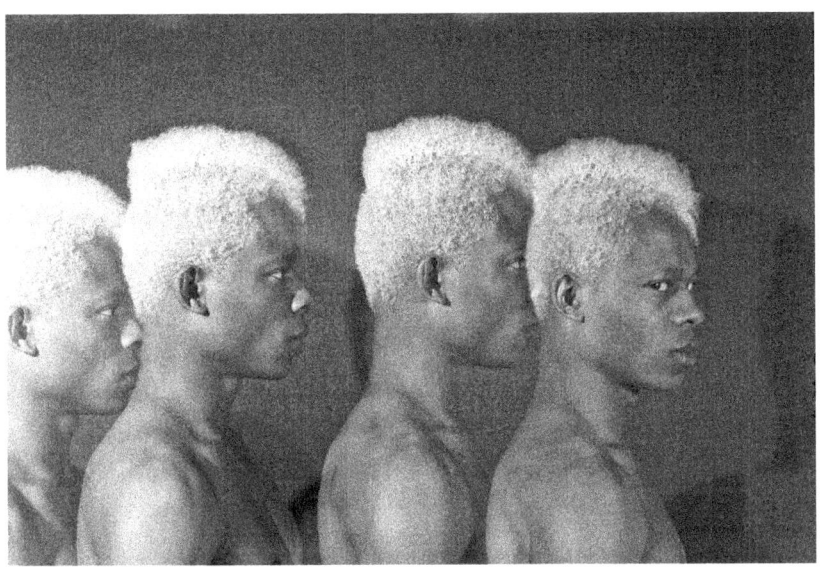

Figure 6.2 Rotimi Fani-Kayode, *Four Twins* (1985). © Rotimi Fani-Kayode / Autograph ABP. Courtesy of Autograph ABP.

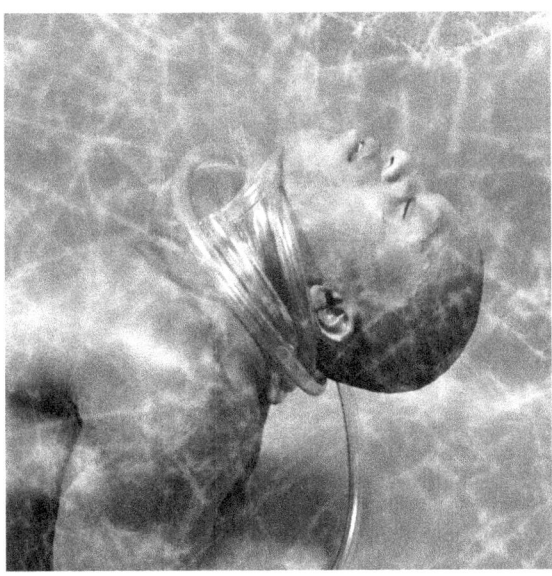

Figure 6.3 Rotimi Fani-Kayode, *Abiku* (1988). © Rotimi Fani-Kayode / Autograph ABP. Courtesy of Autograph ABP.

beyond surrealist experimentation, could this young medium tap into even more ancient techniques? Could photographs be talismanic amulets, sites of spiritual encounter, or even wards against disease? And if so, what would that mean during the peak years of the AIDS crisis?

However unfashionable, Fani-Kayode and Hirst were clear about their intentions. As the titles of their last portfolios of 1988–1989 intoned, every moment counted and they, ultimately, had nothing to lose. Hirst argued at this stage that his and Fani-Kayode's project was one of "tragic freedom" and "bewildering intimacy." They sought to inaugurate moments of reenchantment within the long shadow of Wall Street and a suffocating corporatization of the world. They wrote in a 1989 catalog essay entitled "Metaphysick" that, "under the pressure of such lofty enterprises as the 'alchemical' or 'ritual' production of spiritual antibodies, inspiration is squeezed from all those involved."[9] In a concluding endnote, they go further, arguing that their use of color for the C-prints in the exhibition was integral not merely to an aesthetic but to the spiritual exercise that the work in situ attempted. They argued there that the catalog's "black and white reproductions can only provide a shadow to tempt or to remind; A third element of our work—the icons—cannot be included here. We do not wish our gold to be turned back to lead."[10]

This essay by Fani-Kayode and Hirst acknowledges the HIV that would claim the lives of Hirst and countless others. It is also a clear account of their mature approach to image making—by then more fully a collaborative investigation, and newly imbued with color and by-then antique alternate processes. Working in this vein, the artists took the viewer back to the liminal terrain between the Renaissance and the scientific revolution, invoking arcane spiritual practice and the production of thaumaturgic objects. In this text, they draw important distinctions between registers of objects: between the "icons," or sacred forms that are central to the composition of photographs; the photographs themselves; and the *reproduction* of each in the black-and-white of the catalog (or, later, the digital). They are clear to specify orders of materiality and resonance in their work, insisting on a potency that might be dispelled in proportion to the distance of the image from the original. And while Douglas Crimp theorized photography as a simulacral act—copies of copies without original[11]—Fani-Kayode and Hirst suggest just the opposite. They initiated ephemeral moments that the photograph simultaneously activated and delicately recorded. Fani-Kayode and Hirst's concept of the "tempting shadow" is a reference to picture making as a quintessentially indexical process. And, of course, Fani-Kayode wrote elsewhere that his photographs were quite literally "Traces of Ecstasy."

This final chapter contends, then, that Fani-Kayode's last series elaborated the theatrical, high-contrast black-and-whites of 1987–1988 and his formal experiments with pictorialism and surrealism. Specifically, they can be understood as both an ambitious realization of his larger play of temporality and cultural relation and as a direct response to his own mortality. While Fani-Kayode's work fell outside of the mainstream of what might be called AIDS activism (direct political discourse or legislative mobilization), it nonetheless constituted a crucial intervention in the landscape of art during the height of the AIDS crisis by positing nondiscursive modes of address and staging pictures of people with AIDS that were imbued with life or, indeed, the creative and healing force of what Fani-Kayode called "ecstatic antibodies."

BLACK FRIARS

From the years 1987–1989, one can track two major formal movements in Fani-Kayode's photographs: first, a shift from a wider variation of settings to a more disciplined studio practice; and second, a refinement of earlier plays of surrealist technique and erotic pictures toward carefully staged tableaux. By 1989, Fani-Kayode had channeled these impulses into series that are, together, notable for their large-scale printing and their use of saturated color. Not only had Fani-Kayode embraced the reclamation of color in photography initiated a decade earlier by William Eggleston, Richard Misrach, Stephen Shore, and others, but he made clear incursions into the terrain of painting, as well. The works *Nothing to Lose* (*Bodies of Experience* exhibitions) and *Every Moment Counts* (*Ecstatic Antibodies* group show; figure 6.4) are all notable for their clear citation of and formal congruities with seventeenth-century European painting: Baroque classicism that marked a fusion of chromaticism, chiaroscuro, and naturalism and renovated the medium, from the Netherlands down to the Italian states.[12]

Accordingly, works in Fani-Kayode's final series have been compared to the canvases of Caravaggio. The latter was known in his time for thinly-veiled studio autoportraiture. He was also something of an errant and firebrand and, like Fani-Kayode, made pictures that rather bluntly implied eroticism, Dionysian excess, and even sickness. Caravaggio is also known for lushly saturated colors, the incandescent red robes that drape his figures, and an overall tenebrism that produced deep tonal variation—from light on the surface of subjects' skin to deep recessional space that enshrouds them. As earlier passages in this book have made clear, Caravaggio was himself a figure of homoerotic speculation, and his hyperrealistic depictions of muscled young men and luscious fruit were echoed in a variety of ways during the 1980s, such as Derek Jarman's 1986 anachronistic romp (depicting the painter as a roguish Neoromantic antihero). Other examples include Cindy Sherman's deconstruction by way of grotesque masquerade of the 1593 *Young Sick Bacchus*, and Fani-Kayode's 1989 *Grapes* (figure 4.7)—one of his several "black friars" and "transsexual priests" that built on the punk-styled queering of his earlier *Under the Surplice* (figure 3.3). For these reasons, Yinka Shonibare, for one, recalled:

> I looked at one of Rotimi's works recently and I thought, "Where have I seen that before?" I looked at Caravaggio . . . Derek Jarman's Caravaggio film—I thought about the ICA—Peter Greenaway, making those amazing films. This was a retro-postmodern moment when people were returning to classical art. I think about Christian iconography—which is very evident. I haven't seen references to classical iconography in the scholarship. It's been touched on but not expanded on. The Caravaggio and also the context of postmodern art—there was a climate. . . . History was returning to art practice as a subversive mode: "I'm here and I'm not going away" . . . women, black people.[13]

Shonibare's memory of his time in eighties London is consistent with claims made above about the reclamation of history as a subversive or critical gesture, and the value of such a reclamation to groups who had been largely marginalized within Western art making and its historicization. In other words, Shonibare is pointing to poststructuralist appropriation and its negation or disruption of signs or, to a greater extent, artists such as Fani-Kayode ambivalently signifying on canonical painting. Indeed, one unambiguously titled instance of the latter's work from 1989 is a print of a young man draped in cloth, clutching a raised knee and mournfully gazing at the floor. Saturated orange pigment enlivens the picture, and the whole—called *Renaissance Man* (figure 6.5)—connotes a sensuous iconicity.

Another oft-discussed work from 1989, sometimes marked either as from the *Communion* material or from the 1989 *Ecstatic Antibodies* installation curated by Tessa Boffin and Sunil Gupta, is one of several titled *Every Moment Counts*. The title is both a truism and an urgent declaration by a group of young artists who faced, during the wake of the AIDS epidemic, a profoundly shortened horizon. This photograph, a square-format studio portrait, shows its two figures in full regalia. While the men (one larger and bearded, the other smaller and more youthful) are the black nudes typical of Fani-Kayode's practice, here they are costumed, playing the part of a black friar and a young acolyte. The composition clearly parallels aspects of Caravaggio's painting, from the delicate younger man to the opulent pile of red cloth, or the contemplative pathos inscribed in the figure on the left's heavenward gaze. In other ways it departs: the latent homoerotic looking of Caravaggio is made explicit here, and the figures, of course, are black rather than white. These are substitutions and inversion by now familiar in Fani-Kayode's studio work, while the consistent use of color is something that becomes common only after 1988. Finally, a cruciform shape is added here, circumscribed by pearls. It is a multivalent symbol that evokes an early-Renaissance-style halo, Christian crosses or crowns of thorns, or southwestern American medicine wheels, symbolizing cosmic crossroads and healing energy in many native traditions. Similarly, pearls have many symbolic resonances of their own, from Byzantine royalty to Victorian mourning.

Significantly, Fani-Kayode was, at decade's end, not at all alone in his reinvestment in traditional motifs and belief systems. Earlier cultures of the Americas were widely sentimentalized or drawn into pop-cultural representations at this time, and Christianity became of key site of symbolic transgression under the aegis of a then-ascendant conservative, rightwing base in the United States. Other art-world examples included the return of religious references within avant-garde painting;[14] Mapplethorpe translating the crosses that littered his house into a series of hybrid portraits; Andres Serrano scandalously photographing crucifixes and statues of the Madonna immersed in urine. It was, in fact, Mapplethorpe and Serrano who most fully galvanized the forces of "decency" on the American right. But even popular music was rife with Christian iconography, often in the service of collapsing the dyad of sacred and profane, injecting sex into the field of acceptable religious experience. Madonna's album *Like a Prayer* (1989) went even further by depicting a black Jesus figure—complete with stigmata—miraculously brought to life by her love, amid a field of burning crosses. R.E.M.'s "Losing My Religion" video from two years later movingly depicted a wounded angel bearing the hallmarks of the plague figure Saint Sebastian. By 1991, even recordings of Gregorian chanting became wildly popular. Aside from the politics of representation

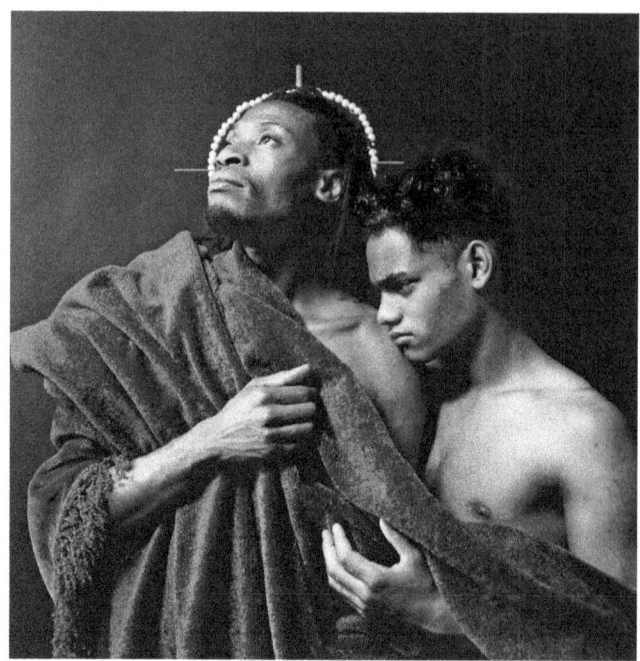

Figure 6.4 Rotimi Fani-Kayode, *Every Moment Counts*
(*Ecstatic Antibodies*) (1989). © Rotimi Fani-Kayode / Autograph ABP.
Courtesy of Autograph ABP.

actively litigated within AIDS activism at the time, Fani-Kayode's yoking of religious forms (both Yoruban and Christian) with homoeroticism and the epidemic was prescient but also typified the larger cultural moment in London and New York. Indeed, 1989 was a watershed year and is notable in the history of artistic censorship. To cite but one example, the religious right in the United States attempted to consolidate its hold on the rhetoric of the divine in order to prevent the display of photographs by Mapplethorpe (some of which dealt explicitly with Catholic iconography themselves).[15]

As to the Baroque and Classical elements in *Every Moment Counts*, the pictures partake in a more general return of early modern motifs across media (even architecture), either as knowing mannerism or fodder for poststructuralist critique during the late 1970s and 1980s. One example that hews toward the latter and that directly foregrounds Fani-Kayode's photographs is the multidecade practice of painter Barkley Hendricks, who produced evoca-

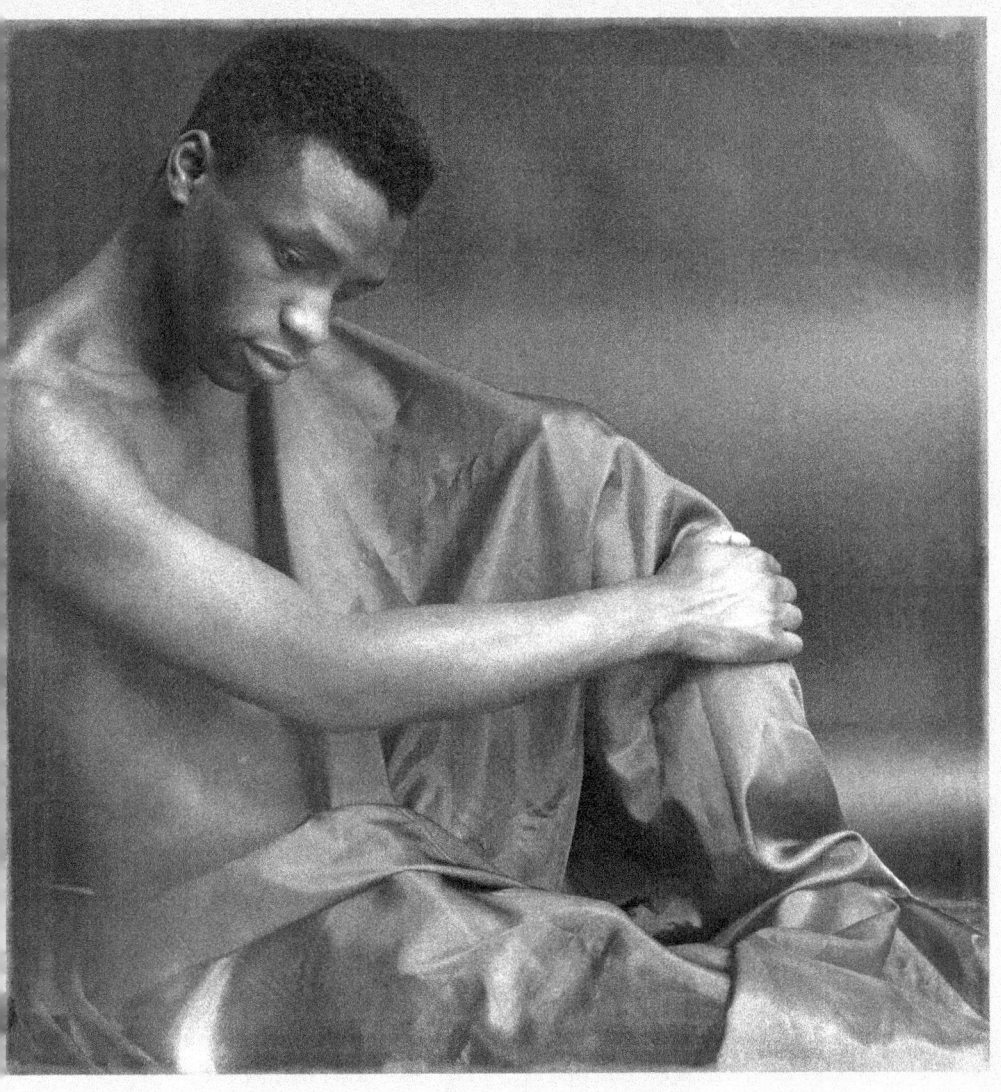

Figure 6.5 Rotimi Fani-Kayode, *Renaissance Man* (1989). © Rotimi Fani-Kayode /
Autograph ABP. Courtesy of Autograph ABP.

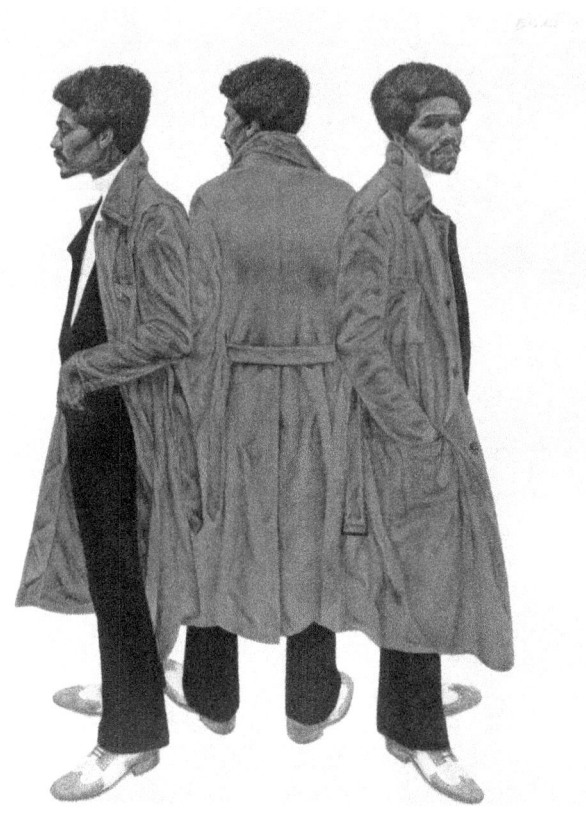

Figure 6.6 Barkley L. Hendricks, *Sir Charles, Alias Willie Harris* (1972), oil on canvas, 84⅛ × 72 in. © Estate of Barkley L. Hendricks. Courtesy of the artist's estate and Jack Shainman Gallery, New York.

tive portraits of contemporaneous black men garbed bold colors. His process knowingly drew on Italian and Dutch traditions. Hendricks's *Sir Charles, Alias Willie Harris* (1972; figure 6.6) stages its subject from three vantages, reminiscent of Fani-Kayode's multiple exposures. Here, Harris sports a sharp Afro and goatee and is outfitted in period-specific two-tone shoes and wide-cut trousers, but his overcoat is of a lustrous, deeply saturated red, like the chromatic robes that marked saints and prophets, from Bronzino and Titian down to Caravaggio. This vision of Willie Harris also clearly echoes the friar figure in *Every Moment Counts*.

Fani-Kayode and Hendricks both seem to differ from their contemporaries in that others tended to import signs whole—readymade—and act upon them through procedures of cancellation, abjection, or anachronistic juxtaposition. Fani-Kayode, in turn, enters directly into a more complex series of citations and elaborations that do not so much undermine or venerate earlier models, but retrofit their best elements to serve his own purposes. In this way, the Renaissance itself provides a compelling model, in which seemingly disparate painters such as Titian and Santi di Tito used poetic license or anachronistic fusions to address their work to contemporary social contexts. In Fani-Kayode's 1980s, such elaborating and disidentifying allowed him to create ambivalent and disruptive interventions in a more subtle register than many of his peers. Where Madonna or Serrano seek to lay their subjects low through sex or waste, or where Hendricks and Yasumasa Morimura (and, later, Kehinde Wiley) benefit from the shock of fusing two fully formed signs (sacred iconography and urban dandy), Fani-Kayode restages his scenes outright, preserving and expanding key methodological and metaphysical conceits of the original. Which is to concede a degree of anachronism at work in Fani-Kayode's photographs, but to deny the merely semiotic characer of that anachronism.[16] In this light, *Every Moment Counts* is neither appropriation as cancellation nor cynical self-identification with the old masters per se. The photograph is in many ways a revival of an earlier mode, albeit with sitters and social resonances suited to Fani-Kayode's immediate context. This is, indeed, a potent political gesture, but it's a form of citation with roots far deeper than the rhetorics of modernism and postmodernism. As a result, elements that seem transgressive in the photograph also serve to remind the viewer of a broader history that was long obscured from view: the presence of blacks in Renaissance Europe and the Mediterranean topographies of the Bible; or the *ars erotica* and general acceptance of the homoerotic from Greco-Roman civilization, segments of the church, and even aspects of life in Victorian England.

Both Hendricks and Fani-Kayode must be read, to an extent, in terms of the signification game proposed by a postmodernist framework that largely set the terms for art interpretation since the 1970s. Nonetheless, the above points to ways in which both artists, to different extents, sought to sidestep such poststructuralist contortions altogether. Indeed, in an interview with Thelma Golden, Hendricks—a noted colorist—suggests that his paintings were not so much about working critically on the Baroque model but elaborating it. He notes that "I would say I love the work of Caravaggio and Rembrandt.... I don't see too many contemporary painters I get inspiration from."[17] Other important clues: as a synthesizer of seemingly discrete cultural and formal valences, Fani-Kayode's photographs borrow both in handling and iconography elements of late-Renaissance Bolognese painting and the atelier of the Carracci. And they share the temporal and spatial cosmopolitanism of the Venetians—Titian, of course, but also the Medicis themselves, with their vast stores of artifacts collected from Africa, East Asia, and the Americas. Beyond these more speculative connections, the 1989 photographs plainly cite the saturated colors and piled fabric in Guido Reni's ecclesiastic portraiture and, more generally, draw on the martyrdom of the plague saint Sebastian (depicted in red by Bronzino's *Saint Sebastian* of 1533). The haloed figure of *Every Moment Counts* borrows less from the abstracted auras of Byzantine painting than from more literally depicted versions, as in Domenichino's *The Vision of Saint Ignatius of Loyola* (1622).

Importantly, the (mostly) northern Italian examples cited above represented, in sixteenth century debates, an emphasis on color and expression rather than the more cognitive "design" specified by the Roman contexts. Such use of color, such poetic handling could in turn, arouse a sensations in the viewer beyond mere intellectual recognition. As Charles Dempsey argues, such paintings could effectively bridge the artifice of the painting with the context everyday life, thus cultivating a sense of devotion in the viewer but also courting danger: releasing a "tiger, for the depiction of a nude . . . could arouse sensations simultaneously devout and carnal."[18] Although possibly an unintended consequence for the late-sixteenth and seventeenth-century painters themselves, Dempsey's description cuts to the center of the wider ambit of Fani-Kayode's practice, of linking the erotic and the spiritual or, more precisely, pursuing the world of the latter by enacting the former.

Such a conjoining was, whatever the artists' intent, a palpable effect for many viewers of late-Renaissance painting. Dempsey points to a function of art long-contested in Europe, one that came to be more steadily repressed throughout the Enlightenment. It was, indeed, the task of the Romantics and the surrealists to work as a counterpoint to this repressive drift, to recuperate the desirous and the marvelous that once pervaded visual art. Perhaps not coincidentally, precisely as Fani-Kayode was at work in Brixton, the art historian David Freedberg published his account of canonical painting, arguing that, historically, art was a site of passionate encounter—of sexual arousal, violence, transcendence, and communion. The power of images is such that they perennially activate old fears: of indecency or idolatry, that art might not only inspire the viewer but bypass the object of inspiration altogether, producing fidelity to the work itself. Freedberg stages the resulting resituating of these works (as illusionistic or visual allegory) in Freudian terms: "we fear the body in the image, we refuse to acknowledge our engagement with it, and we deny recognition of those aspects of our own sexuality that it may seem to threaten or reveal."[19]

In other words, Renaissance and Baroque painting resonated in a different key than the inhibiting debates about the fate of modernism still underway back in New York. A European model rooted in early rather than late modernity, and congruent in some ways with his own explorations of diasporic aesthetics: this would have been a tempting alternative starting point for Fani-Kayode, for a photography of potent materiality, a photography radiating talismanic power and erotic charge that had been complicated by a willful repression, the urge to forget. In short, much as Shonibare argued that Fani-Kayode intentionally bypassed Lagosian modernization to connect with an increasingly marginalized Yoruban past,[20] he may also have sought, in 1989, to elide games of signification and representation by looking to forms of synthetic image making that could directly conjure divinity. It is not accidental that Hirst referred to aspects of their work as icons: a description of saintly portraiture but, in the context of postmedieval Europe, also a genre of objects imbued with tremendous spiritual and social power.

BONDAGE

Ambivalence toward seemingly powerful works of art—this is not a new story. The sixteenth and seventeenth centuries provide an important context for understanding not only the fascination-cum-repulsion long felt toward sacred or mystical objects but also the early encounters between Europe and its others that would come to define many of the antinomies within modernity itself. In this sense, to look backward, to the early days of mercantile exchange, was consistent with Fani-Kayode's ever expanding range of referents, as he mapped the broad constellations of exchange and relation through which difference is produced.

In several passages in this book, the term *fetish* has emerged—to describe the gamut of sexual activities and sartorial codes specified by S/M, or to theorize ways of looking that, drawing on Freudian theories of castration and ambivalence, are implicated in a process of objectification and scopophilic voy-

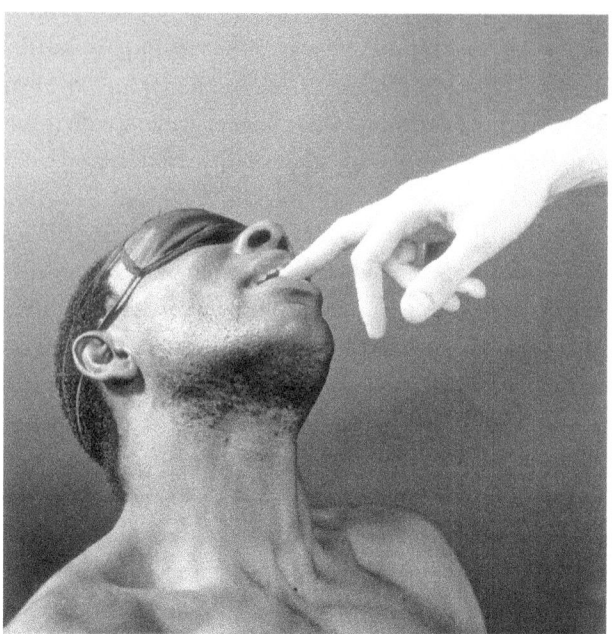

Figure 6.7 Rotimi Fani-Kayode, *Untitled* (1988–1989). © Rotimi Fani-Kayode / Autograph ABP. Courtesy of Autograph ABP.

eurism. Within the context of economics and anthropology, however, fetish takes on other resonances: for one, Karl Marx's conception of the commodity fetish, a power object that reifies an invisible array of relations of production in a system; or fetish as the modernist avant-garde might have understood it, as an substrate bearing excessive energy—something mundane invested with social or spiritual energy.[21] In Fani-Kayode's case, one untitled image from 1988 (figure 6.7) draws these multiple associations together—a blindfolded figure kneels before an outstretched white hand, taking communion, drawing life from a divine force, reveling in prostrate submission to the unknown.

To understand the fetish in anthropological or primitivist terms, one might look to the *nkisi nkondi* hunter figures described above, or the *bocio* of the Fon people of Benin—distressed figurative sculpture that is often physically damaged, bound with cord, or placed on the perimeter of one's home to act as an uncanny talisman. As Suzanne Preston Blier has argued, *bocio* occupy a liminal space—they are simulacral decoys of the living but also small cadavers with lifelike properties, loci of powerful investment and transference and mediators between worlds.[22] And it is from European contact with this very part of the world—the western African territory of the Fon, Yoruba, and Edo kingdoms along the Bight of Benin—that William Pietz famously developed a comprehensive theory of the fetish. The word is derived from the Portuguese and, later, the Dutch, who alternately controlled trade and slaving routes along the western African coast during the fifteenth to seventeenth centuries.

Feticio functioned as a term for specific talismanic artifacts belonging to the Europeans' African interlocutors, but it also described a larger slippage between systems of valuation between the parties. In particular, the Portuguese traders noted that items possessing "real value" (such as gold) were valued for their spiritual associations but not for their commensurate monetary value; at the same time, trifles and trinkets were highly prized by the West African traders. As such, the concept of fetish arose to describe the primal moment of encounter during the early modern period between Europe and Africa. It has ramified in meaning but consistently refers to an investment of inordinate value onto a material object.[23] In short, fetish does not specify actual difference but, instead, the psychic and material space through which difference is desired, repelled, constituted, and repressed—and it is precisely these complexities that allow it to productively describe in contemporary terms both plays of power and historical economies of subjugation.

Fani-Kayode, for his part, mediated the ambivalent spectrum of meanings contained in fetishism in several ways. One that should be clear by now is his inclusion of metal-studded, leather bondage gear in several obvious instances. The *Black Male/White Male* picture *Bondage* (figure 5.14) references Brassaï's corset portrait; and in 1989's *Nothing to Lose IX* from the *Bodies of Experience* portfolio, a figure in a harness seems to pray before one of Hirst's "icons." The latter is a sculptural assemblage that takes on an array of dualisms—partly object, partly divine reliquary, capped with a mask that evokes Eshu, the orisha of divination, creative energy, and the crossroads. Here as elsewhere, Fani-Kayode seems to link the African origins of fetish with the contemporary subcultural register.

An antecedent to the 1989 series is *Sonponnoi* (1987; figure 6.10)—a black-and-white image of a seated man with beaded necklaces that demarcate a head cropped from the image just above the mouth. A burning candle is metonymically placed in the genital area and the figure sits in repose, in not quite frontal profile. The candle's flame and the polka dots on the figure's skin are brought eerily to life by hand-applied pink and yellow on the surface of the photo paper—a nod to both pictorialist materiality and to Hans Bellmer's seeming animation of his uncanny dolls through vivid tinting. *Sonponnoi*, carefully selected from a contact sheet of otherwise playful images, generates for the viewer a sense of vitality, of living resonance that exceeds the mere visuality of a portrait photograph.

Such citational and material density was almost certainly Fani-Kayode's intent, as the title of the image creates a twofold reading. On the one hand the image is hagiographic, depicting the orisha dispatched by the creator god, Olorun, to dispense divine justice, afflicting people with the plague and attendant social exile of smallpox, marked by the dots on his skin. Sonponnoi (also spelled Sonpona) is traditionally a rural deity, recognized through altars that are "dotted" with the orisha's signature markings.[24] On the other hand, given the near-acephaletic quality of the picture's sitter, the presence of the candle suggests a transmutation of the body as an altar in its own right and, as a result, a site of communion with the divine plane. The figure occupies a liminal status—both he and the photograph are imbued with energy through an act of transference. The picture, like it subject, acts as a talismanic ward not unlike the *bocio*.

But beyond Fani-Kayode's invocation of Yoruba tradition, we must also reckon with the fetish as object of avaricious pursuit or compulsive fascination—like Mapplethorpe's bronzed and sculpted bodies. Christina Sharpe, for example, has compellingly explored the confluence of the disciplining of desire, the persistence of "African chattel slavery's continued relationship to the production of black (queer) bodies," and the power of reopening representations of same within early modernity. Her analysis of Isaac Julien's *The Attendant* (1993) frames the eight-minute film in terms of uncanny bodies, the "kinky, haunted spaces" of the museum, and the ambivalent desire—the ongoing sadomasochism—derived from fetishism's primal scenes, which continues to articulate "everyday black life."[25] While Julien works, here, on painterly interventions framed by encounters and hierarchies within the museum, Fani-Kayode's studio practice draws together similar elements from within his own counterarchive. Most evidently, he does this with 1989's *Cargo of Middle Passage* (figure 6.8), the black-and-white version of which later appeared on the cover of a noted Henry Louis Gates book on Black Atlantic theory. That work is, as we have seen, an economical depiction of chattel slavery, of a subject uncannily converted into object. The enslaved person in this way is

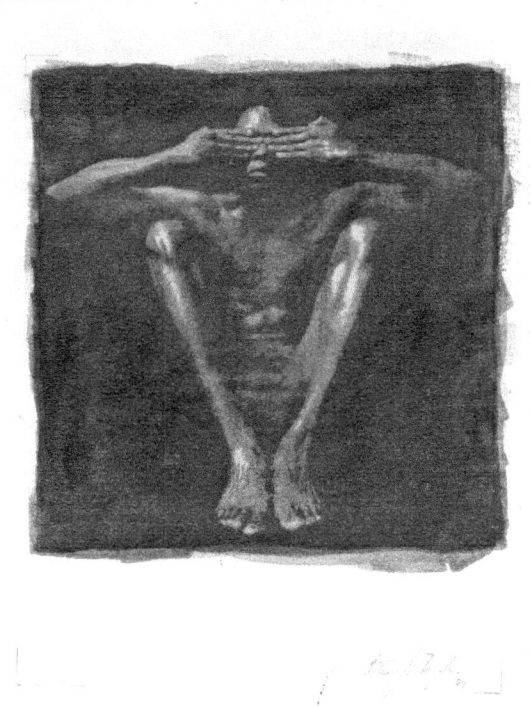

Figure 6.8 Rotimi Fani-Kayode, *Cargo of Middle Passage* (1989).
© Rotimi Fani-Kayode / Autograph ABP. Courtesy of Autograph ABP.

also made double, both a commodity fetish, and a source of production—of master/slave libidinal investment and sadistic regulation. The figure in Fani-Kayode's picture guards his eyes, symbolically unable to bear witness, and visually contorted into a headless (desubjectified) assemblage of muscled limbs.

As a cosmopolitan and mobile contemporary African subject, Fani-Kayode would certainly have experienced the reverberations that Julien (and Sharpe) elaborate—the ways in which black queer subjectivity continued to be structured by such originary fetishisms. But Fani-Kayode is perhaps least effective in his literal depictions, such as *Cargo of Middle Passage*. More powerful was his ability to frame the fluidity and ambivalence, the push and pull, that undergirded the economic flows of an early modernity structured by mercantilist exchange and the traffic of people. The several photographs of 1988–1989, for instance (untitled or called *Gold Phallus*, the latter figure 3.13) employ feathers, the *ororo* mask, and the play of uncanny substitution in order to reopen earlier sites of encounter, and their ramification into Fani-Kayode's own lifetime. In these pictures, the sitter is naked, save for the gold paint on his penis, which in turn mirrors the proboscis of the beaked mask.

In contrast to its appearance atop a calabash (described elsewhere), the mask here covers the wearer's face. In its formal similarity to the gold-painted phallus, the mask suggests an interchangeability between it and the "golden head," or, in Hirst's description, the "higher phallus" echoed in the multivalent picture *Bronze Head* (figure 3.6). Steven Nelson's reading of *Bronze Head* points to a powerful confluence of signifiers of the Yoruban cultural patrimony and its political position in a multiethnic state. *Gold Phallus* makes such associations even more literal, almost in the extreme. As Nelson argues, works that deal with the "higher phallus" could also refer to Fani-Kayode's familial loss, his physical separation from spiritual forces (god), juridical power (Law) and, in particular, the validation of his of father. Each of these "lacks" constitute potential sites of castration—a theme that Fani-Kayode played with in other instances, such as *Snap Shot* (figure 5.8).

Fetishism, according to Freud, is directly connected to such a confluence of family history and anxiety around castration. It can be understood as an act of substitution that keeps at bay the trauma of castration (signaled by maternal lack) by investing a third object with inordinate power. But Fani-Kayode's use of the golden phallus here does not quite reproduce the framework to which he seems so obviously to gesture. As should be clear, he was deeply invested in making images that knowingly, even jubilantly, embraced gender bending and forms roleplaying centered around obscuring and distorting genitalia, making them ambivalent or alien. In these particular images, by so brazenly displaying the phallus rather than its metonymic twin in the fetish, Fani-Kayode at once invokes the structure of fetish symbolically but denudes that structure of its power—the castrated member is revealed in plain sight.

This humorous hiding in plain sight is amplified by another of Fani-Kayode's knowing prods—rendering the phallus in gold. Here's Hirst: many people have this idea that "black men are studs. We wanted to challenge that. The gold makes the dick the center of attention but the string shows the burden is too much to live up to."[26] But I contend that this is not merely a picture about performing and subverting virility: for a pair of artists with a clear sense of art-historical precedent, gold itself was an important choice. As the original material around which fetishism was generated, it was invested with inordinate value. And gold is, according to Bataille, the heterological equivalent of both divinity and base materiality (shit), a reading confirmed in Nelson's analysis of *Bronze Head*. Castration and, by extension fetish itself, are for Fani-Kayode forms not of loss so much as possibility and transmutation. If anything, *Gold Phallus*'s detachable penis becomes a *part object*—one not connected to the body as such, but a potent object unto itself.[27]

All of which reiterates the fetish as a site of both generative "sexual perversion" and spiritual rite—an object (or objectified body) that bridges sacred and profane and wards off mortal danger. Ultimately, these pictures are still haunted by the specter of death—anxiety toward which was traditionally displaced in the psyche by making oneself immortal through portraiture, or celebrating the forced plenitude of still life. In Fani-Kayode's case, the macabre is diffused throughout his last portfolios as a constant reminder of the mortality of their creators, and the epidemic that raged in the wake of that creation. In form and content, then, these photographs constitute a deft and complex repurposing of the fetish, envisioned as a means of drawing vitality from, rather than repressing, the unknown.

But the 1989 portfolios also go a step further. While the symbolic and historical excesses of the fetish were already evident in Fani-Kayode's 1987–1988 pictures, the final series connect us to one last coordinate on the early modern map: Dutch still life. Indeed, the most glaring addition made by the *Nothing to Lose* series to Fani-Kayode's broader oeuvre is their plenitude of flowers and fruit. They add a vegetal liveliness and chromatic potency to photographs that are, in contrast to the *Black Male/White Male* works, easily legible *tableaux vivants* (see, for example, figure 6.9).

As a paradigmatic genre of still life, the Dutch *pronk* paintings of the seventeenth century arose at least in part due to early colonial encounters between the Protestant Dutch, their Catholic rivals, and various peoples of western Africa. And while the Dutch rejected the religious dimension of fetishism—of an object imbued with sacralized power—according to Hal Foster, *pronk* paintings nonetheless relied on the logic of fetish. Faced with the heterological pressure of a trade- and finance-based prosperity—with its influx of foreign goods and reliance on a fluctuating, capitalist system of valuation—Dutch artists and patrons were able to intuit or partially reconcile

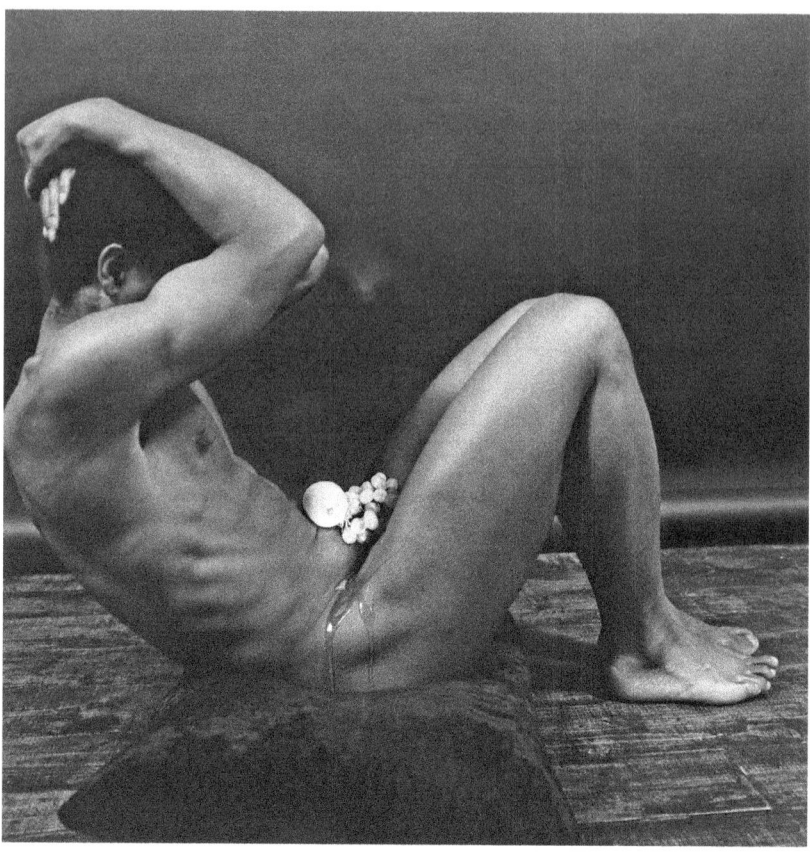

Figure 6.9 Rotimi Fani-Kayode, *Nothing to Lose XII* (*Bodies of Experience*) (1989). © Rotimi Fani-Kayode / Autograph ABP. Courtesy of Autograph ABP.

tensions within the new system (including the "castrating" fear of economic collapse) by transmuting through art the very objects of consumption and exchange. Foster argues that, for Marx, "commodity fetishism is equivalent to religious projection," and that objects of still life, which arose from a protocolonial matrix, "have a mana [secret power] of their own—a mana, moreover, that redounds to the mana or value of painting."[28]

Two key examples that Foster cites to support his claim that Dutch painting of this sort was a "negotiation of divergent representations and dangerous realities" are the *pronk* updates of Greek and Roman table still life (here stripped of "gift" value and accorded commodity value) and their recurrent mixture of objects from near and far. In the case of the latter, food and flowers, goblets and seashells, local commodities and foreign fauna were displayed—made equivalent—in the painted tableaux. The effect of such a leveling and reproduction was to underscore the objects' lack of inherent value. Value was, in effect, shown to be imbued from without, through the transposition of subjects and objects and the persistence of displacement-overvaluation of things that was increasingly understood to be part and parcel of capitalism itself. And while none of Fani-Kayode's pictures depict objects at the expense of subjects as such, the play of metonymy and synecdoche abounds. Recall his uncanny substitutions of masks for heads, or the conversion in *Sonponnoi* (figure 6.10) of an acephaletic body into a literal altar. Similarly, in almost every color image, there are lush, once-vital products or spiritually imbued "exotic" materials on display. One example is the mask array in *Nothing to Lose IX (Bodies of Experience)* (figure 6.11) that is granted a near subjective status. And the men figured in the larger series alternate between prostration to—or erotic consumption of—luxurious, chromatically saturated objects.

Fani-Kayode concisely joins these strands in a single image—an untitled color picture from 1989 (figure 6.12). It is blacked out to a darkened abyss, from which part of a man's face emerges as if in candlelight. One can glimpse the edges of a right hand drawn to his face. His left eye subtly, knowingly, connects with the viewer through the twilight. Most of the room is obscured from view, but one can make out the figure's mouth as it wraps around a glossy red orb—perhaps biting into a succulent tomato or other *pronk* delectable. Maybe it is he who is to be consumed, like an apple-dressed Sunday roast. Or, further still, in this dark cabinet scene, perhaps this symbolically resonant fruit is meant to connote a leather-strapped red ball-gag typical of S/M. There are, in short, some rather obvious articulations of fetish and its significations here. But it is also important to consider the profusion of other vegetal forms in the 1989 pictures—the stems and flowers that, in fact, unite all of Fani-Kayode's portfolios. This should come as no surprise: according to Foster, one tell-tale recurrence in *pronk* painting was the tulip, a flower bound up in the volatile cycles of agricultural production and commercial export. Fittingly, the gum bichromate prints with which this book opens are themselves called *Tulip Boy* (see figures Intro.1 and Intro.2).

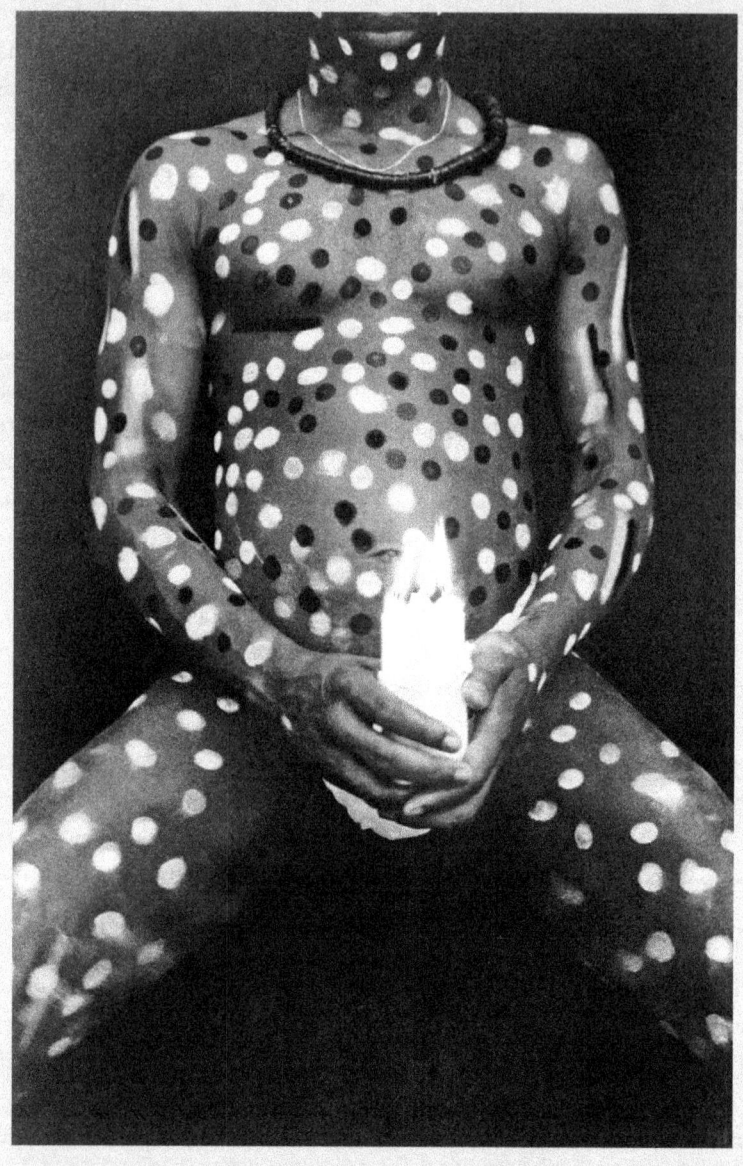

Figure 6.10 Rotimi Fani-Kayode, *Sonponnoi* (1987). © Rotimi Fani-Kayode / Autograph ABP. Courtesy of Autograph ABP.

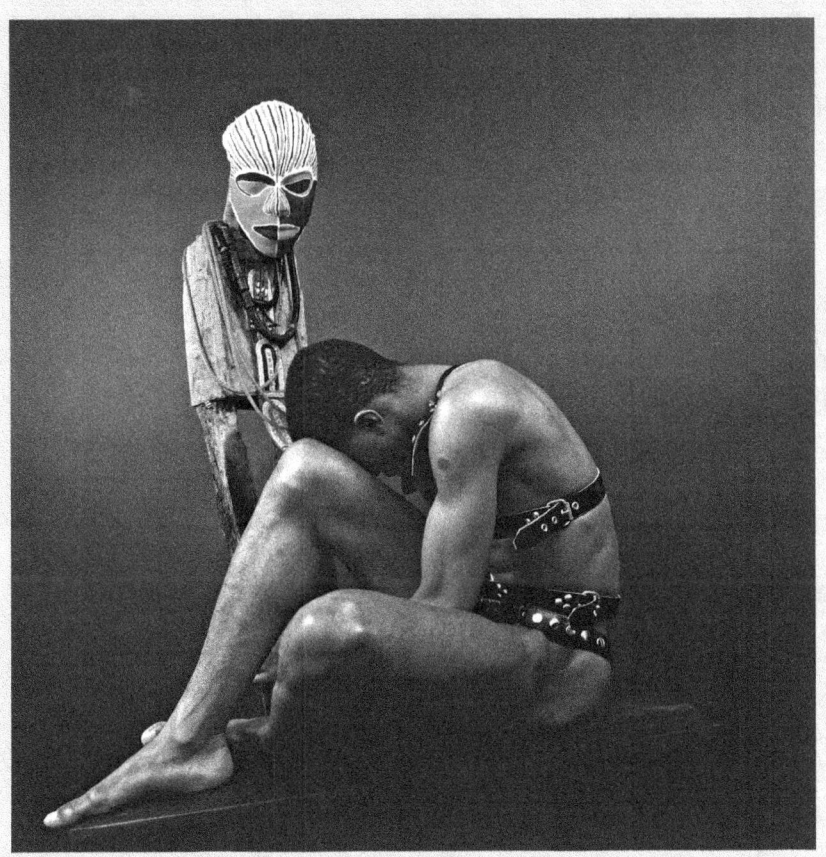

Figure 6.11 Rotimi Fani-Kayode *Nothing to Lose IX* (*Bodies of Experience*) (1989).
© Rotimi Fani-Kayode / Autograph ABP. Courtesy of Autograph ABP.

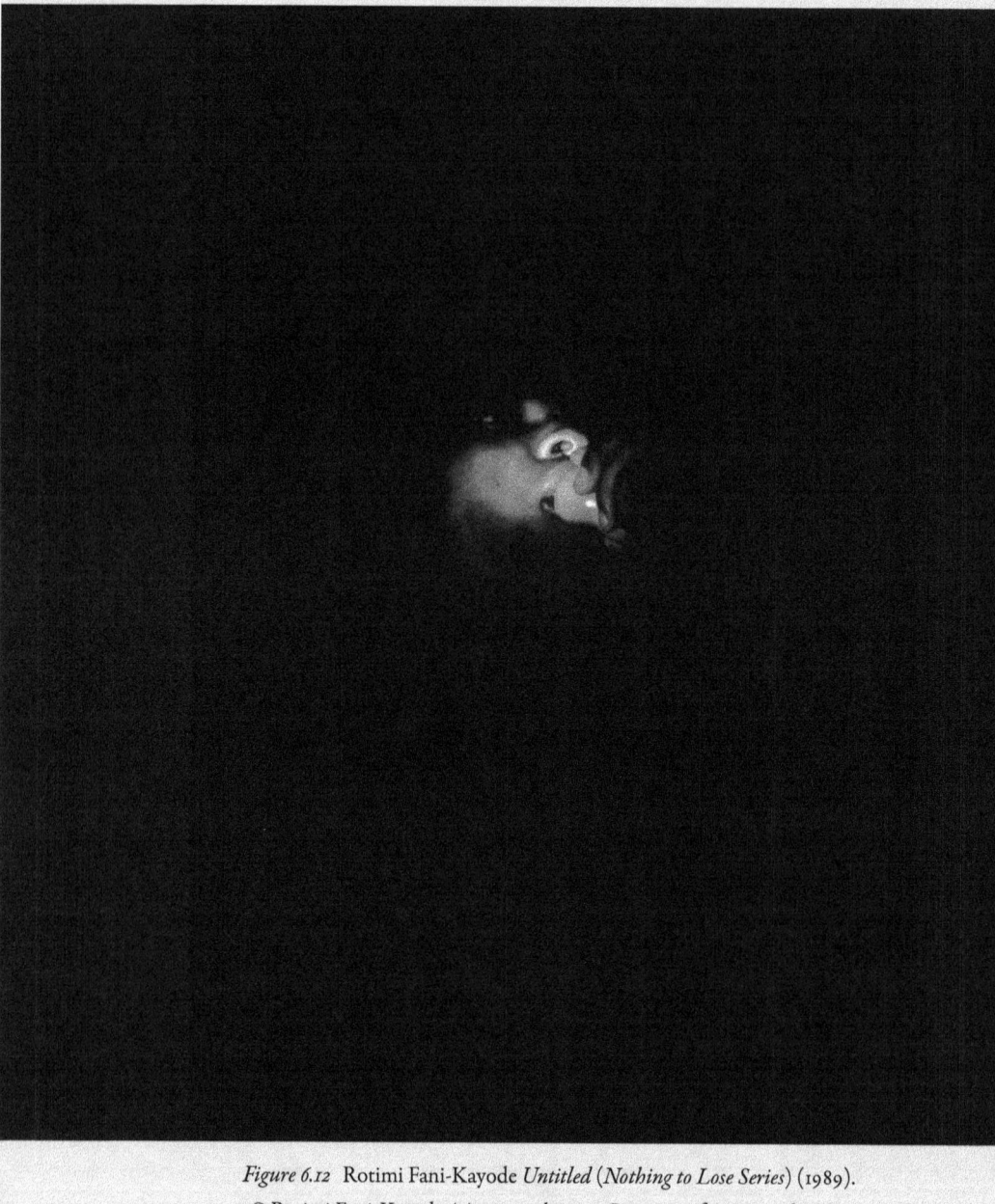

Figure 6.12 Rotimi Fani-Kayode *Untitled* (*Nothing to Lose Series*) (1989).
© Rotimi Fani-Kayode / Autograph ABP. Courtesy of Autograph ABP.

By now it should be apparent that Fani-Kayode was deeply invested in earlier forms of art making that not only promised a vast terrain of disruptive transcoding and signification but also provided him with hidden technologies. Such technologies were increasingly scarce in the midst of the mannerist and poststructuralist current that seemed to suffuse critical literature and the art markets of the day. For instance, in surrealism he recognized the possibility of staging or recording the superreal or supernatural, indexing charged photons onto a material substrate. And from the Yoruban tradition he rediscovered the power of seemingly mundane objects to activate spaces of connection between visible and invisible worlds. These objects included the accoutrements of the diviner and the photographic documentation (and mirror duplication) of twins. The latter often operated in much the same way as traditional *ere ibeji* figures served as mediators between metaphysical planes and as sites of veneration. And from the deeper histories of European painting, he turned repeatedly to objects of ambivalence and talismanic power—the primitivist intermediary and the Dutch still life, Baroque paintings of the Counter-Reformation that awakened the passions and carnal energies of the viewer. Within these forms, he seems to have located the fetishism that structured early modernity itself, what Marx called "the religion of sensuous appetites." These forms of fetish ranged from European obsessions with gold and "precious metals" to a generalized fascination/repulsion with traditional spiritual and religious forms encountered during mercantile exploration.

In drawing these elements together, Fani-Kayode arrived at a provocative theory of the photographic object. In this view, the work acted not merely as representation or documentation—a play in the realm of pure signs or denotation. Instead Fani-Kayode's photographs functioned as talismanic objects, catalysts of passions and drives, gateways to communion with gods and others, and producers of ecstatic antibodies. That same year, 1989, Hirst and Fani-Kayode summarized their relationship with more explicitly mystical modes, the urgency of their adaptation to their own practice, and the limitations thereof:

> At other times, in other places, and with other means, people have approached the mysterious aspects of life with respect. Using their imagination and their practical skills they have developed systems of communication between the

spheres of their understanding and the forces which are beyond it. They have not been able to avoid great public and private calamities but they have been able to prepare themselves in certain ways, spiritual or material, for the unexpected. One can never rely entirely on the kindness of strangers.[29]

This passage, which accompanies the *Bodies of Experience* group show about artistic responses to HIV/AIDS, echoes other statements by Hirst that remark that the wealthy elite—Wall Street, pharmaceutical companies—cannot be counted on. As such, Fani-Kayode and his collaborators took matters into their own hands. It seems clear that they, like the viewer, might not be entirely persuaded of the efficacy of their nocturnal practice (not being able to "avoid public and private calamities"). Yet, in enacting moments of clarity and intensity they might somehow generate a kind of spiritual or psychic inoculation, or steel the participants in the photographs, preparing them for the great unknown that yawned before them.

Hirst and Fani-Kayode had precedent for such belief: they had witnessed instances of traditional communion and transcendence, tracked the mythical and the gothic in photography, revisited Afro-Caribbean modes of Carnival and trance, and elaborated the Dionysian history of bacchanal and its modern equivalents in the heterotopias of the bathhouse, the loft, and the dance club—what Tony Wilson called the cathedral of the postmodern age. For all of that, Hirst expressed doubts about the power of the photographic object itself—recall his anxiety about catalog reproduction turning their "gold into lead." What seems most critical for them by 1989 is not merely a reclamation of the canon or signifying on tropes within art history but, rather, using a larger performative practice to enact a technique of ecstasy and to produce their ecstatic antibodies. In so doing, still life and sculptural forms were built as "icons," and the activities of the studio were documented on film. But as Walter Benjamin argued, no matter how auratic an object might be, its *reproduction*, its duplication and material denaturing, could neutralize the strange distance or enchantment that the painting, monotype, or pictorialist photograph might crystallize. This is, perhaps, why by 1987 (and through 1990) the artists produced alternate process prints of both black-and-white and color pictures. The gum bichromate method, for example, could not be reduplicated precisely, and was notable for its indexing of the artist's hand, its material density, and its atmospheric effects. Notable examples can be found in the reprocessing of the portrait *Adebiyi* (1989), in which the figure holds the Eshu mask aloft, wreathed in a crown of flowering spurge (wild baby's breath), a doubled sign: of martyrdom and death but also renewal and rebirth. That same year, *Cargo of Middle Passage* was printed in deep-red gum bichromate by Fani-Kayode, and Hirst would take up *Ecce Homo* and the *Tulip Boy* photographs in 1990. To a British audience, the latter would likely have struck a chord, as a similar composition began circulating in October 1989 on the cover of singer Kate Bush's celebrated record *The Sensual World*. The songs therein plainly referenced Christian sacrilege and Blakeian mysticism. More broadly, Kate's Bush's catalog conjured a more autochthonous, more paganistic account of British spiritualism. The record's art is a stark black-and-white picture of Bush, and her face exudes surprise and fixation, upper body and mouth occluded by an oversized rose borne in her right hand.

While Kate Bush was likely featured in Fani-Kayode's record bin, it is unclear that he had seen *The Sensual World* before he shot *Tulip Boy* (though as creative projects, they were in process at roughly the same time). What is more likely is that both Bush and Fani-Kayode were repurposing similar material. In their way, both pictures directly cite another, made by the Japanese photographer Eikoh Hosoe in 1961–1962 for a portfolio called *Barakei*, or *Ordeal by Roses*, a title which suggests an arduous rite of passage counterbalanced by the fragility and beauty of a symbolically rich flower—one associated with passion and pain, crimson petals and sharp thorns. (See, for example, figures 6.13 and 6.14.) Hosoe had by 1961 already begun to use surrealist methods— notably uncanny multiplications, gothic tableaux, and solarization—to explore longing and desire, in this case between men and women. The *Barakei* project took place at the home of the noted writer (and, later, political leader) Yukio Mishima (1925–1970). Mishima is a significant touchstone for Fani-Kayode for several reasons: for one, he wrote texts that explored the queer underground of Japan and hinted at his own sexual openness (for example, 1953's *Forbidden Colors*); he also famously resisted the decay of age, preserving his vigor through consistent weight training and committing ritual suicide at age forty-five.

Hosoe noted that, indeed, he dedicated his platinum prints to Mishima, "a man who never allowed his own physical decline. . . . They serve as a permanent record of his immortal beauty, gorgeous at its peak at age thirty-eight."[30] Hirst in turn wrote in 1989 that "I have made a place in my heart for such jokers as [literary critic, poet, and phonic pioneer] Edith Sitwell, [cult comic strip protagonist] Zippy the Pinhead, and Yukio Mishima."[31] *Barakei*, then, was a compelling model—it was a collaboration of a writer and an artist known

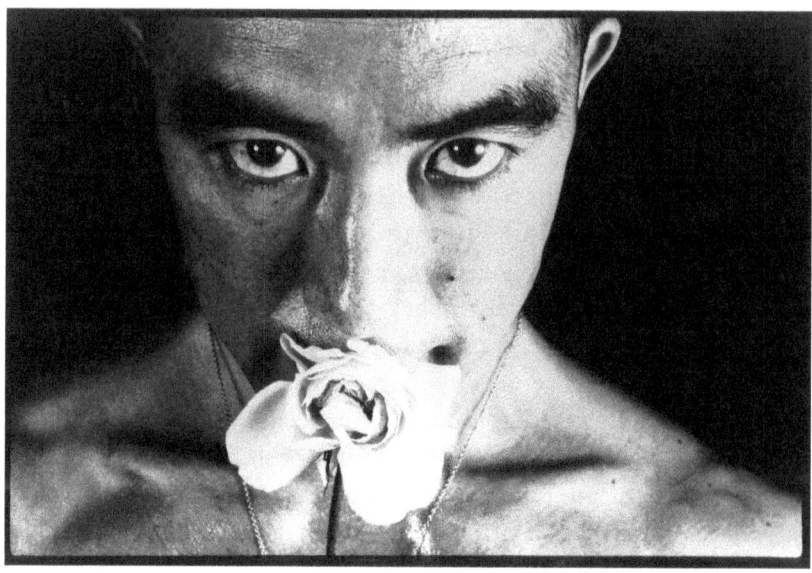

Figure 6.13 Eikoh Hosoe, *Ordeal by Roses #32* (1961). © Eikoh Hosoe.
Courtesy of Taka Ishii Gallery Photography/Film.

for examinations of love and desire, life and death, immortality and transient flesh, and surrealist play with flowers and photographs. One could expend an entire essay recounting the iconographic connections between *Barakei* and the 1988–1989 Fani-Kayode pictures, all the way down to the appearance of black-leather biker gear in a montaged shot by Hosoe of a clock and Guido Reni's plague saint image of the martyred *Saint Sebastian* (1615–1616), another icon of resurrection and homoerotic beauty.[32]

Beyond these more biographical and visual similarities, however, Mishima and Hosoe presented something altogether new and essential. The photograph for them, was not just a charged artifact but a powerful activator. Photography, in short, could frame and engage a moment of lived encounter and exert energy on the very spirit of those involved. Mishima said of *Barakei*—a portfolio documenting prostrate and bound bodies, mirrors, lit candles, ghostly double exposures, and long gazes into the lens—that before the camera "I soon realized that my own spirit, the workings of my mind, had become totally redundant. It was an exhilarating experience, a state of affairs I had long dreamed of."[33] And, as the art historian Ignacio Muñoz has compellingly

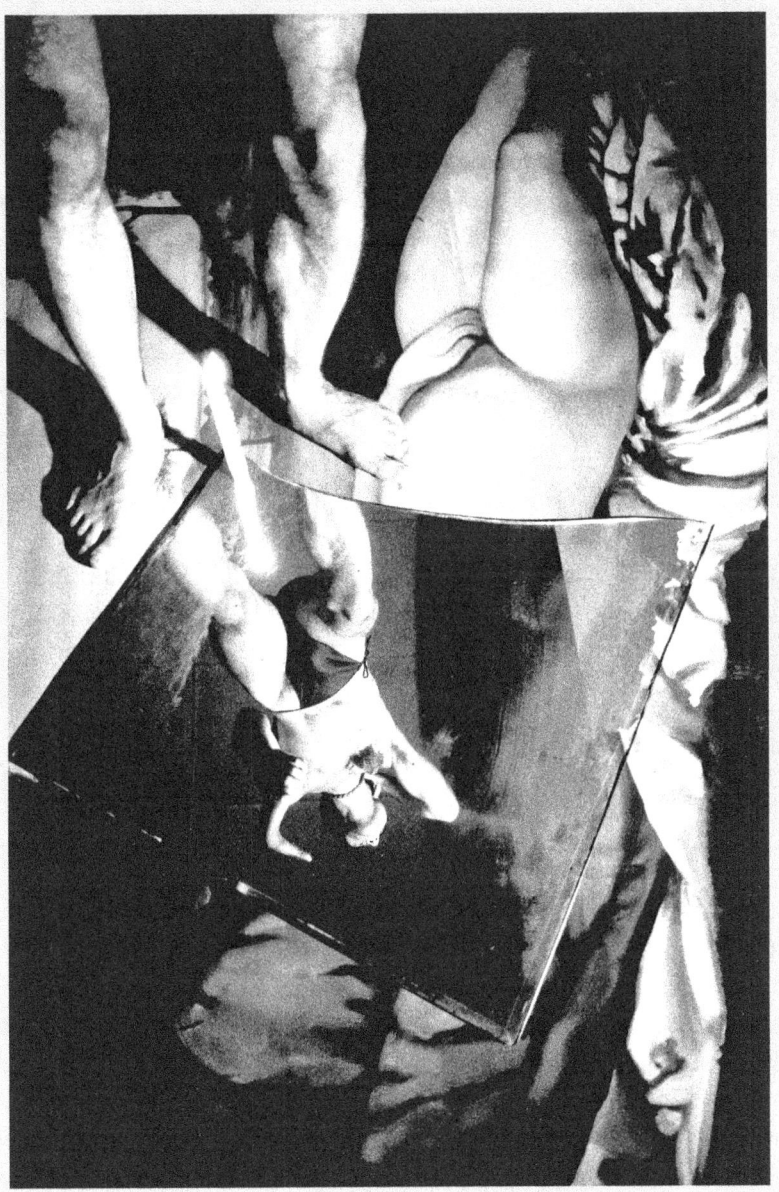

Figure 6.14 Eikoh Hosoe, *Ordeal by Roses #18* (1961). © Eikoh Hosoe.
Courtesy of Taka Ishii Gallery Photography/Film.

argued, Mishima viewed the camera as a vital mechanism that could at once bear witness and also draw into being magically charged environments, condensing time and space. He quotes Mishima, "rather than magical the quality of Hosoe's work was such as that of a machine that produces sorcery. . . . The world I was taken to by the sorcery of his lens was abnormal, twisted, ridiculous, grotesque, savage, pansexual; however in this world one could also hear the murmuring of a clear, cool stream, the undercurrent from within the unseen inside of a gutter."[34] According to Muñoz's reading, the camera could thus serve as a producer of images, but also as a mediator "between this world and Beyond."[35] This mediation, for Mishima, marks a crucial fulcrum at which the photograph moves from the terrain of documentary to *testimony* (*shogensei*); this view disrupts the documentary function of the medium and imbues it with a power to enact spaces of phantasmagoria and communion between worlds. The object, by extension, gives way to performance and the ritual dissolution of the subject—precisely the cosmological and practical setup that Fani-Kayode located in Afro-Caribbean religion, and that Hirst alludes to when he cautions against the diminished potency of mass reproduced images.[36]

A THEATER OF THE INVISIBLE

There was, of course, a strong precedent for moving the terms of art production from simply making objects to simultaneously driving and documenting events to which a viewer might otherwise not have access. One could easily cite the efflorescence of performance art in the 1960s concurrent with the Fluxus "happening," the loft party, or Allan Kaprow's "environments." Similarly, many artists of the 1970s moved beyond the gallery to produce transient or far-flung works directly on the land. Perhaps the most direct corollary for Fani-Kayode in this regard is the Cuban-born Ana Mendieta. Beyond biographical similarities—Mendieta was born to a prominent Cuban family but was, in the aftermath of revolution, exiled to New York—both worked at an oblique angle to larger collectivist narratives that sought to claim the artist as their own ("white feminism" in Mendieta's case). Both also turned explicitly to Afro-Caribbean syncretisms to infuse the work with ritual intensity, to invoke the *orishas* and bring *àshe* into the world. The latter is exemplified in Mendieta's *Silueta* series (for example, 1976 in Mexico), in which she indexed her body into coastal sand and infilled the depression with red flowers. Her

Fetish series rendered such indexes three-dimensional, and she branded the uncanny figures or treated them with blood, recalling both the *bocio* and, explicitly, Cuban Santeria.

As Jane Blocker argues, Mendieta's belief in the universal energy that "reverberates through all organisms . . . magically animates her work with anger, pleasure, hunger, and longing." Such language mirrors almost exactly Fani-Kayode's recollection of the Americas, and the "reverberations" of old Yoruban rhythms he found there. Blocker further contends that such work, with photography as its documentation, worked to short-circuit the essentialism/ antiessentialism binary, with Mendieta showing the "untenability" of collectivist and art-critical rubrics to contain her own (and a range of emerging) intersectional practices.[37] In light of such congruences, Mendieta—the exile, the photographer, the channeler of suppressed aesthestic-spiritual energies—is a vital touchstone for contextualizing Fani-Kayode. But his practices also differed in many ways: he preferred the studio to the land, and he rarely indexed "himself." Instead, he and his cast of sitters performed something more akin to masquerade, operating as players in a larger game designed to transcend the ego-bound subject and temporarily materialize hidden realms.

There are many clues that the 1988 and 1989 pictures oscillated between static tableaux vivants and "stills" of a dynamic activity, of bodies in states motion and devotion. For example, the scenes from the Black Audio Film Collective's *Twilight City* show Fani-Kayode's subjects playing out a calibrated dance on the order of Japanese Noh. His *Fish Vendor* (figure 3.7) and *Milk Drinker*, or *Philip* with his candle (figure 4.4), are all are revealed less as sitters and more as agents in a larger mise-en-scène, behind the closed doors of a nocturnal black box or voyeur's cabinet. Similarly, an untitled shot from the *Nothing to Lose Series* shows its figure in blurred motion, crowned in baby's breath, biting into an orange bird of paradise (that great symbol of both the regal and the exotic). The shutter speed is not fast enough to capture the whip of the stem across the picture plane. Within the same series, Fani-Kayode draws the viewer alongside a man applying makeup to another. One half of the latter's face is a shimmering gold, the other a chalky white, broken by an inky black ocular cavity. This is a theatrical process of transformation, and a reference to the Janus-faced masks of comedy and tragedy.

Taken together, it is clear that Fani-Kayode drew on transcultural traditions of performance and masquerade. This may have been to, as Sealy has observed, "shield" his subjects, keeping them anonymous and talismanically pro-

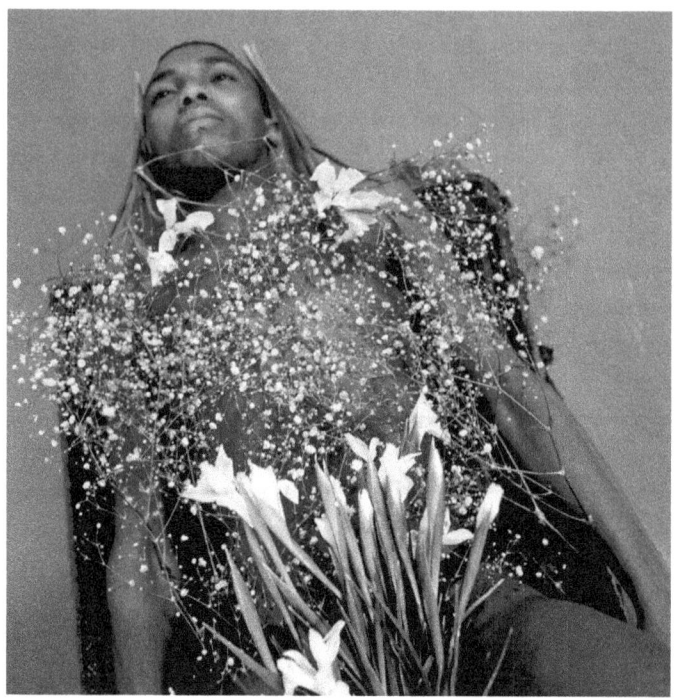

Figure 6.15 Rotimi Fani-Kayode, *Nothing to Lose XI* (1989). © Rotimi Fani-Kayode / Autograph ABP. Courtesy of Autograph ABP.

tected from the audience. But more generally he transformed his studio into an ecosystem in which to enact and picture ruptured boundaries—sexual, ontological, and geographic—and to taunt (or come to grips with) mortality. For, as Roland Barthes has argued, "pictorialism is only an exaggeration of what the Photograph thinks of itself. It is not (it seems to me) by Painting that Photography touches art, but by Theater."[38] Barthes is not referencing, here, the duration and movement of theater but, rather, its connection to death and dying—he invokes several forms of East Asian performance, in particular variants in which the actors are transformed by way of rudimentary masquerade, by painting their faces in a ghostly white. So, too, for Barthes, "photography is a kind of primitive theater, a kind of *Tableau Vivant*, a figuration of the motionless and made-up face beneath which we see the dead."[39]

And so, everything was in place: a theory of the photograph as auratic index of charged photons, a practice in which the camera was a machine for mediating worlds, and a group of performers whose reclamation of old gods and obsolete understandings of art drew them together under Fani-Kayode's carefully calibrated studio lights. In 1988, this produced a series of bleached blond twins, blindfolded young wanderers, vamping white angels, and fluid-drenched supplicants. By 1989, in what were his last photographs, Fani-Kayode orchestrated densely coded but visually electric portrayals of benediction and baptism, consumption and dissolution, frenzy and equanimity. These are moments that balance the high Camp of implied fellatio with the gravity of a funeral pyre and the ferocious gaze of his own priests, hands open and reaching skyward. The photographer Robert Taylor was the model for some of these shoots at Railton Road, donning the bird mask and golden paint for several color prints (for example, figure 3.13, elaborating figure 6.16). Of these collaborations with Hirst and Fani-Kayode, he remembers:

> My experience in the studio for the last photo session related to the golden phallus series is an excellent example of this. I could only see its hindsight that for weeks before the session, even before I'd agreed to do it I was being subtly groomed for it. By the time I'd actually agreed to do it, it was clear that Rotimi and Alex had got it pretty well mapped out. All that was left was to negotiate my reactions to actually performing such an explicit scenario. They were both present in the studio at all times. By the time it came to actually stripping off, the body painting and the "gold penis performance" with the paint, the three had entered a strange little world that was only properly apparent when the lights were cut and "normal" life resumed. Typical portraiture was the furthest thing from any of our minds as far as I was concerned. So many of the results in the studio were directly related to Rotimi's charisma and charm. I trusted him and would have done pretty much anything he asked, pretty secure in the knowledge that it would be very likely fascinating, challenging, and beautiful.[40]

Taylor's recollection seems to confirm in the larger matrix of desire, collaboration, and surrender brought into being through his practice, and the sense of being transported to another plane felt by those in the room, and suffused through his last color series. Beyond a certain point, however, retrospective descriptions or art historical analysis fail to grasp the thing. Whether Fani-Kayode was successful in his alchemy is a matter of speculation or even faith. What he attempted, however, cannot be stated more plainly than in the texts he left behind or in the radiant scenes recorded by his camera—poor substi-

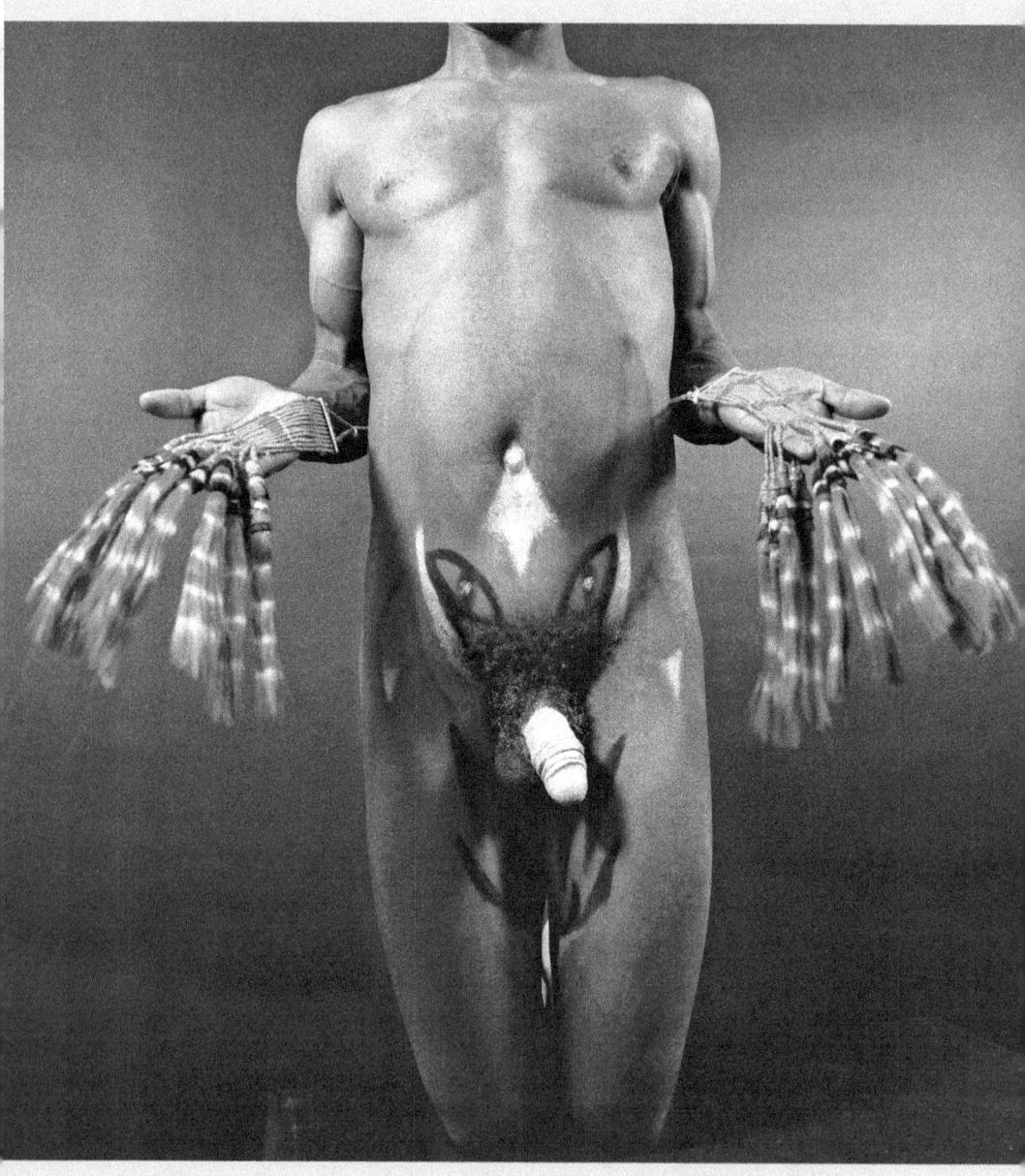

Figure 6.16 Rotimi Fani-Kayode, *Untitled* (1987–1988). © Rotimi Fani-Kayode /
Autograph ABP. Courtesy of Autograph ABP.

tutes for the moment itself, to be sure, but in their way heir to a deeper tradition in which images can induce passion, communion, and even regeneration among their viewers.[41]

PEOPLE WITH AIDS

While in many respects the 1989 photographs mark a coalescing of many impulses already underway in Fani-Kayode's practice, they cannot be understood without considering the context of the AIDS epidemic. As Hirst recalled in *The Last Supper*, the AIDS crisis had by then become an inescapable and daily reality. And many of the works made in 1989 were shown in group shows such as *Bodies of Experience* and *Ecstatic Antibodies*. The title of the latter, in fact, summates the underlying ambitions of Fani-Kayode and Hirst's studio practice that year—producing through the shearing forces of ecstasy a sort of inoculation against the virus, even if that inoculation yielded only the metaphorical immortality of photographs that would survive the artists. In the essay for *Ecstatic Antibodies* they even specify a new meaning for the "golden phallus" of the eponymous picture: "We pay circumspect 'homage' then, to the dragqueen of 'Liberty' in whose ambiguous shadow our erections have turned from base and shameful dross into amulets sporting golden condoms."[42]

Amulets and condoms alike suggest protection against infection or dark energies. This passage also alludes to the artists' ambivalent relationship with New York City itself, a place of contradiction in which artists under the aegis of ACT-UP militated against a complex of pharmaceutical companies and federal policy makers—those who negligently failed to reckon with what was, for much of the decade, ghettoized as an illness of the gay community. As Jarman recalled in 1992, "friends have just disappeared before anyone knew. One young man died of pneumonia—it seemed strange at the time as he was in his early twenties and very strong. . . . I worry about the blindness and degeneration of the mental faculties; I worry about the disfigurement of Kaposi's Sarcoma. I am not afraid of death but I am afraid of dying."[43] In Fani-Kayode and Hirst's estimation, they were out of options—it was incumbent on them to "construct ephemeral prayers in the eternal sand while Wall Street, oblivious, disputes the price of miracles."[44]

Which is to say, suspecting his own end was imminent and surrounded by AIDS-related death, Fani-Kayode's final series of photographs placed him in the company of artists on both sides of the Atlantic seeking to reconcile the existential terror of impending mortality with a political need to reclaim the representational and discursive apparatus of religion, AIDS, and queerness from reactionary elements in government, media, and NGOs.[45] The talismanic photograph or testimonial rite marks a powerful contrast to more literal polemics or representations in the field of art production. For Fani-Kayode, photography and the photograph were a source of material power and metaphysical protection that crosscut zones of transcultural and metaphysical contact, shielding its bearer from malevolent forces. It is worth recalling that in his own brief summation, Fani-Kayode very clearly described his camera and, by extension, his images as *weapons*, defensive survival tools.[46] Other artists working with photographs in response to the epidemic—such as Nan Goldin and Félix González-Torres—relied on the image's mimetic power to combat a more literal erasure in the field of representation, to give physical substance to the transient. As Jarman noted, "*The Last of England* was actually shot before I discovered I was HIV positive. . . . But then, everyone was HIV positive, at least in the world I lived in, from the moment it was actually isolated in 1984. So as far as I'm concerned, even if you haven't been tested, there was a probability, and even if you weren't nearly everyone you knew was, there was that atmosphere . . . so it did alter everything."[47]

But perhaps predictably, given Fani-Kayode's general ambivalence about collective politics or the public address of protest, his contributions to an emerging archive of AIDS-oriented art differed substantially from the activism that floresced in the United States (for example, that of Gran Fury).[48] Instead, Fani-Kayode's approach was, as should be clear, one executed using the tools of art qua art, but also as "metaphysickal" intervention. As he and Hirst observed, "we have drawn on transcultural and transhistorical techniques to offer our response to a phenomenon which is specific only in terms of the individuals it affects here and now. . . . We (happen to) have been inspired in this by ancestral African, ecclesiastical, and contemporary 'Western'/erotic images. HIV has forced us to deal with dark ambiguities."[49]

Still other clues, other evidence of this "transhistorical approach" further mark these last series as addressed to the AIDS crisis. For one, the white *ororo* mask discussed above, the one connecting Africa and Venetian Carnival, also resembles the facial shielding of a Renaissance-era "plague doctor." Depicted in, for example, the woodcutting *Der Doctor Schnabel von Rom* by Paul Fürst (1656; figure 6.17), this class of healer was enlisted in various forms throughout Europe to make rounds among populations sickened with successive

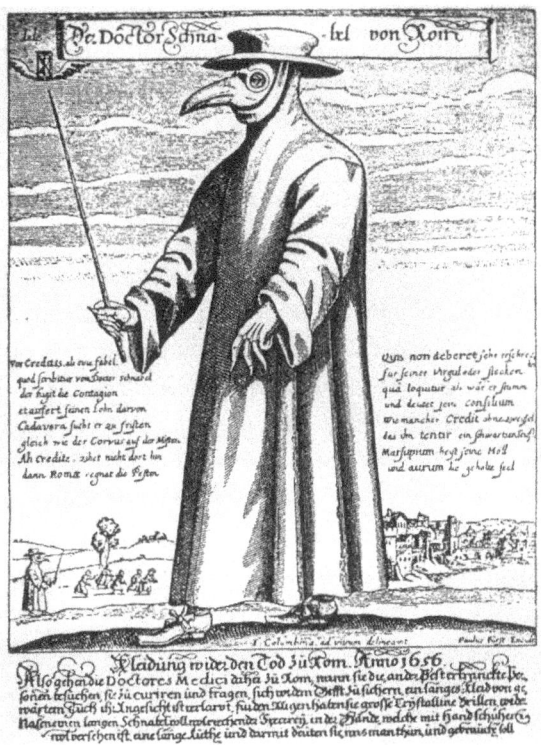

Figure 6.17 Paul Fürst, *Der Doctor Schnabel von Rom*
(Holländer version) (1656).

waves of sickness. While the germ theory of disease was still several hundred years away, such doctors wore protective garb, such as waxed cloth robes, a wide-brimmed hat, and a mask with shielded eyes and a long, curved "beak" packed with aromatic herbs, in order to keep the surrounding pestilence at bay. Schnabel, of course, translates into "bill," like that of a bird. Thinking back to those red-robed "black friars," all haloed in cruciform, Fani-Kayode repeatedly places the viewer squarely in the terrain of Renaissance iconography, here through the figure of "Dr. Bill," and also of the plague saints themselves—European corollaries of *Sonponnoi* figures associated all with pestilence and its mediation.

Indeed, while the Dr. Bill mask functions as a depiction of a quotidian pestilence worker invoked by the *ororo*, one can scarcely look at Fani-Kayode's "transsexual priests" and passionate initiates without calling to mind that contingent of Catholic saints—including Charles Borromeo, Roch, and Sebastian—who were invoked by plague victims or their families during times of need. Sebastian is of particular interest because he was frequently featured in Renaissance painting (by Reni, El Greco, and others) as shot with arrows in a field under orders from Diocletian. He was appropriated as a plague saint because, as legend has it, the arrows that wounded him could not kill him. He suffered martyrdom, but though pierced and wounded he was nonetheless resurrected. Throughout the early modern period, however, Sebastian was notably depicted as a beautiful, scantily clad young man; as a consequence, his portraits have subsequently been read as instances of homoeroticism in which the iconography takes on a coded set of double meanings: the Roman soldiers' arrows as those of Eros; or Sebastian himself as a vehicle through which to desirously depict actual young men. Such a case has, indeed, been made in the case of Agnolo Bronzino's *Portrait of Young Man as Saint Sebastian* from 1533.[50] Typically, then, Fani-Kayode used *Communion* and related series to create tableaux of multiaccentual significance, elaborating existing iconographic resonances in a new sociopolitical context while also making evident more latent or coded meanings in the originals (e.g. homoeroticism). But who are these portraits of plague saints and resurrected angels, frenzied scenes of ecstasy, and charged latter-day *pronk* photographs for?

It seems, initially, that Fani-Kayode was working on behalf of those in the room: after all, those studio shots worked to catalyze and bear witness to seemingly arcane acts that happened, as he said, to enact the "'ritual' production of spiritual antibodies" in which "inspiration is squeezed from all those involved." Like the American "Action Painter" or Fluxus performer, what mattered was in the room, as it were. The works, in this sense, might merely be a record of an event, an afterimage. Fani-Kayode posited those studio projects as a kind of collaboration, like the work of a group of players performing for the gods. The finished work is thus only credited to Fani-Kayode and Hirst because "this world insists on imagining that 'art' or 'science' has to be blamed on individuals. . . . The Queens of Heaven and Earth, along with their handsome male helpers, are also depicted here, to watch over our enterprise and to show off their finery." But they continue, below, to suggest that their more localized efforts stand as an act also on behalf of an "unnamed multitude," those who, in the face of a complacent and adversity, have "constantly resisted . . . who refuse to die in total darkness."[51]

But for a viewer reading now, or for those who, like Gregg Bordowitz, might insist on something more concrete, less ephemeral, there are two ways to reconcile Fani-Kayode's process. One is to acknowledge, like Freedberg or Benjamin, the surrealists and Mishima, or Fani-Kayode's improvised troupe that, for generations "multitudes" have recognized the power of images. Images have power not only to represent, but to conjure passions, to witness and testify and enact material sorcery, and maybe even to heal or produce "ecstatic antibodies." The other option, for the stubborn realists and ardent Marxists, is to consider that Fani-Kayode produced something else in these multivalent and incandescent images: singular pictures of people with AIDS (PWAS).[52]

As Douglas Crimp wrote so poignantly at the time,[53] positive images of PWAS were in short supply, as activists debated whether it was possible to continue loving in the wake of an epidemic. High-profile photographers from Nicholas Nixon to Nan Goldin notably depicted men in states of decay, suffering the wasting effects of the virus. By contrast, to the end Fani-Kayode framed himself and those around him in their prime, radiating erotic energy to be sure—but also humor, love, and even beatific serenity. The purpose of those last series was to use an "atmosphere of West African belief to create pictures that weren't about people dying. . . . AIDS is about life and death, anything goes. In this world everything is directly and indirectly about AIDS, whether you acknowledge it, or realise it, or not."[54] Of course, Fani-Kayode and Hirst would not escape the literal death then ordained for those diagnosed positive. But in those final pictures, outfitted in the regalia of saints and sinners, wreathed in vegetal symbols of resurrection and rejuvenation, they were alive, vital, reminding us that every moment counts.

HOMECOMING

The Nigerian minister of culture stands before a crowd in the bustling Yaba neighborhood of Lagos. This is a day of celebration: a local hero has finally returned—not physically, but in the form of an exhibition of photographs. She remarks that this "is an invaluable and enlightening event which demonstrates the possibilities and the power of art and culture in our lives and in our society."[1] Rotimi Fani-Kayode was right after all. His photographs were, in some crucial way, Yoruban, legible and meaningful not only to those practitioners of the "old ways" in the Nigerian countryside but also to those in the heart of its largest city. And while he worried about the reaction those pictures might generate, imagining himself as a modern-day Socrates in the *Crito*, in the end the more inclusive, humane world he envisioned in his photographs had come to pass. He had died some twenty-five years earlier, but after decades of physical and institutional exile, Fani-Kayode was, in a sense, home.

This is a moving fantasy, and one at least partially fulfilled. It is drawn from an essay by the Nigerian curator Bisi Silva, marking a 2014 touring exhibition of Fani-Kayode's pictures (many on loan from the collection of Yinka Shonibare, MBE) to the South African National Gallery in Cape Town.[2] The return to Lagos would have to wait, however. Silva's speculative exhibition was envisioned not for 2014 but instead for 2039: an index of both the often glacial pace of change and the degree to which Fani-Kayode was ahead of his time. As I have argued, the signal strength of Fani-Kayode's brief career was that he recuperated a deep and transnational array of cultural practices but also looked toward the future, enacting new social horizons marked by more open conviviality and love; to cite Kellie Jones, such conviviality posits a "notion of community—national and outernational—one where we choose the better parts of our histories and ourselves."[3] She cites Paul Gilroy, who argues that conviviality is not an all-or-nothing proposition but a form of negative dia-lectics. Conviviality relies on the constant pressure of a constellation of small acts.[4] These small acts unfold day to day in London and, indeed, Lagos. Bisi Silva concedes that Fani-Kayode was right that his photographs would have "caused a riot" there, but also that "in spite of the controversies . . . and the chaotic aftermath of Nigeria's promulgation into law of the antihomosexual bill, as well as the contestations that we have witnessed across Africa up to today, there is a place for his work now, more than at any time in our recent cultural history."[5]

And so, in looking at his various portfolios, Polaroids, and contact sheets, I also think of the late cultural theorist Mark Fisher, who wrote about the ev-eryday power of art and music, and of their potentially radical social potential. In looking back on the past thirty years—on eighties music and its progeny, Fisher came to define one last theoretical term that is helpful in understanding Fani-Kayode from our current vantage: *hauntology*. That is, we might ask, are the photographs described in the preceding pages important, on the far side of the 1980s, precisely because they are hauntological? For Fisher, hauntol-ogy resonates in the same key as the myriad Romanticisms, surrealisms, and techniques of ecstasy that animated the second half of this book, alluding both to the spectral textures of mortality and melancholia and to the tempo-rality of the uncanny. In this light, earlier cultural formations are never dead and gone, and those who proposed potential futures—escape hatches from a ruined present—are of particular interest. A hauntology of these moments wonders what happened to the harbingers of futures that never arrived, and what those futures might have looked like.[6]

Silva's fantasy positions Fani-Kayode as a kind of hauntological subject, as a Yoruban visionary who elaborated and complicated his cultural patrimony in revelatory and liberating new directions. Maybe the world developed in his photographs and lived in his studio might arrive someday in Lagos but not, alas, today. For Silva, politics and society must either be revised by scores of other dreamers and rebels like Fani-Kayode, or it must change on its own timeline, to be made ready to receive such works. Otherwise, the photographs that populate this book will remain hauntological—documents of an elusive future, a world that existed only fleetingly on the shores of Brighton, in the bedrooms of Harlem, the nocturnal incantations on Railton Road, and the ectoplasmic halides onto which they were inscribed.

But if we zoom out, the question becomes more complex. Did Fani-Kayode's future arrive, perhaps, back in Brooklyn or Brixton? Was he a bellwether of a world that was to emerge, tragically, only in the years after his death in the closing days of that signal year of 1989? Certainly the familiar narrative of the post-1989 (and certainly post-1993) art-institutional landscape is one of a supposed "global turn" marked by greater inclusiveness and self-criticality played out on an ever-broadening map of contemporary platforms and practices. Such shifts in the museum and gallery were often matched by seeming progress toward forms of multicultural inclusion, or by halting moves toward progressive politics in much of Europe and the United States. And certainly, during the past several decades, a greater range of subjectivities and experiences have come to be represented in the mainstream of the art world: in the British case, Chris Ofili famously served as an emissary to the 2003 Venice Biennale, Steve McQueen has risen to international prominence, and Yinka Shonibare was named a knight of the British Empire, to name just a few prominent examples.

Nonetheless, even in the thrall of these supposed realignments, many critics—Olu Oguibe or Julian Stallabrass, for instance—remain unconvinced. They variously suggest that the globalization at hand is simply an offshoring and expansion of the expeditionary impulses of a commercial gallery system; its gestures toward inclusiveness simultaneously reify stereotypical or palatable iconographies of "difference" while eliding more structural issues of equity and access.[7] More disturbingly, some thirty years on, much of the planet is in the thrall of a rightward lurch back to a nationalist xenopolitics more symptomatic of the 1970s or, indeed, the 1930s. With respect to the intersection of art and politics, the participants of a roundtable convened by *Artforum International* in 2016 argued that while nineties-era critique addressed a problem mediated in many of Fani-Kayode's photographs—namely the homogenizing effect of certain assertions or forms of identity—claims of having arrived at an equitable (and certainly postidentity or postracial) world are naive at best.

As Huey Copeland has argued: "The conversation has changed, but that discursive shift doesn't always correspond to a real shift. Homophobia, antiblackness, sexism, misogyny—all these forms of violence continue apace and are even more spectacularly displayed for us today, whether in the streets or on our phones."[8] More optimistically, however, Copeland and others on the panel noted the ongoing contestation by many artists and curators, their investigations of questions of intersectionality and discrimination, and their insistence on the dynamic and adaptive quality of identity as a zone of continual renegotiation. As the preceding pages have shown, while Fani-Kayode's photographs often worked in a singular register, in so doing they played a crucial role: complicating art's institutions and histories while elaborating new kinds of subjectivity. His photographs would gain a wider audience slowly, first in small retrospectives or major group shows and, more recently, through what Silva calls an "exponential" increase in interest. Yet, as a touchstone for a range of vital countercultural practices, he succeeded in animating complex discourses of queer, diasporic, and transnational strategies, and he did so within a few short years of his return to London.

One can see elements of his example in subsequent generations of artists—all of whom negotiate challenges integral to what Copeland calls the *longue durée* of struggle for greater equity in the world and in the gallery. Peers such as Zarina Bhimji, Mona Hatoum, Rasheed Araeen, John Akomfrah, and Isaac Julien remain critical voices, working alongside younger generations of black British artists such as Evan Ifekoya, Runa Islam, and Samson Kambalu. And one sees many of the strands of Fani-Kayode's photographs woven into so much of that which followed: ramifications of queer representation in the photography of Catherine Opie, Zanele Muholi, Lyle Ashton Harris, and Brendan Fernandes; the explicitly genealogical processes of Hank Willis Thomas and Lorna Simpson; the persistence of the haunted and grotesque in the art of Latoya Ruby Frasier and Wangechi Mutu; and the blending of radical sonics and visuality by Jennie C. Jones, Rashid Johnson, and the Otolith Group. Even in Nigeria, Lucy Azubuike, Mudi Yahaya, Andrew Esiobo, and others use photography to challenge the contours of subjectivity and its representation.

Beyond the work of Fani-Kayode's peers and the younger generation, versions of his own photographs are now widely circulated, gaining greater exposure with each passing year. This book outlines many of the solo and group exhibitions that include his photographs and, increasingly, marginalia and archival material. As such, much of the work mentioned here has been to elaborate and expand on the new connections starting to be made through Fani-Kayode's treatment in catalogs and anthologies that continue to emerge. One point of confluence, between the original work and the younger black Britons who have attained international recognition, is Shonibare himself, who has spoken in recent years on the import of Fani-Kayode's practice as an inspirational—even foundational—figure.

In autumn 2014 Tiwani Contemporary gallery featured Fani-Kayode's photographs alongside a public program that included a conversation between Autograph ABP director Mark Sealy and Shonibare. Sealy recalled being the only black student at Goldsmiths, University of London in 1982, while Fani-Kayode was in Brooklyn. He described the ensuing decade sharing various spaces—physical and discursive—with him. At Autograph ABP, he is entrusted with the Fani-Kayode archive, heading an organization that emerged in parallel to the artist, concerned with the broader issue of the underrepresentation of black artists in England at the time.[9] Shonibare was a perfect interlocutor: his name was attached to the traveling show *Traces of Ecstasy*, and because he lived between London and Lagos as a child, he offered insight into the difficulties that still surround the reception of Fani-Kayode's photographs in present-day Nigeria.

Shonibare's own career also brings into sharp relief changes in the British and global art worlds over the intervening twenty-five years. At the Tiwani event, Shonibare noted that he met Rotimi: "but I was a student at the time. London was very politicized in the art world. This was a post-Vietnam period—activism was entering into art—feminism, queer politics . . . Stuart Hall, Paul Gilroy becoming important. When I was a student Rotimi did a show in Hammersmith—that's when I first saw the work. I remember wanting to collect the work—they were 200 pounds; I couldn't afford them."[10] Shonibare was a student at Goldsmiths at what turned out to be an auspicious time, and he would be part of a generational shift, in the wave known variously in the media as the yBas (young British artists). Many of these artists—including Damien Hirst, Tracy Emin, Gavin Turk, Sarah Lucas, and Chris Ofili—would achieve international recognition, in no small part due to 1997's touring *Sensation* exhibition, which originated at the Royal Academy of Arts and, famously, attracted the scorn of American conservatives, including the then mayor of New York Rudolph Giuliani.

While a great deal of the work by the yBas dealt with issues of class, taste, and celebrity, artists such as Ofili and Shonibare developed signature modes— elephant dung and psychedelia, or batik wax-imprint fabric—that allowed them to traffic in signifiers (stereotypes, really) of Africanness even as they subverted them. Both artists realized immense fame in the 1990s, garnering the Turner prize, representing the British Pavilion at the Venice Biennale, being knighted, or occupying Trafalgar Square's highly public Fourth plinth. As of 2016 they are among the most noted artists in the world. While they differ in form and emphasis, each seeks to "contaminate" canonical moments in the history of Europe, from Renaissance painting to modernist formalism, Victorian manners to Catholic saints. Such art, replete with hip-hop superheroes, Afro-lunar lovers, and richly dressed British dandies, is, I think, the natural elaboration of the groundwork laid by Fani-Kayode. Taken together, they also ambivalently reveal and respond to different positions in the recent history of postcolonial migration and cultural practice. They are two of many artists from the postcolony that actively mediate at least two decades during which, as Gilroy argues, engagement with issues of race has tended toward either a banal bureaucratization and disavowal of divergent subjectivities or blunt forms of tokenism that preclude political action.

Perhaps then, with Copeland, we can acknowledge that progress is much slower than we might hope, that history does not arc irrevocably toward a more utopian future. But we can also, in the spirit of Gilroy's dialectics of conviviality, acknowledge those individual actors, sites, and objects that help us to see counterhistories so often hidden from view and chart what the next world will look like—even if we are never assured of its arrival. As beautiful, elegiac, and multilayered as Fani-Kayode's pictures are in image and material substance, their project was ultimately this: of searching; of drawing into relation; of mapping rage, desire and, indeed, conviviality in a single frame. He reminded viewers that history rarely moves in a straight line, and that identity is always already implicated with our Others.

In this sense, Fani-Kayode was a crucial transition figure that emerged from the collectivist politics that defined an earlier generation, and at the same time an artist who foreshadowed the challenges endemic to what would come to be defined as the "global contemporary." Fani-Kayode accomplished this with little support and in the face of genuine hardship—financial constraint, social marginalization, and physical disease. To this one must add that he himself was working without a map, as a contemporary African artist during a time in which such an identification was scarcely thinkable, much less commercially or critically viable.

It is unclear if more Fani-Kayode material will come to light. While Autograph ABP has kept him in the public eye, archives of his writing and photographs are not extensive. Working in a small studio in his apartment and dying suddenly, some work that is alluded to or seen in glimpses may have been passed on to friends and collectors, or lost altogether. Which is to say, this volume is not necessarily exhaustive but has sought to place what we do have of Fani-Kayode—mostly recollections, written statements, and dozens of photographs—in as deep a historical and theoretical context as possible. In so doing, I have positioned him in the wider terrain of the music, urban counterpublics, and cultural politics of the 1980s to bring into focus many layers of this vital but still little-explored history. It is my hope that in the years ahead *Bloodflowers* will contribute to an ongoing and open-ended dialogue about that decade. Certainly Fani-Kayode's presence and his pictures resonated in very different keys during those years relative to now, as his story has made its way to new audiences and new sociopolitical contexts. I have worked to balance both vantages, but the power of the photographs described here is that they will necessarily outlive a given moment, and continue to take on new meanings.

This is fitting: Fani-Kayode's statement "Traces of Ecstasy" consistently made reference to recurrences, to the undeniable continuities in human history, across time and across seemingly unbridgeable distances. Indeed, he concludes that statement by mourning the censorship of his work by the Ovalhouse theater in Brixton, a community group that he believed cast him aside, fearing a PR scandal. He seems rueful here, lonely, but nonetheless optimistic that his art might one day return to Nigeria as Bisi Silva predicted. Speculating about the rural Yorubaland of his youth, he ventures a guess that might also define any of us looking at his photographs some thirty years later: "Perhaps they would recognize my smallpox Gods, my transsexual priests, my images of desirable Black men in state of sexual frenzy, or the tranquility of communion with the spirit world. Perhaps they have less fear of encountering the darkest of Africa's dark secrets by which some of us seek to gain access to the soul."[11]

NOTES

INTRODUCTION

1. This made the gum process especially important in the protomodernist era of photography in the 1890s, before the Lumière brothers developed their Autochrome in 1907.

2. See, for example, Kobena Mercer, *Welcome to the Jungle: New Positions in Black Cultural Studies* (New York: Routledge, 1994). See also the exhibit *Transforming the Crown: African, Asian, and Caribbean Artists in Britain, 1966–1996*, which ran at the Caribbean Cultural Centre in London through autumn 1997 and was accompanied by a catalog of the same title edited by M. Franklin Sirmans and Mora J. Beauchamp-Byrd (Chicago: University of Chicago Press, 1997).

3. Okwui Enwezor, Clare Bell, and Octavio Zaya, eds., *In/sight: African Photographers, 1940 to the Present*, exhibition catalog, Solomon R. Guggenheim Museum, 24 May–29 September 1996 (London: Harry N. Abrams, 1996).

4. Okwui Enwezor in Brent Hayes Edwards, *Snap Judgments: New Positions in Contemporary African Photography* (New York: ICP, 2006), part 3, n.p.

5. See, for example, Catherine Lord and Richard Meyer, eds., *Art and Queer Culture* (London: Phaidon, 2013), 150, and Helen Anne Molesworth, Johanna Burton, and Claire Grace, eds., *This Will Have Been: Art, Love and Politics in the 1980s* (Chicago: Museum of Contemporary Art, 2012), 159–170.

6. Rotimi Fani-Kayode, "Traces of Ecstasy," in *Reading the Contemporary: African Art from Theory to the Marketplace*, ed. Olu Oguibe and Okwui Enwezor (Cambridge: MIT Press / London: Iniva, 1999), 276.

7. From the Cure song "Bloodflowers," 2000.

8. From Robert Herrick's poem "To the Virgins, to Make Much of Time" (published 1648).

9. Fani-Kayode's pictures in *Black Male/White Male* are a thoroughgoing investigation into the transient and transformational nature of mirrors.

10. It is a veritable survey of a gothic Romantic tradition. See Charles Baudelaire, *Les fleurs du mal*, trans. Richard Howard (Boston: David R. Godine, 1985).

11. See, for example, Walter Benjamin from the Exposé of 1935, in "Paris, the Capital of the Nineteenth Century," in *The Arcades Project*, trans. Howard Eiland and Kevin McLaughlin (Cambridge, MA: Belknap Press of Harvard University, 2002), 10–12.

12. This is theorized in depth in Fred Moten, *In the Break: The Aesthetics of the Black Radical Tradition* (Minneapolis: University of Minnesota Press, 2003).

13. Reports of routine and institutionalized homophobia and violence in Nigeria and elsewhere (e.g., Uganda) continue to make headlines as of this writing.

14. See, for example, the accompanying essays for the unpaginated catalog edited by Mark Sealy and Jean Loup Pivin, *Rotimi Fani-Kayode and Alex Hirst* (London: Revue Noire and Autograph ABP, 1996).

15. Steven Nelson, "Transgressive Transcendence in the Photographs of Rotimi Fani-Kayode," *Art Journal* 64, no. 1 (spring 2005): 4–19.

16. An ongoing, multivolume project to produce an archive of such visualizations of black subjects in art can be found in David Bindman and Henry Louis Gates Jr., eds., *The Image of the Black in Western Art* (Cambridge, MA: Belknap Press of Harvard University Press, 2010).

17. Mark Sealy, "A Note from Outside on Rotimi Fani-Kayode," in *Rotimi Fani-Kayode (1955–1989)* (Syracuse, NY: Light Work, 2015), n.p. This version of the essay is a near reproduction of its original from twenty years prior, featured in the book *Communion* (London: Autograph ABP, 1995).

18. Alex Hirst, introduction to *Black Male/White Male* (London: Gay Men's Press, 1988), 3.

19. Defining modernity is a Herculean task, and not one that I fully attempt here. Of course, the thrust of this book is to align Fani-Kayode with expanded but, in the eighties, contested visions of the field of modernity, in the work of Paul Gilroy, Henry Louis Gates Jr., and many others. For an excellent analysis in this direction, see Susan Buck-Morss, "Hegel and Haiti," *Critical Inquiry* 26, no. 4 (summer 2000): 821–865.

20. See, for one, Hal Foster's "The 'Primitive' Unconscious of Modern Art," *October* 34 (autumn 1985): 45–70.

21. See Paul Gilroy's "Sounds Authentic: Black Music, Ethnicity, and the Challenge of a 'Changing Same,'" *Black Music Research Journal* 11, no. 2 (autumn 1991): 111–136. Michael Warner's theorization of counterpublics is in *Publics and Counterpublics* (New York: Zone, 2002).

22. See Brent Hayes Edwards's *The Practice of Diaspora: Literature, Translation, and the Rise of Black Internationalism* (Cambridge, MA: Harvard University Press, 2003), 15. For Edwards, "it is exactly such a haunting gap or discrepancy that allows the African diaspora to 'step' and 'move' in various articulations."

23. Conversation with the author, 19 May 2017.

24. Édouard Glissant, *Poetics of Relation*, trans. Betsy Wing (Ann Arbor: University of Michigan Press, 1997), 18.

25. Mercer, "Iconography after Identity," in *Shades of Black: Assembling Black Arts in 1980s Britain*, ed. David A. Bailey, Ian Baucom, and Sonia Boyce (Durham, NC: Duke University Press in collaboration with the Institute of International Visual Arts and the African and Asian Visual Artists Archive, 2005), 49–58.

26. Paul Gilroy, *Postcolonial Melancholia* (New York: Columbia University Press, 2006), 145–146.

27. Kobena Mercer, "Busy the Ruins of the Wretched Phantasia," in *Travel and See: Black Diaspora Art Practices since the 1980s* (Durham, NC: Duke University Press, 2016), 66.

28. George Baker, *The Artwork Caught by the Tail: Francis Picabia and Dada in Paris* (Cambridge, MA: MIT Press, 2007), 14.

29. Baker, *The Artwork Caught by the Tail*, 15–16.

30. See Anthony Gardner, *Politically Unbecoming: Postsocialist Art against Democracy* (Cambridge, MA: MIT Press, 2015).

31. Keith Piper, "Wait, Did I Miss Something?," in Baily, Baucom, and Boyce, *Shades of Black*, 35.

32. See Sean Wilentz, *The Age of Reagan: A History, 1974–2008* (New York: HarperPerennial, 2009); and David Harvey, *A Brief History of Neoliberalism* (Oxford: Oxford University Press, 2007).

33. This is the diagnostic, of course, of Fredric Jameson, who argued in 1984 that postmodernism in culture and politics more broadly is merely a neoliberal mode of production made manifest.

34. Hirst, *Black Male/White Male*, 3.

35. Molesworth, *This Will Have Been*, 14–46.

36. Kaja Silverman, *The Miracle of Analogy; or, The History of Photography, Part 1* (Stanford, CA: Stanford University Press, 2015), 67–85.

37. Derek Conrad Murray, "Base Materialism: Meditations on the Intersection of Blackness and Form," paper given at the Annual Meeting of the College Art Association, 16 February 2017.

ONE / BRIXTON

1. Alex Hirst, introduction to Rotimi Fani-Kayode and Alex Hirst, *Black Male/White Male* (London: Gay Men's Press, 1988), 3.

2. The common practice is to date all pictures from the collection as 1983–1987, reflecting the period after Fani-Kayode finished graduate school and before the publication of *Black Male/White Male*. Given that many of these images have been posthumously reprinted and resized, it is difficult to ascribe an exact date to most

beyond speculation or inference. I was only able to access contact sheets for later works, that is, those of 1988–1989.

3. On the latter, see, for example, the scholarship of Cécile Fromont and Suzanne Preston Blier, or T. F. Earle and Kate J. P. Lowe, eds., *Black Africans in Renaissance Europe* (Cambridge: Cambridge University Press, 2010).

4. See T. J. Demos, "The Ends of Exile: Towards a Coming Universality?," in *Altermodern: Tate Triennial*, ed. Andrew Barnett and Nicolas Bourriaud (London: Tate Publishing, 2009), n.p.

5. Teju Cole, "Far Away from Here," *New York Times*, 27 September 2015, MM27.

6. Rotimi Fani-Kayode, "Traces of Ecstasy," in *Reading the Contemporary: African Art from Theory to the Marketplace*, ed. Okwui Enwezor and Olu Oguibe (Cambridge, MA: MIT Press; London: InIVA, 1999), 276.

7. See Alex Hirst, "Obituary: Rotimi Fani-Kayode," *Independent* (London), 28 December 1989; and "Fani-Kayode—The Facts and Not Fiction," *This Day* (Lagos), 7 December 2009.

8. Édouard Glissant, "Imaginary," in *Poetics of Relation*, trans. Betsy Wing (Ann Arbor: University of Michigan Press, 1997), 18.

9. Glissant, "Imaginary," 18.

10. See Paul Gilroy, *The Black Atlantic: Modernity and Double Consciousness* (Cambridge, MA: Harvard University Press, 1993), 36–37; and Naomi Beckwith and Dieter Roelstraete, eds., *The Freedom Principle: Experiments in Art and Music, 1965 to Now* (Chicago: University of Chicago Press, 2015).

11. Cole, "Far Away from Here."

12. Paul Gilroy, "Sounds Authentic: Black Music, Ethnicity, and the Challenge of a 'Changing' Same," *Black Music Research Journal* 11 (autumn 1991): 111–136.

13. Precisely because of its usage as a normalizing reference to a certain type of white Englishness, "Britishness" became a site of appropriation and revision for an intentional recoding of the contours of nation to reflect the lived demographic realities and cultural priorities of the United Kingdom in the late twentieth century. As such, I retain the usage here except when geographic location demands greater precision.

14. Gilroy, *The Black Atlantic*, xi.

15. Reprinted as "Art of Darkness: Black Art and the Problem of Belonging to England," in Paul Gilroy, *Small Acts: Thoughts on the Politics of Black Cultures* (London: Serpent's Tail, 1993), 75.

16. For example, in "Nationalism, History and Ethnic Absolutism," in Gilroy, *Small Acts*, 63–73.

17. See "The Notting Hill Riots," *Guardian*, 2 September 1958.

18. For a detailed history of the 1960s and the reactionary National Front, which was instrumental in advocating for racist policies, see Chris Mullard, *Black Britain* (London: Allen and Unwin, 1973); and Paul Gilroy, *"There Ain't No Black in*

the Union Jack": The Cultural Politics of Race and Nation (Chicago: University of Chicago Press, 1987).

19. See Enow Eshun's memoir, *Black Gold of the Sun: Searching for Home in Africa and Beyond* (New York: Pantheon, 2005), 65, and the historical overview provided in Michael Eldridge, "The Rise and Fall of Black Britain," *Transition* 74 (1997): 32–43. Eshun recalls that Prime Minister Margaret Thatcher "worried that Britain was in danger of being 'swamped' by 'people with a different culture,'" which is to say, not British (*Black Gold*, 69).

20. *The Other Story* was curated by the artist and critic Rasheed Araeen, who had been active since the 1970s with publications such as *Black Phoenix* and, later, the influential journal *Third Text*. See Araeen's catalog *The Other Story: Afro-Asian Artists in Post-War Britain* (London: Hayward Gallery, 1989).

21. The HMT *Empire Windrush* sailed from Jamaica to England in 1948, with nearly five hundred Jamaican passengers (and over eight hundred Caribbean passengers total), many bound for jobs in the reconstruction of a country decimated by war.

22. Jean Fisher, "The Other Story and the Past Imperfect," *Tate Papers* 12 (2009): 5–6.

23. Eddie Chambers, *Black Artists in British Art: A History since the 1950s* (London: I. B. Tauris, 2014)

24. Fisher, "The Other Story," 5–6.

25. David A. Bailey, Ian Baucom, and Sonia Boyce, eds., *Shades of Black: Assembling Black Arts in 1980s Britain* (Durham, NC: Duke University Press in collaboration with the Institute of International Visual Arts and the African and Asian Visual Artists Archive , 2005), 3. See also Eddie Chambers, *Annotations 5: Run through the Jungle; Selected Writings by Eddie Chambers*, ed. Gilane Tawadros and Victoria Clark (London: Iniva, 1999).

26. Stuart Hall, "New Ethnicities," in *Stuart Hall: Critical Dialogues in Cultural Studies*, ed. David Morley and Kuan-Hsing Chen (New York: Routledge, 1996), 441. Reprinted from Kobena Mercer, ed., *ICA Documents 7: Black Film, British Cinema* (1989).

27. Gilroy, "Art of Darkness," 85.

28. Keith Piper, "Wait, Did I Miss Something?," in Bailey, Baucom, and Boyce, *Shades of Black*.

29. Citing both Chambers and the Guyanese-British-American painter Frank Bowling, however, Piper concludes in favor or "the strategic use of the term 'black art' as a tool for launching intervention into the various debates around contemporary practice—and eventually to ensuring that the contributions of black artists were fully acknowledged as an integral part of contemporary art practice." See Keith Piper, "Wait, Did I Miss Something?," in Bailey, Baucom, and Boyce, *Shades of Black*, 36–37.

30. On the Black Arts Movement, see, for example, Lisa Gail Collins and Margo Natalie Crawford, eds., *New Thoughts on the Black Arts Movement* (New Brunswick, NJ: Rutgers University Press, 2006). For many of the original documents, see Amiri Baraka and Larry Neal, eds., *Black Fire: An Anthology of Afro-American Writing* (Baltimore: Black Classics Press, 2007).

31. See Eddie Chambers, "Black Art Now," *Third Text* 15 (summer 1991): 91–96.

32. For Hall, the determinant factor in the United States was the persistent legacy of slavery and subsequent jurisprudence; in the United Kingdom, by contrast, slavery and the more immediate question of decolonization, independence, and migration were all at issue—a complex that he theorized at length under the heading of "new ethnicities."

33. Jeff R. Donaldson, "AfriCOBRA Manifesto: 'Ten in Search of a Nation,'" *Nka: Journal of Contemporary African Art* 30 (2012): 80.

34. Remi Fani-Kayode, *Blackism* (Lagos: n.p., 1965), 34.

35. Fani-Kayode cited in "Couples," *Square Peg* (1987): 33.

36. See "Interview with Rita Keegan" (video), in the online archive Sam the Wheels: Local Brixton Films 1960–2008, http://www.samthewheels.co.uk/video_image/487.

37. "Interview with Rita Keegan."

38. "Rotimi Fani-Kayode," artist file, MoMA Archives, New York, n.p.

39. Quoted in Stuart Taylor, "Rita Keegan on Digital Diversity and Colour of Computers," *Mute* 1, no. 7 (10 January 1997), http://www.metamute.org/editorial/articles/rita-keegan-digital-diversity-and-colour-computers.

40. See Alwyn W. Turner, *Rejoice! Rejoice! Britain in the 1980s* (London: Aurum, 2010), 77–82.

41. See, for example, "Greater London Council Abolished," BBC Archive, 31 March 1986, http://news.bbc.co.uk/onthisday/hi/dates/stories/march/31/newsid_2530000/2530803.stm.

42. Adeola Solanke, "Juggling Worlds," in *From Two Worlds*, ed. Rasheed Araeen, Rachel Kirby, and Nicholas Serota (London: Trustees of the Whitechapel Art Gallery, 1986), 14.

43. Autograph ABP was founded as an association and agency to work on behalf of black photographers. Its initial steering committee consisted of Monika Bake, Fani-Kayode, Armet Francis, Sunil Gupta, Michael Jess, and Merle Van Den Bosch. See "Autograph Sees Light of Day," *British Journal of Photography*, 4 August 1988, unpaginated archival material. See also "Come On, Get Snappy!," *The Voice* (UK), 9 August 1988.

44. Mark Sealy, public lecture held at Tiwani Contemporary in London, 1 November 2014, transcript of audio recording by the author.

45. "Rotimi Fani-Kayode," artist file, MoMA Archives, New York, n.p.

46. "Rotimi Fani-Kayode," n.p.

47. Conversation with the author, 19 May 2017.

48. Quoted on the current distribution portal for Akomfrah's projects (including a 2014 film on Stuart Hall), http://www.smokingdogsfilms.com/projects/film /handsworth-songs/.

49. Such a project is not unlike the postindustrial blight pictured by, for instance, Martin Parr, but it adds the crucial third term of race to an implicitly Marxist (that is, class-based) social analysis.

50. Linton Kwesi Johnson, "Di Great Insohreckshan," in *Linton Kwesi Johnson: Selected Poems* (London: Penguin, 2006), https://www.poetryarchive.org/poem/di -great-insohreckshan. "Scarman" is a reference to the November 1981 report by Lord Scarman commissioned by the Home Secretary to determine the cause of the April riots in Brixton. See Ben Bowling, "Facing the Ugly Facts," *Guardian*, 16 February 1999.

51. Fred Moten, *In the Break: The Aesthetics of the Black Radical Tradition* (Minneapolis: University of Minnesota Press, 2003), 7; see also Kodwo Eshun, *More Brilliant Than the Sun: Adventures in Sonic Fiction* (London: Quartet, 1999).

52. AfriCOBRA cofounder Barbara Jones-Hogu sought a "new international consciousness" that might be inaugurated by visual and sonic forms alike, calling on artists to produce works that "mark the spot where real and unreal, the objective and the non-objective, the plus and the minus, meet." Quoted in Naomi Beckwith, "Only Poetry," in Beckwith and Roelstraete, *The Freedom Principle*, 45.

53. From the Massive Attack song "Blue Lines" (1991). "Budokan headset" refers at once to the storied Tokyo venue and, relatedly, to the Sony WM-DD100 Boodo Khan, a high-end Walkman tape player issued in 1987 and paired with DJ-style over-ear headphones. The Boodo Kahn was noted for its next-generation bass amplification capabilities and intensity at low volumes.

54. See Rosalind Krauss, "A Note on Photography and the Simulacral," *October* 31 (winter 1984): 49–68.

55. Consider Maya Deren's classic film *Divine Horsemen: The Living Gods of Haiti*, filmed between 1947 and 1954 and released more widely in 1985. It documents the fusion of sacralized visual form and sonic pulsation integral to creating ruptures in the quotidian, opening on to invisible realms of the *loa*, aspects of the divine.

56. Yve-Alain Bois and Rosalind E. Krauss, *Formless: A User's Guide* (New York: Zone, 1997), 32.

57. Bois and Krauss, *Formless*, 32–34.

58. For more on corporate appropriations of black musical formations, see Ellis Cashmore, *The Black Culture Industry* (London: Routledge, 1997).

59. Moten, *In the Break*, 197.

60. Moten, *In the Break*, 223.

61. The roster of people who lived at the Brixton Housing Co-op at Railton and Shakespeare Roads in Brixton was provided by another resident, and current activist, Ajamu Ikwe-Tyehimba. Correspondence with the author, 5 October 2015.

62. See Kobena Mercer, "Black Hair/Style Politics" in *Welcome to the Jungle: New Positions in Black Cultural Studies* (New York: Routledge, 1994), 97–128.

63. Mercer, "Black Masculinity and the Sexual Politics of Race," in *Welcome to the Jungle*, 131–170.

64. See, for example, Joseph Murphy, *Santería: African Spirits in America* (Boston: Beacon Press, 1993); and Robert Farris Thomson, *Flash of the Spirit: African and Afro-American Art and Philosophy* (New York: Vintage, 1984), 1–100.

65. Mark Sealy, "A Note from Outside on Rotimi Fani-Kayode," in *Communion* (London: Autograph ABP, 1995), n.p.

66. Fani-Kayode, "Traces of Ecstasy," 280.

67. Sealy, "A Note from Outside," n.p.

68. Sealy, "A Note from Outside," n.p.

69. Huey Copeland, *Bound to Appear: Art, Slavery, and the Site of Blackness in Multicultural America* (Chicago: University of Chicago Press, 2013), 136.

70. Robert Farris Thompson, "An Aesthetic of the Cool," *African Arts* 7, no. 1 (1973): 40–43, 64–67.

71. Kobena Mercer, "Eros and Diaspora," reprinted in *Reading the Contemporary: African Art from Theory to the Marketplace*, ed. Olu Oguibe and Okwui Enwezor (Cambridge, MA: MIT Press / London: InIVA, 1999), 282–293.

72. See Suzanne Preston Blier, "King Glele of Danhomè, Part One: Divination Portraits of a Lion King and Man of Iron," *African Arts* 23, no. 4 (October 1990): 42–53.

73. Derek Bishton, "A Black British Photographer," in *Rotimi Fani-Kayode and Alex Hirst*, ed. Mark Sealy and Jean Loup Pivin (Paris: Revue Noire, 1996), n.p. This collection provides several firsthand accounts that shore up the available primary documentation on Fani-Kayode in the late eighties.

74. This is the phrase used by Ajamu X in outlining a left politics that addresses issues for a range of people who "were treated like outsiders" in Thatcher's England. Correspondence with the author, 5 October 2015.

TWO / RAGE AND DESIRE

1. Quoted in the short film *Rage and Desire*, dir. Ruppert Gabriel (San Francisco: Frameline, 1992).

2. Quoted in *Rage and Desire*.

3. These larger early works are held in the Autograph ABP archives and are not, at the time of this writing, available for reproduction.

4. Rotimi Fani-Kayode and Stedman Scribner, "Paint Cut React (Razor's Aftershave)," *Square Peg* 3 (1983). *Archives of Sexuality and Gender*, accessed 3 February 2017, http://tinyurl.galegroup.com/tinyurl/6acNfX.

5. This framework echoes the protean zone of relation enacted by Fani-Kayode

in his *Black Male/White Male*, and will continue to be instructive in exploring his uses of surrealism.

6. These quotations all appear in Frantz Fanon, *Black Skin, White Masks*, trans. Richard Philcox (New York: Grove Press, 2008), 94.

7. A 1959 artist's book produced by Guy Debord and Asger Jorn, by then both central to the Situationist International.

8. Rotimi Fani-Kayode and Alex Hirst, "Metaphysick: Every Moment Counts," in *Ecstatic Antibodies: Resisting the AIDS Mythology*, ed. Tessa Boffin and Sunil Gupta (London: Rivers Oram, 1990), 83.

9. Kobena Mercer in "Neo-Romantic, Afro-Atlantic," in *Rotimi Fani-Kayode: Nothing to Lose* (New York: Walther Collection, 2012), n.p. For an overview of this period, see Patti Smith, *Just Kids* (New York: Ecco, 2010); Alan Parker, *Sid Vicious: No One is Innocent* (London: Orion, 2008); and for ramifications into the 1980s hardcore and indie scenes, Michael Azerrad, *Our Band Could Be Your Life: Scenes from the American Indie Underground 1981–1991* (New York: Back Bay Books, 2002).

10. Much of this was captured on tape and is available in digitally dubbed versions of WGTB's programming. School leadership virtually gave away the license to the station in 1979. For a discussion of Georgetown's internal politics and cultural impact during the 1970s, see Guy Raz, "Radio Free Georgetown," *Washington City Paper*, 29 January 1999.

11. Carlo McCormick contends that the simultaneous emergence of punk in the two cultural capitals of New York and London is unsurprising—both cities were flooded by a wave of young art students who had graduated into relative "wastelands," cities denuded by years of economic stagnation and industrial decline. As early as 1984, curator Janet Kardon organized with McCormick an iconic show of "East Village" art in Philadelphia, quite literally mapping its terrain in the associated catalog. See their *The East Village Scene* (Philadelphia: ICA, 1984). See also Phoebe Hoban, *Basquiat: A Quick Killing in Art* (New York: Penguin, 2004).

12. As a symbol of the avant-garde outsider for the punk era, Basquiat is depicted making his way through a dilapidated but hallucinatory Lower East Side in Edo Bertoglio's cult film *Downtown 81*. For photographs and a historic overview, see Marvin J. Taylor, ed., *The Downtown Book: The New York Art Scene 1974–1984* (Princeton, NJ: Princeton University Press, 2005).

13. Punk was a name given by critics and impresarios, such as the boutique merchant and band manager Malcolm McLaren. But the music itself, as played by the Ramones or the Sex Pistols, was simply a sped-up rock and roll and most at the time would have referred to it as such.

14. The Sex Pistols' cover art was designed as a series, made from photocopies and newsprint by Jamie Reid in 1977. Reid is a multimedia artist and self-proclaimed anarchist influenced by the Situationist International and, according

to his former personal website, "the English tradition of Radical dissent that would include, for example, William Blake, Wat Tyler and Gerrard Winstanley," accessed winter 2017, http://www.jamiereid.org/about/.

15. Director Penelope Spheeris's 1981 documentary *The Decline of Western Civilization* followed the careers of an emerging Los Angeles hardcore scene and helped to circulate the sartorial codes of American punk to a wider audience.

16. See Greil Marcus, *Lipstick Traces: A Secret History of the Twentieth Century* (1989; twentieth anniversary ed., Cambridge, MA: Belknap Press of Harvard University Press, 2009), 16–17.

17. See, for example, Paul Morley, "The Sex Pistols Play the Lesser Free Hall," *Guardian*, 13 June 2011.

18. See, for instance, Mat Collishaw's deadpan images of wounds and congenital illness from 1988–1989, or Gavin Turk's revival of the dead Pistols bassist, Sid Vicious, in a sculptural send-up (*POP*, 1993) of Andy Warhol's *Triple Elvis*.

19. Mark Sealy, introduction to Syd Shelton, *Rock against Racism*, 15.

20. Gilroy, "Rebel Souls: Dance-Floor Justice and the Temporary Undoing of Britain's Babylon," in Shelton, *Rock against Racism* , 25.

21. Ajamu X, correspondence with the author, 5 October 2015.

22. For an excellent overview of specific venues, see Tim Burrows, *From CBGB to the Roundhouse: Music Venues through the Years* (London: Marion Boyars, 2009).

23. The precise origins of punk—especially geographically—are still contested. Malcolm McLaren brought the fusion of queer, biker, glam, and punk styles together concurrently at his Chelsea (London)-based boutique, SEX, which he ran with the designer Vivienne Westwood. Here, bondage gear, New York subway–style graffiti, and subversive imagery came together to form the stylistic template for UK punk.

24. Gilroy, "Rebel Souls," 24.

25. Quoted in Burrows, *From CBGB to the Roundhouse*, 122.

26. Discussed in a rapidly edited sequence of interviews with members of Scream, Fugazi, and a range of local bookers and producers in Dave Grohl's documentary *Foo Fighters: Sonic Highways*, episode 2, "Washington, D.C." (2014).

27. Quoted in Cynthia Connolly, Leslie Clague, and Sharon Cheslow, eds., *Banned in DC: Photos and Anecdotes from the DC Punk Underground (79–85)* (Washington, DC: self-published, 1986), 7.

28. Connelly, Clague, and Cheslow, *Banned in DC*, 1.

29. For an excellent oral history and compilation of archival material on The Clash during this period, see the 2000 documentary film by Don Letts, *The Clash: Westway to the World*.

30. Jon Savage has called the Clash's approach "humanist" and "multicultural." See his "The World's End: London Punk 1976–1977," in Gerald Matt and Thomas

Miessgang, *Punk: No One Is Innocent. Art-Style-Revolt* (Vienna: Kunsthalle Wien, 2008), 40–47.

31. Rotimi Fani-Kayode, "Traces of Ecstasy," in *Reading the Contemporary: African Art from Theory to the Marketplace*, ed. Olu Oguibe and Okwui Enwezor (Cambridge, MA: MIT Press / London: Iniva, 1999), 278.

32. Fani-Kayode, "Traces of Ecstasy," 280.

33. Mark Sealy, "A Note from Outside on Rotimi Fani-Kayode," in *Rotimi Fani-Kayode (1955–1989)* (Syracuse: Light Work, 2015), 3.

34. Lisa E. Farrington, "Black Light," in Farrington and Faith Ringgold, *Faith Ringgold* (Petaluma: Pomegranate, 2004), 32.

35. Farrington, "Black Light," 32.

36. Rosetta Brooks, "Rip It Up, Cut It Off, Rend It Asunder," in *Panic Attack! Art in the Punk Years*, ed. Mark Sladen and Ariella Yedgar (London: Merrell, 2007), 48–49.

37. See Jon Savage, *England's Dreaming, Revised Edition: Anarchy, Sex Pistols, Punk Rock, and Beyond* (New York: St. Martin's Press, 2002).

38. Brooks, "Rip It Up," 48.

39. See the excellent sociological study by Richard Lloyd, *Neo-Bohemia: Art and Commerce in the Postindustrial City* (New York: Routledge, 2010).

40. Jay McInerney, "The Death of (the Idea of) the Upper East Side," *New York*, 24 October 2007.

41. Mapplethorpe also made a flag picture: 1977's *American Flag* shows the standard flag, tattered at the edges, but waving proudly in the sunlight (even here, a frozen beauty and sense of erectness predominates in his pictures).

42. Given their shared interests in Afro-diasporic syncretisms one might chart many affinities between Fani-Kayode and Basquiat. Certainly this chapter only gives Basquiat a cursory treatment, to elaborate key differences in the production and reception of art by those who might be identified as punk or black punk in their tactics and ambitions. See, for example, Robert Farris Thompson, "Three Works by Basquiat," in *Basquiat and the Bayou*, ed. Franklin Sirmans (New York: Prestel, 2014), 30–51.

43. On the commercialization of graffiti and the confluence of hip-hop and the East Village scene, see my "Graffiti's Discursive Spaces," *Chicago Art Journal* 17 (2007): 56–83.

44. See Ingrid Sischy's "A Society Artist," in *Robert Mapplethorpe*, ed. Richard Marshall (New York: Whitney Museum of American Art, 1990), n.p.; and Jack Fritscher, *Mapplethorpe: Assault with a Deadly Camera: A Pop Culture Memoir, an Outlaw Reminiscence* (Mamaroneck, NY: Hastings House, 1994), 19–21.

45. See, for example, Richard Shone, "From 'Freeze' to *House*: 1988–94," in *Sensation: Young British Artists at the Saatchi Collection*, ed. Norman Rosenthal (Lon-

don: Thames and Hudson, 1997); and Sarah Kent, "Nine Years," in *Young British Art: The Saatchi Decade*, ed. Robert Timms et al. (London: Booth-Clibborn, 1999).

46. See Goldin, "The Ballad of Sexual Dependency," in *The Cinematic*, ed. David Campany (London: Whitechapel; Cambridge, MA: MIT Press, 2007), 66.

47. Quoted in Morrisroe, *Mark Morrisroe* (Santa Fe, NM: Twin Palms, 1999), front layout (n.p.), 98.

48. Such observations are clear from looking at the works themselves, but Morrisroe's process is described in more detail by Klaus Ottman in "Mark Morrisroe and His Words," in Morrisroe, *Mark Morrisroe*, n.p.

49. José Esteban Muñoz, *Disidentifications: Queers of Color and the Performance of Politics* (Minneapolis: University of Minnesota Press, 1999), 93–104.

50. Savage, "The World's End," 42.

51. Of course, the disco was not the only such site, and Hirst's account also invokes broader themes of exhausted, hungover mornings-after and desirous cruising so integral to an emerging subculture rooted in gay liberation. Douglas Crimp recalls his aerial view at 12 West of throngs of bodies moving in the dark, a scene reminiscent of author Samuel Delany's account of his own youth in downtown bathhouses in *The Motion of Light in Water: Sex and Science Fiction Writing in the East Village: 1960–1965* (New York: Plume, 1989). Crimp draws a distinction between discos, which, though often gay, were fundamentally about the pleasures and experience of dancing, and the bathhouses, which provided the framework for predictably sexual encounters. These two "forbidden" spaces, however, fit hand in glove: Crimp argues that "the liberation ethos developed into a new sexual culture, and that culture fed into the new dance scene. It's not surprising that one of the earliest gay dance parties in New York happened at a bathhouse: the Continental Baths introduced disco in 1970." See Douglas Crimp, "*Disss*-Co (A Fragment)," *Criticism* 50, no. 1 (2008): 15.

52. José Esteban Muñoz, *Cruising Utopia: The Then and There of Queer Futurity* (New York: New York University Press, 2009).

53. Quoted in Isaac Julien's 2008 film *Derek*.

54. Dramatized in Michael Winterbottom's narrative-cum-documentary *24 Hour Party People* (2002). See also Peter Hook, *The Hacienda: How Not to Run a Club* (London: Simon and Schuster, 2010).

55. Michel Foucault, "Of Other Spaces" (1967), trans. Jay Miskowiec, available online at http://foucault.info/documents/heteroTopia/foucault.heteroTopia.en.html.

56. Bill Brewster and Frank Broughton, *Last Night a DJ Saved My Life: The History of the Disc Jockey* (New York: Grove Press, 1999), 148.

57. Ernestine, "The Clubhouse" (1978), available online, along with other collected oral and popular history, at: http://rainbowhistory.omeka.net/items/show/3.

58. Stephen Johnson, "Colonel Abrams," *Whazzup! Magazine*, December 1996, 18.

59. Hence the *fa* in "Fani." One gets a sense of both dominant sexual and class imperatives within a few hours of deplaning in Lagos, where the Fani-Kayode family conducts its business. Fani-Kayode's father, Chief Remilekun, was the former deputy prime minister of the western (Yoruban) region, and his mother hailed from a notable Hausa (northern Muslim) family. See Alex Hirst, "Obituary: Rotimi Fani-Kayode," *Independent* (London), 28 December 1989; and "Fani-Kayode—The Facts and Not Fiction," *This Day* (Lagos), 7 December 2009.

60. This is an emerging and primarily oral history, but, as mentioned previously, many of the participants in the DC scene are interviewed by the musician Dave Grohl in his 2014 documentary series *Foo Fighters: Sonic Highways*.

61. For an exceptional overview of the early history of dance music and its connections with the utopian currents of the postwar avant-garde, see Tim Lawrence, *Love Saves the Day: A History of American Dance Music Culture, 1970–1979* (Durham, NC: Duke University Press, 2003).

62. Foucault, "Of Other Spaces."

63. Michael Warner, *Publics and Counterpublics* (New York: Zone, 2005).

THREE / MAGNOLIA AIR

1. Catherine Lord and Richard Meyer, eds., *Art and Queer Culture* (London: Phaidon, 2013); Helen Anne Molesworth, Johanna Burton, and Claire Grace, eds., *This Will Have Been: Art, Love, and Politics in the 1980s* (Chicago: Museum of Contemporary Art, 2012).

2. Lord and Meyer, *Art and Queer Culture*, 150.

3. Kobena Mercer's project of theoretical definition is presented in a range of essays in his *Travel and See: Black Diaspora Art Practices since the 1980s* (Durham, NC: Duke University Press, 2016.

4. That is, the AIDS Coalition to Unleash Power, formed in 1987. For more on the New York context, see Douglas Crimp, *AIDS: Cultural Analysis/Cultural Activism* (Cambridge, MA: MIT Press, 1988).

5. Simon Watney, *Policing Desire: Pornography, AIDS and the Media* (Minneapolis: University of Minnesota Press, 1987), 14.

6. Rotimi Fani-Kayode, "Traces of Ecstasy," in *Reading the Contemporary: African Art from Theory to the Marketplace*, ed. Olu Oguibe and Okwui Enwezor (Cambridge, MA: MIT Press; London: Iniva, 1999), 276.

7. Fani-Kayode, "Traces of Ecstasy," 279.

8. Fani-Kayode, "Traces of Ecstasy," 280.

9. *Camp* is not consistently capitalized, but it appears as such in some of its earlier theorization. As such, I capitalize it as a noun but not as an adjective.

10. In 2013 an essay for a survey by the Walther Collection was brought to my attention—Kobena Mercer's "Neo-Romantic, Afro-Atlantic" piece discussed in the

first chapter. Toward the end of that essay, in suggesting a wider reading of Fani-Kayode's career, Mercer invokes Day's *An Ethiopian Chief* (ca. 1897). Given that Mercer worked alongside Fani-Kayode in South London, this suggestion confirms that it is plausible to imagine Fani-Kayode considering Day as he staged his own photographs.

11. Kristin Schwain, "F. Holland Day's *Seven Last Words* and the Religious Roots of American Modernism," *American Art* 19, no. 1 (2005): 32–59.

12. This connection was initially suggested to me by an Americanist art historian, Randall Griffin of SMU, in early 2012.

13. See Estelle Jussim, "F. Holland Day's 'Nubians,'" *History of Photography* 2 (April–June 1983): 131–141. The identity of the "Nubian" is subject to debate, though it seems likely that it was a Boston-area model.

14. Ethiopia during this period was notable not for its chiefdoms but for its Christian lineage and resistance to colonialism. The figure's regalia is not particularly indicative of Ethiopian garb. Similarly, Day's dubbing of his figures as "Nubians" points more toward a late Victorian orientalism that included Egypt and the southern Nile than to the actual (likely western African) heritage of his sitter.

15. On the definition of homosexuality and the discursive production of deviance, especially in the late nineteenth century, see Michel Foucault, *The History of Sexuality, Volume 1: An Introduction*, trans. Robert Hurley (New York: Vintage, 1978).

16. Schwain, "F. Holland Day's *Seven Last Words*," 48.

17. Schwain is citing the work of James Crump in *F. Holland Day: Suffering the Ideal* (Santa Fe, NM: Twin Palms, 1995).

18. Emmanuel Cooper, *Fully Exposed: The Male Nude in Photography* (London: Routledge, 1989).

19. See Cooper, *Fully Exposed*, 49–60, 183–235.

20. Richard Meyer, "'Los Angles Meant Boys': David Hockney, Bob Mizer, and the Lure of Physique Photography," in *Pacific Standard Time: Los Angeles Art 1945–1980*, ed. Rebecca Peabody, Andrew Perchuk, Glenn Phillips, and Rani Singh (Los Angeles: Getty Research Institute, 2011), 183–185.

21. Reproductions of the stamps are accessible online. See, for example, James Nichols, "Tom of Finland Stamps to be Released in Finland," *Huffington Post*, 15 April 2014, http://www.huffingtonpost.com/2014/04/15/tom-of-finland -stamps_n_5153034.html.

22. Cooper, *Fully Exposed*, 191.

23. Cooper, *Fully Exposed*, 173. See also Steven Haas and Allen Ellenzweig, eds., *George Platt Lynes: The Male Nudes* (New York: Rizzoli, 2011).

24. Alex Hirst, "Unacceptable Behaviour: A Memoir," in *Rotimi Fani-Kayode: Photographer* (London: 198 Gallery, 1990), n.p.

25. Laura Mulvey, "Visual Pleasure and Narrative Cinema," *Screen* 16, no. 3 (autumn 1975): 6–18.

26. Such stories are recounted in great detail in Jack Fritscher, *Mapplethorpe: Assault with a Deadly Camera; A Pop Culture Memoir, an Outlaw Reminiscence* (Mamaroneck, NY: Hastings House Press, 1994).

27. Cooper, *Fully Exposed*, 188.

28. On this, see Richard Meyer, "Barring Desire: Robert Mapplethorpe and the Disciplining of Photography," in *Outlaw Representation: Censorship and Homosexuality in Twentieth-Century American Art* (Boston: Beacon Press, 2002), 158–223.

29. Meyer, "Barring Desire," 168–204.

30. For more on power and the paternal in psychoanalysis, see Joan Copjec, *Read My Desire: Lacan against the Historicists* (Cambridge, MA: MIT Press, 1996).

31. See Rotimi Fani-Kayode and Alex Hirst, "Metaphysick: Every Moment Counts," in *Ecstatic Antibodies: Resisting the AIDS Mythology*, ed. Tessa Boffin and Sunil Gupta (London: Rivers Oram, 1990), 78–79.

32. Alex Hirst, introduction to *Black Male/White Male* (London: Gay Men's Press, 1988), 3.

33. As Hal Foster has compellingly argued, surrealism was dually fixated with abundance, in the form of return to maternal unity, and with persistent anxiety related to fears of paternal castration. Both rendered its desublimatory landscape a "masculinist domain" that may not genuinely "trouble masculine identity." See Hal Foster, *Compulsive Beauty* (Cambridge, MA: MIT Press, 1995), 208.

34. Theorized concurrently with Fani-Kayode's own practice by Julia Kristeva in *Powers of Horror: An Essay on Abjection*, trans. Leon S. Roudiez (New York: Columbia University Press, 1982).

35. Fritscher, *Mapplethorpe*, 56.

36. Isaac Julien and Kobena Mercer, "True Confessions: A Discourse on Images of Black Male Sexuality," in *Brother to Brother: Collected Writings by Black Gay Men*, ed. Essex Hemphill and Joseph Beam (Boston: Alyson, 1991), 170.

37. Julien and Mercer, "True Confessions," 172.

38. Julien and Mercer, "True Confessions," 172.

39. Sontag's "Notes on 'Camp'" was originally published in *Partisan Review* 31, no. 4 (1964) and has been collected in several reprintings of her criticism, for example, in *Against Interpretation: And Other Essays* (New York: Picador, 2001), 275–292. Each note in the essay is numbered, and I reference them in those terms; for example, "(50)" for the above quotation.

40. See, for example, *Slate* magazine's LGBTQ editor's multipart assessment of Camp in the twenty-first century: J. Bryan Lowder, "Postcards from Camp," *Slate*, 1–3 April 2013, http://www.slate.com/articles/arts/culturebox/features/2013 /postcards_from_camp/camp_is_not_dead.html.

41. Alex Hirst and Seymour Kelly, "Sex and Sensibility," *Square Peg* 3 (1983), n.p.

42. The tenor of queer politics in the United Kingdom shifted throughout the

eighties. See Larry Gross, *Contested Closets: The Politics and Ethics of Outing* (Minneapolis: University of Minnesota Press, 1993).

43. Lowder, "Postcards from Camp."

44. Taped interviews with Jarman are excerpted at length in Isaac Julien's 2008 film *Derek*.

45. Sontag, "Notes on Camp," (26).

46. A colleague at Oxford University recently wrote to me, after seeing a private showing of the 1989 C-prints, that, if nothing else, they were visually exquisite: "If you can't see Caravaggio, this is the next best thing."

47. Sontag, "Notes on Camp,"(53).

48. Described in interview footage in Julien, *Derek*.

49. Jarman quoted in *At Your Own Risk: A Saint's Testament* (Woodstock, NY: Overlook Press, 1992), 91.

50. Fani-Kayode was part of a larger network that included Isaac Julien, whose documentary *Derek* was released fourteen years after the latter's death. Jarman's film *Sebastiane* (1976) was also an early instance of both actual gay sex being documented as art practice (rather than as pornographic commerce) and the overt recasting of Saint Sebastian as a queer figure.

51. The latter form of performance/dance was, of course, made famous by Madonna in her 1990 single "Vogue." The following year saw the release of Jennie Livingston's documentary *Paris Is Burning*, which explored balls, drag, and voguing as part of a larger set of queer counteraesthetics, especially in the black and Latinx communities of New York.

52. Sontag, "Notes on Camp," (14).

53. See Cooper, *Fully Exposed*, 155–157.

54. Mark Booth, *Camp* (London: Quartet, 1983).

55. Described in Charles Baudelaire, *The Painter of Modern Life and Other Essays*, trans. Jonathan Mayne (London: Phaidon, 1970), 26–29.

56. The actor and artist quoted in Julien, *Derek*.

57. Rosalyn Deutsche has written about the "future anterior" as political praxis in "Hiroshima after Iraq: A Study in Art and War," *October* 131 (winter 2010): 3–22.

58. Sontag, "Notes on Camp," (2).

59. Martin Humphries, introduction to *Tongues Untied*, ed. Dirg Aarb-Richards (London: Gay Men's Press, 1987), 5.

60. See Hazel V. Carby, "White Woman Listen! Black Feminism and the Boundaries of Sisterhood," in *Black British Feminism: A Reader*, ed. Heidi Safia Mirza (London: Routledge, 1997), 49.

61. This, emphatically, is not to elide the complexities of the formation and representation of transgendered and cisgendered subjects; it is only to say that while pieces such as *Bronze Head* and *Snap Shot* complicate the biological operations of gender and work at times to invaginate the typically phallic logic of picture tak-

ing, there is little evidence of transgendered subjects, as such, being central to the photographs.

62. Carby, "White Woman Listen!," 48. The complexities resulting from an "intersectional" account of subjectivity and domination were notably articulated by the legal theorist Kimberle Crenshaw in her 1989 essay "Mapping the Margins: Intersectionality, Identity Politics, and Violence against Women of Color," *Stanford Law Review* 43 (July 1991): 1241–1299.

63. Correspondence with the author, 5 October 2015.

64. Riggs was based in the San Francisco Bay Area. Nonetheless, one can map a gay topography of the 1970s and 1980s that comprises a set of cities linked through air travel and the movement of shared cultural production in film, magazines, art photography, fashion, and literature. See Joseph Beam, ed., *In the Life: A Black Gay Anthology* (Boston: Alyson, 1986).

65. As of this writing, Simmons is the director of Us Helping Us, a nonprofit aimed at reducing HIV/AIDS in African American communities, particularly black gay/same-gender-loving men. These quotations are from his account "Joe, Essex, Marlon, and Me," in *Black Gay Genius: Answering Joseph Beam's Call*, ed. Steven G. Fullwood and Charles Stephens (New York: Vintage Entity Press, 2014), 54–55.

66. See Manthia Diawara, "The Absent One: The Avant-Garde and the Black Imaginary in *Looking for Langston*," in *Representing Black Men*, ed. Marcellus Blount and George Philbert Cunningham (New York: Routledge, 1996), 206.

67. Quoted in Alexis Pauline Gumbs, "Queer Relative, Joseph Beam, Audre Lorde, and the Diasporic Poetics of Survival in the 1980s," in Fullwood and Stephens, *Black Gay Genius*, 221.

68. Hirst, "Unacceptable Behaviour," n.p.

69. There is a larger history here, beyond the scope of this book. For an overview of the internecine debates in American gay activism in the eighties, see Charles Kaiser, *The Gay Metropolis: 1940–1996* (New York: Houghton Mifflin, 1997), 284–325.

70. Many of these poems are collected in Essex Hemphill and Joseph Beam, *Brother to Brother*, and Hemphill's collection *Ceremonies: Prose and Poetry* (San Francisco: Cleis Press, 2000). For more on Stanford and black poetry in the eighties, see Sonya L. Jones, ed., *Gay and Lesbian Literature since World War II: History and Memory* (New York: Routledge, 1998). For more on the radical formalism of black sonics, see Fred Moten, *In the Break: The Aesthetics of the Black Radical Tradition* (Minneapolis: University of Minnesota Press, 2003).

71. Simmons, "Joe, Essex, Marlon, and Me," 59.

72. Hemphill quoted by Robert F. Reid-Pharr in "Stronger, in This Life: Loving the Genius of Essex Hemphill and Joseph Beam," in Fullwood and Stephens, *Black Gay Genius*, 52.

73. Gupta quoted in "Conversation with Saleem Kidwai," in *Queer* (Munich: Prestel, 2011), 37.

74. Gupta, "Conversation with Saleem Kidwai," 39.

75. Gupta, "Conversation with Saleem Kidwai," 39.

76. See José Esteban Muñoz, *Disidentifications: Queers of Color and the Performance of Politics* (Minneapolis: University of Minnesota Press, 1999), 11.

77. The artist Gregg Bordowitz recalls this transition point in mid-eighties New York in "My Postmodernism," originally published in *Artforum* (2003) and collected in *The AIDS Crisis Is Ridiculous and Other Writings, 1986–2003* (Cambridge, MA: MIT Press, 2004), 222–239.

78. This is part of his larger theorization of counterpublicity and politics in Michael Warner, *Publics and Counterpublics* (New York: Zone, 2002), especially 91–124.

79. As Warner wrote in the introduction to his seminal 1994 collection *Fear of a Queer Planet*, queer culture, whatever "else it might be, it is not autochthonous. It cannot even be in diaspora, having no locale from which to wander." I would argue that queerness functions like diasporic practice in short-circuiting the dichotomy of exclusion/inclusion by questioning the historical terrain in which difference is figured, resisting the "reification of identity." Michael Warner, ed., *Fear of a Queer Planet: Queer Politics and Social Theory* (Minneapolis: University of Minnesota Press, 1993), xvii–xviii.

80. "Rotimi," *Square Peg* (1990), 10.

81. "An Exhibition of Photographs by Rotimi Fani-Kayode Opens at the Submarine Gallery," *Capital Gay*, 10 June 1988, 15.

82. Antoinette Azolakov, "Book Club," *Campaign*, March 1989, 60.

83. Alex Hirst, introduction to Rotimi Fani-Kayode and Alex Hirst, *Black Male/White Male* (London: Gay Men's Press, 1988), 3.

84. Hirst, *Black Male/White Male*, 3.

85. Mapplethorpe's compilation of images of black men, *Black Book* (New York: St. Martin's Press, 1988), was published in the same year as *Black Male/White Male* in a strikingly similar square format.

86. See Miwon Kwon, "One Place After Another: Notes on Site Specificity," *October* 80 (Spring 1997): 109.

87. See David Wojnarowicz, *In the Shadow of the American Dream: The Diaries of David Wojnarowicz*, ed. Amy Scholder (New York: Grove Press, 2000), e.g. 115–131. On the "indexical" sculptural forms that emerged in the 1970s, see Rosalind Krauss, "Notes on the Index: Seventies Art in America, Part II," *October* 4 (Autumn 1977): 58–67.

88. See Douglas Crimp, *Before Pictures* (Chicago: University of Chicago Press, 2016).

89. Brewster and Broughton, *Last Night*, 133–174. The fallout of the HIV epidemic in queer populations, and the subsequent contraction of the sexual freedom that imparted places such as the bathhouse with its liminal power, were described in

both Leo Bersani, "Is the Rectum a Grave?," *October* 43 (winter 1987): 197–222; and Douglas Crimp, "How to Have Promiscuity in an Epidemic," in *Melancholia and Moralism: Essays on AIDS and Queer Politics* (Cambridge, MA: MIT Press, 2002), 43–82.

90. See again, Crimp, especially his "Melancholia and Moralism: An Introduction," *Melancholia and Moralism*, 1–26.

91. Fani-Kayode and Hirst, "Metaphysick," 80.

92. Jarman, *At Your Own Risk*, 117.

FOUR / THE QUEEN IS DEAD

1. A black-and-white picture from 1934 of the same name. The Minotaur's association with cultic activity and ritual sacrifice dovetailed with a deeper interest of Georges Bataille, who used the creature as the title of his journal of 1933–1939. The figure of the headless man—echoed directly by Fani-Kayode's *Torso*—became the titular figure of Bataille's five-issue journal and secret society of 1936–1939, *Acéphale*.

2. A compelling history in its own right, brought into focus by Edward Said's classic *Orientalism* (New York: Vintage, 1978) and connected to European painting by Linda Nochlin in "The Imaginary Orient," in *The Politics of Vision: Essays on Nineteenth Century Society* (New York: Harper and Row, 1989), 33–59.

3. There is evidence, described in subsequent chapters, that Fani-Kayode staged many of his pictures in direct dialogue with earlier moments of modernism and modernist primitivism—notably in the work of Paul Gauguin.

4. Magritte, *Treachery of Images* (1928–1929).

5. From Coleridge's archetypical Romantic poem "Kubla Khan" (1797)—at least apocryphally thought to have been written under the influence of opium as the poet contemplated accounts from central Asia.

6. The specific term for this white clay is *mpemba*, literally meaning "cemetery" and "land of the dead." These figures are written about widely, but see Wyatt MacGaffey, "Fetishism Revisited: Kongo 'Nkisi' in Sociological Perspective," *Africa: Journal of the International Africa Institute* 47 (1977): 172–184.

7. Alex Hirst, untitled text caption to group show materials in *Bodies of Experience: Stories about Living with HIV*, ed. Arabella Plouviez (London: Camerawork/ The Photo Co-op, 1989), n.p.

8. Ann Magnuson, in a catalog for the Grey Gallery at NYU. See Marvin J. Taylor, ed., *The Downtown Book: The New York Art Scene 1974–1984* (Princeton, NJ: Princeton University Press, 2005), 46.

9. A term common among critics of the period, describing a late-night world of artist-run spaces, often managed out of bathrooms and living rooms, and connected to a vibrant music scene centered around CBGB on the Bowery. See Steven Hager, *Art after Midnight: The East Village Scene* (New York: St. Martin's Press, 1986).

10. Consider work such as Tehching Hsieh's *One Year Performance (Time Piece)* (1980–1981) and oral histories of the early eighties scene in New York (when Fani-Kayode was at the Pratt Institute) compiled at http://www.nyu.edu/greyart/exhibits/downtown/sublime1.html, accessed winter 2017. The authors argue here that "'Sublime Time' not only encompasses mesmeric or meditative artworks and compositions, but also conjures the atmosphere of the late-night club scene and even New York City itself, where time—even without the mind-altering drugs then so prevalent—often seemed to either slow down inexorably or speed by in a blinding flash." See also https://greyartgallery.nyu.edu/exhibition/the-downtown-show-011006-040106/.

11. In 1983 the Royal Drummers of Burundi themselves would appear on the droning "Zimbo," the B-side to the twelve-inch recording of "The Cutter" by the mournful Liverpool band Echo and the Bunnymen. In that year the single "The Cutter" became immediately notable for its languid (if poppy) faux-sitar melody.

12. For more on the emergence of punk and Neoromantic fashion in London, see Simon Easton, *Clothes for Heroes: The Punk Fashions of Vivienne Westwood and Malcolm McLaren* (New York: Abrams, 2014).

13. David Johnson, "Spandau Ballet, the Blitz Kids and the Birth of the New Romantics," *Guardian*, 3 October 2009.

14. Morrissey, *Autobiography* (New York: Putnam, 2013), 3.

15. Of course, Manchester is notable for its own creative efflorescence in the eighties, around the "Madchester" scene anchored by Factory Records. A gothic undercurrent nonetheless connected the distinct projects in the Midlands and greater London.

16. Johnson, "Spandau Ballet."

17. Parr also shot pictures of everyday life, scenes of British family, manners, and kitsch, largely working in a photojournalistic mode. See Val Williams, ed., *Martin Parr* (London: Phaidon, 2002).

18. According to the curator's display caption at the Tate Gallery, Britain.

19. On this, see David Sylvester's interview-cum-portfolio *Francis Bacon* (New York: Pantheon, 1975). Bacon notes that "when you're outside a tradition, as every artist is today, one can only want to record one's own feelings about certain situations as closely to one's own nervous system as one possibly can" (43).

20. Kobena Mercer, "Neo-Romantic, Afro-Atlantic," in *Rotimi Fani-Kayode: Nothing to Lose* (New York: Walther Collection, 2012), n.p.

21. See Isaiah Berlin's outstanding overview, *The Roots of Romanticism* (Princeton, NJ: Princeton University Press, 1999), 16–17. Berlin's focus, here, is the intellectual-historical and, to an extent, the literary.

22. The original archetype is defined at length by Marsha Morton, who argues that artists such as Carl Wilhelm Kolbe, Caspar David Friedrich, and Julius Schnorr von Carolsfeld viewed art as an emotional exercise not unlike religious devotion.

See Morton, "German Romanticism: The Search for 'A Quiet Place,'" *Art Institute of Chicago Museum Studies* 28, no. 1 (2002): esp. 8–12.

23. Morton, "German Romanticism," 10.

24. Morton, "German Romanticism," 11.

25. See Mark Edmundson, "Nightmare on Main Street: Angels, Sadomasochism and the Culture of Gothic" (1997), in *The Gothic*, ed. Gilda Williams (London: Whitechapel and MIT Press, 2007), 31–32.

26. T. J. Clark thus sums up the poet W. B. Yeats as a modernist for believing in ghosts, for believing "in the possibility of endless agony, fueled forever by a life unfulfilled—not stopped for a minute by mere physical extinction." See Clark, "Modernism, Postmodernism, and Steam," *October* 100 (spring 2002): 154–174.

27. Walter Benjamin, "Paris, Capital of the Nineteenth Century" (exposé of 1935), in *The Arcades Project*, trans. Howard Eiland and Kevin McLaughlin (Cambridge, MA: Belknap Press of Harvard University Press, 2002), 3–13.

28. Alex Hirst, introduction to Rotimi Fani-Kayode and Alex Hirst, *Black Male/ White Male* (London: Gay Men's Press, 1987). This quotation has been taken from the German version (Berlin: Borderline, 1988), 3.

29. This is what T. J. Clark called a "disenchanting" of the world under capitalism, in Clark, "Modernism, Postmodernism, and Steam."

30. Johnson, "Spandau Ballet."

31. Art historically, this dynamic has principally surfaced in both Freudian/psychoanalytic interpretation (with its emphasis on repressed drives and traumas that manifest in unpredictable ways) and also by way of structuralism, which posits hidden and unresolvable contradictions that perennially reemerge in the field of culture, a mytholinguistic system that governs our behaviors while remaining ceaselessly elusive.

32. Rotimi Fani-Kayode and Alex Hirst, "Metaphysick: Every Moment Counts," in *Ecstatic Antibodies: Resisting the AIDS Mythology*, ed. Tessa Boffin and Sunil Gupta (London: Rivers Oram, 1990), 83–84.

33. Michael Taussig writes about this as a problem of anthropological methodology in his "Viscerality, Faith, and Skepticism: Another Theory of Magic," in *Walter Benjamin's Grave* (Chicago: University of Chicago Press, 2006), 121–155.

34. David Marriot, *Haunted Life: Visual Culture and Black Modernity* (New Brunswick, NJ: Rutgers University Press, 2007), 226. Art historically, Huey Copeland examines the persistence of slavery in recent art; see his *Bound to Appear: Art, Slavery, and the Site of Blackness in Multicultural America* (Chicago: University of Chicago Press, 2013). Similar insights have been brought to the fore more locally in literature, too: the incursion of seemingly past trauma and violence into waking life was described in the work, most notably, of Toni Morrison, in books such as *Sula* (1973) and *Beloved* (1987).

35. Such structures will likely be familiar to students of sub-Saharan Africa and, especially, of religions of the African diaspora, such as Haitian voudou.

36. See T. J. Demos, *Return to the Postcolony: Specters of Colonialism in Contemporary Art* (Berlin: Sternberg Press, 2013).

37. Haunting has been an interpretive mode for dealing with literature and art on trauma, especially slavery and its legacy. See, e.g., Jenny Sharpe, *Ghosts of Slavery: A Literary Archaeology of Black Women's Lives* (Minneapolis: University of Minnesota Press, 2002). At the 2014 Arts Council of the African Studies Association (ACASA) Triennial, spectral time appeared, for example, in Rachel Nelson's paper "Specters in the City: Kiluanji Kia Henda and Luanda Past and Present" (Brooklyn, 21 March 2014).

38. In the context of twenty-first-century neoliberalism, the historian Jonathan Crary has gone as far as to argue that reengineering one's relationship to sleep and nonproductive states is the next frontier of capitalism's biopolitics (i.e., the regulation of the subject within a productive, growth-oriented economy). See Crary, *24/7: Late Capitalism and the Ends of Sleep* (London: Verso, 2014).

39. This is squarely the territory of the surreal, a movement that gained momentum in the years after Sigmund Freud's publication of his 1919 theory of the uncanny—of things existing out of place or out of time . . . recurrences that make the subject herself feel disjointed, her home made "unhomely."

40. Berlin, *Roots of Romanticism*, 104.

41. The "cybernetic" vision was outlined, for instance, in literary genres such as cyberpunk (e.g., in the work of William Gibson and Philip K. Dick, and in related movies such as 1982's *Blade Runner*), and also in the theoretical work of Marxists and poststructuralists alike. For retrospective diagnostics, see Jean Baudrillard, *Cool Memories* (London: Verso, 1990), and Fredric Jameson, *Postmodernism, or, the Cultural Logic of Late Capitalism* (Durham, NC: Duke University Press, 1992).

42. In his famed overview of the early eighties New York scene, Ricard describes graffiti as a visual language for the decayed ruins of New York and writes of an East Village suffused with vitality: a time when Fani-Kayode was across the river earning an MFA. See Rene Ricard, "The Radiant Child," *Artforum* (December 1981): n.p.

43. For a trove of oral history on life in England during the 1970s, see BBC News, "Your 1970s: Strikes and Blackouts," 7 June 2007, http://news.bbc.co.uk/2/hi/uk _news/magazine/6729683.stm. By 1979, Margaret Thatcher's Conservative Party would oust the left government, aided by the public relations talent of (future art collector) Charles Saatchi, who famously produced a billboard featuring a crowded dole line with the concise heading "Labour Isn't Working."

44. See Okwui Enwezor, "Coalition Building: Black Audio Film Collective and Transnational Post-Colonialism," in *The Ghosts of Songs: The Film Art of the Black Audio Film Collective, 1982–1998*, ed. Kodwo Eshun and Anjalika Sagar (Liverpool: Liverpool University Press, 2007), 113.

45. This is the date provided by the BAFC's current offices. Other publications

date the film as 1989, which accords with Eshun's specifying the Fani-Kayode photograph of a fish vendor as a work from 1988. Both later dates, however, could easily refer to public release, with prints (or versions of prints) of both completed as early as 1987.

46. See Jean Fisher, "In Living Memory . . . Archive and Testimony in the Films of the Black Audio Film Collective," in Eshun and Sagar, *Ghosts of Songs*, 16–30.

47. Interview with the author, 6 October 2017.

48. See, for example, Sven Beckert, *Empire of Cotton: A Global History* (New York: Vintage, 2015).

49. Kodwo Eshun, "Drawing the Forms of Things Unknown," in Eshun and Sagar, *Ghosts of Songs*, 84.

50. Eshun, "Drawing the Forms of Things Unknown," 84.

51. Eshun, "Drawing the Forms of Things Unknown," 84

52. Alex Hirst, introduction to *Rotimi Fani-Kayode*, 3.

53. Tobias Wofford, "Afrofutures: Africa and the Aesthetics of Black Resistance," *Third Text* 31, nos. 5–6 (2017): 633–649.

54. These quotations are taken from Steven Nelson, "Transgressive Transcendence in the Photographs of Rotimi Fani-Kayode," *Art Journal* 64, no. 1 (spring 2005): 14.

55. Nelson, "Transgressive Transcendence," 19.

56. Fani-Kayode, "Traces of Ecstasy," 279.

57. For example, see Kobena Mercer, "The Fragile Inheritors," in *Travel and See: Black Diaspora Art Practices since the 1980s* (Durham, NC: Duke University Press, 2016), 39–49.

58. In Abigail Solomon-Godeau, "Playing in the Fields of the Image," in *Photography at the Dock* (Minneapolis: University of Minnesota Press, 1991), 86–102.

59. Quoted in *Rage and Desire*, dir. Ruppert Gabriel (San Francisco: Frameline, 1992).

60. Cited in Johnson, "Spandau Ballet."

FIVE / MIRROR WORLDS

1. This included a range of film types, including Kodak 5060 in the early years, and Kodak Pantomic-X, which was discontinued in 1987 but may have remained in his storage until the end of his life. A move to Ilford FP4 sometime in 1987 correlates to a general increase in tonal quality and finish in the prints and, it seems, a gradual turn to medium format from 35 mm.

2. This is Abigail Solomon-Godeau's formulation, writing of new accounts of the emerging photographic canon in the early eighties. Generally, she refers to conventions solidified in the writing of Clement Greenberg and Beaumont Newhall and curators such as the Museum of Modern Art's John Szarkowski. Szarkowski's catalog

The Photographer and the American Landscape (New York: Doubleday, 1963) is exemplary.

3. André Breton, for one, reiterated the influence of Romantic poetry and the emerging gothic writing of the Victorian era, citing Comte de Lautréamont (Isidore Ducasse), Rimbaud, Baudelaire, Mallarmé, Shelley, Poe, and Gustave Moreau.

4. Outlined in Dawn Ades and Simon Baker, eds., *Undercover Surrealism: Georges Bataille and DOCUMENTS* (Cambridge, MA: MIT Press, 2006). See also Georges Bataille, *The Tears of Eros*, trans. Peter Connor (San Francisco: City Lights Books, 2002).

5. See Julie Caniglia, "Joseph Cornell and White Magic," https://walkerart.org /magazine/joseph-cornell-and-white-magic.

6. This line of argument is in the work of Rosalind Krauss, e.g. in *The Optical Unconscious* (Cambridge, MA: MIT Press, 1994) and Yve-Alain Bois and Rosalind Krauss, *Formless: A User's Guide* (New York: Zone, 1997).

7. See contemporary curatorial iterations of these impulses in Jennifer Blessing and Nat Trotman, eds., *Haunted: Contemporary Photography, Video, Performance* (New York: Guggenheim Museum, 2010); and in Jane Alison, ed., *The Surreal House* (New Haven, CT: Yale University Press, 2010).

8. See Alison, *The Surreal House*, 238–271; and Jeffrey Fraenkel, ed., *The Unphotographable* (San Francisco: Fraenkel Gallery, 2013).

9. They became strange notably in the uncanny and fetishistic objectification of bodies in the hands of 1930s-era photographers. See Rosalind Krauss, "Corpus Delicti," *October* 33 (summer 1985): 31–72; and "The Photographic Conditions of Surrealism," in *The Originality of the Avant-Garde and Other Modernist Myths* (Cambridge, MA: MIT Press, 1986), 87–118.

10. See Krauss, "Corpus Delicti," 32–36.

11. Steven Nelson, "Transgressive Transcendence in the Photographs of Rotimi Fani-Kayode," *Art Journal* 64, no. 1 (spring 2005): 4–19.

12. Claire Grace, "Rotimi Fani-Kayode," in *This Will Have Been: Art, Love and Politics in the 1980s*, ed. Helen Anne Molesworth, Johanna Burton, and Claire Grace (Chicago: Museum of Contemporary Art, 2012), 335.

13. See James A. Snead, "Repetition as a Figure in Black Culture," in *Out There: Marginalization and Contemporary Culture*, ed. Russell Ferguson, Martha Gever, Trinh T. Minh-Ha, and Cornel West (Cambridge, MA: MIT Press, 1989), 222.

14. Here I rely on Huey Copeland's reading of black artists signifying in the field of postminimal sculpture, notably in *Bound to Appear: Art, Slavery, and the Site of Blackness in Multicultural America* (Chicago: University of Chicago Press, 2013), 150.

15. See Rebecca Zorach, "The Positive Aesthetics of the Black Arts Movement," in *The Freedom Principle: Experiments in Art and Music, 1965 to Now*, ed. Naomi Beckwith and Dieter Roelstraete (Chicago: University of Chicago Press, 2015), 103.

16. Robin D. G. Kelley, *Freedom Dreams: The Black Radical Imagination* (Boston: Beacon Press, 2002), 197.

17. Bois and Krauss, *Formless*, 71.

18. Brent Hayes Edwards, "The Ethnics of Surrealism," *Transition* 78 (1998): 84–135. See, in particular, 86–91, 115–131. For his part, André Breton would travel to Martinique in 1941 and collaborate with the foundational theorist of Négritude, Aimé Césaire (who also instructed Fanon).

19. Black internationalist and diasporic developments are well documented. See, for example, Franklin Rosemont and Robin D. G. Kelley, eds., *Black, Brown, and Beige: Surrealist Writings from Africa and the Diaspora* (Austin: University of Texas Press, 2010).

20. Kelley, *Freedom Dreams*, 159. In this formulation, the surrealist relationship to the colonial periphery can be understood less as anthropological taxonomy or misbegotten romanticism but, rather, a localization of both a cause and method of psychic and political awakening.

21. This reduction, especially as it translated into mid-century visions of Négritude, was of concern to Fanon in particular. See Frantz Fanon, *Black Skin, White Masks*, trans. Richard Philcox (New York: Grove Press, 2008), 100–109.

22. Nelson, "Transgressive Transcendence," 8–9.

23. While Man Ray fused the ethnographic with the aesthetic, the impulse to collect masks was articulated elsewhere. For an exceptional visual and historical accounting of these themes (and many others) in Bataille's journals, see Ades and Baker, *Undercover Surrealism*.

24. Hal Foster, "'Primitive' Scenes," *Critical Inquiry* 20 (autumn 1993): 69–102. See also Abigail Solomon-Godeau, "Going Native: Gauguin and the Invention of Primitivist Modernism," *Art in America* 77 (7 July 1989): 118–129.

25. See Krauss, "Corpus Delicti," 42–44.

26. See Craig Owens, "Photography *en abyme*," *October* 5 (summer 1978): 73–88; it is reprinted in Scott Bryson, ed., *Beyond Recognition: Representation, Power, and Culture* (Berkeley: University of California Press, 1992), 16–30.

27. For example, Hal Foster, "The 'Primitive' Unconscious of Modern Art," *October* 34 (autumn 1985): 45–70.

28. Mark Sealy, "A Note from Outside on Rotimi Fani-Kayode," in *Rotimi Fani-Kayode (1955–1989)* (Syracuse: Light Work, 2015), 3. This is a reprinting of an earlier version of the essay from the *Communion* book, hence the citation of the year 1995 above.

29. Nelson, "Transgressive Transcendence," 7. *Olympia* marked a tectonic shift when it debuted in Paris at the 1865 Salon, hung alongside verse by the poet Zacharie Astruc. Looking back now, we see foundational gestures of modernism in its formalist mode (as self-reflective, flat) and also its twin, avant-garde guise—as

a violent rupture, a visualization of Paris hidden in plain sight, and a debasing of classical beauty.

30. See, for one, Guerrilla Girls, *The Guerrilla Girls' Bedside Companion to the History of Western Art* (New York: Penguin, 1998).

31. This interpretation is laid out in the various printings of Mercer, "Eros and Diaspora," e.g. in *Rotimi Fani-Kayode and Alex Hirst: Photographs*, ed. Mark Sealy and Jean Loup Pivin (London: Revue Noire and Autograph, 1996), n.p.

32. Nelson, "Transgressive Transcendence," 8.

33. Nelson, "Transgressive Transcendence," 6–10.

34. See Fanon, *Black Skin, White Masks*, chaps. 4–5.

35. Quotations on this page are from Nelson, "Transgressive Transcendence," 8.

36. Such strategies were typified in Bataille's varied publications. He worked at the intersection of economics, anthropology, and art criticism and was associated with the journals *Documents* (which he edited, and of which fifteen issues were published in 1929–1930), *Minotaure* (1933–1939), and *Acéphale* (1936–1939).

37. For example, in Yasumasa Morimura, *Daughter of Art History: Photographs by Yasumasa Morimura* (New York: Aperture, 2005).

38. See Nicolas Bourriaud, "Michel Foucault: Manet and the Birth of the Viewer," in Michel Foucault and Nicolas Bourriaud, *Manet and the Object of Painting*, trans. Matthew Barr (London: Tate Publishing, 2010), 18–19. According to Bourriaud, this is "the discrete yet decisive role of painting in the theoretical work of Foucault: absolute heterotopia, a one-way mirror in which the mastery of man is effaced in his real life."

39. David A. Bailey and Stuart Hall, "The Vertigo of Displacement," in *The Photography Reader*, ed. Liz Wells (London: Routledge, 2002), 380–386.

40. For example, Krauss, "Corpus Delicti," 32–37.

41. Foster, "'Primitive' Scenes," 72–83.

42. This is elaborated in Gauguin's notes on "Manao Tupapau," in *Theories of Modern Art*, ed. Herschel B. Chipp (Berkeley: University of California Press, 1984), 66–69 (originally written as part of *Cahier pour Aline* [1893]).

43. Kobena Mercer, "Reading Racial Fetishism: The Photographs of Robert Mapplethorpe" and "Dark and Lovely: Black Gay Image Making" (1991), in *Welcome to the Jungle: New Positions in Black Cultural Studies* (New York: Routledge, 1994), 221–232.

44. For example, Paul Landau and Deborah Kaspin, eds., *Images and Empire: Visuality in Colonial and Postcolonial Africa* (Berkeley: University of California Press, 2002).

45. Hirst, introduction to Rotimi Fani-Kayode and Alex Hirst, *Black Male/White Male* (London: Gay Men's Press, 1988), 3.

46. It is important to note that several of Fani-Kayode's interlocutors—both

Hirst and Sealy—insist that Fani-Kayode's was a distinct practice that was reductively conflated with Mapplethorpe's. I would argue that such a distinction simply insists on the former's practice as being specific rather than derivative.

47. Michael Warner's distinction bears repeating: to be gay is an *identification*; queerness is a *process* that undoes the structures by which those identifications are figured.

48. James is (particularly among Fani-Kayode's models) obviously black. My assessment is largely a formal one, and it is the operation of the camera and the image's position within the artist's book that makes this brief moment of uncertainty of interest. On the whole, however, Fani-Kayode seems unconcerned with the slippage between physiognomy and stereotype (Fanon's "dermal schema") that is so central to discussions of passing and in the work of, say, Adrian Piper. See, for example, John P. Bowles, "Adrian Piper as African American Artist," *American Art* 20 (fall 2006): 108–117.

49. See Bois and Krauss, *Formless*, 164. This "dictionary" in which one finds the subheading "pulse" was itself a secret map of the sunken cities that at once cancelled and subverted modernism, but which also configured it by relation (in this case, through the psychoanalytic metaphor of repression and the unconscious).

50. See, for example, Rosalind Krauss, "Francesca Woodman: Problem Sets," in *Bachelors* (Cambridge, MA: MIT Press, 1999), 161–178; and Abigail Solomon-Godeau, "Just Like a Woman," in *Photography at the Dock* (Minneapolis: University of Minnesota Press, 1991), 238–255. Relatedly, exhibitions of Man Ray's work were widespread in the United States and Europe throughout Fani-Kayode's adult life, including at the Venice Biennale in 1976, the Centre Georges Pompidou in 1981 and 1982, the Knoedler Gallery in London in 1981, and the Zabriskie Gallery in New York in 1982.

51. See Ades and Baker, "Sacrifice," in *Undercover Surrealism*, 103–114. Lacan's initial version of "The Mirror Stage as Formative of the Function of the I as Revealed in Psychoanalytic Experience" has its origins in a 1936 paper and report on the "mirror phase," itself indebted to Roger Caillois's 1935 essay "Mimicry and Legendary Psychasthenia," published in Bataille's *Minotaure*.

52. Rotimi Fani-Kayode, "Traces of Ecstasy," in *Reading the Contemporary: African Art from Theory to the Marketplace*, ed. Olu Oguibe and Okwui (Cambridge, MA: MIT Press London: Iniva, 1999), 276.

53. Henry Louis Gates Jr., *The Signifying Monkey: A Theory of African-American Literary Criticism* (Oxford: Oxford University Press, 1988), 3–43, 220–225.

54. Gates, *Signifying Monkey*, 49.

55. For example, the preferences of Douglas Crimp, or of Solomon-Godeau in "Photography after Art Photography," in Solomon-Godeau, *Photography at the Dock*, 103–123.

56. Fani-Kayode, "Traces of Ecstasy," 276.

57. Mark Sealy, "A Note from Outside: On Rotimi Fani-Kayode," in *Rotimi Fani-Kayode (1955–1989)* (Syracuse: Light Work, 2015), 4.

58. See Richard Goldstein, "A Night at the Continental Baths," *New York*, 17 September 1973.

59. Brassaï quoted by Catherine Lord in "Stepping Out," in *Art and Queer Culture*, ed. Catherine Lord and Richard Meyer (London: Phaidon, 2013), 85.

60. Lord, "Stepping Out," 85.

61. Butler quoted in Lord, "Stepping Out," 40.

62. Owens, "Photography *en abyme*," 22–25.

63. Owens, "Photography *en abyme*," 17.

64. Deferral and Carnival appear in, for example, Mikhail Bakhtin, *Problems of Dostoevsky's Poetics*, ed. Caryl Emerson (Minneapolis: University of Minnesota Press, 1984). See also William R. Handley, "The Ethics of Subject Creation in Bakhtin and Lacan," in *Mikhail Bakhtin: Carnival and Other Subjects*, ed. David G. Shepherd (Amsterdam: Rodopi, 1993), 144–162.

65. Sigmund Freud, "The Uncanny" (1919), in *The Standard Edition of the Complete Psychological Works of Sigmund Freud, Volume 17 (1917–1919): An Infantile Neurosis and Other Works*, ed. and trans. James Strachey (London: Hogarth Press, 1955), 217–256.

66. One example is the citation in the journal of a film version of Mark Connelly's play *The Green Pastures*. The latter explores a fantasy world in which heaven is populated by black angels and overseen by "De Lawd." It was Michel Leiris (reading W. E. B. Du Bois's journal *The Crisis*) who came across the story, which posits a colonial-era hierarchy inverted by color, not unlike Fani-Kayode's handling of *White Bouquet*. On angels and Connelly, see Ades and Baker, *Undercover Surrealism*, 230–233. This treatment builds on even earlier investigations in Paul Klee's *Angelus Novus* (1920) and Walter Benjamin's adaptation of that angel in his 1940 "Theses on the Philosophy of History," in *Illuminations: Essays and Reflections*, trans. Harry Zohn (New York: Schocken, 1969), 253–264.

67. See Robert Farris Thompson, *Flash of the Spirit: African and Afro-American Art and Philosophy* (New York: Vintage, 1984), 163–191.

68. That is, in Deren's film and accompanying book *Divine Horsemen: The Living Gods of Haiti* (book with Joseph Campbell; Kingston, NY: McPherson, 1983).

69. Georges Bataille, from his theory of eroticism, "The Object of Desire and the Totality of the Real," in *The Bataille Reader*, ed. Fred Botting and Scott Wilson (Oxford: Blackwell, 1997), 265.

70. Sealy, "A Note from Outside: On Rotimi Fani-Kayode," 4 (citing Wendy Grossman).

71. Sealy, ""A Note from Outside: On Rotimi Fani-Kayode," 4.

72. Suzanne Preston Blier, "Kings, Crowns, and Rites of Succession: Obalufon

Arts at Ife and Other Yoruba Centers," *The Art Bulletin* 67 (September 1985): 383–401. See also Margaret Thompson Drewal, "Projections from the Top in Yoruba Art," *African Arts* 11, no. 1 (1977): 43–50.

73. In Thompson, *Flash of the Spirit*, 79–82. This cross-reading of Fani-Kayode emerges, then, from the same portion of text that Mercer cites in his declaration that the mask is the *ororo* of Osanyin (see n75 in this chapter).

74. See Ades and Baker, "Places of Pilgrimage," in *Undercover Surrealism*, 77–81.

75. Kobena Mercer, "Eros and Diaspora," in Oguibe and Enwezor, *Reading the Contemporary*, 282–294.

76. Thompson, *Flash of the Spirit*, 11–12.

77. A visual and textual survey of the Carnival tradition is found in Barbara Mauldin, ed., *Carnaval!* (Seattle: University of Washington Press, 2004).

SIX / NIGHT MOVES

1. The film aired shortly after its release at the Museum of Modern Art in the series Speaking Out: Film and Video about AIDS. See "The Museum of Modern Art Observes 'A Day without Art.'" Press release, November 1992.

2. Alex Hirst, in *Bodies of Experience: Stories about Living with HIV*, ed. Arabella Plouviez (London: Camerawork/The Photo Co-op, 1989), n.p.

3. Pas Paschali, "Alex Hirst," *Capital Gay*, 22 October 1993, 18.

4. Alex Hirst, *The Last Supper: A Creative Farewell to Rotimi Fani-Kayode* (Wolverhampton: Light House Media Centre, 1992), 9.

5. Quoted in *Rage and Desire*, dir. Ruppert Gabriel (San Francisco: Frameline, 1992).

6. Quoted in *Rage and Desire*.

7. Man Ray, "The Age of Light," in *Classic Essays on Photography*, ed. Alan Trachtenberg (Sedgwick, ME: Leete's Island Books, 1980), 167.

8. These are themes taken up in several essays (e.g., "Surrealism") in Walter Benjamin's collected *Reflections: Essays, Aphorisms, Autobiographical Writings*, ed. Peter Demetz (New York: Schocken, 1986).

9. Rotimi Fani-Kayode and Alex Hirst, "Metaphysick: Every Moment Counts," in *Ecstatic Antibodies: Resisting the AIDS Mythology*, ed. Tessa Boffin and Sunil Gupta (London: Rivers Oram, 1990), 80.

10. Fani-Kayode and Hirst, "Metaphysick," 84. Bataille's heterology was interested in canceling the distinction between high and low forms of value, with gold as a key touchstone. His interest in ritual, and Fani-Kayode's uses of heterology, explored earlier, suggest more affinity than dissonance.

11. Douglas Crimp, "The Photographic Activity of Postmodernism," *October* 15 (winter 1980): 91–101.

12. For a rich discussion of the homoerotic/Baroque axis in Fani-Kayode's later

work, see Evan Moffitt, "Rotimi Fani-Kayode's Ecstatic Antibodies," *Transition* 118 (2015): 74–86.

13. Yinka Shonibare, speaking at the Tiwani Gallery, London, November 1, 2014, author's transcript.

14. The so-called neoexpressionist painting of David Salle and Anselm Kiefer, for example, mined biblical references.

15. See Janet Kardon, "The Perfect Moment," in Robert Mapplethorpe, *Robert Mapplethorpe: The Perfect Moment* (Boston: Published for the ICA by Stuff Magazine, 1990), 9–13; and Steven Watson, "In Memory of Their Feelings," *Artforum* 49 (January 2011): 65–66.

16. Importantly, in then-contemporary accounts of artistic and architectural postmodernism, the seeming opposition of "neoconservative pastiche" and "critical deconstruction" were staged in terms of semiotic invocation rather than, as it were, the return of the real. See Hal Foster, "(Post)Modern Polemics," *Perspecta* 21 (1984): 144–153.

17. Thelma Golden, "Conversation with Barkley Hendricks," in *Barkley L. Hendricks: Birth of the Cool*, ed. Trevor Schoonmaker (Durham, NC: Nasher Museum of Art, Duke University, 2008), 69.

18. Charles Dempsey, "Painting in Bologna from the Carracci to Crespi," in *Captured Emotions: Baroque Painting in Bologna, 1575–1725*, ed. Andreas Henning and Scott Schaefer (Los Angeles: Getty Publications, 2008), 3.

19. David Freedberg, *The Power of Images: Studies in the History and Theory of Response* (Chicago: University of Chicago Press, 1989), 12–13.

20. Urban Nigeria is cosmopolitan but also increasingly marked by a balance of secularism and charismatic Christianity. The mores of the latter are widely circulated in Nollywood films, many genres of which are explicitly critical of what is portrayed as the superstition associated with traditional spiritual practices.

21. William Pietz, "The Problem of the Fetish, I," *Res: Anthropology and Aesthetics* 9 (spring 1985): 5–17.

22. See Suzanne Preston Blier, *African Vodun: Art, Psychology, and Power* (Chicago: University of Chicago Press, 1995), 95–132.

23. See Hal Foster, "The Art of Fetishism," *The Princeton Journal* 4 (1992): 6–19; and William Pietz, "The Problem of the Fetish, II: The Origin of the Fetish," *Res: Anthropology and Aesthetics* 13 (1987): 23–45.

24. See Emefie Ikenga-Metuh, "Religious Concepts in West African Cosmogonies: A Problem of Interpretation," *Journal of Religion in Africa* 13 (1982): 11–24; and Michael Worton, "Behold the (Sick) Man," in *National Healths: Gender, Sexuality and Health in a Cross-Cultural Context*, ed. Michael Worton and Nana Wilson-Tagoe (London: UCL Publishing, 2004), 157–158.

25. Christina Sharpe, *Monstrous Intimacies: Making Post-slavery Subjects* (Durham, NC: Duke University Press, 2010), 111–146.

26. Alex Hirst, "Interview with Ruppert Gabriel," in *The Last Supper*, 10.

27. In Mignon Nixon's psychoanalytic reading of the part object in the work of Jasper Johns and Louise Bourgeois, the phallus's posing as such desublimates it, removes it from the realm of signification—the "lack" imposed by castration, of male dominance and virility, in the post-seventies feminist conception—and more fully into the realm of the *real* of the base drives. In short, "the scopic drive is displaced by the oral and anal drives, and libidinal desire by the death drive." See Mignon Nixon, "Posing the Phallus," *October* 92 (spring 2000): 102.

28. Foster, "Art of Fetishism," 9.

29. Alex Hirst and Rotimi Fani-Kayode, in Plouviez, *Bodies of Experience*, n.p.

30. Eikoh Hosoe, "Photography and I," in *Meta* (Los Angeles: Curatorial Assistance, 1991), 25.

31. Hirst, in Plouviez, *Bodies of Experience*, n.p.

32. See, for an overview of this wide array of scholarship, Nicholas Burka, "Bronzino's *Portrait of a Man as Saint Sebastian*: Allegory, Love, Passion, and Homoeroticism in a Renaissance Portrait (and In Modern Oblivion)" (MA thesis, University of Chicago, 2009).

33. Yukio Mishima quoted in Eikoh Hosoe, *Eikoh Hosoe: Meta* (Los Angeles: Curatorial Assistance, 1991), 25. Mishima's description of "cool waters" echoes the strong association in diaspora and present-day western African religions between water and the spirit world. This can be seen in the Edo (Kingdom of Benin) cosmology of southern Nigeria, the everyday veneration of *Mami Wata*, or the *loa*, the spirits who reside underwater in the case of Haiti. See also Wade Davis, *The Serpent and the Rainbow* (New York: Simon and Schuster, 1985), 172–176.

34. Ignacio Muñoz, "Melancholy Sites: The Affective Politics of Marginality in Post-Anpo Japan (1960–1970)" (PhD diss., Duke University, 2011), 139.

35. Muñoz, "Melancholy Sites," 141–145.

36. See Robert Farris Thomson, *Face of the Gods: Art and Altars of Africa and the African Americas* (New York: Museum for African Art, 1993).

37. Jane Blocker, *Where Is Ana Mendieta? Identity, Performativity, and Exile* (Durham, NC: Duke University Press, 1999), 18, 47–50.

38. Roland Barthes, *Camera Lucida: Reflections on Photography*, trans. Richard Howard (New York: Hill and Wang, 2010), 31.

39. Barthes, *Camera Lucida*, 32.

40. Interview with Robert Taylor, 18 August 2017 (author's transcript).

41. See Jacques Mercier, *Art That Heals: The Image as Medicine in Ethiopia* (New York: Prestel, 1997).

42. Fani-Kayode and Hirst, "Metaphysick," 83–84.

43. Derek Jarman, *At Your Own Risk: A Saint's Testament* (Woodstock, NY: Overlook Press, 1992), 113.

44. Jarman, *At Your Own Risk*, 113.

45. Such considerations are trenchantly detailed in Douglas Crimp, "Portraits of People with AIDS," in *Melancholia and Moralism: Essays on AIDS and Queer Politics* (Cambridge, MA: MIT Press, 2002), 83–107. See also Leo Bersani, "Is the Rectum a Grave?," *October* 43 (winter 1987): 197–222.

46. Rotimi Fani-Kayode, "Traces of Ecstasy," in *Reading the Contemporary: African Art from Theory to the Marketplace*, ed. Olu Oguibe and Okwui Enwezor (Cambridge, MA: MIT Press / London: Iniva: 1999), 276.

47. Filmmaker Derek Jarman, quoted in Isaac Julien's 2008 feature *Derek*.

48. For example, the filmmaker and critic Gregg Bordowitz, writing in 2003 of his initiation to AIDS activism in the eighties, recalled that as "an artist I felt I had a unique contribution to make to AIDS activism: I could use my skills as manipulator of images to document the movement from the point of view of activists. I was biased. I was partisan. And I was not alone. A generation of artists joined the cause and freely gave their time and expertise to produce a vibrant culture in the interest of people with AIDS." Bordowitz, "My Postmodernism," in *The AIDS Crisis Is Ridiculous and Other Writings, 1986–2003* (Cambridge, MA: MIT Press, 2004), 233. See also Douglas Crimp, *AIDS: Cultural Analysis/Cultural Activism* (Cambridge, MA: MIT Press, 1988).

49. Fani-Kayode and Hirst, "Metaphysick," 82.

50. See, for example, Burka, "Bronzino's *Portrait of a Man as Saint Sebastian*."

51. Fani-Kayode and Hirst, "Metaphysick," 80.

52. This was, broadly, the aim of the *Bodies of Experience* and *Ecstatic Antibodies* group shows, both of which featured an array of representations of people with AIDS.

53. Crimp, "Portraits of People with AIDS," 98–107.

54. Hirst, *The Last Supper*, 9.

EPILOGUE

1. Bisi Silva, "Reflections on a Native Son," in *Rotimi Fani-Kayode (1955–1989)*, ed. Stephanie Baptist (London: Tiwani Contemporary, 2014), 48–57.

2. The exhibition in Cape Town was one of a sequence of crucial solo exhibitions organized by Renée Mussai and Mark Sealy through Autograph ABP. These included a 2009 show at the W. E. B. Du Bois Research Institute at Harvard, and subsequent projects at Rivington Place in London in 2011, and Tiwani Contemporary in 2014.

3. Kellie Jones, *EyeMinded: Living and Writing Contemporary Art* (Durham, NC: Duke University Press, 2011), 26.

4. See Paul Gilroy, *Postcolonial Melancholia* (New York: Columbia University Press, 2006), 139–151.

5. Silva, "Reflections on a Native Son," 52.

6. See Mark Fisher, *Ghosts of My Life: Writings on Depression, Hauntology and Lost Futures* (London: Zero Books, 2014).

7. This is an argument made by a range of historians and critics in an ongoing way. But Stallabrass is especially trenchant here, in *Art Incorporated: The Story of Contemporary Art* (Oxford: Oxford University Press, 2004).

8. "Collective Consciousness: A Roundtable," *Artforum* 54, no. 10 (summer 2016): 267.

9. Interview with Mark Sealy, 3 October 2014 (author's transcript).

10. Interview with Mark Sealy, 3 October 2014.

11. Rotimi Fani-Kayode, "Traces of Ecstasy," in *Reading the Contemporary: African Art from Theory to the Marketplace*, ed. Olu Oguibe and Okwui Enwezor (Cambridge, MA: MIT Press / London: Iniva, 1999), 281.

BIBLIOGRAPHY

Aarb-Richards, Dirg, ed. *Tongues Untied: Poems*. London: Gay Men's Press, 1987.

Ades, Dawn, and Simon Baker, eds. *Undercover Surrealism: Georges Bataille and DOCUMENTS*. Exhibition catalog, London, Hayward Gallery, 11 May–30 July 2006. Cambridge, MA: MIT Press, 2006.

Alison, Jane, ed. *The Surreal House*. New Haven, CT: Yale University Press, 2010.

Araeen, Rasheed. *The Other Story: Afro-Asian Artists in Post-War Britain*. London: Hayward Gallery, 1989.

Araeen, Rasheed, Rachel Kirby, and Nicholas Serota, eds. *From Two Worlds*. London: Trustees of the Whitechapel Art Gallery, 1986.

Azerrad, Michael. *Our Band Could Be Your Life: Scenes from the American Indie Underground 1981–1991*. New York: Back Bay Books, 2002.

Bailey, David A., Ian Baucom, and Sonia Boyce, eds. *Shades of Black: Assembling Black Arts in 1980s Britain*. Durham, NC: Duke University Press in collaboration with the Institute of International Visual Arts and the African and Asian Visual Artists Archive, 2005.

Bailey, David A., and Stuart Hall, eds. *Critical Decade: Black British Photography in the 80s*. Birmingham, Eng.: Ten. 8 Ltd., 1992.

Baker, George. *The Artwork Caught by the Tail: Francis Picabia and Dada in Paris*. Cambridge, MA: MIT Press, 2007.

Baldwin, James. *No Name in the Street*. New York: Vintage, 2007.

Baptist, Stephanie, ed. *Rotimi Fani-Kayode (1955–1989)*. Exhibition catalog, Tiwani Contemporary Gallery, 19 September–1 November 2014. London: Tiwani Contemporary, 2014.

Baraka, Amiri, and Larry Neal, eds. *Black Fire: An Anthology of Afro-American Writing*. Baltimore: Black Classics Press, 2007.

Barnett, Andrew, and Nicolas Bourriaud, eds. *Altermodern: Tate Triennial*. London: Tate Publishing, 2009.

Barthes, Roland. *Camera Lucida: Reflections on Photography*. Translated by Richard Howard. New York: Hill and Wang, 2010.

Bataille, Georges. *The Tears of Eros*. Translated by Peter Connor. San Francisco: City Lights Books, 2002.

Baudelaire, Charles. *Les fleurs du mal*. Translated by Richard Howard. Boston: David R. Godine, 1985.

Baudelaire, Charles. *The Painter of Modern Life and Other Essays*. Translated by Jonathan Mayne. London: Phaidon, 1970.

Baudrillard, Jean. *Cool Memories*. London: Verso, 1990.

Beam, Joseph, ed. *In the Life: A Black Gay Anthology*. Boston: Alyson, 1986.

Beckert, Sven. *Empire of Cotton: A Global History*. New York: Vintage, 2015.

Beckwith, Naomi, and Dieter Roelstraete, eds. *The Freedom Principle: Experiments in Art and Music, 1965 to Now*. Chicago: University of Chicago Press, 2015.

Benjamin, Walter. *The Arcades Project*. Translated by Howard Eiland and Kevin McLaughlin. Cambridge, MA: Belknap Press of Harvard University, 2002.

Benjamin, Walter. *Illuminations: Essays and Reflections*. Translated by Harry Zohn. New York: Schocken, 1969.

Benjamin, Walter. *Reflections: Essays, Aphorisms, Autobiographical Writings*. Edited by Peter Demetz. New York: Schocken, 1986.

Berlin, Isaiah. *The Roots of Romanticism*. Princeton, NJ: Princeton University Press, 1999.

Bersani, Leo. "Is the Rectum a Grave?" *October* 43 (winter 1987): 197–222. https://doi.org/10.2307/3397574.

Bersani, Leo, and Ulysse Dutoit. *Caravaggio's Secrets*. Cambridge, MA: MIT Press, 1998.

Bindman, David, and Henry Louis Gates Jr., eds. *The Image of the Black in Western Art*. Cambridge, MA: Belknap Press of Harvard University Press, 2010.

Blanning, T. C. W. *The Romantic Revolution: A History*. New York: Random House, 2011.

Blessing, Jennifer, and Nat Trotman, eds. *Haunted: Contemporary Photography, Video, Performance*. New York: Guggenheim Museum, 2010.

Blier, Suzanne Preston. *African Vodun: Art, Psychology, and Power*. Chicago: University of Chicago Press, 1995.

Blier, Suzanne Preston. "King Glele of Danhomè, Part One: Divination Portraits of a Lion King and Man of Iron." *African Arts* 23, no. 4 (1990): 42–53.

Blier, Suzanne Preston. "King Glele of Danhomè, Part Two: Dynasty and Destiny." *African Arts* 24, no. 1 (1991): 44–55. https://doi.org/10.2307/3336871.

Blier, Suzanne Preston. "Kings, Crowns, and Rites of Succession: Obalufon Arts at Ife and Other Yoruba Centers." *Art Bulletin* 67 (September 1985): 383–401.

Blier, Suzanne Preston. *Kingship and Art in Africa*. New York: Harry N. Abrams, 1995.

Blocker, Jane. *Where Is Ana Mendieta? Identity, Performativity, and Exile*. Durham, NC: Duke University Press, 1999.

Blount, Marcellus, and George Philbert Cunningham. *Representing Black Men*. New York: Routledge, 1996.

Boffin, Tessa, and Sunil Gupta, eds. *Ecstatic Antibodies: Resisting the AIDS Mythology*. London: Rivers Oram, 1990.

Bois, Yve-Alain, and Rosalind E. Krauss. *Formless: A User's Guide*. New York: Zone, 1997.

Booth, Mark. *Camp*. London: Quartet, 1983.

Bordowitz, Gregg. *The AIDS Crisis Is Ridiculous and Other Writings, 1986–2003*. Cambridge, MA: MIT Press, 2004.

Botting, Fred, and Scott Wilson, eds. *The Bataille Reader*. Oxford: Blackwell, 1997.

Bourland, Ian. "Graffiti's Discursive Spaces." *Chicago Art Journal* 17 (2007): 56–83.

Bowles, John B. *Adrian Piper: Race, Gender, and Embodiment*. Durham, NC: Duke University Press, 2011.

Bowles, John P. "Adrian Piper as African American Artist." *American Art* 20 (fall 2006): 108–117.

Breton, André. *Mad Love*. Translated by Mary Ann Caws. Lincoln: University of Nebraska Press, 1988.

Brewster, Bill, and Frank Broughton. *Last Night a DJ Saved My Life: The History of the Disc Jockey*. New York: Grove Press, 1999.

Bryson, Scott, ed. *Craig Owens: Beyond Recognition: Representation, Power, and Culture*. Berkeley: University of California Press, 1992,

Buck-Morss, Susan. "Hegel and Haiti." *Critical Inquiry* 26, no. 4 (summer 2000): 821–865. https://doi.org/10.1086/448993.

Burrows, Tim. *From CBGB to the Roundhouse: Music Venues through the Years*. London: Marion Boyars, 2009.

Cahan, Susan E. *Mounting Frustration: The Art Museum in the Age of Black Power*. Durham, NC: Duke University Press, 2017.

Cameron, Dan, Liza Kirwin, and Alan W. Moore. *East Village USA*. New York: New Museum of Contemporary Art, 2005.

Campany, David, ed. *The Cinematic*. London: Whitechapel and MIT Press, 2007.

Carby, Hazel V. *Cultures in Babylon: Black Britain and African America*. London: Verso, 1999.

Cashmore, Ellis. *The Black Culture Industry*. London: Routledge, 1997.

Centre for Contemporary Cultural Studies. *Empire Strikes Back: Race and Racism in 70s Britain*. London: Routledge, 1982.

Chambers, Eddie. *Annotations 5: Run through the Jungle; Selected Writings by Eddie Chambers*. Edited by Gilane Tawadros and Victoria Clark. London: Iniva, 1999.

Chambers, Eddie. *Black Artists in British Art: A History since the 1950s*. London: I. B. Tauris, 2014.

Chambers, Eddie. "Black Art Now." *Third Text* 15 (summer 1991): 91–96.

Chipp, Herschel B. *Theories of Modern Art*. Berkeley: University of California Press, 1984.

Clark, T. J. "Modernism, Postmodernism, and Steam." *October* 100 (spring 2002): 154–174.

Collins, Lisa Gail, and Margo Natalie Crawford, eds. *New Thoughts on the Black Arts Movement*. New Brunswick, NJ: Rutgers University Press, 2006.

Connolly, Cynthia, Leslie Clague, and Sharon Cheslow, eds. *Banned in DC: Photos and Anecdotes from the DC Punk Underground (79–85)*. Washington, DC: self-published, 1986.

Cooper, Emmanuel. *Fully Exposed: The Male Nude in Photography*. London: Routledge, 1989.

Copeland, Huey. *Bound to Appear: Art, Slavery, and the Site of Blackness in Multicultural America*. Chicago: University of Chicago Press, 2013.

Copjec, Joan. *Read My Desire: Lacan against the Historicists*. Cambridge, MA: MIT Press, 1994.

Cosentino, Donald. *Sacred Arts of Haitian Vodou*. Los Angeles: UCLA Fowler Museum of Cultural History, 1995.

Cotter, Holland. "Rotimi Fani-Kayode: 'Nothing to Lose.'" *New York Times*, May 10, 2012.

Crary, Jonathan. *24/7: Late Capitalism and the Ends of Sleep*. London: Verso, 2014.

Crenshaw, Kimberle. "Mapping the Margins: Intersectionality, Identity Politics, and Violence against Women of Color." *Stanford Law Review* 43 (July 1991): 1241–1299.

Crimp, Douglas. *AIDS: Cultural Analysis, Cultural Activism*. Cambridge, MA: MIT Press, 1988.

Crimp, Douglas. *Before Pictures*. Chicago: University of Chicago Press, 2016.

Crimp, Douglas. "*Disss*-Co (A Fragment)." *Criticism* 50, no. 1 (2008): 1–18.

Crimp, Douglas. *Melancholia and Moralism: Essays on AIDS and Queer Politics*. Cambridge, MA: MIT Press, 2002.

Crimp, Douglas. *On the Museum's Ruins*. Cambridge, MA: MIT Press, 1993.

Crimp, Douglas. "The Photographic Activity of Postmodernism." *October* 15 (winter 1980): 91–101.

Crump, James. *F. Holland Day: Suffering the Ideal*. Santa Fe, NM: Twin Palms, 1995.

Danto, Arthur Coleman, and Robert Mapplethorpe. *Mapplethorpe*. New York: Random House, 1992.

Davis, Wade. *The Serpent and the Rainbow*. New York: Simon and Schuster, 1985.

Delany, Samuel R. *The Motion of Light in Water: Sex and Science Fiction Writing in the East Village, 1960–1965*. New York: Plume, 1989.

Demos, T. J. *The Exiles of Marcel Duchamp*. Cambridge, MA: MIT Press, 2007.

Demos, T. J. *Return to the Postcolony: Specters of Colonialism in Contemporary Art.* Berlin: Sternberg Press, 2013.

Deren, Maya, and Joseph Campbell. *Divine Horsemen: The Living Gods of Haiti.* Kingston, NY: McPherson, 1983.

Deutsche, Rosalyn. "Hiroshima after Iraq: A Study in Art and War." *October* 131 (winter 2010): 3–22.

Diawara, Manthia. *African Cinema: Politics and Culture.* Bloomington: Indiana University Press, 2001.

Diawara, Manthia. "Noir by Noirs: Towards a New Realism in Black Cinema." *African American Review* 27, no. 4 (1993): 899–911. https://doi.org/10.2307 /3041886.

Diawara, Manthia. "One World in Relation: Édouard Glissant in Conversation with Manthia Diawara." *Nka: Journal of Contemporary African Art* 28 (2011): 4–19. https://doi.org/10.1215/10757163-1266639.

Donaldson, Jeff R. "AfriCOBRA Manifesto: 'Ten in Search of a Nation.'" *Nka: Journal of Contemporary African Art* 30 (2012): 76–83. https://doi. org/10.1215/10757163-1496489.

Drewal, Henry John, John Pemberton, Rowland Abiodun, and Allen Wardwell, eds. *Yoruba: Nine Centuries of African Art and Thought.* New York: Center for African Art in Association with Harry N. Abrams, 1989.

Drewal, Margaret Thompson. "Projections from the Top in Yoruba Art." *African Arts* 11, no. 1 (1977): 43–50. https://doi.org/10.2307/3335223.

Earle, T. F., and Kate J. P. Lowe. *Black Africans in Renaissance Europe.* Cambridge: Cambridge University Press, 2010.

Easton, Simon. *Clothes for Heroes: The Punk Fashions of Vivienne Westwood and Malcolm McLaren.* New York: Abrams, 2014.

Edwards, Brent Hayes. *Archive Fever: Uses of the Document in Contemporary Art.* New York: International Center of Photography, 2008.

Edwards, Brent Hayes. "The Ethnics of Surrealism." *Transition* 78 (1998): 84–135. https://doi.org/10.2307/2903180.

Edwards, Brent Hayes. *The Practice of Diaspora: Literature, Translation, and the Rise of Black Internationalism.* Cambridge, MA: Harvard University Press, 2003.

Eldridge, Michael. "The Rise and Fall of Black Britain." *Transition* 74 (1997): 32–43. https://doi.org/10.2307/2935372.

English, Darby. *How to See a Work of Art in Total Darkness.* Cambridge, MA: MIT Press, 2010.

Enwezor, Okwui. *Snap Judgments: New Positions in Contemporary African Photography.* Göttingen: Steidl, 2006.

Enwezor, Okwui, ed. *Events of the Self: Portraiture and Social Identity; Contemporary African Photography from the Walther Collection.* Göttingen: Steidl, 2010.

Enwezor, Okwui, Clare Bell, and Octavio Zaya. *In/sight: African Photographers,*

1940 to the Present. Exhibition catalog, Solomon R. Guggenheim Museum, 24 May–29 September 1996. London: Harry N. Abrams, 1996.

Eshun, Ekow. *Black Gold of the Sun: Searching for Home in Africa and Beyond.* New York: Pantheon, 2005.

Eshun, Kodwo. *More Brilliant Than the Sun: Adventures in Sonic Fiction.* London: Quartet, 1999.

Eshun, Kodwo, and Anjalika Sagar, eds. *The Ghosts of Songs: The Film Art of the Black Audio Film Collective, 1982–1998.* Liverpool: Liverpool University Press, 2007.

Fani-Kayode, Remi. *Blackism.* Lagos: n.p., 1965.

Fani-Kayode, Rotimi, and Alex Hirst. *Black Male/White Male.* London: Gay Men's Press, 1988.

Fanon, Frantz. *Black Skin, White Masks.* Translated by Richard Philcox. New York: Grove Press, 2008.

Fanon, Frantz. *Toward the African Revolution: Political Essays.* Translated by Haakon Chevalier. New York: Grove Press, 1967.

Farrington, Lisa E., and Faith Ringgold. *Faith Ringgold.* Petaluma: Pomegranate, 2004.

Ferguson, Russell, Martha Gever, Trinh T. Minh-Ha, and Cornel West, eds. *Out There: Marginalization and Contemporary Culture.* Cambridge, MA: MIT Press, 1989.

Fisher, Jean. "The Other Story and the Past Imperfect." *Tate Papers*, no. 12 (autumn 2009).

Fisher, Mark. *Ghosts of My Life: Writings on Depression, Hauntology and Lost Futures.* London: Zero Books, 2014.

Foster, Hal. "The Art of Fetishism." *Princeton Journal* 4 (1992): 6–19.

Foster, Hal. *Compulsive Beauty.* Cambridge, Mass.: MIT Press, 1995.

Foster, Hal. "(Post)Modern Polemics." *Perspecta* 21 (1984): 144–153.

Foster, Hal. "'Primitive' Scenes." *Critical Inquiry* 20 (autumn 1993): 69–102.

Foster, Hal. "The 'Primitive' Unconscious of Modern Art." *October* 34 (autumn 1985): 45–70. https://doi.org/10.2307/778488.

Foucault, Michel. *The History of Sexuality, Volume 1: An Introduction.* Translated by Robert Hurley. New York: Vintage, 1978.

Foucault, Michel. "Of Other Spaces" (1967), translated by Jay Miskowiec. Accessed 18 June 2018. http://foucault.info/documents/heteroTopia/foucault.heteroTopia.en.html.

Foucault, Michel, and Nicolas Bourriaud. *Manet and the Object of Painting.* Translated by Matthew Barr. London: Tate Publishing, 2010.

Fraenkel, Jeffrey, ed. *The Unphotographable.* San Francisco: Fraenkel Gallery, 2013.

Freedberg, David. *The Power of Images: Studies in the History and Theory of Response.* Chicago: University of Chicago Press, 1989.

Freud, Sigmund. "The Uncanny" (1919). In *The Standard Edition of the Complete Psychological Works of Sigmund Freud, Volume 17 (1917–1919): An Infantile Neurosis and Other Works*, edited and translated by James Strachey, 217–256. London: Hogarth Press, 1955.

Fritscher, Jack. *Mapplethorpe: Assault with a Deadly Camera. A Pop Culture Memoir, an Outlaw Reminiscence*. Mamaroneck, NY: Hastings House, 1994.

Fullwood, Steven G., and Charles Stephens. *Black Gay Genius: Answering Joseph Beam's Call*. New York: Vintage Entity Press, 2014.

Gardner, Anthony. *Politically Unbecoming: Postsocialist Art against Democracy*. Cambridge, MA: MIT Press, 2015.

Gates, Henry Louis, Jr. *The Signifying Monkey: A Theory of African-American Literary Criticism*. Oxford: Oxford University Press, 1988.

Gates, Henry Louis, Jr. *Tradition and the Black Atlantic: Critical Theory in the African Diaspora*. New York: Civitas Books, 2008.

Gilroy, Paul. *Against Race: Imagining Political Culture beyond the Color Line*. Cambridge, MA: Belknap Press of Harvard University Press, 2001.

Gilroy, Paul. *The Black Atlantic: Modernity and Double Consciousness*. Cambridge, MA: Harvard University Press, 1993.

Gilroy, Paul. *Postcolonial Melancholia*. New York: Columbia University Press, 2006.

Gilroy, Paul. *Small Acts: Thoughts on the Politics of Black Cultures*. London: Serpent's Tail, 1993.

Gilroy, Paul. "Sounds Authentic: Black Music, Ethnicity, and the Challenge of a 'Changing' Same." *Black Music Research Journal* 11, no. 2 (autumn 1991): 111–136. https://doi.org/10.2307/779262.

Gilroy, Paul. *"There Ain't No Black in the Union Jack": The Cultural Politics of Race and Nation*. Chicago: University of Chicago Press, 1987.

Glissant, Édouard. *Poetics of Relation*. Translated by Betsy Wing. Ann Arbor: University of Michigan Press, 1997.

Golden, Thelma. *Black Male: Representations of Masculinity in Contemporary American Art*. New York: Whitney Museum of American Art, 1994.

Gross, Larry. *Contested Closets: The Politics and Ethics of Outing*. Minneapolis: University of Minnesota Press, 1993.

Guerrilla Girls. *The Guerrilla Girls' Bedside Companion to the History of Western Art*. New York: Penguin, 1998.

Gupta, Sunil. *Queer*. Munich: Prestel, 2011.

Haas, Steven, and Allen Ellenzweig. *George Platt Lynes: The Male Nudes*. New York: Rizzoli, 2011.

Hager, Steven. *Art after Midnight: The East Village Scene*. New York: St. Martin's Press, 1986.

Hall, James Baker, ed. *Minor White: Rites and Passages*. New York: Aperture, 1978.

Hall, Stuart, Sarat Maharaj, Sarah Campbell, and Gilane Tawadros. *Modernity and Difference*. London: Institute of International Visual Arts, 2001.

Hall, Stuart, and Mark Sealy. *Different: Contemporary Photographers and Black Identity*. London: Phaidon, 2001.

Harvey, David. *A Brief History of Neoliberalism*. Oxford: Oxford University Press, 2007.

Hemphill, Essex. *Ceremonies: Prose and Poetry*. San Francisco: Cleis Press, 2000.

Hemphill, Essex, and Joseph Beam, eds. *Brother to Brother: New Writings by Black Gay Men*. Boston: Alyson, 1991.

Henning, Andreas, and Scott Schaefer, eds. *Captured Emotions: Baroque Painting in Bologna, 1575–1725*. Los Angeles: Getty Publications, 2008,

Hirst, Alex. *The Last Supper: A Creative Farewell to Rotimi Fani-Kayode*. Wolverhampton: Light House Media Centre, 1992.

Hirst, Alex. "Unacceptable Behaviour: A Memoir." In *Rotimi Fani-Kayode: Photographer*. London: 198 Gallery, 1990.

Hoban, Phoebe. *Basquiat: A Quick Killing in Art*. New York: Penguin, 2004.

Hook, Peter. *The Hacienda: How Not to Run a Club*. London: Simon and Schuster, 2010.

Hook, Peter. *Substance: Inside New Order*. New York: William Morrow, 2017.

Hosoe, Eikoh. *Eikoh Hosoe: Meta*. Los Angeles: Curatorial Assistance, 1991.

Ikenga-Metuh, Emefie. "Religious Concepts in West African Cosmogonies: A Problem of Interpretation." *Journal of Religion in Africa* 13 (1982): 11–24.

Jameson, Fredric. *Postmodernism, or, the Cultural Logic of Late Capitalism*. Durham, NC: Duke University Press, 1992.

Jarman, Derek. *At Your Own Risk: A Saint's Testament*. Woodstock, NY: Overlook Press, 1992.

Johnson, Linton Kwesi. *Linton Kwesi Johnson: Selected Poems*. London: Penguin, 2006.

Jones, Kellie. *EyeMinded: Living and Writing Contemporary Art*. Durham, NC: Duke University Press, 2011.

Jones, Sonya L., ed. *Gay and Lesbian Literature since World War II: History and Memory*. New York: Routledge, 1998.

Jussim, Estelle. "F. Holland Day's 'Nubians.'" *History of Photography* 2 (April–June 1983): 131–141.

Kaiser, Charles. *The Gay Metropolis: 1940–1996*. New York: Houghton Mifflin, 1997.

Kardon, Janet, Carlo McCormick, and Irving Sandler, eds. *The East Village Scene*. Philadelphia: ICA, 1984.

Kelley, Robin D. G. *Freedom Dreams: The Black Radical Imagination*. Boston, MA: Beacon Press, 2002.

Krauss, Rosalind. *Bachelors*. Cambridge, MA: MIT Press, 1999.

Krauss, Rosalind. "Corpus Delicti." *October* 33 (summer 1985): 31–72. https://doi
.org/10.2307/778393.

Krauss, Rosalind. "A Note on Photography and the Simulacral." *October* 31 (1984):
49–68. https://doi.org/10.2307/778356.

Krauss, Rosalind. *The Optical Unconscious*. Cambridge, MA: MIT Press, 1994.

Krauss, Rosalind. *The Originality of the Avant-Garde and Other Modernist Myths*.
Cambridge, MA: MIT Press, 1986.

Kristeva, Julia. *Powers of Horror: An Essay on Abjection*. Translated by Leon S.
Roudiez. New York: Columbia University Press, 1982.

Kwon, Miwon. "One Place After Another: Notes on Site Specificity." *October* 80
(spring 1997): 85–110.

Landau, Paul Stuart, and Deborah D. Kaspin, eds. *Images and Empires: Visuality in
Colonial and Postcolonial Africa*. Berkeley: University of California Press, 2002.

Lawal, Babatunde. "Orí: The Significance of the Head in Yoruba Sculpture." *Journal
of Anthropological Research* 41, no. 1 (1985): 91–103. https://doi.org/10.1086
/jar.41.1.3630272.

Lawrence, Tim. *Love Saves the Day: A History of American Dance Music Culture,
1970–1979*. Durham, NC: Duke University Press, 2003.

Lloyd, Richard. *Neo-Bohemia: Art and Commerce in the Postindustrial City*. New
York: Routledge, 2010.

Locke, Alain. *The New Negro*. New York: Simon and Schuster, 1997.

Lord, Catherine, and Richard Meyer, eds. *Art and Queer Culture*. London: Phaidon,
2013.

MacGaffey, Wyatt. "Fetishism Revisited: Kongo 'Nkisi' in Sociological Perspective."
Africa: Journal of the International Africa Institute 47 (1977): 172–184.

Mapplethorpe, Robert. *Black Flowers*. Madrid: Fernando Vijande, 1985.

Mapplethorpe, Robert. *Robert Mapplethorpe: The Perfect Moment*. Exhibition catalog, Institute of Contemporary Art, Boston, 1 August–4 October, 1990. Boston,
MA: Published for the ICA by Stuff Magazine, 1990.

Mapplethorpe, Robert. *A Season in Hell*. New York: Limited Editions Club, 1986.

Mapplethorpe, Robert, and Herbert Muschamp. *Mapplethorpe: The Complete Flowers*. Düsseldorf: TeNeues, 2006.

Marcus, Greil. *Lipstick Traces: A Secret History of the Twentieth Century*. Twentieth-
anniversary ed. Cambridge, MA: Belknap Press of Harvard University Press,
2009.

Marriott, David. *Haunted Life: Visual Culture and Black Modernity*. New Brunswick, NJ: Rutgers University Press, 2007.

Marshall, Richard, ed. *Robert Mapplethorpe*. New York: Whitney Museum of American Art, 1990.

Mauldin, Barbara, ed. *Carnaval!* Seattle: University of Washington Press, 2004.

Matt, Gerald, and Thomas Miessgang. *Punk. No One Is Innocent: Art, Style, Revolt.*

Kunsthalle Wien, 16 May–7 September, 2008. Vienna: Kunsthalle Wien, 2008.

Mbembe, Achille. *Critique of Black Reason.* Translated by Laurent Dubois. Durham, NC: Duke University Press, 2017.

Mercer, Kobena, ed. *Discrepant Abstraction.* London: Iniva, 2006.

Mercer, Kobena. "Neo-Romantic, Afro-Atlantic." In *Rotimi Fani-Kayode: Nothing to Lose.* New York: Walther Collection, 2012.

Mercer, Kobena. *Travel and See: Black Diaspora Art Practices since the 1980s.* Durham, NC: Duke University Press, 2016.

Mercer, Kobena. *Welcome to the Jungle: New Positions in Black Cultural Studies.* New York: Routledge, 1994.

Mercier, Jacques. *Art That Heals: The Image as Medicine in Ethiopia.* New York: Prestel, 1997.

Meyer, Richard. *Outlaw Representation: Censorship and Homosexuality in Twentieth-Century American Art.* Boston: Beacon Press, 2002.

Michalak, Thomas, ed. *Mark Morrisroe 1959–1989.* Berlin: NGBK, 1998.

Mirza, Heidi Safia, ed. *Black British Feminism: A Reader.* London: Routledge, 1997.

Moffitt, Evan. "Rotimi Fani-Kayode's Ecstatic Antibodies." *Transition* 118 (2015): 74–86.

Molesworth, Helen Anne, Johanna Burton, and Claire Grace, eds. *This Will Have Been: Art, Love and Politics in the 1980s.* Chicago: Museum of Contemporary Art, 2012.

Morimura, Yasumasa. *Daughter of Art History: Photographs by Yasumasa Morimura.* New York: Aperture, 2005.

Morley, David, and Kuan-Hsing Chen, eds. *Stuart Hall: Critical Dialogues in Cultural Studies.* London: Routledge, 1996.

Morrisroe, Mark. *Mark Morrisroe.* Santa Fe, NM: Twin Palms Publishers, 1999.

Morrissey. *Autobiography.* New York: Putnam, 2011.

Morton, Marsha. "German Romanticism: The Search for 'A Quiet Place.'" *Art Institute of Chicago Museum Studies* 28, no. 1 (2002): 8–23, 106–107. https://doi.org/10.2307/4113048.

Moten, Fred. *In the Break: The Aesthetics of the Black Radical Tradition.* Minneapolis: University of Minnesota Press, 2003.

Mullard, Chris. *Black Britain.* London: Allen and Unwin, 1973.

Mulvey, Laura. "Visual Pleasure and Narrative Cinema." *Screen* 16, no. 3 (autumn 1975): 6–18.

Muñoz, Ignacio. "Melancholy Sites: The Affective Politics of Marginality in Post-Anpo Japan (1960–1970)." PhD diss., Duke University, 2011.

Muñoz, José Esteban. *Cruising Utopia: The Then and There of Queer Futurity.* New York: New York University Press, 2009.

Muñoz, José Esteban. *Disidentifications: Queers of Color and the Performance of Politics*. Minneapolis: University of Minnesota Press, 1999.

Murphy, Joseph M. *Santería: African Spirits in America*. Boston: Beacon Press, 1993.

Murray, Derek Conrad. "Base Materialism: Meditations on the Intersection of Blackness and Form." Paper given at the Annual Meeting of the College Art Association, 16 February 2017.

Nelson, Steven. "Transgressive Transcendence in the Photographs of Rotimi Fani-Kayode." *Art Journal* 64, no. 1 (spring 2005): 4–19. https://doi.org/10.2307 /20068359.

Nin, Anaïs. *Cities of the Interior*. Athens: Swallow Press/Ohio University Press, 1993.

Nixon, Mignon. "Posing the Phallus." *October* 92 (spring 2000): 98–127. https:// doi.org/10.2307/779235.

Nochlin, Linda. *The Politics of Vision: Essays on Nineteenth-Century Art and Society*. New York: Harper and Row, 1989.

Nugent, Richard Bruce, and Thomas H. Wirth. *Gay Rebel of the Harlem Renaissance: Selections from the Work of Richard Bruce Nugent*. Durham, NC: Duke University Press, 2002.

Oguibe, Olu, and Okwui Enwezor, eds. *Reading the Contemporary: African Art from Theory to the Marketplace*. Cambridge, MA: MIT Press / London: Iniva, 1999.

Owens, Craig. "Photography *en abyme*." *October* 5 (summer 1978): 73–88.

Parker, Alan. *Sid Vicious: No One Is Innocent*. London: Orion, 2008.

Peabody, Rebecca, Andrew Perchuk, Glenn Phillips, and Rani Singh, eds. *Pacific Standard Time: Los Angeles Art 1945–1980*. Los Angeles: The Getty Research Institute and the J. Paul Getty Museum, 2011.

Pietz, William. "The Problem of the Fetish, I." *Res: Anthropology and Aesthetics* 9 (spring 1985): 5–17.

Pietz, William. "The Problem of the Fetish, II: The Origin of the Fetish." *Res: Anthropology and Aesthetics* 13 (1987): 23–45. https://doi.org/10.1086 /resv13n1ms20166762.

Pinder, Kymberly N. *Race-ing Art History: Critical Readings in Race and Art History*. New York: Routledge, 2002.

Plouviez, Arabella, ed. *Bodies of Experience: Stories about Living with HIV*. London: Camerawork/The Photo Co-op, 1989.

Ricard, Rene. "The Radiant Child." *Artforum* (December 1981): n.p.

Rosemont, Franklin, and Robin D. G. Kelley, eds. *Black, Brown, and Beige: Surrealist Writings from Africa and the Diaspora*. Austin: University of Texas Press, 2010.

Rosenthal, Norman, ed. *Sensation: Young British Artists from the Saatchi Collection*. London: Thames and Hudson, 1998.

Said, Edward. *Orientalism*. New York: Vintage, 1978.

Savage, Jon. *England's Dreaming, Revised Edition: Anarchy, Sex Pistols, Punk Rock, and Beyond*. New York: St. Martin's Press, 2002.

Schoonmaker, Trevor, ed. *Barkley L. Hendricks: Birth of the Cool.* Durham, NC: Nasher Museum of Art, Duke University, 2008.

Schwain, Kristin. "F. Holland Day's *Seven Last Words* and the Religious Roots of American Modernism." *American Art* 19, no. 1 (2005): 32–59. https://doi.org /10.1086/429974.

Sealy, Mark. *Communion.* London: Autograph ABP, 1995.

Sealy, Mark. *Rotimi Fani-Kayode (1955–1989).* Syracuse, NY: Light Work, 2015.

Sealy, Mark, ed. *Vanley Burke: A Retrospective.* London: Lawrence and Wishart, 1993.

Sealy, Mark, Roger Malbert, and Alice Lobb, eds. *Documenting Disposable People: Contemporary Global Slavery.* London: Hayward, 2008.

Sealy, Mark, and Jean Loup Pivin, eds. *Rotimi Fani-Kayode and Alex Hirst: Photographs.* Exhibition catalog. Paris: Revue Noire and Autograph ABP, 1996.

Sharpe, Christina. *Monstrous Intimacies: Making Post-slavery Subjects.* Durham, NC: Duke University Press, 2010.

Sharpe, Jenny. *Ghosts of Slavery: A Literary Archaeology of Black Womens' Lives.* Minneapolis: University of Minnesota Press, 2002.

Shelton, Syd. *Rock against Racism.* London: Autograph ABP, 2015.

Silverman, Kaja. *The Miracle of Analogy; or, The History of Photography, Part 1.* Stanford, CA: Stanford University Press, 2015.

Sirmans, Franklin, ed. *Basquiat and the Bayou.* New York: Prestel, 2014.

Sirmans, M. Franklin, and Mora L. Beauchamp-Byrd, eds. *Transforming the Crown: African, Asian, and Caribbean Artists in Britain, 1966–1996.* Exhibition catalog. Chicago: University of Chicago Press, 1997.

Sladen, Mark, and Ariella Yedgar, eds. *Panic Attack! Art in the Punk Years.* London: Merrell, 2007.

Smith, Patti. *Just Kids.* New York: Ecco, 2010.

Solomon-Godeau, Abigail. "Going Native: Gauguin and the Invention of Primitivist Modernism." *Art in America* 77 (7 July 1989): 118–129.

Solomon-Godeau, Abigail. *Photography at the Dock: Essays on Photographic History, Institutions, and Practices.* Minneapolis: University of Minnesota Press, 1991.

Sontag, Susan. *Against Interpretation: And Other Essays.* New York: Picador, 2001.

Sontag, Susan, and Elizabeth Hardwick. *A Susan Sontag Reader.* Harmondsworth: Penguin Books, 1983.

Sprague, Stephen. "Yoruba Photography." In *Photography's Other Histories,* edited by Christopher Pinney and Nicolas Peterson, 240–260. Durham, NC: Duke University Press, 2003. https://doi.org/10.1215/9780822384717-013.

Squiers, Carol. *Over Exposed: Essays on Contemporary Photography.* New York: New Press, 1999.

Stallabrass, Julian. *High Art Lite.* London: Verso, 1999.

Sylvester, David. *Francis Bacon.* New York: Pantheon, 1975.

Szarkowski, John. *The Photographer and the American Landscape*. New York: Doubleday, 1963.

Taussig, Michael. "Viscerality, Faith, and Skepticism: Another Theory of Magic." In *Walter Benjamin's Grave*, 121–155. Chicago: University of Chicago Press, 2006.

Taylor, Marvin J., ed. *The Downtown Book: The New York Art Scene, 1974–1984*. Princeton, NJ: Princeton University Press, 2005.

Taylor, Stuart. "Rita Keegan on Digital Diversity and Colour of Computers." *Mute* 1, no. 7 (10 January 1997). http://www.metamute.org/editorial/articles /rita-keegan-digital-diversity-and-colour-computers.

Thompson, Robert Farris. "An Aesthetic of the Cool." *African Arts* 7, no. 1 (1973): 40–43, 64–67. https://doi.org/10.2307/3334749.

Thompson, Robert Farris. *Face of the Gods: Art and Altars of Africa and the African Americas*. New York: Museum for African Art, 1993.

Thompson, Robert Farris. *Flash of the Spirit: African and Afro-American Art and Philosophy*. New York: Vintage, 1984.

Timms, Robert, et al., eds. *Young British Art: The Saatchi Decade*. London: Booth-Clibborn, 1999.

Trachtenberg, Alan, ed. *Classic Essays on Photography*. Sedgwick, ME: Leete's Island Books, 1980.

Turner, Alwyn W. *Glam Rock: Dandies in the Underworld*. London: V and A Publications, 2013.

Turner, Alwyn W. *Rejoice, Rejoice! Britain in the 1980s*. London: Aurum, 2010.

Warner, Michael, ed. *Fear of a Queer Planet: Queer Politics and Social Theory*. Minneapolis: University of Minnesota Press, 1993.

Warner, Michael. *Publics and Counterpublics*. New York: Zone, 2002.

Watney, Simon. *Policing Desire: Pornography, AIDS, and the Media*. Minneapolis: University of Minnesota Press, 1987.

Watson, Steven. "In Memory of Their Feelings." *Artforum* 49 (January 2011): 65–66.

Wells, Liz, ed. *The Photography Reader*. London: Routledge, 2002.

Wilentz, Sean. *The Age of Reagan: A History, 1974–2008*. New York: Harper-Perennial, 2009.

Williams, Gilda, ed. *The Gothic*. London: Whitechapel; Cambridge, MA: MIT Press, 2007.

Williams, Val, ed., *Martin Parr*. London: Phaidon, 2002.

Wojnarowicz, David. *In the Shadow of the American Dream: The Diaries of David Wojnarowicz*. Edited by Amy Scholder. New York: Grove Press, 2000.

Wofford, Tobias. "Afrofutures: Africa and the Aesthetics of Black Resistance." *Third Text* 31, nos. 5–6 (2017): 633–649.

Wolf, Sylvia, ed. *Polaroids: Mapplethorpe*. Munich: Prestel, 2013.

Wollen, Peter. *Raiding the Icebox: Reflections on Twentieth-Century Culture*. London: Verso, 2008.

Worton, Michael, and Nana Wilson-Tagoe, eds. *National Healths: Gender, Sexuality and Health in a Cross-Cultural Context*. London: UCL Publishing, 2004.

INDEX

Page numbers in *italics* indicate photographs or other figures.

bathhouses, 87–88, 140, 142, 145, 199, 236, 268n51, 274n89

Battersea Arts Centre, 32

Baudelaire, Charles, 7, 127, 172, 184, 280n3

Bauhaus (rock band), 163

Beam, Joseph, 133, 135, 138, 273n70

Bearden, Romare, 177, 208

"Beautiful Black Men" (Blackberri song), 137

Bell, Claire, 141

Bellas, Bruce (Bruce of Los Angeles), 108

Bellmer, Hans, 3, 141, 173, 226

Bellocq, E. J., 189

Belly, Léon, 149

Benin art and culture, 53, 199, 224–225, 287n33

Benjamin, Walter, 166, 212, 236, 246, 284n66, 285n8

Berlin, Isaiah, 160, 164

Bhabha, Homi, 165

Biafra, 4, 26

birds and bird masks, 159, 205, 207, 241, 243, 247

Birmingham Centre for Contemporary Cultural Studies, 28

The Birthday Party (band), 163

Bishton, Derek, 9, 56, 264n73

Black and Gay Lesbian Centre, 95

Black and White (Man Ray), 176, 179

black art, 15, 20, 31, 33, 80, 261n29

black artists, 29, 37–38, 80, 97, 177–178, 254, 261n29, 280n14

Black Arts Movement (BAM), 31–33, 78, 261–262n30

Black Atlantic, 4, 12, 20, 27–30, 47, 60, 141–143, 226

The Black Atlantic (Gilroy), 28–31

Black Audio Film Collective (BAFC), 40–41, 95, 165–168, 241, 278n45. See also Handsworth Songs; Twilight City

Black Book (Mapplethorpe photo series), 4, 92, 192, 274n85

Black British Arts Movement, 30

"A Black British Photographer" (Bishton), 264n73

black friars, 157, 159, 216–217, 247

black gay artists/art, 75, 94, 97, 131, 137

black gay consciousness/culture, 14, 21, 24, 118, 129

black gay photography, 7–8, 75, 92, 95, 97, 113

black gay/queer subjectivity, 53, 94, 128–129, 133, 137–138, 227, 239

black identity, 29, 32–34, 41, 47, 50, 63, 77

black internationalism, 281n19; black diasporic art, 269n3

black liberation, 11

Black Light (Ringgold photo series), 77

Black Male/White Male (Fani-Kayode photo portfolio): Africa in, 142; and HIV/AIDS, 145; art-historical connections in, 43–44, 198; and Bataille, 185; Bondage in, 225; and Brassaï, 225; British contexts in, 27; Bronze Head in, 188; camera motif in, 115; and The Clubhouse, 89; Crucifix, 100; and Day, 99–101; described, 23–25; Ebo Òrìsà in, 188; and the female body, 117; formalism and, 55, 198; gothic modes in, 149; hairstyles in, 50; Hirst on, 141–142, 161, 190; and Looking for Langston, 189; and Lord, 95; and Mapplethorpe, 142, 189; mirrors and mirrored imagery in, 198, 257n9; One in Three in, 43; and postmodernism, 160; primitivism in, 173, 175, 179–180, 182, 188; pulse in, 46; signification in, 198; Snap Shot in, 190; Struggle in, 43; and surrealism, 43–44, 264n5; and Tongues Untied, 128; Torso in, 147–148; untitled photos in, 100

black nationalism, 33

Black Panther movement, 30

Black Phoenix (art journal), 140

Chocolate City (Washington, DC), 89, 134–135

Christian iconography, 98, 100–101, 168

Christianity, 28, 99, 102, 157, 169, 216–218, 237, 270n14, 286n20

Cimabue (Italian painter), 157

civil rights, 17, 32, 38, 94, 96, 103, 121–122

Clague, Leslie, 72, *73*

Clam Twins (Morrisroe and Tashjian), 83

Clark, T. J., 277n26, 277n29

The Clash, 72, 266nn29–30

class, social, 5, 133

Clover, Lee, 72–74, *74*

club nightlife: and HIV/AIDS, 145; and F-K, 57, 61, 63, 66–67, 89–91; and Foucault, 88, 90; as heterotopia, 88–90; in London, 59, 61, 63–64, 86–87, 154–155; in New York, 20, 59, 61, 275–276n10; resistance represented by, 59, 140; as ritualistic, 162; as transgressive, 88–89

The Clubhouse (DC), 88–90, 135

Cole, Teju, 23, 26

Coleridge, Samuel Taylor, 149, 153, 275n5

Colonel Abrams (DJ), 89

colonialism, 6, 33, 179, 184, 187, 229, 270n14, 281n20. *See also headings under post-colonial*; neocolonialism

Combat Rock (The Clash album), 72

Communion (Fani-Kayode photo series), 75, 155, 216, 248, 258n17

Community Copyart (arts organization), 35

conk hairstyles, 50

conservatism: in the 1970s and 1980s, 14, 17; in the British film industry, 123; F-K vs., 27, 57, 96; of Gauguin, 188–189; GLC vs., 37; Mapplethorpe galvanizing, 217; resistance to, 59; resurgence in England, 14, 17, 28, 37, 57, 59, 96, 123, 165; Serrano galvanizing, 217; in the US, 145

Cooper, Emmanuel, 103–104, 106–108, 111–114

Copeland, Huey, 53, 252–253, 255, 277n34, 280n14

Copyart (Community Copyart organization), 35

Cornell, Joseph, 172

counterpublics: in artist communities, 97; black gay counterpublics, 132; of Brixton, 32; of civil rights movements, 121; counterpublicity of, 20, 90, 142, 274n78; of DC, 4; defined, 11; and F-K, 4, 7, 18, 20, 90, 121, 127, 138–139, 255–256; and gay liberation, 21, 138; gay liberation in, 21; as heterotopia, 90, 140; of London, 57; marginalization of, 7, 11, 138; musical counterpublics, 90, 97; of New York, 4; performance of, 139–140; queer counterpublics, 57; radical counterpublics, 11; strategies of, 140; subaltern counterpublics, 138; Warner on, 139–140, 258n21. *See also* subcultures

Crimp, Douglas, 143, 145, 214, 249, 268n51, 288n45

Cronenberg, David, 195

Crucifix (Fani-Kayode photo), 100

cultural politics, 14, 18, 28, 40, 57, 192–193, 256

The Cure, 6, 153, 257n7

Curtis, Ian, 163

Dada/Dadaism, 16, 75

Dance Hall Style (reggae album), 42–43

dandies and dandyism, 6, 49–50, 121, 136–137, 154, 162, 221

Darcus Howe in Lewisham (Shelton photo), 30, *31*

Davis, Angela, 49

Davis, Vaginal, 86

Day, F. Holland, 3, 98–100, *100*, 127, 192, 269–270n10, 270n14

"Daydreaming" (del Naja song), 42

Death Be Not Proud (Donne poem), 145

house music, 42, 89, 204

Howe, Darcus, 30, *31*, 71

HR (Bad Brains' frontman), 71–72

HR of the Bad Brains Performing at the 9:30 Club in Washington, DC, on April 29, 1982 (Clague), *73*

Hsieh, Tehching, 275–276n10

Hughes, Langston, 133–134, 136. See also *Looking for Langston*

Hujar, Peter, 143, 145

"I Want Candy" (Bow Wow Wow song), 153–154

identity politics, 18, 91, 129, 139

Ifá (Yoruban diviner priests), 4, 25, 56–57, 205

Ife (Yoruban ancient city), 51, 54

Igbo culture, 4, 26

In the Life (black gay anthology), 130, 133–134

Ingres, Jean August Dominique, 149, 182

Inner London Education Authority (ILEA), 34–35

In/sight: African Photographers, 1940 to the Present exhibition, 5, 141

Institute of Race Relations (London), 71

intersectionality among cultures: and black gay subjectivity, 272–273n62; and black subjects, 9–10, 13, 139; as central to F-K's work, 5–9, 12–13, 59–60, 140; Crenshaw on, 272–273n62; as disidentification, 140; and gay collectivity, 140; Glissant on, 12; and intersectional identities, 57, 264n74; and marginalization, 131; Mercer on, 49–50, 55, 66–67; punk music/culture's complications of, 86; and queer subjects, 10; with Yoruban culture, 10

Jamaica, 261n21

James (Fani-Kayode photo), 192, *193*, 283n48

James, C. L. R., 34, 47

James in Brixton (Fani-Kayode photo), 201, *202*

Jameson, Fredric, 259n33

Jantjes, Gavin, 32, 37

Jarman, Derek: on HIV/AIDS, 245; *The Angelic Conversation*, 124; on British conservative resurgence, 123; on Brixton, 123; Caravaggio in films of, 216; on club nightlife, 88; dandyism of, 127–128; on death and art, 145; film-viewing parties of, 123; and F-K, 122, 124, 136, 166; and F-K's Polaroids, 84–85; as HIV positive, 246; interviews with, 271n44; *Jubilee*, 123; *The Last of England*, 246; Neoclassicism of, 155; and punk music/culture, 84–86, 122; *Sebastiane*, 124, 272n50; *The Tempest*, 124; transgression in the work of, 84–85, 124–125

Jarrell, Wadsworth, 49

jazz music, 71–72, 136, 176, 178–179

Joe (Mapplethorpe photo), 118

Johnson, Alan, 136

Johnson, Claudette, 32

Johnson, David, 154–155, 162

Johnson, Linton Kwesi, 34, 41, 48, 71, 263n50

Johnson, Rasheed, 41

Joining of Equal Forces (Fani-Kayode photo), 173, *194*, 201

Joy Division, 163

Jubilee (Jarman film), 123

Julien, Isaac: *The Attendant*, 226; and black gay subjectivity, 227; dandyism of, 128; in DC, 136; *Derek*, 271n44, 272n50; and disidentification, 15; and F-K, 204; F-K and Mapplethorpe compared by, 118–119, 129, 189–190; *Looking for Langston*, 124, 133–134, 136, 189, 204; and surrealism, 204

Kaprow, Allan, 240

Keegan, Rita, 34–36, *36*

Manet, Édouard, 75, 134, 154, 180, 182–184, 186–187, 281n29, 282n38. See also *Olympia*

Mann, Sally, 195

mannerism, 127, 183, 218, 235

Mapplethorpe, Robert: *Ajitto*, 95, 192; *American Flag*, 267n41; autobiographical photography of, 190; *Black Book*, 85, 92, 192, 274n85; black male subjects of, 113, 118, 189; and *Black Male/White Male*, 142, 189; and Brassäi, 192; camera a gift to, 81; and castration, 112; Christian iconography in, 216; conservatism galvanized by, 217; cultural racism of, 189; *Derrick Cross*, 192; *Dominick and Elliott*, 111–112, *113*; and F-K, 4, 80–81, 97, 112–115, 117–119, 129, 141, 189–190, 192, 282n46; as gay artist, 80; and gay liberation, 114; and gender issues, 190; *Joe*, 118; *Leigh Lee*, 192, *193*; lifestyle of, 113–114, 119; and *Looking for Langston*, 189; *Man in a Polyester Suit*, 95; marginalization of, 80–81, 118, 190; *Marty Gibson*, 192; neoprimitivism of, 189; phallocentrism of, 117; Polaroid photographs by, 81, 190; racial fetishism of, 97, 113, 118, 139, 190; *Self Portrait with Whip*, 119; *Standing Male Nude*, 111; *Stedman*, 61, 81, *82*; success of, 80; *Thomas*, 192; as transgressive, 81; women photographed by, 111, 115, 117; *X Portfolio*, 92

Marcus, Greil, 68, 75, 79

marginalization: of Basquiat, 80; of black art, 80; of the black body in art, 184, 187; of blacks, 129; of countercultures/counterpublics, 7, 11, 138; and cultural intersectionality, 131; demarginalization of the global contemporary, 13; double marginalization, 129; of F-K, 7, 15, 57, 59, 86, 97, 138, 169, 184, 223, 255; F-K's transcending of, 169; and gay clubs, 87;

of gays, 129; of London neighborhoods, 35; of Mapplethorpe, 80–81, 118, 190; of people with AIDS, 16, 18; reclamation from, 216; of South London neighborhoods, 35. *See also* subcultures

Marriot, David, 163

Martin, Gary, 133

Marty Gibson (Mapplethorpe photo), 192

Marx, Karl, 177, 224, 230, 235

Marxists and Marxism, 37, 47, 71, 212, 224, 230, 244, 249, 263n49, 278n41

Mary Boone Gallery, 81

masks: in *Black and White*, 179; *in Black Skin, White Masks*, 64; in *Bodies of Experience*, 107; Carnival masks, 115, 207; in *Ebo Òrìsà*, 92; in *Farewell to Meat*, 119; in F-K's work, 15; in *Gold Phallus*, 228; in Noh theater, 149; *ororo* masks, 207, 246–247, 284n73; and *Philip*, 149; in Razor's work, 61; in *Sonponnoi*, 231; in Wojnarowicz's work, 67; of the Yoruba, 54. *See also* birds and bird masks

masquerades: Barthes on, 242; in Brassäi's work, 200; Carnival masks and masquerades, 202; in East Asian performance, 242; and F-K's work, 15, 24, 48, 56, 61, 182–183, 202, 204, 241; in Morrisroe's work, 84; in Noh theater, 149; in Sherman's work, 159, 216; in Yoruban culture, 204

Massive Attack (British band), 42–43, 263n53

Matisse, Henri, 24

Matta-Clark, Gordon, 143

Mbembe, Achille, 163

McCarthy, Paul, 195

McCormick, Carlo, 58, 265n11

McInerney, Jay, 80

McKendry, John, 81

McLaren, Malcolm, 153, 265n13, 266n23

Medicis, the, 222

melancholia, 14, 26, 251

Mémoires (Debord), 66

Mendieta, Ana, 240–241

Mercer, Kobena: on black gay photography, 112–113; "Communion: Love Will Tear Us Apart," 163; on Day, 98; on DC, 136; on defiant dandyism, 49; on diasporic art, 92, 94, 269n3; on *Every Moment Counts*, 207; on F-K, 13, 163, 170; as F-K advocate, 5; F-K and Day compared by, 112; F-K and Mapplethorpe compared by, 118–119, 129, 189–190; F-K and Sherman compared by, 168; on intersectionality among cultures, 49–50, 55, 66–67; on Mapplethorpe, 114, 139; on masks, 284n73; on New York, 136; on punk music/culture, 50; in South London, 269–270n10; on *White Bouquet*, 183–184; Yoruban art and culture romanticized by, 169

Meshes of the Afternoon (Deren and Hammid film), 203–204, 207

"Metaphysick" catalogue (Fani-Kayode and Hirst entry), 214

Meyer, Richard, 103–104, 114, 118

Michael French of Arcachon (Fani-Kayode photo), 53–54, *54*

Milk Drinker (Fani-Kayode photo), 168, 241

minkisi (Kongolese spirit figures), 149, 203

Minotaur, the, 149, 203

Minotaur (Bataille), 275n1, 282n36, 283n51

mirror worlds, 143, 186, 196, 203

mirrors and mirrored imagery: in African art, 203; Akomfrah on, 171; in *Black Male/White Male*, 198, 257n9; in Brassaï's work, 200; in "Fire in Cairo," 153; in F-K's work, 173, 185, 201–202, 203–204, 257n9; and the Freudian doppelgänger, 202; in Kongolese art, 203; in Lacan's work, 196, 283n51; Mabille on, 171; in Manet's work, 186; in *Meshes of*

the Afternoon, 203; in Mishima's work, 237; Owens on, 200 201; in surrealism, 173, 201, 203; viewer/photographer and camera as, 200; in Woodman's work, 195, 198; in Yoruban culture, 235

Misfits exhibition, 141

Mishima, Yukio, 4, 237–238, 240, 249, 287n33

Misrach, Richard, 215

Mizer, Robert, 103–104, 114

modernism: black performativity in, 41; British parochialism vs., 29; and Camp, 127; demythologized, 59; ending of, 19; European modernism, 195; and *Every Moment Counts*, 221; fetishism in, 182; F-K's modes of, 5, 55–56, 196, 275n3; formalism in, 61, 172, 255, 281n29; hegemonies of, 143; in New York, 164; in painting, 9; vs. postmodernism, 5, 160; primitivism in, 180, 211, 273n3; as progressive, 162; and punk music/culture, 66; and Romanticism, 152, 160, 168; signification of, 195; and surrealism, 172, 177, 180

modernity, 258n16, 258n19; and black gay bodies, 226; and black radicalism, 172; countercultures of, 10, 143; difficulties in defining, 258n19; F-K's modes of, 11–13, 59; microhistories of, 11; as progressive, 162; queer diasporic modernity, 92, 95; repressive aspects of, 124–125; and Romanticism, 160–161, 168, 170; and surrealism, 172, 177

Morimura, Yasumasa, 182, *183*, 186–187, 221

Morrell, Frances, 35

Morrison, Toni, 134, 277n34

Morrisroe, Mark, 83–86, *85*, 268n48

Morrissey (Smiths lead singer), 6, 124, 146, 154–155

Morton, Marsha, 161, 276n22

Moten, Fred, 41–43, 46, 176, 258n12, 273n70

Sealy, Mark: as Autograph ABP director,
9; on the black British movement, 13; on
economic systems impacting black culture, 53; on England after World War I, 69;
on Eurocentrism, 199; on F-K, 9, 11, 13,
51, 75, 182, 199–200, 205, 241–242, 254,
282n46; *Les Rencontres d'Arles* organized
by, 141; *Rotimi Fani-Kayode and Alex
Hirst*, 264n73, 282n31; on uprisings in
Caribbean populations, 40
Sebastian (Saint), 217, 222, 238, 248, 272n50,
287n32. *See also* Bronzino, Agnolo; Reni,
Guido
Sebastiane (Jarman film), 124, 272n50
Self Portrait with Whip (Mapplethorpe
photo), 119
Self-Deceit #1, Rome (Woodman photo), 195
The Sensual World (Bush record), 237
Serota, Nicholas, 37
Serrano, Andres, 217
Sex Pistols, 69–70, 77, 123, 265nn13–14,
266n18

Shango (Yoruban king), 63, 197
Sharpe, Christina, 226–227
Shelton, Syd, 30, 33, 69, 73–74
Sherman, Cindy, 159, 186–187, 216
Shonibare, Yinka, 209, 216, 223, 250,
252–254
Shore, Stephen, 215
Sidibé, Malick, 211
signification: by Basquiat, 81; of black
homoeroticism, 133; in *Black Male/
White Male*, 198; of black power, 49; by
Day, 102; diasporic signification, 15, 196;
in disidentification, 134; of European
modernism, 195; of European painting,
180; by F-K on Mapplethorpe, 190;
F-K's practice of, 21, 143, 195; Gates on,
176; of imperialism, 77; of modernist
history, 177–178; of pan-Africanism,

78; postmodernist signification, 221; of
priest figures, 157; on primitivism, 182,
188; queer signification, 50; as a strategy,
207; on surrealism, 176–177, 185; of urban
blackness, 48; of Yoruban culture, 223
Silueta (Mendieta series), 240–241
Simmons, Ron, 133–134, 136, 273n65
Siouxsie and the Banshees, 163
Sir Charles, Alias Willie Harris (Hendricks
photo), 220, *220*
Sischy, Ingrid, 81
Sisters of Mercy, 163
Situationist International movement, 68,
75, 265n7, 265n14
ska, 40, 47–48, 69, 71, 73
slavery and the slave trade: in contemporary
art, 277n34; in England, 41, 166–167,
262n32; in F-K's work, 6, 10, 24–25, 51,
163, 166–167, *167*; and haunting, 278n37;
Hirst on, 141; legacy of, 6; in the Nether-
lands, 225; Sharpe on, 226; in the
US, 262n32. *See also Cargo of Middle
Passage*
"Sledgehammer" (Gabriel song), 195
Smith, Graham, 155, *156*, 167
Smith, Patti, 67, 80, 164, 265n9
Smith, Robert, 6–7
The Smiths, 6, 154
The Smoker (Day photo), 98–99
Snap Shot (Fani-Kayode photo), 100, 115,
190, *191*, 228, 272n61
Snead, James, 187
Solanke, Adeola, 37
Solomon-Godeau, Abigail, 188, 279n2
sonics: and black radicalism, 18, 20, 28–29,
47, 50, 139, 273n70; black sonic traditions,
135; and F-K's photography, 14, 46–47, 85,
87, 90; in *Handsworth Songs*, 40; of New
Romanticism, 155; poetry building from,
135; radical sonics, 9, 47, 70, 94; under-
ground, in London, 20; visualization of,

www.ingramcontent.com/pod-product-compliance
Lightning Source LLC
Chambersburg PA
CBHW051209170526
45166CB00005B/1821